# RHETORIC

*A Study of the Communicative and Aesthetic
Dimensions of Language*

## Paul Newell Campbell

Queens College of the City University of New York

Dickenson Publishing Company, Inc.
Belmont, California and Encino, California

Copyright © 1972 by Paul Newell Campbell. All rights
reserved. No part of this book may be reproduced, stored in a retrieval
system, or transcribed, in any form or by any means—electronic, mechanical,
photocopying, recording, or otherwise—without the prior written permission
of the publisher, 16561 Ventura Boulevard, Encino, California 91316.

Library of Congress Catalog Card Number: 75-178179
Printed in the United States of America
10   9   8   7   6   5   4   3   2   1

It is a difficult thing to unite public and private universes of discourse, yet the degree and depth of my indebtedness regarding this book requires just that. There are three levels on which I must publicly express my appreciation to my wife, Professor Karlyn Kohrs Campbell.

Because of her extensive academic and intellectual preparations in the areas of Philosophy and Rhetoric, because of her deep knowledge of existential, dialectical, and phenomenological modes of thought, and particularly because of her near-unique abilities as a Sartrean scholar, I must acknowledge the hundreds of ways she has helped in the thinking, writing, and rewriting that have resulted in this work.

Because love and work are fused in our lives, because Karlyn is so integral to all of me, I must acknowledge her—not for any act or series of acts—simply, I must acknowledge her.

And because this is a book about words by one who lives by words, I must proclaim the endless thanks I owe her for endless hours of that most precious form of discourse—pillow talk.

# Contents

Preface     xi
Introduction    1
Part I    RHETORIC    11
   1   Rhetoric: A Thesis    12
      *The Nature and Scope of Rhetoric*    *15*
      *Invention*    *22*
         *Ethical Proofs*    *22*
         *Emotional Proofs*    *36*
         *Logical Proofs*    *55*
      *Disposition*    *81*
      *Style*    *96*
         *Individual Style*    *99*
         *Rhetorical Style*    *101*

   2   Rhetoric: An Anti-Thesis    117
      *Minor Problems in the Neo-Aristotelian View of Rhetoric*    *118*
      *Major Problems in the Neo-Aristotelian View of Rhetoric*    *120*

Part II    RITUAL    131
   3   Ritual: A Thesis    132
      *The Forms of Ritual*    *140*
      *Poetic Form*    *140*
         *Poetic Rhythm*    *140*
         *Metaphorical Language in Poetry*    *146*
      *Prose Form*    *149*
         *Exposition*    *150*
         *Description*    *151*
         *Narration*    *155*
         *Prose: A Combined Form*    *164*
      *Dramatic Form*    *166*
      *The Content of Ritual*    *172*
         *Lexical and Contextual Meaning*    *172*
         *The Universality of Ritual*    *180*

4   Ritual: An Anti-Thesis      184

Part III   RHETORIC-RITUAL      191
   5   Rhetoric-Ritual      192
         *Ritual as the Ground of Rhetoric*      203
               *Language as Intrapersonal Process*      203
               *Language as Poetic Process*      208
         *Rhetoric and Ritual as the Limits of Language*      213
         *Rhetoric: A Synthesis*      220
               *Persuasion Reconsidered*      220
                     *The Rhetorician and His Rhetoric*      223
                     *The Rhetorical Road to Freedom of Choice*      226
                     *The Success or Failure of Rhetoric*      228
         *Ritual: A Synthesis*      239
               *Ritual as Drama*      240
                     *Language as Drama*      241
                     *Ritualists as Actors*      244
                     *The Personae of Poetry, Prose, Verse, and Non-poetry*      252
               *The Hierarchies of Ritual*      259
         *Ritual versus Rhetoric*      269

   Epilogue      274
   Bibliography      275
   Index      295

I wish to express my gratitude to several persons for their help in the creation of this book. Miss Christine Jordan's efforts, as my research assistant, were invaluable, and I look forward to reading her own books in the near future. Professors Carroll Arnold, Theodore Clevenger, Jr., Sammy Danna, Joseph DeVito, Chester Clayton Long, Mary McEdwards, and Jeré Veilleux all read the complete manuscript, and their comments, positive and negative, were of great importance in the shaping and reshaping of this work. And finally, I am particularly grateful to Professor Wayne Brockriede, of the University of Colorado, Professor Robert Cathcart, of Queens College of the City University of New York, and Professor Robert Scott, of the University of Minnesota, who provided the detailed and insightful criticisms without which a book of this sort cannot exist.

The proper study of mankind is no longer merely man, but man as he possesses and is possessed by his language. It's in these twin processes of possessing and being possessed that man perceives, creates, and changes his world, himself, and his fellow men.

Although my main concern in this book is the nature of language, most of what I shall say necessarily involves comments, direct or indirect, on the nature of man and on his relationship to his environment. Such an approach is admittedly complex and difficult, but is also required, in my opinion, by the state of knowledge and consciousness in which we exist.

# *Preface*

*reason let others give and realness bring—*
*ask the always impossible of me*
*—E. E. Cummings*

On the one hand, then, I must warn that few simple answers will be found herein. In one sense there are no answers that I can offer; there is only the act that is this book, and it's a *single* act that must be perceived as such. Like MacLeish, I intend not that it mean, but that it be.

On the other hand, I must ask for patience and, strangely, playfulness. The patience will be needed because, since I can give no comfortably fixed rules or laws, and since such attempts are promising at first, but embittering finally, my efforts will constantly be aimed at synthesis, interrelatedness, unity. Further, since the book itself is a unit, a whole, it cannot be profitably dealt with in parts; and since each part must be seen through the prism of all the other parts, something more than the ordinary degree of patience is requested.

The playfulness, too, will be needed because it is impossible, at least for me, to handle shifting, intertwined, continually changing phenomena by attacking them with brusque, intellectual aggressiveness. Rather, you must toy with the ideas, seriously for a moment, then whimsically. Forget them for a while, then return. Laugh at them, then try to make them work. And with luck, probably during one of the lighter intervals, some of these notions may acquire a local habitation and a name.

*My Method*

For a great many centuries, man has felt or fought his way through life in one of two modes of thought—the analytical or the dialectical. He has viewed himself and his universe either as a huge complex of interacting forces and elements that could be subdivided into discrete, separate units that were knowable, if not known, or as a single, complicated process that was in no real or meaningful sense divisible. To put it simply, throughout recorded history man has placed his primary philosophical and personal faith in either analysis or synthesis.

Certainly the two names that tower philosophically above all others in western thought are Plato and Aristotle. Plato was a dialectician, Aristotle an analyst. Yet despite the familiarity of these names, despite the ancient and

# *Introduction*

*when man determined to destroy
himself he picked the was
of shall and finding only why
smashed it into because*[1]
—E. E. Cummings

honorable heritages of these philosophical methods, you will, if I guess correctly, be comfortable and familiar with the one, unfamiliar and ill at ease with the other.

The terms "analysis," "analytic," and "analyst" are known in a simple, workaday sense to all of us. More important, the analytical process is not only known but seems to be supported and validated by both personal experience and the whole movement of western civilization. Discoveries are made, experimentation is carried on, the entire scientific endeavor rests, apparently, on the foundation of analytical thought. In our personal experiences we are used to dividing things up into their component parts, thus reducing matters to what seem to be basic units or building-blocks. Analysis is very nearly an intellectual way of life for most of us.

[1] The excerpts from E. E. Cummings' poetry used here as chapter sub-headings are reprinted from *Poems 1923–1954*, copyright, 1923, 1931, 1935, 1940, 1944, renewed, 1951, 1959, by E. E. Cummings; renewed 1963, 1966, 1968, by Marion Morehouse Cummings; copyright 1926, by Horace Liveright; renewed, 1954 by E. E. Cummings. Reprinted by permission of Harcourt, Brace & World, Inc.

Indeed, especially in recent Anglo-American traditions, any other approach is little known or practiced.[2]

On the other hand, "dialectic" and "dialectician" are, I imagine, either completely unknown or only vaguely familiar terms to most of you. The word "synthesis" is, of course, an old stand-by. But the usual interpretation given to it is merely "the combination of previously separated items," or something similar. Many of us use the phrase "the whole is more than the sum of its parts" in relation to synthesis, although the specific relationship is usually unclear, and this simple phrase can give the basic clue to the nature of the dialectical process. We seem to have little difficulty in agreeing that a whole is, in experiential fact, something more, something other than the simple sum of its parts. A man isn't just x number of chemical compounds, he's a man, and man-ness means more than chemicals. A song isn't just a series of notes, it's a song, possessing qualities that notes do not have; a song can be haunting, sad, lilting, martial, etc., but notes cannot. A championship team isn't just so many individual athletes. It's a team that wins because of its wholeness, its team-ness.

Well and good. The whole is more than the sum of its parts. But the reverse of this statement, or the importance of reversing this statement, seems to have escaped attention. If the whole is *more than,* or something *other than* the sum of its parts, it must follow that the parts are *less than,* or something *other than* the items that make up the whole. Man is characterized by his abilities to think, to conceive, to symbolize. Chemicals can do none of these things. In this sense chemicals are *not parts* of man. Songs are gay, or depressing, or amusing, but there are no gay, depressing, or amusing notes. Notes, then, are *not parts* of songs. The New York Knickerbockers is (or was) a championship basketball team. The individual players, however, may not all be champions. Only in the team context do they become brilliant shooters, great playmakers, etc. These individuals are *not parts* of the New York Knicks.

My conditioning, like yours, has been analytical. I am steeped in the analytical tradition. When I first became involved in dialectical thought, I reacted to statements like those in the above paragraph something like this: "Well, of course that's true in *one way.* But it's silly to say these things aren't parts of a man, or a song, or what have you. You couldn't have a man or a song *without* these things." And I went on to more frustrated grumblings. Of course, I (and you, if you are reacting similarly) was absolutely right. You *can't* have a team without individual players, a man without chemicals, etc. But the team is *more* than those individual players, and the man is *more* than those chemicals; and conversely, the chemicals and the players are *less* than the constituents of their respective wholes. And right here is the essence of dialectic—here in these frustrating and seemingly contradictory statements.[3]

From a dialectical point of view, the above statements are necessary and

[2] For an excellent statement of this problem see Richard McKeon, "Communication, Truth, and Society," *Ethics* LXVII, 2: 89-99, and "Dialectic and Political Thought and Action," *Ethics* LXV, 1: 1-33, and "Philosophy and Action," *Ethics* LXII, 2: 79-100.

[3] A particularly clear illustration of this essence of dialectic is found in William Barrett's *Irrational Man* (New York: Doubleday & Company, Inc., 1958), pp. 31-36.

noncontradictory. They are necessary because the dialectician is not opposed to analysis; he depends on analysis for his starting point, his foundation. Without the findings of the analytical method, the dialectician would have nothing to synthesize. The statements are noncontradictory because the dialectical method *includes* analysis, but goes beyond it in insisting that, although a whole cannot exist without parts, wholes are more than the sum of their parts, and parts are not units that add up to wholes. For the dialectician, any statement, any description, any discussion must begin at some point; that point will be more or less objective, discrete, analytical in nature; it will deal with such items as the chemicals in man, the notes in a song, etc. But that point, that opening statement, will also be incomplete and inaccurate. So the necessary next step is the adjustment, the revision, the change, or the contradiction of the original statement. It is this change or revision that is the heart of the dialectical method, and it is also the basis of the profound dialectical comment that the truth begins with two.

The analytical and dialectical methods are not mutually exclusive modes of thought. Dialectic includes analysis and adds to it. The basic aim and assumption of the analyst is that it is possible and profitable to abstract parts from given processes and to consider those parts as real entities. The basic aim and assumption of the dialectician is that parts are arbitrary and artificial items and that only wholes or processes may be meaningfully and realistically discussed.

One frequent objection to the dialectional method goes something like this: "It is perfectly correct, in theory, to insist on wholes, to point out the essential unity or interrelatedness of aspects of reality. Unfortunately, we are simply incapable of dealing with wholes, be the whole a tennis serve, a molecule, or a piece of literature. The only way we can understand any phenomenon is to consider it part by part, to analyze it." On one level this objection is quite sound; on another it is self-contradictory, for if something or other won't work in practice, the theory behind it is inadequate and must be revised. True, descriptions of wholes *per se* may well be vague, or at least extremely complicated. For this reason descriptions or explanations must ordinarily *begin* with parts. *Begin,* not *end.* The analyst deals with parts, with component elements, and he assumes that by describing, controlling, and manipulating them he is dealing with the whole. The dialectician also deals with parts in the *beginning,* but he goes on to point out that it is the parts *in combinations and patterns,* the parts as they *interact,* that constitute meaningful wholes. These combinations, patterns, and interactions are not qualities or characteristics of parts, but of wholes. And it is these qualities, these relationships that are of major importance to the dialectician, for he considers them to be the only reality knowable to man.

For example, water is "made up" of oxygen and hydrogen. But water has qualities such as wetness, drinkability, use as a cleaning agent, etc., that are not characteristic of either oxygen or hydrogen. These characteristics are not qualities of the parts, but of the whole. The dialectician would say that you cannot study wetness or rate of evaporation by studying oxygen or hydrogen, for these things have nothing to do with oxygen or hydrogen. They refer solely and directly to the whole, water. Or, reversing the equation, oxygen and hydrogen have nothing to do with wetness or evaporability. Only water has those qualities. In that sense, oxygen and hydrogen are not parts of water. Water includes oxygen and hydrogen and more. But the more, the wetness, drinkability, etc., transcends and changes the parts.

On a more complicated level, attempts have been made to describe human behavior as a series of discrete S-R units: a given stimulus leads to a given response. Those attempts quickly proved inadequate, though they have not yet been completely abandoned.[4] Psychologists then changed the S-R theory to S-O-R. The "O" stands for the human organism and for the changes that the organism brings about, first in the stimulus, then in the response. In place of a passive organism responding to a known S with a predictable R, theorists have postulated a human being who is stimulated, but who, in that very process, alters the stimuli that impinge upon him—eliminating some, emphasizing and elaborating others—until he finally responds to stimuli that he himself has shaped or, at least partially, created. In other words the O not only represents the organism, it stands for part of the stimulus and part of the response. So the change from S-R to S-O-R was a major move away from the analytical method and toward the dialectical method.

Let me emphasize again that the dialectician almost always begins with parts, with analysis. For example, to say that "wetness" alone interests him makes that quality almost meaningless. Water, gasoline, hydrochloric acid, and Chanel No. 5 are all "wet," but distinctions must be made between them. Or, to say that only the organism is important, and that stimuli and responses are insignificant, is to ignore the difference in an organism stimulated by a kiss, an electric shock, or a blow on the head. Analysis is necessary and indispensable. But after the initial analysis, one must recognize the whole, and at this point parts have no separate, independent significance.

I'm writing this book from a dialectical point of view for two reasons. First, I've been forced to adopt the dialectical approach as a result of my own analytical failures. That is, over a good many years of thinking and teaching I've found that analysis simply doesn't work, particularly in relation to the study of language. Concepts that begin with analytical promise end in divisiveness and fragmentation. Too often I've searched futilely (and foolishly, it seems now) for givens, for fixed units, for parts that do not change when looked at from new angles and attitudes. Many of my students have duplicated these failures; they have been quite able to deal with parts, to specify them, define them, even manipulate them. They have been able to write analytically correct and accurate reports, papers, give analytically proper descriptions, speeches, but they have been unable to deal purposefully and richly with wholes, to understand the dramatic nature of the communicative act, to feel the magic of the symbol system called language. Finally, I've been forced to realize that not only am I doing my students a disservice by using analytical viewpoints, but that they can absorb and profit from dialectical thought more easily than I, probably because their analytical conditioning has been less intense and less lengthy than my own.

[4] For an entertaining and, I believe, valid polemic against S-R theories and theorists, see Arthur Koestler, *The Act of Creation* (New York: The Macmillan Company, 1964), especially Book Two, Chapter 12.

Second, although analysis is still the sole or primary investigative method employed in many academic and intellectual areas, the use of the dialectical mode is by no means my own re-discovery or re-innovation. We are, if I read the signs rightly, in the middle of a philosophical revolution that will change our thinking in profound ways. Voices are heard from all sides—philosophy, the physical sciences, letters, the arts and humanities—insisting that man is a part of and is inseparable from the world in which he exists.[5] Contemporary philosophers are using the metaphor "the Copernican revolution" to stress the notion that man is necessarily the center of his universe. In perceiving that universe man will color it, distort it, and confuse it. Therefore any study of that universe is in some sense a study of man and his particular confusions, and any study that presumes to separate man from his universe becomes, sooner or later, meaningless.

In this book I shall, as a dialectician, make statements, qualify, modify, or even contradict those statements, and then attempt to combine the original statements and the qualifications or contradictions into larger wholes. It is this process of change, modification, and fusion that will, I hope, provide a demonstration of the dialectical method.

The organization of the book reflects the dialectical approach. There are five chapters in all. Each of the first two main parts is subdivided into two chapters, the first titled "Thesis," the second "Anti-Thesis." In each Thesis chapter, I shall describe the parts that familiar analytical thought has postulated; in the Anti-Thesis chapters, I shall point out that those analytical postulates are *necessary* but *inadequate*. I use the hyphenated term "Anti-Thesis" rather than "antithesis" because I shall not present a second thesis that is incompatible with the first (a true antithesis), but shall comment on the inadequacies or shortcomings of the previously stated thesis. The process of setting forth incompatible theses and then combining them into a larger synthesis appeals to me, but the method I have decided to use here has even stronger appeals. Thus, I shall set up theses and stress their validity and their limitations. Then in the third part of the book I shall try to provide a synthesis that gives a larger and richer frame of reference to *each* of the first two parts and, at the same time, *fuses* those parts into a greater and more meaningful whole. The third part, the Synthesis, will be one long chapter because it seems to me that language is essentially a single process.

In one sense the Synthesis section is the heart of this book; in that section I shall be directly concerned with relationships, with patterns, with wholes. In another sense the Thesis and Anti-Thesis sections are just as important; without the Thesis there would be nothing for the Anti-Thesis to change or contradict, and without both of these there would be nothing to combine into a Synthesis.

[5] Outstanding among these voices are Kenneth Burke in all his writings, but especially in "What are the Signs of What?" in *Language as Symbolic Action* (Berkeley: University of California Press, 1968), pp. 359-79, Eric H. Lenneberg, *Biological Foundations of Language* (New York: John Wiley & Sons, Inc., 1967), particularly p. 1 and p. 325, Susanne K. Langer, *Philosophy in a New Key* (New York: A Mentor Book, 1948), throughout the book, but especially Chapter 2, and Hugh Dalziel Duncan, *Language and Literature in Society* (Chicago: The University of Chicago Press, 1953), p. 9.

# My Subject

*such*
*great writhing words as, uttering overmuch,*
*stand helplessly before the spirit at bay*
—*E. E. Cummings*

Analytically it is perfectly possible to postulate the symbol system called language and to separate from it the symbol user called man.[6] From my point of view, however, there is no such thing as man separate from his language or language separate from man. *To be human is to use language.* Indeed, with increasing frequency man is being defined as the symbol-using, the language-using animal.[7] Such a definition strongly implies that non-symbol-using animals are not men, that to the extent that symbol systems are not used, the animal involved is not human. The importance of that definition and its implications can be emphasized by describing the nature of a "man" without language. Such a creature would be without words; he could neither speak, understand speech, read, nor write. To the very considerable extent that thought requires the use of words, he could not think. A "man" without language could neither produce nor perceive even the simplest words. But there are further losses that would be entailed, and in order to talk about them I must switch for a moment to a description of language as a symbol system.

I use the term "language" in a sense broad enough to include both verbal and nonverbal symbol systems. Although this usage is not particularly unusual, it deserves stress simply because the prominence of verbal symbols in language tends to make us deemphasize the non- or extraverbal symbols. For instance, we may think of an ordinary conversation as consisting of words. In fact, such nonverbal symbols as posture, gesture, vocal inflection, facial expression, etc., are of great significance in such a conversation, as they are in every speech situation. Further, those nonverbal symbols are not separable from the verbal symbols. It is impossible to utter a word without *some* vocal inflection, or bodily involvement, etc. Thus that seemingly simple conversation is a symbol system that consists of verbal and nonverbal sub-systems. And the same interdependence between the verbal and the nonverbal is found even in the act of silent reading, during which the verbal symbols are thoroughly intermixed with such nonverbal, psychophysical symbolic states as tension, relaxation, and the various "feelings" that accompany and are part of the verbal.

[6] Such a separation has been the basis of much of the work of the structural linguists. Interestingly, though, Noam Chomsky, one of, if not the, leading linguists in the world has sharply questioned this analytical process. For a convenient summary of Chomsky's work, see Francis P. Dinneen, S. J., *An Introduction to General Linguistics* (Holt, Rinehart and Winston, Inc., 1967), Chapter 12.

[7] Kenneth Burke has set forth that definition most tellingly, I think. It is found in concise form in "Definition of Man," in *Language as Symbolic Action*, pp. 3-25, and in *The Rhetoric of Religion: Studies in Logology* (Boston: Beacon Press, 1969), p. 40.

In addition to these nonverbal systems, there are those called music and mathematics. (However, mathematics is nonverbal only on one level. All mathematical statements can be translated into linguistic forms. $\frac{\sqrt{a-b}}{d^m + e^{m+n}}$ means "the square root of a-minus-b over d to the $m^{th}$ power plus e to the $m^{th}$-plus-$n^{th}$ power.) In addition to these, other nonverbal systems allow us to find great meaning in the dancer's movements, the painter's use of colors, and the sculptor's treatment of form and texture. All these are *part* of language, for they are all involved in the processes through which we exchange meanings, affect each other, and contribute to the creation of a distinctly human environment.

Now, returning to the "man" without language, we find that such a creature would not only be completely unable to produce or perceive words, but would also be unable to perceive red as startling or black as sombre. He could not hear the kingly quality in one voice or the sultriness in another. He would not see carved wood or polished marble as needing to be touched. Movements would never seem to him to be frightened, or passionate, or silken. Sounds would never be heard as clashing and angry or solemn and mournful. Mountains would never seem awesomely huge, or chihuahuas foolishly tiny. He would be as unmoved by a ship's horn on a foggy sea as by an infant's first cry.

That creature could in no sense be called human. Without language he could be only an animal, and not a very highly evolved animal at that.

Conversely, *to use language is to be human.* That is to say, it is impossible to use language in the sense in which I have described it and be other than human. The creature who not only uses words, but who perceives the mournfulness of a fog horn and the fierce beauty of a flamenco dancer is necessarily a human being. The use of these symbol systems, verbal and nonverbal, *is* his human-ness. It is not that he *expresses* his humanity *through* such symbolic behavior—that would imply that the humanity was somehow there, ready to be expressed. Instead, it is the possession and the use (and the two are inseparable) of those symbolic powers that make an animal human.

I am concerned with man and his language as they merge, or better, with man as he emerges in language. My interest is in man as a symbol-using being and in language as a human and a humane process. It is here in the fusion of these elements, in the symbolic processes called language, that man finds understanding of, and draws relationships between himself, his fellows, and his world. In a sense it is in and with language that man *creates* himself and his world. It is of course necessary to assume the existence of some "real," "objective," undifferentiated out-there—to assume that it existed before man and that it exists now. But you can know that world only symbolically. There is no direct, totally objective contact that you can make with it. You taste it, feel it, smell it, perceive it in all sorts of ways, every one of which is symbolic. And as soon as you employ these symbolic means of perception, you are no longer simply *reacting to* your environment. Rather, you are *acting on* that environment.[8] For instance, consider the word

[8] Koestler, pp. 447-53.

"chair." By possessing and using that word you affect, you act on your environment. As soon as you own that word you are owned by it, and with it you perceptually structure the world around you.[9] The word is a symbol for your experiences with a particular sort of object, and as a result of those experiences, you've categorized as chairs those things that are man-made, that have arms (sides) and/or a back, and on which you can sit and lean either backwards or sideways. If an object has neither arms nor back you do not perceive it as a chair. Further, if it is not man-made you do not perceive it as a chair. You can sit on the ground and lean back against a tree, but you don't call the right-angled meeting of ground and tree a chair. Even if there's a rock under the tree, and you sit on the rock and recline against the tree trunk, you don't call the combination of rock, ground, and tree a chair (although "chair" might be used metaphorically for such objects). A chair is made by man for man. Its man-madeness is part of its meaning. And with that meaning you perceive and structure the world in which you live (and sit). Suppose that "chair" meant anything on which you could sit. The category that you would then create with that symbol would be far different than it presently is. Depending on your experiences, chair would mean ground, table, rock, lap, stack of books, horse, enemy's head, pillow, piano, and who knows what else. The important thing is that all items within that new category would be perceived as having something in common, just as all of the things you now call chairs seem to have something in common. In other words, you would perceive, would create different relationships between different things. And the word "create" is the appropriate one here, for such relationships are never *in* the objects or events perceived, but are superimposed on them by the perceiver. It is at this level that you, the user of symbols, the symbol system, and the thing symbolized melt into one. The symbol affects you, and with it you affect the reality of which you are a part.

A somewhat similar point was made by Benjamin Lee Whorf in a series of writings.[10] He indicated that a language has a structure of its own, and that when we use that language to describe reality we are unknowingly superimposing the structure of language on the structure of reality. In English, for instance, the simplest structural elements are probably the actors (subjects), acts (verbs), and things acted on (objects). Using this kind of language structure to describe some kinds of reality is fairly satisfactory, as "the falling tree crushed the car," or "the water ruined the painting." But what about statements like "it's raining"? What does "it" mean in that context? What is acting on what? And what about "war is hell," "truth exists by definition," "I feel sad," "she regarded death courteously," and hundreds of hundreds of others. If you unthinkingly assume that the subject-verb-object structure of language also exists in reality, you're in trouble. You may go to the tortuous lengths of postulating a state called "war" which acts in a painful manner called "hell" on the real or potential human condition call "is."

[9] Excellently illustrated in Dorothy Lee's "Lineal and Nonlineal Codifications of Reality" in *Explorations in Communication*, ed. Edmund Carpenter and Marshall McLuhan (Boston: Beacon Press, 1960), especially pp. 136-37.

[10] John B. Carroll, ed., *Language, Thought, and Reality: Selected Writings of Benjamin Lee Whorf* (Cambridge, Mass.: M.I.T. Press, 1956).

If you do you find yourself in the odd linguistic and philosophical spot of having created a thing called war that has the power to affect man; you have, in other words, separated man and war. At that point you will have some trouble finding an example of war on man that is not man-made, that is not man making war on man.

Whorf's notion that the structures of different languages differ has been questioned,[11] but there is no disagreement with the idea that language *per se* possesses a distinct structure. Because of that structure it will always be impossible to avoid distorting reality by using language. We are all trapped in language, though *freed by language* is just as meaningful a description. It is possible, however, to be aware of and partially control the blending of the situation and language that allows for or requires one sort of behavior or another. It is possible, that is, so long as we keep reminding ourselves that language does not merely mirror our responses to the environment, but also constitutes our organization or structuring of that environment. This structuring of or acting on the environment is perhaps most obvious on the linguistic level, but it actually occurs on all levels, in all phases of existence. Arthur Koestler, to whom I shall refer frequently and gratefully in this book, says:

> The lowliest creature and the highest, the moment it is hatched or born, lashes out at the environment, be it liquid, or solid, with cilia, flagellae, or contractile muscle fibre; it crawls, swims, glides, pulsates; it kicks, yells, breeds, feeds, and sucks negative entropy from its surrounding for all its worth.[12]

> In fact, the animal does not merely adapt to the environment, but constantly adapts the environment to itself. It eats environment, drinks environment, fights and mates environment, it modifies, dismantles, analyzes, and reassembles it after its own fashion, converting "noise" into "information."[13]

Language, then, is the medium in which we exist, with which we build the universe around us, and through which we war, and love, and praise. Language is not an element that is added to or imposed on some pre-existing human state; on the contrary, it is central to the nature of mankind, his behavior, and his world.

In the following pages I shall deal with language dialectically, beginning with a conventional analytic discussion, then denying the validity of that discussion, and, lastly, creating a broader context within which the earlier Theses and Anti-Theses function properly and profitably. I shall follow the first part of this procedure twice—once for each of what I take to be the primary language processes. Somewhat arbitrarily, and quite alliteratively, I shall call those processes Rhetoric and Ritual.

First, Rhetoric . . .

[11] Eric H. Lenneberg, *Biological Foundations of Language* (New York: John Wiley & Sons, Inc., 1967), pp. 363-64.
[12] Koestler, p. 447.
[13] Koestler, p. 448.

# Part I

# RHETORIC

When one man speaks honestly and openly to other men, it can be a thing of wonder and magic. It's a mistake to regard that act as commonplace or trivial. For a man to speak his thoughts, his feelings, his desires, and his needs to others requires bravery, for in so speaking that man becomes vulnerable. He places himself before others and opens himself to their acceptance and praise or to their rejection and scorn. The regard and good will of others is important to all of us, and it's in the rhetorical act, the act of speaking, that we run the risk of finding out that we do not have that regard and good will. It's not at all surprising that speaking to others is so often avoided, and is always accompanied by some fear. Rather, it's surprising that so many men have had the courage to speak at times when the risks were enormous. Surprising and fortunate! For very often the words that were spoken

# 1

# *Rhetoric:*

## *A Thesis*

> *driving white spikes of silence into joists*
> *hewn from hugest colour*
> —*E. E. Cummings*

changed the way men thought, the way they viewed their world, and their attitudes toward their fellows. In sum, very often those words changed human history.

Here are statements that men have had the courage and the honor to utter:

Let the word go forth from this time and place, to friend and foe alike, that the torch has been passed to a new generation of Americans—born in this century, tempered by war, disciplined by a hard and bitter peace, proud of our ancient heritage—and unwilling to witness or permit the slow undoing of those human rights to which this nation has always been committed, and to which we are committed today at home and around the world.

—John F. Kennedy
Inaugural Address, January 20, 1961

It is in vain, sir, to extenuate the matter. Gentlemen may cry peace, peace—but there is no peace. The war is actually begun! The next gale that sweeps from the North will bring to our ears the clash of resounding arms! Our brethren are already in the field! Why stand we here idle? What is it that gentlemen wish? What would they have? Is life so dear, or peace so sweet, as to be purchased at the price of chains and slavery? Forbid it, Almighty God! I know not what course others may take; but as for me, give me liberty, or give me death!

—Patrick Henry
Speech delivered before the
Virginia Convention, March 23, 1775

It is not difficult, O Athenians, to escape death, but it is much more difficult to avoid depravity, for it runs swifter than death. And now I, being slow and aged, am overtaken by the slower of the two; but my accusers, being strong and active, have been overtaken by the swifter, wickedness. And now I depart, condemned by you to death; but they condemned by truth, as guilty of iniquity and injustice: and I abide my sentence and so do they. These things, perhaps, ought so to be, and I think that they are for the best.

—Socrates
Speech delivered on his
condemnation to death, 399 B.C.

If you have tears, prepare to shed them now.
You all do know this mantel: I remember
The first time ever Caesar put it on;
'Twas on a summer's evening, in his tent,
That day he overcame the Nervii:
Look, in this place ran Cassius' dagger through:
See what a rent the envious Casca made:
Through this the well-belov'd Brutus stabb'd;
And as he pluck'd his cursed steel away,
Mark how the blood of Caesar follow'd it,
as rushing out of doors, to be resolved
If Brutus so unkindly knocked, or no:
For Brutus, as you know, was Caesar's angel:
Judge, O you gods, how dearly Caesar loved him.
That was the most unkindest cut of all;
For when the noble Caesar saw him stab,
Ingratitude, more strong than traitors' arms,
Quite vanquish'd him: then burst his mighty heart;
And, in his mantle muffling up his face,
Even at the base of Pompey's statue,
Which all the while ran blood, great Caesar fell.
Oh, what a fall was there, my countrymen!
Then I, and you, and all of us fell down.
Whilst bloody treason flourish'd over us.
O, now you weep, and I perceive you feel
The dint of pity: these are gracious drops.
Kind souls, what weep you when you but behold
Our Caesar's vesture wounded? Look you here,
Here is himself, marr'd, as you see, with traitors.

—Mark Antony
Oration on the death of Julius Caesar, 44 B.C.[14]

[14] This work is, of course, the imaginative creation of Shakespeare. However, it is based on the historical writings of Appian, Cicero, Dio Cassius, Nicholas of Damascus, and Plutarch. And it is a rhetorical masterpiece.

I returned, and saw under the sun, that the race is not to the swift, nor the battle to the strong, neither yet bread to the wise, nor yet riches to men of understanding, nor yet favor to men of skill; but time and chance happeneth to them all.

For man also knoweth not his time; as the fishes that are taken in an evil net, and as the birds that are caught in the snare; so are the sons of men snared in an evil time, when it falleth suddenly upon them.

—Ecclesiastes 9: 11-12

These are some of the words that men have spoken. They are, of course, words that had, and that have, an extraordinary importance for and impact on their hearers. Yet at least a tinge of the splendor of such words exists every time one man speaks directly and honestly to a group of listeners.

In the western world the study of words such as these, of the situations in which they were uttered, and of the results of those utterances has been thought to be of great value for many centuries. Since approximately 500 B.C. that study has been known as Rhetoric. During the ancient Greek and Roman cultures the most famous rhetorical theorists and practitioners included Isocrates, Plato, Aristotle, Cicero, and Quintilian. These men developed and practiced the art and the study of Rhetoric primarily for sociological reasons. In Greece the newly formed democratic political system placed much importance on communicative and persuasive (i.e., rhetorical) skills. Greek citizens needed to plead their causes in courts of law, to persuade others to vote for desired social changes in the *Ecclesia*, or general assembly. It seemed apparent that skilled speakers stood a far better chance of influencing judges or of garnering votes than did those that were unskilled. In Rome a somewhat different emphasis was placed on Rhetoric. Although leading figures taught that rhetorical ability was of great educational and philosophical importance, others stressed the ornamental aspects of Rhetoric. This change in emphasis occurred largely because there was often less opportunity for the individual to speak for or against important issues in Rome than there had been in Greece. The Roman political system simply offered less rhetorical freedom, less freedom of speech.

Throughout the centuries the study of Rhetoric has varied in terms of emphasis, purpose, and importance. At various times it has found greater or lesser favor among intellectuals, philosophers, and academicians. However, the study and the belief in its essential value have persisted. Today, perhaps more than any time in history, man's well-being and indeed his very survival depend on an awareness and a knowledge of the nature of the rhetorical act. For instance, in March 1968, in a New Hampshire presidential primary, Eugene McCarthy vividly demonstrated that rhetorical discourse could alter the course of history. A rather different, and certainly more energetic, demonstration was provided by Spiro Agnew following the 1968 elections.

But of all the rhetoricians of the last twenty-five hundred years, and of all the rhetorical concepts that have been advanced, one name and one concept are overwhelmingly important—Aristotle. Aristotelian Rhetoric. It is an oversimplification to use the term "one concept," although Aristotle did propose one basic conceptual approach to Rhetoric. But that approach has been modified over the years, sometimes in ways that were so subtle as to have gone unnoticed. *In fact there may be little similarity between some of today's views of Aristotle's notions and his actual ideas.*[15] In any event the result of Aristotle's teachings, principally a work titled *Rhetoric*, and of the revisions and interpretations of his concepts is an approach that is usually called neo-Aristotelian. It is a traditional approach in the sense that many of its roots go back to Aristotle's original views and in the sense that many contemporary rhetoricians accept it as the most valid and the most profitable of the possible approaches to Rhetoric. It is that neo-Aristotelian approach that will be described in the rest of this chapter, though I shall ring some changes of my own on this traditional theme.

## The Nature and Scope of Rhetoric

Aristotle believed that there were two basic language forms—*Poetic*, which he viewed as discourse that moved men artistically or aesthetically, and *Rhetoric*, which he defined as "the faculty of observing in any given case the available means of persuasion." [16] Modernizing those words a bit, I shall use the following definition in this chapter: *Rhetoric is the theory and practice of persuasion by means of reasoned discourse.* It seems immediately clear that two key terms here require discussion: *reason* and *persuasion*.

The idea of *reason*, of *rationality*, is absolutely basic to neo-Aristotelian Rhetoric. Aristotle believed that men were, at their best, logical and rational beings. He did not deny their emotionality, but he thought that the emotions could and should be subject to the rule of reason, at least in all ordinary situations. Neo-Aristotelian theorists are thoroughly aware of the importance of emotions, and as I shall indicate later in this chapter, they include many emotional factors and processes in their discussions of Rhetoric. Still, the major emphasis is placed on rational language processes. The belief is that audiences *can* be reached by reason, that speakers *can* use reasoned appeals to influence their hearers, and that, though emotional appeals and emotional needs can never be ignored, it is the voice of reason that sounds most clearly in the rhetorical act.

The stress on rationality has the effect of focusing rhetorical theory on logically ordered *verbal* behavior. (Originally Rhetoric was thought of as *oral* discourse largely because the arts of writing and printing were little practiced or unknown. Now Rhetoric includes the written *and* the oral, i.e., *all verbal discourse*.) That focus is perfectly appropriate on one level, but it can be misleading on another. It is quite true that logical patterns are usually expressed in verbal language. However, as I said in the Introduction, the verbal and the nonverbal cannot be separated, and this is as true of rhetorical discourse as it is of other

[15] This notion is argued most persuasively by Edwin Black, *Rhetorical Criticism* (New York: The Macmillan Company, 1965) and by James J. Murphy, "Aristotle's *Rhetoric* in the Middle Ages," *Quarterly Journal of Speech* LII, 2: 109-15.
[16] Aristotle *Rhetorica*, trans. W. Rhys Roberts, *The Works of Aristotle*, Vol. XI (London: Oxford University Press, 1946), i.2. 1355b. 26-27.

language forms. Any discourse will involve both verbal and nonverbal elements. For instance, the pride in Malcolm X's works is certainly of rhetorical importance, but it would seem foolish to try to fit that pride into some verbal category. The dignity and restraint of Senator Eugene McCarthy's speeches was obviously an important part of the impact that they had on the American voting public, but it is difficult to think of dignity and restraint as specifically verbal processes. Thus, though neo-Aristotelian Rhetoric is concerned primarily with *reasoned* and *verbal* language acts, it must be understood that *emotional* and *nonverbal* processes are also involved.

With the second key term, *persuasion*, I am immediately caught up in a problem: although the great majority of theorists from Aristotle to the present have viewed Rhetoric as persuasive discourse, there have been a few who have included "informative" or "expository" language as rhetorical forms. And the difficulty doesn't stop there, for the very term *persuasive* is defined narrowly by some writers, broadly by others. Specifically, the question is how broadly the area of Rhetoric shall be construed, and whether or not "informative" or "expository" uses of language shall be considered as rhetorical processes. For me the answer is simple enough: if used to mean the opposite of, or something other than persuasion, *there is no such thing as "informative" or "expository" language*.

Of course that answer is an extreme one, and it plumps me squarely in the middle of a situation that makes direct argument necessary. That may be unwise at this stage of things, but I see no help for it.

On the one hand, it seems perfectly reasonable to say that presenting facts in a logical and impersonal fashion should be called informative or expository speaking or writing, whereas efforts to change an audience's beliefs or attitudes should be called persuasion. For example, if I simply describe the working of an internal combusion engine, the questions asked by census takers, or the way gasoline is refined, I would seem to be engaged in expository language acts; but if I try to get you to contribute to the NAACP Legal Defense and Educational Fund, or to buy a particular book, or to join the Democratic Party, it would appear that I am about the business of persuasion. Perhaps the most extreme cases would be something like these: if I say 118 plus 247 equals 365, I must be informing; and if I say that you should involve yourself in political activity on the community level, I must be attempting to persuade. The former seems far from persuasive in nature and the latter equally far from the stuff of exposition. I imagine that for many people the difference between the two seems quite clear. In the one case, there is an attempt to change the audience's ideas or attitudes, and that is called persuasion. In the other, there is no attempt made to change the audience; it is merely a matter of offering objective statements that the audience may or may not accept, and that is an informative process.

On the other hand, this very notion of simply laying out objective data before an audience has been sharply questioned by many writers who hold that language is inherently and inescapably persuasive. [17] Richard M. Weaver has said that

[17] Burke has argued this point in nearly all his works. In *A Rhetoric of Motives* (Cleveland: The World Publishing Co., 1962), p. 798, he says "there is, *implicit in*

"language is sermonic." [18] By that he means that all language acts are purposive and persuasive. All our words, phrases, sentences are *ours*, which is to say they reflect *our* views, attitudes, and desires; combining them, we produce statements that have the quality of sermons—small or large preachments that advance and advocate particular outlooks or courses of action. In Weaver's words,

> The condition essential to see is that every use of speech, oral and written, exhibits an attitude, and an attitude implies an act. "Thy speech betrayeth thee" is aphoristically true if we take it as saying, "Your speech reveals your disposition," first by what you choose to say, then by the amount you decide to say, and so on down through the resources of linguistic elaboration and intonation. All rhetoric is a rhetoric of motives, as Kenneth Burke saw fit to indicate in the title of his book. At the low end of the scale, one may be doing nothing more than making sounds to express exuberance. But if at the other end one sits down to compose a *Critique of the Pure Reason*, one has the motive of refuting other philosophers' account of the constitution of being, and of substituting one's own, for an interest which may be universal, but which nonetheless proceeds from the will to alter something. [19]

Thus language is itself persuasive (including the language quoted above), for it is necessarily biased by the views of the speaker or writer. I may try to give an objective view of something, and within certain relative limits I may very well succeed, but that is not to say that I have avoided persuasion, for at the very least I must attempt to persuade my readers or hearers that I am, in fact, giving an objective view. Further, I can never escape the personal viewpoint that is mine rather than yours, or Elizabeth Taylor's, and that means that my idea of what is objective about a certain view will differ from yours, or hers. Of course, with such supremely simple language processes as naming colors, or pointing out obvious differences in size, we may never explore the perceptual and psychological elements that separate us, for we may be content to agree that "that's red," or "this car is longer than that one." If we were to pursue it further, we would quickly discover that my "red" differs slightly or seriously from yours, and that your notion of "longer" is not quite the same as mine. When we are involved in more complex language processes the differences become much clearer. "Love," "democracy," "anxiety," etc., mean something different to each of us, depending on the experiences to which those terms refer. When such terms are used it is the user's meaning that is imposed on them, and therefore, on those who listen or read.

*language itself*, the act of persuasion." And in the same book, he says (p. 696) "wherever there is persuasion there is rhetoric. And wherever there is 'meaning,' there is persuasion." Also, I must here footnote the first of many acknowledgements of the work of Professor Karlyn Kohrs Campbell who writes extensively of this inherent persuasive dimension of language in "The Rhetorical Implications of the Philosophy of Jean-Paul Sartre" (unpublished doctoral dissertation, University of Minnesota, 1968), especially pp. 59-65. And perhaps the simplest and most direct argument for this point of view is found in David K. Berlo's *The Process of Communication* (New York: Holt, Rinehart and Winston, 1960), pp. 8-9 and 228-34.

[18] Richard M. Weaver, "Language is Sermonic," in *Dimensions of Rhetorical Scholarship*, ed. Roger E. Nebergall (Norman Oklahoma: A Publication of the Department of Speech of the University of Oklahoma, 1963), p. 49 ff.

[19] Weaver, pp. 60-61.

It follows that as language is sermonic it is persuasive, and as language is persuasive it is rhetorical. This book is a rhetorical act, for in every page, in every sentence I am, if nothing else, trying to persuade you that what I say is true, or valid, or reasonable. Of course, such a notion greatly expands the scope of Rhetoric, for whereas a narrow definition would limit Rhetoric to those language behaviors that attempted to directly and immediately affect an audience's actions,[20] the definition I am suggesting means that all language includes a rhetorical dimension. That dimension may be of major or minor importance, but it is there.

Some of you will, perhaps, be a bit uneasy with this attitude toward Rhetoric. There may be a reaction something like this: "You mean there's no such thing as information, or informing? Then how do we ever learn anything new—a language, a concept, or a mathematical process?" It's a good question, but there is a good answer. If by "information" you mean new knowledge, new data, a new awareness of some object or event, obviously "information" exists; but if you mean a neutral, impersonal *process* of presenting those data to some audience—a process that differs from the one called persuasion—I repeat, there is no such thing. If I read a book about White racism, and in the reading I am informed of certain ways in which White Americans have oppressed Black Americans, what has really happened is that I have been persuaded that this oppression has occurred by having certain data presented to me. Those data constitute information, yes. But the presentation of this information is a persuasive act.

Put differently, if I relate to you certain facts, and if I relate them in a manner that makes you accept them, I am being persuasive; I am persuading you that those facts are believable and logical.[21] And of course, to the extent that I persuade you that fact A is credible, I have persuaded you that contradictory fact B is incredible. In a word, *facts are persuasive*; there is nothing cold, or remote, or unfeeling about them. You may say that facts are more or less meaningful or significant, but as long as there is *any* meaning or significance there is persuasive power. Facts influence people, change opinions, create new attitudes. To use facts, then, *is* to persuade.

Thus as I see it, there is only one rhetorical process—persuasion. The words "informative" and "expository" are not going to disappear from the language, nor would I wish them to. Rather I would urge closer attention to them. For instance, in the Harcourt, Brace & World *Standard College Dictionary*, the first meaning listed for "inform" is "To acquaint (someone) with facts, data, opinion, etc.; make something known to; notify." And notice the second meaning that is given: "To pervade or animate; give quality or character to." And a rare third meaning is "To shape or form (the mind, character, etc.)." Clearly, the second and third meanings can easily be understood as forms of persuasion, but so, I believe, can the first one.

[20] For illustrations of this narrower view, see any of the standard texts on Rhetoric. Alan H. Monroe and Douglas Ehninger, *Principles and Types of Speech,* sixth ed. (Glenview, Ill.: Scott, Foresman and Co., 1967) is one of the more popular texts.
[21] This point is argued in a slightly more restrained fashion by Ivan Preston, "The Forum: 'Communication: Is It Always Persuasion?'," *Quarterly Journal of Speech* LV, 3: 312-15.

I find nothing in *any* of these listings that requires me to understand that informing entails an impersonal and objective procedure. Therefore the act of informing, the act of presenting facts, seems to me to be part of the larger persuasive act.

Here are two examples of rhetorical discourse that demonstrate the oneness of the informing-persuading process. The first is one of the famous speeches of this century. It was delivered to the Congress of the United States by President Franklin Delano Roosevelt one day after the Japanese attack on Pearl Harbor.

Yesterday, December 7, 1941—a date which will live in infamy—the United States of America was suddenly and deliberately attacked by naval and air forces of the Empire of Japan.

The United States was at peace with that nation and, at the solicitation of Japan, was still in conversation with its government and its Emperor looking toward the maintenance of peace in the Pacific. Indeed, one hour after Japanese air squadrons had commenced bombing in Oahu, the Japanese Ambassador to the United States and his colleague delivered to the Secretary of State a formal reply to a recent American message. While this reply stated that it seemed useless to continue the existing diplomatic negotiations, it contained no threat or hint of war or armed attack.

It will be recorded that the distance of Hawaii from Japan makes it obvious that the attack was deliberately planned many days or even weeks ago. During the intervening time the Japanese government had deliberately sought to deceive the United States by false statement and expressions of hope for continued peace.

The attack yesterday on the Hawaiian Islands has caused severe damage to American naval and military forces. Very many American lives have been lost. In addition American ships have been reported torpedoed on the high seas between San Francisco and Honolulu.

Yesterday the Japanese government also launched an attack against Malaya.

Last night Japanese forces attacked Hong Kong.
Last night Japanese forces attacked Guam.
Last night Japanese forces attacked the Philippine Islands.
Last night Japanese forces attacked Wake Island.
This morning the Japanese attacked Midway Island.

Japan has, therefore, undertaken a surprise offensive extending through the Pacific area. The facts of yesterday speak for themselves. The people of the United States have already formed their opinions and well understand the implications to the very life and safety of our nation.

As Commander in Chief of the Army and Navy I have directed that all measures be taken for our defense.

Always will we remember the character of the onslaught against us.

No matter how long it may take us to overcome this premeditated invasion, the American people in their righteous might will win through to absolute victory.

I believe I interpret the will of the Congress and of the people when I assert that we will not only defend ourselves to the uttermost but will make very certain that this form of treachery shall never endanger us again.

Hostilities exist. There is no blinking at the fact that our people, our territory, and our interests are in grave danger.

With confidence in our armed forces—with the unbounded determination of our people—we will gain the inevitable triumph—so help us God.

I ask that the Congress declare that since the unprovoked and dastardly attack by Japan on Sunday, December 7, a state of war has existed between the United States and the Japanese Empire.

This speech is commonly considered to be an outstanding example of persuasive discourse, and I thoroughly agree with that estimate of its nature and worth. But what is it that makes this speech persuasive? If you examine it carefully, you will find that except for the famous phrase "a date which will live in infamy" and the brief next-to-the-last paragraph, the entire speech lies well within the bounds of the "informative" process. Indeed, if you set up separate informative and persuasive patterns, and if you consider that informative discourses are those that consist of factual statements or that "acquaint (someone) with facts," it seems to me that you will be forced to call this an informative speech. After all, President Roosevelt cited fact after fact after fact: the Japanese attack, the hypocrisy of the Japanese diplomatic mission, the realization that the attack was planned days or weeks in advance, the American losses, the places attacked—Malaya, Hong Kong, Guam, the Philippines, Wake Island, Midway Island. These were facts. Cold, impersonal facts? No, of course not, but that's the point, isn't it? If you say that informing means setting forth facts, and that that is a process that is something other than persuasive, then you must call this an informative (a nonpersuasive) discourse. And that is obviously absurd. It would be hard to imagine a more dramatic address, one more distant from the objective and the impersonal than this one delivered by the president of a crippled nation that had not even yet prepared to defend itself. This discourse was anything but informative in that sense. But if you admit that, I think you must go on to talk about the persuasive nature of the facts that President Roosevelt used. For they were facts; he did present information. But those facts and that information functioned persuasively. And if you concede that point, you will have abolished the ill-considered informing-persuading dichotomy. Once you begin to talk about the persuasive nature of facts or of information, you must abandon the idea that there are two rhetorical processes and grant that the business of rhetoric is always persuasion.

Now for the second and very different discourse. And one of a sort that you may not be used to thinking of as rhetorical. These are the opening words of the first chapter of a book that I regard as extraordinarily important for all students of language. They are from Eric H. Lenneberg's *Biological Foundations of Language*.

Ever since man first mused about his own nature, it has been the gift of language that has surprised him most. If we search through the most primitive and the most ancient evidence of intellectual activity, through myths, magic, or religions, we will find one question that is repeated over and over: from what source comes the power of speech? Answers offered are either of a mystical or rational nature. The first type does not concern us here; the second, which is still prevalent today, is based on the principles of "discovery and rational utilization of inarticulate sounds." Explanations of this type propose that someone discovered certain advantages arising from accidental or instinctive vocalizations, and that one small discovery after another was incorporated into a communication system adopted by an ever-increasing range of individuals. The verbal behavior that came into existence in this manner proved to be so advantageous to those who adopted it in the struggle for survival, that it affected survival rates and natural selection, resulting in a strain that was endowed with "enlarged intellectual capacities," enabling even small children to learn the complicated natural languages as we know them today. A major objective of this monograph is to take issue with this type of formulation and to show that reason, discovery, and intelligence are concepts that are as irrelevant for an explanation of the existence of language as for the existence of bird songs or the dance of the bees.[22]

Compared to Roosevelt's address, these words seem calm, measured, and deliberate. These statements are far less dramatic than were Roosevelt's, but this is an unmistakably rhetorical use of language. The author is getting ready to propose a point of view. You can't tell what it is yet; at least you can't tell with any specificity. But you can tell what it is not. It's not going to be the conventional notion that language developed because of the social and communicative needs of the human animal. The author is going to argue against that idea; in his words, he is going to "take issue with" this notion. That is, he is going to set forth some idea(s) of his own, and he is going to advocate those ideas. He is going to (indeed, he has already begun to) *persuade*.

It's certainly possible to note some differences between the two examples I've given. My point is that both are rhetorical, that both present attitudes, that both attempt to persuade. But that immediately raises the question, "What sort of language behavior, if any, is *not* rhetorical?" The first answer is *none,* for I've already said that all language includes a rhetorical dimension. Every utterance is intended by the utterer to be heard, accepted, acted on, judged valid, or deemed meaningful. All of these are examples of persuasion, at least in the sense that, when I spell *judgment* j-u-d-g-m-e-n-t, I am trying to persuade you that I have spelled the word correctly. The second answer is that those language acts that we commonly call poetic, or literary, or artistic, or aesthetic are "not" rhetorical. As language, such forms include a rhetorical dimension, but that is not the function or the quality that we find most significant in them: so, logically, that is not the name by which we know them.

*Rhetoric is the theory and practice of persuasion by means of reasoned discourse.* I intend that definition to be a broad one. The major emphasis is on *reasoned discourse,* i.e. verbal language, but nonverbal and nonrational processes are necessarily included. "Persuasion" is a term that I use to cover all language that is

[22] Lenneberg, p. 1.

*primarily* concerned with expressing attitudes, positing points of view, or delineating certain outlooks. Such language includes the forms that have been called informative or expository, for language is a dynamic and personal process, and the very act of informing means that at a minimum the informer wishes to persuade the hearer or reader of the rightness of his information.

With this statement of the nature and scope of Rhetoric, I shall go on to inquire into the ways the speaker or writer discovers and develops his materials, the patterns into which he arranges and organizes those materials, and the qualities and kinds of language he chooses for his discourses. Since the classical period, these rhetorical issues have been titled Invention *(Inventio)*, Disposition *(Dispositio)*, and Style *(Elocutio)*.

## Invention

When you set out to persuade someone that something is true, false, should or should not be done, obviously you must first of all gather together the materials you plan to use. (I don't mean to imply that there are clear chronological divisions between Invention, Disposition, and Style; in fact, there's a great deal of overlapping. Still, Invention is necessarily the beginning.) Those materials may be vague notions or precise statements, quotations from authoritative sources or your own prejudices, but if they are to function as the ideas, data, and arguments in a discourse, they must first be found and then refined. The word *Invention* is appropriate in that the rhetorician *invents* the materials *as they finally appear.* I don't mean that he simply makes them up, but rather that he changes, modifies, and combines them so that their final form is one that is newly made and that can well be called *invented.*

In other words, Invention is the process of readying the persuasive elements that are to be used. Traditionally, those elements have been described as *proofs,* as the ways in which the speaker or writer "proves his point," and they have been divided into the *ethical* (those that consist of the rhetorician's behavior during the discourse), the *emotional* (those that are made up of appeals to the psychological needs and desires of the audience), and the *logical* (those that are provided by the evidence and argument of the discourse itself). Together, these processes offer a framework within which a good many rhetorical functions and effects can be discussed, as I shall try to show.

### Ethical Proofs

Audiences' responses are based in large part on the character of the speaker or writer. That is, reactions depend a great deal on *who* is speaking, not merely on what is being said. The various appeals that the rhetorician exerts simply by being the person that he is are called *ethos,* or ethical proofs. A distinction must be made, however, between the ethical proofs that depend on the rhetorician's fame or reputation and those that depend on the discourse itself. We often listen to celebrities more readily or with more interest than to unknown writers or speakers. There is no mystery in this, and it is a simple enough matter to understand and even to calculate in advance that a particular person is likely to be listened to by a particular audience just because he is a famous athlete, or movie star, or cabinet member.

Not only is this sort of ethical appeal easy to understand, there is relatively little to be done about it one way or the other, at least from the viewpoint of the speaker or writer. If you're not famous, you're not famous, and audiences are not going to behave as if you were. There's no way you can become famous for a special audience or occasion. Or, if you are famous, you are, and you can't put off your fame and behave as though it didn't exist. Aristotle pointed out the difference between *ethos* based on prior reputation and that based on behavior during the discourse, and I shall follow his lead in limiting the rest of this discussion to the ethical appeals created by the discourse. My primary reason for doing so is that a rhetorician has a great deal of control over his conduct during the brief period of time of the discourse, but far less over the past. There is much that can be done to change or increase the *ethos* that depends on the discourse, and to the extent that a reputation earned *during* a rhetorical act changes the image or the reputation that the speaker or writer had prior to that act, the rhetorician can control the past; to the extent that rhetorical acts do not alter prior reputations, the past is uncontrollable. *Ethos* is created, changed, diminished, increased in the present, in the rhetorical act that affects the past to varying degrees.[23]

In talking about ethical appeals, the first thing to get clear is the idea that we very often follow or support people, not because of what they say, but because of their character or personality. Indeed we may disagree rather directly with them and still consider that they are "right" or are doing a good job. A perfect example is found in the amazing political turmoil of 1968; Senator Eugene McCarthy, who based his campaign largely on opposition to the Vietnam war, was found to have many supporters who didn't agree with him at all. A column by pollster Louis Harris that appeared in the *Los Angeles Times*, August 22, 1968, stated that,

> The real key to the popular support for the McCarthy candidacy, despite all the speculation to the contrary, does not rest on the substance of the Vietnam war issue alone. Rather, the Senator has caught fire with sizable majorities of the American people for his personal and political courage and his new style of politics, whether or not they agree with his positions on Vietnam.

The fact that over twenty percent of McCarthy's supporters voted for George Wallace in the actual election seems to lend weight to the above comments, for it is hard to think of candidates who were further apart in their views on all issues than those two. And if some "McCarthy people" were able to vote for Wallace, it would appear either that they had not agreed with McCarthy's position on Vietnam (which was almost diametrically opposed to Wallace's) or that they were not

[23] For a pertinent article on this issue, see William R. Brown, "Television and the Democratic Convention of 1968," *Quarterly Journal of Speech* LV, 3: 237-46.

agreeing with Wallace's view but were, in one or both cases, voting on the basis of ethical appeals made by the two candidates.

This is really a perfectly ordinary matter and one that is part of our everyday actions. For instance, the man whom I most respect in my own field is one with whom I disagree very often on professional issues. Nevertheless, his honesty is like looking down a gun barrel, and his dedication to his work, to our field, and to academe is unblemished and unassailable. Compared with these qualities, the fact of my disagreements is unimportant; I would support him willingly and freely.

You will discover examples of your own, I'm sure: a friend whose preoccupation with, say, astrology borders on the absurd, but who is a warm and accepting person; another who is fairly brainless, but who has a vast tenderness for all troubled beings; or, on the other side, someone who is eminently sensible (that is, who feels much the way you do) about most important matters, but who is somehow a rather cold and remote person.

The point is that we react to the *person* speaking or writing, and at times we are quite capable of ignoring what is said and honoring our affection for, or aversion to, the person behind the words.

The ethical appeals exerted by rhetoricians during discourses are based primarily on their attitudes toward the subject or toward the audience, since these are the attitudes that we as hearers or readers perceive most readily. It's hard to draw a dividing line between these two attitudes, for careful accuracy or honesty toward a particular subject is likely to be mirrored in attitudes of honesty toward the audience, and *vice versa.* So I shall treat them as separate only because it's convenient, not because they are realistically separable.

Pertinent at this point is a group of studies that attempted to explore the importance and efficacy of *one-sided* versus *two-sided* persuasion.[24] "One-sided" means a discourse that presents only those arguments favoring the speaker or writer's view, "two-sided," a discourse that gives the arguments for *and* against a proposition, with the stress on the pro side. It seems to me highly significant that the findings generally have favored two-sided persuasion. In fact, one-sided persuasion can apparently be used advantageously only with audiences who already favor the point of view that's being advanced or who are relatively uneducated. Two-sided persuasion turned out to be more effective with relatively well educated audiences, with audiences who were neutral or opposed to the idea presented, and with audiences who were later exposed to counter-propaganda or persuasive efforts aimed at the opposing viewpoint (audiences exposed to two-sided persuasion resisted counter-propaganda far better than those exposed to one-sided persuasion). As with most such studies, these conclusions can be applied only tentatively in broad terms, for there were factors in those studies that may invalidate them in relation to other discourses and audiences. For example, the study referred to most frequently involved soldiers in World War II who were persuaded that the war would probably last another two years, and that they, therefore, would have to

[24] Carl I. Hovland, I. L. Janis, and H. H. Kelley, *Communication and Persuasion* (New Haven: Yale University Press, 1953), pp. 105-111.

fight that much longer. Clearly, such an audience may differ considerably from, say, a group of students being drafted today, or a bunch of over-thirty establishment members listening to Vice President Spiro Agnew.

Nevertheless, the very terms "one-sided" and "two-sided" are provocative. They suggest various attitudes and actions on the part of the rhetorician that must be evaluated ethically. I assume we would all agree that there are few issues of any significance today that can be treated simply or as if one knew the perfect answer. Despite some efforts to turn the cultural clock back a century or two, it appears that most of us are aware of the complexity of the times and troubles in which we live. What, then, shall we say of the speaker or writer who presents the simple answer, who offers only one side of the problem? It's tempting to say that he or she is not being entirely candid or has not done his research carefully enough. And similarly, we may wish to say of the user of two-sided persuasion that he trusts his audience enough to let them make up their own minds and that his thorough treatment of the subject makes him seem trustworthy to them. There are, of course, limits to this point of view; for example, I cannot imagine an explanation of our treatment of the American Indian that would make that aspect of our national character attractive to me. And I think I would be enormously suspicious of anyone who attempted such an explanation. So I must concede that there are some subjects or some occasions when two-sidedness is simply impossible, even though I am aware that we may determine those occasions and subjects differently.

In most instances, though, there is something to be said for the other side(s), though it will vary greatly in significance. And in most instances the rhetorician who takes the trouble to acquaint the audience with the negative aspects of his case will enhance the positive aspects of that case. There is a sense in which "positive" and "negative" may be better terms for the process I am describing than the notion of "sides," for many subjects do not have sides, as such. For example, I may wish to write about the values placed on art in preclassical societies; there are really no *sides*, to such a discourse, but there are positive and negative aspects thereof, as least in the simple sense that some things can be known quite clearly and definitely and positively, while others must be admitted to be questionable and vague, i.e., negative in relation to the affirmative movement of the discourse. And that brings up another point that needs comment.

It's possible to misinterpret this business of two-sided persuasion to mean that the rhetorician merely sets forth all the available facts and lets the audience do with them as it will. I intend nothing of the sort by my use of the label "two-sided." The speaker or writer who employs two-sided persuasion advocates a point of view; he affirms. He offers the audience the other side(s), the negative statements, because he wants to present the entire case honestly. But that is not to say that he is neutral in the matter. Because he is the persuader, he is, by definition, biased. He wishes the audience to believe or behave in a certain fashion, and he may well confront them with reasons for not behaving in such a manner simply in order to strengthen the conflicting reasons that will, he hopes, lead to just that behavior.

Here's a discourse that is an unusual example of this process. Unusual because one of the "sides" here is the speaker himself. It's a discourse by an "old" man that is addressed, at least partially, to "young" men. This creates a great many pitfalls for the writer. That he avoids them is almost rhetorical magic, and in the avoidance a discourse is created that is, in my opinion, an exceedingly important rhetorical act. I shall refer to it several times in pages to come.

## The Children's Crusade[25]

I am of two minds about this country's present convulsions. My heart is in the highlands with the hellers. But my head tells me . . . It's an old head, mine, without much wool on the top of it in the place where the wool ought to grow. Let me tell you what it is like to be old in the United States of America at the tail end of the nineteen-sixties.

My generation accepted the precepts of its parents, and they were the same precepts our parents had accepted from theirs. We violated the precepts, naturally; but we accepted them. The new generation rejects them. We were wrong and the new generation is right. Our precepts were good precepts, but still the new generation is right. They are right because preceptorial is as preceptorial does. We were—and, of course, are—pious frauds. They are impious Abelards.

That's the one big change. Another one is this: except for the remnantal remains of Gopher Prairie, the America of my youth is vanished without a trace; *Spurlos versunken*. In its perfectly splendid isolation, the rest of the world, being out of sight, was out of mind. My father didn't know whether Korea was in the Caribbean or the Mediterranean, or whether the Congo was a Spanish dance, a Hindu god, or a chocolate bar; he didn't care, and he didn't have to care.

It was an unjust America, of course. Blacks were Negroes, Negroes were niggers, and niggers were ineducable and would therefore always be menial. Jews knew their place and did not take forcible possession of the boardroom of the college or country club that refused to practice participatory democracy. It was an uncouth America, but a generous America and a visionary America. Its golden door was open and the lamp was bright beside it. Its very existence was a terror to tyranny everywhere, lest its spirit be infectious. In its pre-scientific and anarchic ardor it cultivated the techniques, if not the arts and institutions, of peace. In the first eight years of my life in Chicago, I never once saw a soldier. America was still, as it was intended to be, a refuge from chauvinistic horrors. If someone had told my father that he had to take a loyalty oath, he would have said, "What do you think this is—Russia?"

Gone, all gone now, to be replaced by the garrison state and the last best hope of preserving the status quo ante all over the world. If, then, you can understand what it is to be old in this country at the tail end of the nineteen-sixties, you will be able to understand why I am of two minds about the present convulsions: on balance, the changes I have seen in my time have been for the worse. I am afraid. But about certain aspects of the situation I am of one mind.

First: The revolution of the young blacks, formerly Negroes, is nothing but the Jim Crow branch of the American Children's Crusade. What the

[25] "The Children's Crusade" by Milton Mayer reprinted by permission of *The Center Magazine, a publication of the Center for the Study of Democratic Institutions.*

American Negroes are saying to the American whites is what the American young are saying to the American old: "I don't dig you. I don't love you. I don't honor you. I don't obey you." Whether it's Vietnam and "Hell, no, we won't go," or the ghetto and "Hell, no, we won't stay," the message is the same. The parochial concern of the Negro should not obscure the common cause against an America whose promises were made with its fingers crossed.

Second: The revolution of the young Americans—white, black, red, or pink—is nothing but the American branch of the world revolution of the rising generation—and the American branch is behind the times. The French branch has pulled down de Gaulle. The Spanish and Japanese branches have driven Franco and Sato up the wall. The Italian branch has made it impossible to govern Italy. The German branch has paralyzed Prussianism, and the Czech branch has immobilized communism. In our characteristic American provincialism we suppose that we have something special going here. The only thing that is special, indeed unique, is the elders' effort to persuade the young to call themselves kids in the hope that they won't take themselves seriously.

Third: The revolution is overdue—the revolution which Jeremiah and Jefferson invoked when they said that God's justice would not sleep forever. The evils that were containable under kings are no longer containable under politicians. A world that spends more on war than it does on health and education combined is not susceptible of reform. It calls for revolution. But revolution is not the same thing as rebellion. The aftermath of the Russian Revolution instructs us that revolution is not a matter of systems but of men; as the men are, so will the revolution be.

John Locke never heard of law and order, but he had heard of divine right. "When men are miserable enough," said Locke, "they will rebel, cry up divine right how you will." I think he should have said "desperate enough" instead of "miserable enough." The difference between submissive misery and desperate rebellion is hope. And the difference between rebellion and revolution is intelligence. The young everywhere, black, white, poor, rich, have the desperate certitude of hope along with the adolescent possibility of intelligence. The young don't need God *or* the big battalions on their side. All they need is the actuarial table, and they've got it. My object here is to persuade them to win a revolution instead of a rebellion—to make their victory stick. No revolution—not the French, not the American, and not the Russian—has ever stuck.

What is wanted is intelligence. That the status quo is unintelligent is superbly self-evident. But the revolution against it is not *ipso facto* intelligent. If it strikes with the wrong weapons at the wrong people for the wrong reasons, it will prove to have been unintelligent. If it assumes that there is nothing wrong with power and that a transfer or redistribution of power will improve the human condition, it will prove to have been unintelligent. He who says, "This ruler is a fool, but when I am a ruler I will not be a fool" is already a fool. It is not power that corrupts, but the unintelligent belief that power is not necessarily corrosive.

The revolution has to be intelligent, and the Negro's revolution has to be especially intelligent because he is its natural leader and is fighting in an exposed position. If he acts unintelligently he will go down faster than the white revolutionary whose pallor restrains (though it does not disable) the counter-revolution. To ask the Negro to be more intelligent than the white is only to ask him to use the intelligence he already has. But if all he has learned through his suffering is how to burn, baby, burn, he hasn't learned anything more than the white man, whose technological triumph consists of burning babies.

If the Negro does not use his superior intelligence, he is lost, because an ignorant little man cannot beat an ignorant big one. Whitey has overkill; blackie has underkill. The inference is inescapable. Along toward the end of 1941—but prior to December 7th of that year—Professor Morris Cohen listened while a Jewish colleague said, "I just want to bash in a few Nazi heads before I die." Somebody turned to Cohen and said, "And what do you think?" "I think," said Cohen, "that bashing heads is for the ninety-six per cent — not for the four per cent."

Even the ninety-six per cent cannot win that way now. It took the winners of the First World War fifteen years to realize that they had lost it. It took the winners of the Second World War only five. What keeps the winners of the third world war from launching it is the suspicion that they have lost it in advance of its launching. They can't bash in a few Russian or American heads without being bashed back. Their unintelligent alternative, as every schoolboy knows, is a balance of terror which is ruinous in any terms and in its own terms unreliable. Their only hope is to save their faces: It is an open secret that the Americans will agree to surrender to the Vietcong if the Vietcong will agree to proclaim an American victory. Old whitey seems to be at the end of the road. The inventor of the lynching bee at Calvary, the auction block at Charleston, and the shoot-out at Verdun seems to have no more inventions.

The young—above all, those who are non-Caucasian and therefore preconditioned to use their intelligence—are called upon to go out and turn the world upside down. Like the Apostles of Jesus, they do not need any baggage. They do not need black studies, because intelligence is not absorbed through the epidermis. They do not need black dormitories, because intelligence is not contracted by sleeping with people. They do not need black awareness, because intelligence is aware of itself and everything else. They need the intelligence they acquired in the course of their suffering, nothing more.

It is not enough for them to do their thing; the thing has to be the sensible thing to do. The sensible thing to do is not to demand a debased education on the ground that a debased education is what the young, and especially the Negro young, are fit for. The sensible thing to do is to demand a good education plus the compensatory qualifications of which they have been deprived.

A good education is not vocational training. The purpose of education is human freedom. We don't want Dow Chemical or R. O. T. C. off the campus; we want everything off the campus that has nothing to do with education for human freedom. That takes care not only of Dow Chemical and R. O. T. C. but also the placement office, home economics, physical education, business administration, journalism, speech, fraternities, and all the other goodies with which the old have tricked out higher learning in the hope of keeping the young quiet in a rest home for rich adolescents. We don't want war research off the campus; we want everything off the campus that has nothing to do with education for human freedom—including war research and industrial and commercial and labor research. We don't want theology, law, medicine, and engineering off the campus, but across the street where we can take advantage of pure research without diverting it from its purity.

Their motto has to be the motto of my alma mater, and it has to be properly parsed. The motto of my alma mater is, "Let knowledge grow more and more, that human life may be enriched." My alma mater abandoned the enrichment for the knowledge, the end for the means, and achieved the first self-sustaining nuclear chain reaction; the enrichment of human life in Hiroshima astonished the world.

There is nothing the young can do to disrupt the American college campus that hasn't been done by their elders. They should not connive with their elders in its disruption. They should revolutionize it—revolutionize it intelligently on the intelligent ground that it has forfeited its legitimacy and prostituted its independence. A university fifty per cent of whose budget is provided by the producers of overkill is monopolized by them and every one of its procedures tainted. (The Supreme Court once held that control of six per cent of the market for automobile magnetos was enough to constitute a monopoly in the industry.)

Education has always presupposed authority—the rightful authority, in respect of teaching, of those who know over those who don't know. It has lost its authority because its practitioners have lent themselves to the production and perpetuation of deadly error. Authority stripped of its rightfulness is authoritarianism. The young are right in repudiating authoritarianism. But they are mortally wrong if they think that they will improve their situation by replacing their elders' authoritarianism with their own.

Their intelligence, as it rejects authoritarianism, rejects the struggle for Negro rights as such and for student rights as such. Such a struggle is self-interested and is therefore no different in principle from the self-interest that disgraces their elders. There is no such category as Negro rights or student rights because there is no such category as Negro or student. Either there are human rights or there are none. Either we are first of all men, and only then black men or white men, or we are nothing. Because blacks are men, they are not to be badgered. Because they are men, they are not to be manipulated. Because they are men, they are not to be conscripted or enslaved. When the Negro was a slave, and the white man called him a black, he said, "I am a man."

The Negro does not have to be superhuman or saintly. He has only to be intelligent. What was good about Martin Luther King was his intelligence. He would not lift a finger to save one man or one country. His race was the one race, man, without regard to the amount of melanin in his skin. He knew the perdurable agony of man in his own person. Persecution was his teacher, and he learned from his teacher how to speak for man.

Who else will speak for man? Not whitey. Whitey has battened on partiality—on racism, on nationalism, on the exploitation of his brother, black and white. Whoever fights for partiality is playing whitey's game and playing into whitey's hands, perpetuating the intolerable separation of man into species. Separatism is for the birds; there is only one surviving species of the class *Homo,* and that is *Homo sapiens.* Whoever speaks for man must refuse to let any man be segregated by anybody—even by himself.

Just as there must be one world or none, so there must be one culture or none. That culture is man's. Asian and African and European studies in America are justified only by the American's ignorance of Asia, Africa, and Europe; that is, they are not justified at all. The black culture of the African-descended American, like the Irish culture of the Irish-descended American, is an atavism that denies the common manhood and asserts a tribalism which is always and everywhere barbarian. If I cannot understand the writings of Eldridge Cleaver because of my skin color, then Eldridge Cleaver cannot understand the writings of Shakespeare because of his. Everybody, and not just the Nazis, will burn the books.

What is wanted here is unanswerable argument. Attack education for its present debasement, and you are unanswerable. Assert your right to live without killing, and you are unanswerable. Demand justice and not advantage, and you are unanswerable. Call upon the church, not for five hundred million dollars in special reparations for the Negro but for five hundred billion dollars in general justice for the poor, and you are unanswerable. But call policemen "pigs" and you are answerable by those who remember the Nazis calling the Jews *Schweinehunde.* Call public officials "fascists" and you are answerable by those who remember fascism. Call for power and you are answerable by those who remember the Caesars and the Hapsburgs and the Romanovs. Call for black faculties and black curricula and you are answerable by those who call for humanistic faculties and humane curricula. Call for separatism and you will have on your side—though they kill you—the supremacists who have the necessary overkill to maintain the separatism you call for. Do you want separate but equal opportunity? You will get the separate opportunity and suffer the inequality that follows ineluctably from the separation of the minority from the majority.

The Negro racist, like the white racist, bases his racism on dignity. But men cannot shoot or burn or brawl their way to dignity; if they could, the American white man would be the most dignified man on earth. Does it make the young feel good to occupy an administration building and horrify the straights and terrify the timid and license the governor to turn on the tear gas? Do they want to feel good or to be intelligent? Do they want a rebellion or a revolution? Dignity is not a matter of feeling good—of the mumbo-jumbo of "black is beautiful" or "America the beautiful." America is no more beautiful than Africa and black is no more beautiful than blue.

I wish that the young could make their demands negotiable, but I don't see how they can if they make them intelligent. I don't see how overkill can be negotiated. I don't see how a ghetto or nerve gas research or the C. I. A. can be negotiated. But properly non-negotiable objectives cannot be achieved by throwing a rock through a window on the ground that the owner of the window understands nothing but force. He understands force, all right, and he has it. His level of intelligence has to be raised to the point where he can comprehend that the travesty of the campus and the ghettos and the battlefield is finished. A generation which elects a Lyndon Johnson or a Richard Nixon has no visible intention to negotiate. It will pay lip service to negotiation, provided that the shape of the table is right and as long as it doesn't have to stop doing the only thing it knows how to do. Harvard University had three hundred years to clean house on the basis of negotiable demands. The people who rightfully deplore the claim of the riotous young to amnesty have amnestied themselves since the world began. There may be those who recall Cain's general demurrer to the complaint that he had failed to discharge his responsibility to his brother.

Old whitey may be unintelligent and out of steam, but he still has his pristine cunning. If he is persistently pushed he will propose gradualism, by which he means gradually wearing blackie down. Whitey isn't wicked. He is unconcerned. His unconcern is not immoral. It is unintelligent. By power possessed, he cannot understand what Paul meant by saying that we are all members one of another. He cannot understand what Jesus meant by saying that he who takes the sword will perish by it. He cannot understand what the prophet meant by proclaiming the greater damnation of those who devour widows' houses and make long prayers for a pretense. He didn't mean to be like this. Power benighted him, and he walks in the noonday as in the night. If I may paraphrase an eminent Harvard alumnus—a hundred generations of people like us is enough. If the new generation turns out to be the hundred and first, it is lost.

The old have torn down Vietnam and kept the ghettos in their place, and now they say that the young want to tear things down without having anything to put in their place. The old are not competent to complain, and the complaint is an empty one anyway. The young don't have to have anything to put in the place of the present shambles. The Lord God Jehovah did not tell their ancestors and mine what to put in the place of Sidon and Tyre; he told them, "You shall walk in My path and I will show you My way." It is easy to think up the right thing. What is hard is to stop doing the wrong one. The Lord did not tell their ancestors and mine to do good. He told them, "Cease to do evil—learn to do good." They need only to be intelligent.

If they are intelligent, the totalitarian spirit—which unintelligently obeys all laws—will call them anarchists. But they should not be dismayed. True, anarchy is the second worst condition of human society. The worst is tyranny. He who, like the intelligent founders of this republic, will not have tyranny, must take his chances on anarchy. The Nuremberg decision of the International Military Tribunal in 1946 *requires* anarchy of the soldier who is ordered to perform inhuman acts. Disorder is no worse than injustice, which is the institutionalization of disorder. When the laws are rooted in violence and maintained by violence, they must not be obeyed. Socrates was right, not wrong, when he said, "Men of Athens, I love you, but I shall obey God rather than you." John Brown was right. Mohandas Gandhi was right. Martin Luther King was right. And Thomas Aquinas was right seven centuries ago when he said that an unjust law is no law and does not bind a man in conscience.

There is a higher law. The higher law does not have to be very high to be higher than the Selective Service Act or the Internal Revenue Act, only more intelligent. The young should study the German experience of the nineteen-thirties, when the most literate nation on earth, mistaking literacy for intelligence, elevated ignorance to power and cut its own head off. They should study the German experience and learn that neither the government nor the majority is by definition a good judge of justice. Civil disobedience may be treasonable. It is not necessarily unpatriotic. A patriot will set his country right if he can, but in no case will he contribute to its continued delinquency.

I am one of the elders of whom I speak. The young terrify me. They terrify me because I have mine, which I got by the exercise of the good precepts I learned from my parents plus being white and landing on my feet every time I fell on my face. The young do not terrify me with their popguns; I have ten machine guns for every one of their popguns. They terrify me because they show some small sign of social maturity, of civic responsibility and human concern. Their elders, like me, are nice people, but they did not mature. The young have seen them playing cops and robbers at home and overkill in their worldwide playpen. Television reveals the infantilism of the adults' attention span. They cannot talk; they can sit mesmerized, or they can shout or mumble. They made the young mumble, "One nation, indivisible," and after they had mumbled it a few thousand times, some subversive told them that five per cent of the American people have twenty per cent of the nation's income and twenty per cent have five per cent of it, and they began to become what their elders call cynical; that is, intelligent. The day the young complete the process their elders will fall off the stage of history; they won't even have to be pushed.

The President of Notre Dame says that "we need a rebirth of academic, civic, and political leadership—a sharing of those youthful ideals and dreams, whether they are impossible or not." The President of Notre Dame is right. But whose fault is it that we need such a rebirth? How did we come to be so needy, with so rich a heritage and so profligate a land? How are we to be reborn? What does "a sharing of those youthful ideals and dreams" mean? What have the elders got to offer as their share? Not youth or ideals or dreams.

The ideals of the elders are money, fame, and power, and they dream of bigger and better sugarplums. They are starved for soul food, and chicken every Sunday has not filled them. They are obese, but unfilled. Now they have run out of time. They have run out of time to choose to free the Negroes or to fight a civil war to enslave them. All they can do now is cry up the divine right of law and order and shudder for themselves as they see it in action and observe the lawlessness and disorder it brings in its train.

Our black brethren are freeing themselves impatiently. For three centuries they waited patiently—so patiently that whitey, who takes impatience for manliness, took them for sheep who look up to be fed and look down when they aren't. They waited at the end of the line, and no matter how short the line got they were still waiting. They waited at the back of the bus, and no matter how empty the bus was they were still at the back. Their patience is beginning to be exhausted.

Whitey had no intention of living up to his profession that all men are created equal. As this country's sovereign he could not and can not pass the buck for its derelictions. What the country was was his doing; was, and is. His tragic flaw was his possession by power and the consequent corruption of his intelligence. He did not understand that no man can free another because no man can enslave another. Whitey wanted blackie to act like a freedman. But blackie isn't a freedman; no man is. He is a free man, and a free man because he is a man. Therein lies his dignity—not in the grace of his master—and he loses it not by being in chains but by chaining himself to the humiliating values of his master. Whoever would want to be and do and have what the American white man is and does and has is not a man but a slave and, like the American white man, an unhappy slave at that.

The only hope of the old is the intelligence of the young. Their intelligence may be undeveloped, but it is not yet corrupted. They are still young. They have been forced by the American educational process to undertake their own education. They are not to be put down or put off, because they have been set to wondering. What set them to wondering was, I suppose, the two victorious world wars their elders waged and lost in the process of winning them. Coming in the wake of these wingless victories, they would have had to be catatonic epileptics not to have wondered. Wonder is the beginning of wisdom. The young are wising up. All they have not to do is what what E. E. Cummings called up-grow and down-forget.

Their intelligence tells them that the only solution to racialism is miscegenation. There was a time when an Irishman could not be elected President. There was a time when a Catholic could not be elected President. There was even a time when a fighting Quaker couldn't be elected President. The change in our national attitude was the result of what we Dixiecrats call mixing. Hybrid corn and hybrid pigs are of higher quality than the original stocks, and there is no evidence whatever that hybrid man is not. Since seventy percent of all the American "blacks" are part "white" and millions of American "blacks" have passed unknowingly into the so-called white race, the racist who says he wouldn't want his daughter to marry a Negro—or a white man—has no way of knowing whether she does or doesn't and neither has she or her fiancé. As long as pigmentation provides our society with the one discernible other, and as long as whitey is ineducable by anthropology, psychology, and theology, the only solution is to make indiscernible others of us all.

Five hundred years would do it. But then five hundred years of education for freedom would make intelligent human beings of us and it wouldn't matter anymore what color we were. But we have run out of time. It isn't the future that's dark—it's the present. If the young do not bring light to the world, if they spurn a little suffering undergone for the sake of intelligence, the wave of the present will roll over them and, like their elders, they will be heard of no more.

—Milton Mayer

The first thing that strikes me about this discourse is the enormous difference between it and the majority, the great majority of the sentiments regularly voiced by the old. This speaker may be, as he says, old. But he possesses a precious combination of qualities—age and honesty. Consider the things that he has *not* said:

he has *not* told the young they are right to be dissatisfied, *but* that they must realize that changes of the sort they desire require a great deal of careful thought and planning; he has *not* argued that many changes must certainly be made, *but* that the young must be very careful not to destroy what is valuable along with what is valueless; he has *not* talked piously of the American social system as the best in the world, *despite* the problems that we face ("and we face them together, my young friends"); he has emphatically *not* said a word to the effect that most of the disruptions and demonstrations have been caused by the misguided *few* who have swallowed the terrible bait of a foreign ideology, while the *many* are really fine American lads and lasses who are a bit confused by these confusing times; and he has very carefully and clearly *not* said that the young are ready enough to tear down, *but* that they have nothing, and certainly nothing better, to put in the place of what they will destroy.

He has not said any of these things—these mouthings that are the too frequent utterances of the frightened old to the angry young. Instead he has said, *first of all,* that he has mixed feelings, that his "heart is in the highlands with the hellers," but that his head is cautious, even cynical. And that comment sets the tone for the whole essay; it's the beginning of the process of pointing out both sides.

Put in their simplest terms, the sides in question here are the favorable and unfavorable attitudes toward the discontent of the young. In somewhat more complicated terms, the sides are the positive and negative aspects of the rebellion of the young and the positive and negative aspects of the social order the old have created and the young have inherited. This discourse is, as I said, an unusual example of two-sided persuasion because the rhetorician points out the validity in both the favorable and unfavorable views of youthful discontent, discusses both the positive and the negative aspects of the revolution of youth, and even deals with the worthy and the worthless elements of the social order of the old. And he does all this, not by pretending to report facts in some impersonal fashion, but within the limits of an intensely personal and warmly positive statement to and about the young.

First, the undeniable right of the young to be discontented, to express that discontent, and to change the society in which they live is not only admitted, but is stressed. He says bluntly, "We (the old) were wrong and the new generation is right." He adds, "The revolution is overdue. . . . The evils that were containable under kings are no longer containable under politicians. A world that spends more on war than it does on health and education combined is not susceptible of reform. It calls for revolution." These are not the words of a man who is playing it safe; they are extreme—extreme and passionate. But they are only one side of the picture, and if he had stopped there the discourse would have not stirred me. He does not stop, though; he goes on to the notion that the young are too often rebelling, not mounting a revolution.

Second, in his constant emphasis on the need for intelligence he points out that the young are right in repudiating authoritarianism, in attacking education because it has been cheapened, in demanding an end to killing, in asking help for the poor. All these are positive aspects of the international youth movement. But he adds the negative ones: calling police and officials "pigs" and "fascists," using the American white man's violent tactics, and wanting "to feel good" more than to be intelligent. A major strength of this discourse is the fact that the author never says that the young should listen to him. I find no hint here of the familiar, "Now, if you young people will follow the advice. . . . " Indeed he has completely eliminated the possibility of any such whining by saying, "The young don't need God *or* the big battalions on their side. *All they need is the actuarial table, and they've got it.*" (Italics mine.) I understand that to mean that the young are going to "win." The only question concerns revolution versus rebellion, not victory versus defeat.

Third, he talks truthfully about the ills and evils the old have created. "We were wrong. . . . We were—and, of course, are—pious frauds." "It was an unjust America." "Old Whitey seems to be at the end of the road. The inventor of the lynching bee at Calvary, the auction block at Charleston, and the shoot-out at Verdun seems to have no more inventions." And that flat comment, "A generation which elects a Lyndon Johnson or a Richard Nixon has no visible intention to negotiate." But again, if he had stopped here it would all have come to little, for the man who has only ill to speak of himself and his kind has nothing to say to those who have already charged him with these ills. And silence might add more significance to the charges than merely echoing one's accusers. It's important that he said, "Our precepts were good precepts. . . . It was an uncouth America, but a generous America and a visionary America. Its golden door was open and the lamp was bright beside it." And even the tepid, "Their elders, like me, are nice people, but they did not mature." These qualities *must* be added to the longer list of evils, for without them not only is there a weakness in this rhetorician's voice and view, but the young will have no strength, no good, no grace on which to build their history. It is imperative that the two sides be told.

Most impressive of all, to me, is the intimate and personal honesty of this author. I respect him and am moved by him when he writes, "I am one of the elders of whom I speak. The young terrify me. They terrify me because I have mine. . . ." I respect him and am moved by him when he says, "I wish that the young could make their demands negotiable, but I don't see how they can if they make them intelligent." And I respect him and am moved by him and when he utters those bleak words, "A hundred generations of people like us is enough." I think that this is the highest form of two-sided persuasion—the ability to speak as a member of a disliked or despised group of oppressors to the group that is fighting to resist that very oppression, to tell of the shortcomings and virtues of both groups, to admit the fear and the guilt that accompanies the telling, and even to confess the wish that the young not be so resolute, adding at once that intelligence requires just that resoluteness.

This is an important and extremely well made rhetorical discourse. Much more might be written about it, and its strengths might be explored from various points of view. One of those strengths, however, and a major one, is the two-sidedness of the persuasion involved here. And that means that it was the *writer* who made these words lustrous. It was the *ethos*, the man himself that worked this rhetorical magic. It was the strikingly and uncompromisingly ethical attitude toward his subject and his audience that made these words memorable. Or if you prefer, reverse the equation: His utter honesty toward his audience was reflected in the care and thoroughness with which he handled his subject. The two go together; where there is one the other will be found.

For me, the effect of this sort of ethical behavior can easily outweigh other aspects of the discourse. And I am in good company here, for Aristotle wrote that the rhetorician's "character may almost be called the most effective means of persuasion he possesses."[26] It often seems so to me, particularly in the case of discourses such as this one. The very fact that Professor Mayer presents with such meticulous care the various sides of the issues involved makes me feel that his own viewpoint must be a powerful one indeed. Anyone who can treat opposing views so directly and honestly must have profound faith in his own position and in his reasons for holding it. And of course that feeling leads me to listen carefully, to take those reasons very seriously. I am, in other words, prepared to be convinced.

So, as I said earlier, the very act of doing justice to the other side is likely to strengthen your own. Obviously there are not many cases of ethical appeals as firmly based as those in this discourse. And there are many subjects with which it would be difficult or impossible to exhibit this sort of extraordinary honesty, for there are many subjects that do not have "sides" in this sense. Still, every speaker or writer has the opportunity to admit completely and gracefully the validity of the views that he opposes, the questions for which he has no answers, and the shortcomings of the concepts that he advocates. Such admissions are likely to stand the rhetorician in extremely good persuasive stead, for they present him to his audience as an ethical man.

### Emotional Proofs

The act of appealing to an audience's emotions presents, or can present, a problem for theorists and practitioners of Rhetoric which can be stated something like this: If Rhetoric is primarily a rational process, it would seem that the very use of emotional appeals would be, at best, incidental to, and at worst, degrading to the rhetorical process. Presumably the rhetorician will prefer rational approaches and will use emotional appeals only as an added rhetorical fillip or when he is unsure of the power of his logical statements and wishes to prod the audience into act or attitude. And presumably, the audience will need emotional appeals only when they are unable to understand the logical reasons for behaving in a given manner or have not been moved rationally to such behavior. If you take this view, you carry neo-Aristotelianism to an indefensible extreme, for you say, in effect, that emotional appeals work, but that they work only because of the unfortunate flaws in the nature of human beings, and that responsible rhetoricians should be wary of using this rhetorical technique even though it may be the most effective one they have. A few writers have taken this position, as witness these quotes from a textbook on persuasion:

[26] Aristotle *Rhetorica* i. 2. 1356a. 14-15.

Emotional appeals have always been somewhat suspect because of the quite proper assumption that they befuddle the hearer's judgment.[27]

(Indirect suggestion) operates best when the subject's thinking is *dissociated;* that is, when his thought processes are so fully occupied with an irrelevant problem that the speaker's point can slip through without critical examination.[28]

Suggestion is of value to the persuasive speaker when he needs to secure a decision in a hurry, when his audience is incapable of following through a long and involved logical argument, when the audience is sufficiently predisposed toward the proposal so that it needs only direction—not proof—and when the speaker's prestige is so great that the audience wants to know only what he believes, not why he believes it.[29]

As I understand them, the first of the above quotes covers all emotional appeals with a blanket of suspicion, for who would trust decisions made with the judgment befuddled; the second points out quite clearly that the rhetorician who uses indirect suggestion best is a sort of con man who tricks the audience into believing him; and the third seems to say that the writer or speaker should use suggestive techniques only when he hasn't time to be rational (although the suggestive appeals must be stronger or more effective than the rational because they do the job in a hurry), when his audience is too stupid to understand logical reasoning, when his audience needs to know only what to think and will not worry about why they should do so, and when the audience is willing to ape the speaker or writer slavishly no matter what his beliefs are. I have put these comments rather strongly, but they do not distort the quoted matter given above, to the best of my judgment.

This point of view seems to me unfortunate if only because the rhetorical process is cheapened, and those (i.e., all of us) who engage in it are characterized as sharpsters or fools. This viewpoint is dismayingly like one I found in an old book on salesmanship. Compare the following words with the above excerpts:

All men want things. All men want many things which they feel, for one reason or another, they cannot have. Some of these wants become so strong that they become passions, and when a want has arrived at that state, it is usually satisfied. Most men, however, have learned to control such passions and to try to think things out rationally, and even when their emotions have affected their judgments, they feel that it was brought about by reasoning. The task of the salesman at this point is to appeal to the emotions of the prospect and to let him feel that the sound reasoning which he used earlier in the sale led him to these logical conclusions. The salesman must bear in mind, however, that no one likes to realize that he is being appealed to through his emotions. It is one of the psychological laws that when people know they are having their emotions "played on," they immediately develop antipathy for the person appealing to them, and in some people this develops into intense

[27] Robert T. Oliver, *The Psychology of Persuasive Speech* (New York: Longmans, Green and Co., 1942), p. 170.
[28] *Ibid.*, p. 233.
[29] *Ibid.*, p. 250.

anger, harbored animosity, and, occasionally, violence. The salesman must always be *most* sincere at a time like this.[30]

A pretty naked and ugly statement, isn't it? The direct admission that the salesman's job is to fool the customer—manipulate him without letting him know it. The comic naivete in the proclamation of a psychological law. And the strangest idea of all—the notion that feelings are so ugly that we wish to ignore them, and that we will so resent appeals that arouse feeling responses that we may resort to violence. And of course, that incredible final statement that in the middle of his manipulation the salesman "must always be *most* sincere."

What is most troublesome to me is that the same attitudes are present in the three short quotes given first as in the longer paragraph above. The hucksters of the world have often been criticized for unethical behavior, but are we to say that this business of selling is one of the two basic language currents in which we all move? Look at the similarities: the unworthiness of emotional responses combined with the fact that they are more powerful than rational ones; the idea that both the rhetorician and the salesman fool their audiences; and the belief that the audience is so psychologically and intellectually limited that they cannot control their own behavior, but will jerk like obedient puppets when the emotional strings are pulled. If these comments are to apply to all those language acts through which men persuade their fellows, we are indeed beset by a problem—the problem of the thoroughly shoddy nature of Rhetoric itself!

That problem seems to be based on one simple assumption, namely, that you can choose to *use* emotional appeals or *not to use* them; put differently, the assumption is that some language is logical and some is emotional, and that the two can be separated. This is the basis of the problem because it is only by assuming that you may or may not appeal to an audience emotionally that the issues of when and how to employ such appeals are created. If the original assumption were that the speaker or writer was *always* using emotional appeals, because language itself was an emotional process, the whole fuss about suggestion, fooling the audience, and manipulating people without letting them know it would not exist, *could not* exist. For to assume that emotional appeals are always being made is to say that the rhetorician cannot avoid making them, that they are simply part of the reality of language, and that there are no special occasions when emotional appeals are made because reason has failed.

In a sense I've already dealt with this problem by insisting that all language is persuasive, that impersonal and objective uses of language do not exist. The idea of logical appeals is surely similar to the idea of factual, informative language, and of emotional appeals to persuasive language forms. So by arguing that all language acts are biased and persuasive, I've pretty much argued that all those acts are emotional.

Obviously I don't mean that all my (or your) language behaviors are emotional and *nonfactual* or *nonlogical*; I mean that they are *emotional and logical*. I said earlier that facts are persuasive, and I would restate it now, "Logic is emotionally effective." President Roosevelt delivered a rhetorical address to

[30] Charles H. Fernald, *Salesmanship* (New York: Prentice-Hall, Inc., 1933), pp. 247-48.

Congress; it was rhetorical because it was persuasive, and it achieved persuasiveness primarily by using factual or logical statements in an emotionally effective manner.

To put it simply, every possible utterance has an emotional dimension, no matter how unimportant that dimension may seem.

But all this merely relieves you of the need to decide that certain statements or discourses *are or are not* logical or emotional, for they are all logical *and* emotional. But it does nothing to help you decide that certain statements or discourses function *more* or *less* logically or emotionally *for certain audiences* than do others. The simple comment that Lincoln's "Gettysburg Address" and Emerson's essay "The Poet" both include logical and emotional elements is important in that it prohibits the disastrous view that the emotional appeals of one or both of these works were deliberately brought into play after the processes of reason had failed, and that those emotional aspects are, consequently, to be scorned as inferior rhetorical efforts. But it *is* a simple comment, and it will not help you discern the important differences between these (or other) discourses. What is needed is another notion.

That notion is found in the idea that the rhetorical act is a *discourse.* I've used that word frequently, and I intend by it its most usual meaning: *systematic or connected statements that communicate thoughts and feelings to listeners or readers.* A discourse is *addressed to someone*, it communicates *with* some audience. And therein lies the nature of emotional appeals, for it's not by some measure of the emotions that are objectively *in* the discourse that meaningful comparisons can be made, but by an evaluation of the discourse *as it affects a particular audience.* A discourse is emotionally stirring or disappointing only *for some audience.* Without the audience there is no discourse. If no one reads it, this book will not exist as a rhetorical event; it will exist only as ink squiggles on pages. So it's the direct relationship between the discourse and the audience that determines the emotional appeals being used. The degree to which the writer/speaker focuses on his audience, speaks *to them*, and frames his statements in relation to the needs and desires of that specific audience determines the emotional impact and elicits emotional responses.

I do *not* mean that, like the worst salesmen and politicians, the rhetorician merely tells his audience what they want to hear. That sort of behavior might, I suppose, be called *direct*, but it clearly rules out any possible ethical position on the part of the rhetorician. (And interestingly, I know of no evidence that supports the idea that the unethical speaker or writer is likely to be more successful than the ethical one.) Rather, I mean that the rhetorician who addresses his audience, who constructs his discourse in such a way that his statements are *meaningful* and *important* to that audience is the one who is using the strongest emotional appeals. The whole process of fitting the discourse to the audience in this fashion has been called "audience adaptation."

*Audience adaption* is an appropriate and significant term, so long as you realize that the simple business of "selling out" ethically is not involved. Discourses must be adapted to audiences, for without the audience there is no discourse. One of the first problems that occurs with audience adaptation is the simple difficulty of adapting to certain audiences. I may fairly easily build a discourse that is adapted to a group of academic philosophers; it would be considerably harder to adapt a discourse to an audience of American college students; and it would be extremely difficult to adapt a talk or an essay to the American public. The first of these groups is relatively small and homogeneous (despite the glaring differences between some of its members), the second, large and varied in hundreds of ways, and the third, enormous and enormously complex. So in general, the larger and more varied the audience, the harder it is to adapt to that audience. Still, it must be attempted if the discourse itself is to be attempted.

An idea that has functioned well for me as a key to the complexities of audience adaptation is the notion that so-called facts or objective statements are not single linguistic entities, but are pluralistic and relativistic phenomena. That is, a fact is not simply *a fact*; it is *one of several* ways of saying something. *One of several.* We tend, I think, to assume that a fact is a fact is a fact, and that's all there is to it. But not so, there's much more to it. For example, several years ago the city of San Francisco asked its citizens to vote on whether or not they wanted U.S. military forces withdrawn from Vietnam. About a third voted "yes." The Los Angeles papers reported that "fact" about like this: "San Franciscans Vote Overwhelmingly Against Vietnam Withdrawal." Now of course, you will say that the word "overwhelmingly" is the villain because it's an emotionally loaded word. And you're right. But what happens if you merely eliminate that word? You're left then with "San Franciscans Vote Against Vietnam Withdrawal." That's a "fact," yes. But it's not very specific. What was the vote? Well, the simplest solution might seem to be: "San Franciscans Vote 2 to 1 Against Vietnam Withdrawal." This is quite obviously a "fact," but equally obvious would be the "fact" that "San Franciscans Vote 1 to 2 For Vietnam Withdrawal." And the two "facts" are not the same. More than that, neither is a very complete or thoroughly stated fact, for that 2 to 1 or 1 to 2 vote might be either a huge outpouring of public feeling in a certain context or a disappointing trickle in another. As I write this page, all political theorists agree that the vast majority of Americans is in favor of ending the Vietnam War, and that it's possible that a majority actually favors unilateral withdrawal. Today, then, a third of the people favoring withdrawal would be a surprisingly small group. When the vote was actually taken in San Francisco, the drums were still beating, and we were still talking about maintaining our honorable commitments in Asia no matter what the cost. Thus, the third who favored withdrawal was a surprisingly large group for that time. The 2 to 1 or 1 to 2 was one thing then, and would be quite a different thing today. Given the temper of the times (not the *Los Angeles Times*, though), the headlines might well have read "Surprisingly Large San Franciscan Vote Favors Vietnam Withdrawal," for it is a "fact" that it *was* a surprisingly large vote, and the surprising size of the vote is part of its factualness. You can't ignore or eliminate that part without distorting the "fact" that is being reported. Of course you can also distort it by moving to the other extreme: "Huge San Franciscan Vote Against Vietnam War." That's a "fact," too.

One comment frequently made in these cases is that two things are involved—the "fact" and its significance. It's argued that some statements are entirely factual and can be reported without distortion. Statements of significance, it's added, may distort, but they can be eliminated without affecting the "fact." This argument is made less impressive, in my opinion, by the "fact" that the examples used are almost never the normally complex language events that affect us most deeply (notice the distortion on my part here); instead, extremely simple utterances are used as evidence. It's asserted that statements such as "The pencil is on the table" are entirely factual. But even with these simple language acts the argument can be refuted. Consider this approach: You begin by saying that there is no universal sense in which the statement is a "fact," for there *are* tables with no pencils on them; in other words, the statement can be true only of a particular table and a particular pencil; then you go on to describe the sort of situation in which someone might say, "The pencil is on the table," and you emphasize the idea that the statement is necessarily arbitrary in the sense that it is but one of several statements that might have been made; for example, depending on the rhetorical elements involved, you might say "The pencil is on the table," or "The pencil is on the left-hand corner of the brown table," or "The pencil is exactly three-quarters of an inch from the lower left-hand corner of the dark brown table in front of the window," or . . .etc., etc., etc.; and you finish by stressing the "fact" that *all* these statements are "facts" in that particular situation, and that the reasons for using one rather than another are *rhetorical,* not *logical.* If you think your audience is concerned only with knowing whether the pencil is on the table or on the chair, you utter the first statement; if you think your audience wants or needs more detail, you utter the second, or third, or some other statement. The point is that *you choose* the "fact" that *seems to you* most effectively *adapted to your audience.*

(The argument isn't likely to end so easily. Very often the next step is a resort to mathematics or an attempt to find a situation in which there are two equally probable possibilities, the choice between which is made by the communication of a "fact." Then it's argued that this is a *pure fact.* However, the battle can be waged on this level, too, as I shall describe in Chapter 5.)

The concept of the relative nature of facts becomes much clearer when you are involved in social questions. "The pencil is on the table" may *seem* at first glance to be totally factual, but "America must remain the strongest nation in the world," is not likely to be considered in such a simple light. And similarly, the vote in San Francisco was far from a simple factual matter. It was a "fact" that "One Third of the Voters in San Francisco Favor Withdrawal From Vietnam," and it was *also* a "fact" that "Two Thirds of the Voters In San Francisco Oppose Withdrawal From Vietnam," and it made a difference whether it was put the one way or the other. Thus "facts" are never ready made items that you simply pass on to your audience; you must *choose* from various statements the one that you present as "fact," and your choice will be rhetorically determined by *your* estimate of the *emotional impact* that that "fact" will have on *a certain* audience.[31]

[31] For an interesting development of this point, see Robert L. Scott, "On Viewing Rhetoric as Epistemic," *Central States Speech Journal* XVIII, 9-17.

So, returning to the business of audience adaptation as a process of exerting emotional appeals by addressing hearers or readers directly, the first principle is that all discourses, even the most factual ones, *must* be adapted to the audience, and the fact of audience adaptation is the basis of the emotional appeals involved. Now I don't mean to say that only facts have emotional value. There are many emotionally effective statements that we would wish to call nonfactual. Rather, I have been trying to demonstrate my belief that there is no such thing as a completely unemotional, factual, impersonal, and objective statement. In other words, all statements, all language acts are emotional to some degree, though that degree may vary considerably.

Partly because language events differ greatly in the intensity of their emotional appeals, and partly because today's audiences are rather sophisticated, contemporary rhetoricians must use emotional proofs pretty carefully if they are not to alienate their audiences. At least this care is indicated if I am at all representative of today's audiences. Recently I received an invitation to join a discount club that promised huge savings on all sorts of purchases. Those savings may or may not be possible, but I quickly decided I wouldn't join the organization under any circumstances, and I decided after reading these words:

> I'd like to assure you that this offer isn't for just anyone. If you don't spend at least $100 annually on merchandise, or if you are not a real go-getter and can't dig up that much business, just put this offer aside. YOU WILL be wasting your time and money. First, you must invest $5.00 in this opportunity. Second, you will have to buy $100 worth of merchandise a year to effect a real good savings or earn any kind of decent profit.
>
> I REPEAT. If $5.00 for a membership fee scares you forget this whole offer. It isn't for you. We are organized to service the SERIOUS BUYER ONLY! We don't need and don't want your money if you can't profit or save handsomely by membership in a FACTORY BUYING CLUB. But if you are really serious I invite you to read on. We don't have to sell you on the value of our unique service. That is readily evident to any thoughtful person.

There are a few flaws in this rhetorical monstrosity that you might call factual, I suppose, but these are the least of the rhetorical crimes that are committed here. My immediate reaction was that I was the object of a hard-sell routine delivered by a salesman who was both stupid and snotty. The absolutely childish attempt to put me in the category of big spenders by talking of $100 a year was bad enough. But the idiocy of trying to pressure or shame me into joining by asking if the $5.00 membership fee scared me was far worse. And the utterly transparent attempt at a kind of proud independence by saying that they didn't want or need my money (in the middle of the very act of asking for that money) unless I promised to be a SERIOUS BUYER was too much. By that time I was so alienated by this drivel that I was commenting to myself on the writer's basic inabilities with the English language, as witness the gem, "effect a real good savings."

This is a rather extreme example, though you could probably find worse. But precisely because it's so clear an instance of the unfortunate emotional effects resulting from poor audience adaptation, it illustrates the concept well. This sort of discourse is especially unfortunate today when audiences are aware of the ways in which they are being rhetorically assailed. I may react a bit more strongly than would some readers, but I find it difficult to believe that any significant number of positive responses would occur after reading this passage. Unless the rhetorician is certain that his audience's intelligence is minimal, he would do well to avoid such techniques.

The object, then, is to fit the discourse to the audience, and that object is especially important today. There are various ways that the writer/speaker may try to adapt to his audience, and they all begin with the need for knowledge about the audience. That knowledge will include or emphasize some or all of the following: the age of audience members, sex distribution, educational background, political affiliation, religious orientation (if any), group memberships, general social point of view, and if possible, attitude toward the subject being presented. The importance of these sorts of knowledge is apparent. Just as a fact is not merely *one* simple thing, a discourse is not something that is predetermined, but is formed to fit the needs and interests of an audience. You would talk about, say, the idea that Beauty and Progress are incompatible differently to an audience under twenty than to one over fifty, to an audience of men than to one of women, to college graduates than to high school dropouts, to liberals than to conservatives, to Bible Belt fundamentalists than to atheists, to Rotarians than to members of Students for a Democratic Society, to militants than to establishment members, and to those who favor Progress than to those who favor Beauty.

How do you create these differences? By what you say. An argument against air and water pollution might best be presented to a group of businessmen by stressing the economic losses involved, to a group of housewives and mothers by emphasizing the dangers to their families' health, and to a group of psychologists by talking of the psychic damage inflicted on the population. In every case some of the same facts may be used, but it's probable that many different points will be emphasized with each audience. Those points will indicate the degree of audience adaptation and the degree of emotional impact that has been achieved.

Here is a discourse on precisely this problem, and I want to use it as an example of the emotional tension that a discourse can create.

## Eco-Catastrophe![32]

The end of the ocean came late in the summer of 1979, and it came even more rapidly than the biologists had expected. There had been signs for more than a decade, commencing with the discovery in 1968 that DDT slows down photosynthesis in marine plant life. It was announced in a short paper in the technical journal, *Science*, but to ecologists it smacked of doomsday. They knew that all life in the sea depends on photosynthesis, the chemical process

[32] Copyright 1969 Paul R. Ehrlich. Reprinted with the permission of the author and the Editors of *Ramparts* Magazine.

by which green plants bind the sun's energy and make it available to living things. And they knew that DDT and similar chlorinated hydrocarbons had polluted the entire surface of the earth, including the sea.

But that was only the first of many signs. There had been the final gasp of the whaling industry in 1973, and the end of the Peruvian anchovy fishery in 1975. Indeed, a score of other fisheries had disappeared quietly from over-exploitation and various eco-catastrophes by 1977. The term "eco-catastrophe" was coined by a California ecologist in 1969 to describe the most spectacular of man's attacks on the systems which sustain his life. He drew his inspiration from the Santa Barbara offshore oil disaster of that year, and from the news which spread among naturalists that virtually all of the Golden State's seashore bird life was doomed because of chlorinated hydro-carbon interference with its reproduction. Eco-catastrophes in the sea became increasingly common in the early 1970's. Mysterious "blooms" of previously rare microorganisms began to appear in offshore waters. Red tides—killer outbreaks of a minute single-celled plant—returned to the Florida Gulf coast and were sometimes accompanied by tides of other exotic hues.

It was clear by 1975 that the entire ecology of the ocean was changing. A few types of phytoplankton were becoming resistant to chlorinated hydrocarbons and were gaining the upper hand. Changes in the phytoplankton community led inevitably to changes in the community of zooplankton, the tiny animals which eat the phytoplankton. These changes were passed on up the chains of life in the ocean to the herring, plaice, cod and tuna. As the diversity of life in the ocean diminished, its stability also decreased.

Other changes had taken place by 1975. Most ocean fishes that returned to fresh water to breed, like the salmon, had become extinct, their breeding streams so dammed up and polluted that their powerful homing instinct only resulted in suicide. Many fishes and shellfishes that bred in restricted areas along the coasts followed them as onshore pollution escalated.

By 1977 the annual yield of fish from the sea was down to 30 million metric tons, less than one-half the per capita catch of a decade earlier. This helped malnutrition to escalate sharply in a world where an estimated 50 million people per year were already dying of starvation. The United Nations attempted to get all chlorinated hydrocarbon insecticides banned on a worldwide basis, but the move was defeated by the United States. This opposition was generated primarily by the American petrochemical industry, operating hand in glove with its subsidiary, the United States Department of Agriculture. Together they persuaded the government to oppose the U.N. move—which was not difficult since most Americans believed that Russia and China were more in need of fish products than was the United States. The United Nations also attempted to get fishing nations to adopt strict and enforced catch limits to preserve dwindling stocks. This move was blocked by Russia, who, with the most modern electronic equipment, was in the best position to glean what was left in the sea. It was, curiously, on the very day in 1977 when the Soviet Union announced its refusal that another ominous article appeared in *Science*. It announced that incident solar radiation had been so reduced by worldwide air pollution that serious effects on the world's vegetation could be expected.

Apparently it was a combination of ecosystem destabilization, sunlight reduction, and rapid escalation in chlorinated hydrocarbon pollution from massive Thanodrin applications which triggered the ultimate catastrophe. Seventeen huge Soviet-financed Thanodrin plants were operating in under-developed countries by 1978. They had been part of a massive Russian "aid offensive" designed to fill the gap caused by the collapse of America's ballyhooed "Green Revolution."

It became apparent in the early '70s that the "Green Revolution" was more talk than substance. Distribution of high yield "miracle" grain seeds had caused temporary local spurts in agricultural production. Simultaneously, excellent weather had produced record harvests. The combination permitted bureaucrats, especially in the United States Department of Agriculture and the Agency for International Development (AID), to reverse their previous pessimism and indulge in an outburst of optimistic propaganda about staving off famine. They raved about the approaching transformation of agriculture in the underdeveloped countries (UDCs). The reason for the propaganda reversal was never made clear. Most historians agree that a combination of utter ignorance of ecology, a desire to justify past errors, and pressure from agro-industry (which was eager to sell pesticides, fertilizers, and farm machinery to the UDCs and agencies helping the UDCs) was behind the campaign. Whatever the motivation, the results were clear. Many concerned people, lacking the expertise to see through the Green Revolution drivel, relaxed. The population-food crisis was "solved."

But reality was not long in showing itself. Local famine persisted in northern India even after good weather brought an end to the ghastly Bihar famine of the mid-'60s. East Pakistan was next, followed by a resurgence of general famine in northern India. Other foci of famine rapidly developed in Indonesia, the Philippines, Malawi, the Congo, Egypt, Colombia, Ecuador, Honduras, the Dominican Republic, and Mexico.

Everywhere hard realities destroyed the illusion of the Green Revolution. Yields dropped as the progressive farmers who had first accepted the new seeds found that their higher yields brought lower prices—effective demand (hunger plus cash) was not sufficient in poor countries to keep prices up. Less progressive farmers, observing this, refused to make the extra effort required to cultivate the "miracle" grains. Transport systems proved inadequate to bring the necessary fertilizer to the fields where the new and extremely fertilizer-sensitive grains were being grown. The same systems were also inadequate to move produce to markets. Fertilizer plants were not built fast enough, and most of the underdeveloped countries could not scrape together funds to purchase supplies, even on concessional terms. Finally, the inevitable happened, and pests began to reduce yields in even the most carefully cultivated fields. Among the first were the famous "miracle rats" which invaded Philippine "miracle rice" fields early in 1969. They were quickly followed by many insects and viruses, thriving on the relatively pest-susceptible new grains, encouraged by the vast and dense plantings, and rapidly acquiring resistance to the chemicals used against them. As chaos spread until even the most obtuse agriculturists and economists realized that the Green Revolution had turned brown, the Russians stepped in.

In retrospect it seems incredible that the Russians, with the American mistakes known to them, could launch an even more incompetent program of aid to the underdeveloped world. Indeed, in the early 1970's there were cynics in the United States who claimed that outdoing the stupidity of American foreign aid would be physically impossible. Those critics were, however, obviously unaware that the Russians had been busily destroying their own environment for many years. The virtual disappearance of sturgeon from Russian rivers caused a great shortage of caviar by 1970. A standard joke among Russian scientists at that time was that they had created an artificial caviar which was indistinguishable from the real thing—except by taste. At any rate the Soviet Union, observing with interest the progressive deterioration of relations between the UDCs and the United States, came up with a solution. It had recently developed what it claimed was the ideal insecticide, a highly lethal chlorinated hydrocarbon complexed with a special agent for penetrating the external skeletal armor of insects. Announcing that the new pesticide, called Thanodrin, would truly produce a Green Revolution, the Soviets entered into negotiations with various UDCs for the construction of massive Thanodrin factories. The USSR would bear all the costs; all it wanted in return were certain trade and military concessions.

It is interesting now, with the perspective of years, to examine in some detail the reasons why the UDCs welcomed the Thanodrin plan with such open arms. Government officials in these countries ignored the protests of their own scientists that Thanodrin would not solve the problems which plagued them. The governments now knew that the basic cause of their problems was overpopulation, and that these problems had been exacerbated by the dullness, daydreaming, and cupidity endemic to all governments. They knew that only population control and limited development aimed primarily at agriculture could have spared them the horrors they now faced. They knew it, but they were not about to admit it. How much easier it was simply to accuse the Americans of failing to give them proper aid; how much simpler to accept the Russian panacea.

And then there was the general worsening of relations between the United States and the UDCs. Many things had contributed to this. The situation in America in the first half of the 1970's deserves our close scrutiny. Being more dependent on imports for raw materials than the Soviet Union, the United States had, in the early 1970's, adopted more and more heavy-handed policies in order to insure continuing supplies. Military adventures in Asia and Latin America had further lessened the international credibility of the United States as a great defender of freedom—an image which had begun to deteriorate rapidly during the pointless and fruitless Viet-Nam conflict. At home, acceptance of the carefully manufactured image lessened dramatically, as even the more romantic and chauvinistic citizens began to understand the role of the military and the industrial system in what John Kenneth Galbraith had aptly named "The New Industrial State."

At home in the USA the early '70s were traumatic times. Racial violence grew and the habitability of the cities diminished, as nothing substantial was done to ameliorate either racial inequities or urban blight. Welfare rolls grew as automation and general technological progress forced more and more people into the category of "unemployable." Simultaneously a taxpayers' revolt occurred. Although there was not enough money to build the schools, roads, water systems, sewage systems, jails, hospitals, urban transit lines, and all the other amenities needed to support a burgeoning population, Americans refused to tax themselves more heavily. Starting in Youngstown, Ohio in 1969 and followed closely by Richmond, California, community after community was forced to close its schools or curtail educational operations for lack of funds. Water supplies, already marginal in quality and quantity in many places by 1970, deteriorated quickly. Water rationing occurred in 1723 municipalities in the summer of 1974, and hepatitis and epidemic dysentery rates climbed about 500 per cent between 1970-1974.

Air pollution continued to be the most obvious manifestation of environmental deterioration. It was, by 1972, quite literally in the eyes of all Americans. The year 1973 saw not only the New York and Los Angeles smog disasters, but also the publication of the Surgeon General's massive report on air pollution and health. The public had been partially prepared for the worst by the publicity given to the U.N. pollution conference held in 1972. Deaths in the late '60s caused by smog were well known to scientists, but the public had ignored them because they mostly involved the early demise of the old and sick rather than people dropping dead on the freeways. But suddenly our citizens were faced with nearly 200,000 corpses and massive documentation that they could be the next to die from respiratory disease. They were not ready for the scale of disaster. After all, the U.N. conference had not predicted that accumulated air pollution would make the planet uninhabitable until almost 1990. The population was terrorized as TV screens became filled with scenes of horror from the disaster areas. Especially vivid was NBC's coverage of hundreds of unattended people choking out their lives outside of New York's hospitals. Terms like nitrogen oxide, acute bronchitis and cardiac arrest began to have real meaning for most Americans.

The ultimate horror was the announcement that chlorinated hydrocarbons were now a major constituent of air pollution in all American cities. Autopsies of smog disaster victims revealed an average chlorinated hydrocarbon load in fatty tissue equivalent to 26 parts per million of DDT. In October, 1973, the Department of Health, Education and Welfare announced studies which showed unequivocally that increasing death rates from hypertension, cirrhosis of the liver, liver cancer and a series of other diseases had resulted from the chlorinated hydrocarbon load. They estimated that Americans born since 1946 (when DDT usage began) now had a life expectancy of only 49 years, and predicted that if current patterns continued, this expectancy would reach 42 years by 1980, when it might level out. Plunging insurance stocks triggered a stock market panic. Giants of the petrochemical industry, attempting to dispute the indisputable evidence, launched a massive pressure campaign on Congress to force HEW to "get out of agriculture's business." They were aided by the agro-chemical journals, which had decades of experience in misleading the public about the benefits and dangers of pesticides. But by now the public realized that it had been duped. The Nobel Prize for medicine and physiology was given to Drs. J. L. Radomski and W. B. Deichmann, who in the late 1960's had pioneered in the documentation of the long-term lethal effects of chlorinated hydrocarbons. A Presidential Commission with unimpeachable credentials directly accused the agro-chemical complex of "condemning many millions of Americans to an early death." The year 1973 was the year in which Americans finally came to understand the direct threat to their existence posed by environmental deterioration.

And 1973 was also the year in which most people finally comprehended the indirect threat. Even the president of Union Oil Company and several other industrialists publicly stated their concern over the reduction of bird populations which had resulted from pollution by DDT and other chlorinated hydrocarbons. Insect populations boomed because they were resistant to most pesticides and had been freed, by the incompetent use of those pesticides, from most of their natural enemies. Rodents swarmed over crops, multiplying rapidly in the absence of predatory birds. The effect of pests on the wheat crop was especially disastrous in the summer of 1973, since that was also the year of the great drought. Most of us can remember the shock which greeted the announcement by atmospheric physicists that the shift of the jet stream which had caused the drought was probably permanent. It signalled the birth of the Midwestern desert. Man's air-polluting activities had by then caused gross changes in climatic patterns. The news, of course, played hell with commodity and stock markets. Food prices skyrocketed, as savings were poured into hoarded canned goods. Official assurances that food supplies would remain ample fell on deaf ears, and even the government showed signs of nervousness when California migrant field workers went out on strike again in protest against the continued use of pesticides by growers. The strike burgeoned into farm burning and riots. The workers, calling themselves "The Walking Dead," demanded immediate compensation for their shortened lives, and crash research programs to attempt to lengthen them.

It was in the same speech in which President Edward Kennedy, after much delay, finally declared a national emergency and called out the National Guard to harvest California's crops, that the first mention of population control was made. Kennedy pointed out that the United States would no longer be able to offer any food aid to other nations and was likely to suffer food shortages herself. He suggested that, in view of the manifest failure of the Green Revolution, the only hope of the UDCs lay in population control. His statement, you will recall, created an uproar in the underdeveloped countries. Newspaper editorials accused the United States of wishing to prevent small countries from becoming large nations and thus threatening American hegemony. Politicians asserted that President Kennedy was a "creature of the giant drug combine" that wished to shove its pills down every woman's throat.

Among Americans, religious opposition to population control was very slight. Industry in general also backed the idea. Increasing poverty in the UDCs was both destroying markets and threatening supplies of raw materials. The seriousness of the raw material situation had been brought home during the Congressional Hard Resources hearings in 1971. The exposure of the ignorance of the cornucopian economists had been quite a spectacle—a spectacle brought into virtually every American's home in living color. Few would forget the distinguished geologist from the University of California who suggested that economists be legally required to learn at least the most elementary facts of geology. Fewer still would forget that an equally distinguished Harvard economist added that they might be required to learn some economics, too. The overall message was clear: America's resource situation was bad and bound to get worse. The hearings had led to a bill requiring the Departments of State, Interior, and Commerce to set up a joint resource procurement council with the express purpose of "insuring that proper consideration of American resource needs be an integral part of American foreign policy."

Suddenly the United States discovered that it had a national consensus: population control was the only possible salvation of the underdeveloped world. But that same consensus led to heated debate. How could the UDCs be persuaded to limit their populations, and should not the United States lead the way by limiting its own? Members of the intellectual community wanted America to set an example. They pointed out that the United States was in the midst of a new baby boom: her birth rate, well over 20 per thousand per year, and her growth rate of over one per cent per annum were among the very highest of the developed countries. They detailed the deterioration of the American physical and psychic environments, the growing health threats, the impending food shortages, and the insufficiency of funds for desperately needed public works. They contended that the nation was clearly unable or unwilling to properly care for the people it already had. What possible reason could there be, they queried, for adding any more? Besides, who would listen to requests by the United States for population control when that nation did not control her own profligate reproduction?

Those who opposed population controls for the U.S. were equally vociferous. The military-industrial complex, with its all-too-human mixture of ignorance and avarice, still saw strength and prosperity in numbers. Baby food magnates, already worried by the growing nitrate pollution of their products, saw their market disappearing. Steel manufacturers saw a decrease in aggregate demand and slippage for that holy of holies, the Gross National Product. And military men saw, in the growing population-food-environment crisis, a serious threat to their carefully nurtured Cold War. In the end, of course, economic arguments held sway, and the "inalienable right of every American couple to determine the size of its family," a freedom invented for the occasion in the early '70s, was not compromised.

The population control bill, which was passed by Congress early in 1974, was quite a document, nevertheless. On the domestic front, it authorized an increase from 100 to 150 million dollars in funds for "family planning" activities. This was made possible by a general feeling in the country that the growing army on welfare needed family planning. But the gist of the bill was a series of measures designed to impress the need for population control on the UDCs. All American aid to countries with overpopulation problems was required by law to consist in part of population control assistance. In order to receive any assistance each nation was required not only to accept the population control aid, but also to match it according to a complex formula. "Overpopulation" itself was defined by a formula based on U.N. statistics, and the UDCs were required not only to accept aid, but also to show progress in reducing birth rates. Every five years the status of the aid program for each nation was to be re-evaluated.

The reaction to the announcement of this program dwarfed the response to President Kennedy's speech. A coalition of UDCs attempted to get the U.N. General Assembly to condemn the United States as a "genetic aggressor." Most damaging of all to the American cause was the famous "25 Indians and a dog" speech by Mr. Shankarnarayan, Indian Ambassador to the U.N. Shankarnarayan pointed out that for several decades the United States, with less than six per cent of the people of the world had consumed roughly 50 per cent of the raw materials used every year. He described vividly America's contribution to worldwide environmental deterioration, and he scathingly denounced the miserly record of United States foreign aid as "unworthy of a fourth-rate power, let alone the most powerful nation on earth."

It was the climax of his speech, however, which most historians claim once and for all destroyed the image of the United States. Shankarnarayan informed the assembly that the average American family dog was fed more animal protein per week than the average Indian got in a month. "How do you justify taking fish from protein-starved Peruvians and feeding them to your animals?" he asked. "I contend," he concluded, "that the birth of an American baby is a greater disaster for the world than that of 25 Indian babies." When the applause had died away, Mr. Sorensen, the American representative, made a speech which said essentially that "other countries look after their own self-interest, too." When the vote came, the United States was condemned.

This condemnation set the tone of U.S.-UDC relations at the time the Russian Thanodrin proposal was made. The proposal seemed to offer the masses in the UDCs an opportunity to save themselves and humiliate the United States at the same time; and in human affairs, as we all know, biological realities could never interfere with such an opportunity. The scientists were silenced, the politicians said yes, the Thanodrin plants were built, and the results were what any beginning ecology student could have predicated. At first Thanodrin seemed to offer excellent control of many pests. True, there was a rash of human fatalities from improper use of the lethal chemical, but, as Russian technical advisors were prone to note, these were more than compensated for by increased yields. Thanodrin use skyrocketed throughout the underdeveloped world. The Mikoyan design group developed a dependable, cheap agricultural aircraft which the Soviets donated to the effort in large numbers. MIG sprayers became even more common in UDCs than MIG interceptors.

Then the troubles began. Insect strains with cuticles resistant to Thanodrin penetration began to appear. And as streams, rivers, fish culture ponds and onshore waters became rich in Thanodrin, more fisheries began to disappear. Bird populations were decimated. The sequence of events was standard for broadcast use of a synthetic pesticide: great success at first, followed by removal of natural enemies and development of resistance by the pest. Populations of crop-eating insects in areas treated with Thanodrin made steady comebacks and soon became more abundant than ever. Yields plunged, while farmers in their desperation increased the Thanodrin dose and shortened the time between treatments. Death from Thanodrin poisoining became common. The first violent incident occurred in the Canete Valley of Peru, where farmers had suffered a similar chlorinated hydrocarbon disaster in the mid-'50s. A Russian advisor serving as an agricultural pilot was assaulted and killed by a mob of enraged farmers in January, 1978. Trouble spread rapidly during 1978, especially after the word got out that two years earlier Russia herself had banned the use of Thanodrin at home because of its serious effects on ecological systems. Suddenly Russia, and not the United States, was the *bête noir* in the UDCs. "Thanodrin parties" became epidemic, with farmers, in their ignorance, dumping carloads of Thanodrin concentrate into the sea. Russian advisors fled, and four of the Thanodrin plants were leveled to the ground. Destruction of the plants in Rio and Calcutta led to hundreds of thousands of gallons of Thanodrin concentrate being dumped directly into the sea.

Mr. Shankarnarayan again rose to address the U.N., but this time it was Mr. Potemkin, a representative of the Soviet Union, who was on the hot seat. Mr. Potemkin heard his nation described as the greatest mass killer of all time as Shankarnarayan predicted at least 30 million deaths from crop failures due to overdependence on Thanodrin. Russia was accused of "chemical aggression," and the General Assembly, after a weak reply by Potemkin, passed a vote of censure.

It was in January, 1979, that huge blooms of a previously unknown variety of diatom were reported off the coast of Peru. The blooms were accompanied by a massive die-off of sea life and of the pathetic remainder of the birds which had once feasted on the anchovies of the area. Almost immediately another huge bloom was reported in the Indian ocean, centering around the Seychelles, and then a third in the South Atlantic off the African coast. Both of these were accompanied by spectacular die-offs of marine animals. Even more ominous were growing reports of fish and bird kills at oceanic points where there were no spectacular blooms. Biologists were soon able to explain the phenomena: the diatom had evolved an enzyme which broke down Thanodrin; that enzyme also produced a breakdown product which interfered with the transmission of nerve impulses, and was therefore lethal to animals. Unfortunately, the biologists could suggest no way of repressing the poisonous diatom bloom in time. By September, 1979, all important animal life in the sea was extinct. Large areas of coastline had to be evacuated, as windrows of dead fish created a monumental stench.

But stench was the least of man's problems. Japan and China were faced with almost instant starvation from a total loss of the seafood on which they were so dependent. Both blamed Russia for their situation and demanded immediate mass shipments of food. Russia had none to send. On October 13, Chinese armies attacked Russia on a broad front. . . .

A pretty grim scenario. Unfortunately, we're a long way into it already. Everything mentioned as happening before 1970 has actually occurred; much of the rest is based on projections of trends already appearing. Evidence that pesticides have long-term lethal effects on human beings has started to accumulate, and recently Robert Finch, Secretary of the Department of Health, Education and Welfare expressed his extreme apprehension about the pesticide situation. Simultaneously the petrochemical industry continues its unconscionable poison-peddling. For instance, Shell Chemical has been carrying on a high-pressure campaign to sell the insecticide Azodrin to farmers as a killer of cotton pests. They continue their program even though they know that Azodrin is not only ineffective, but often *increases* the pest density. They've covered themselves nicely in an advertisement which states, "Even if an overpowering migration [sic] develops, the flexibility of Azodrin lets you regain control fast. Just increase the dosage according to label recommendations." It's a great game—get people to apply the poison and kill the natural enemies of the pests. Then blame the increased pests on "migration" and sell even more pesticide!

Right now fisheries are being wiped out by over-exploitation, made easy by modern electronic equipment. The companies producing the equipment know this. They even boast in advertising that only their equipment will keep fishermen in business until the final kill. Profits must obviously be maximized in the short run. Indeed, Western society is in the process of completing the rape and murder of the planet for economic gain. And, sadly, most of the rest of the world is eager for the opportunity to emulate our behavior. But the underdeveloped peoples will be denied that opportunity—the days of plunder are drawing inexorably to a close.

Most of the people who are going to die in the greatest cataclysm in the history of man have already been born. More than three and a half billion people already populate our moribund globe, and about half of them are hungry. Some 10 to 20 million will starve to death *this year.* In spite of this, the population of the earth will increase by 70 million souls in 1969. For mankind has artificially lowered the death rate of the human population, while in general birth rates have remained high. With the input side of the population system in high gear and the output side slowed down, our fragile planet has filled with people at an incredible rate. It took several million years for the population to reach a total of two billion people in 1930, while a *second two billion will have been added by 1975!* By that time some experts feel that food shortages will have escalated the present level of world hunger and starvation into famines of unbelievable proportions. Other experts, more optimistic, think the ultimate food-population collision will not occur until the decade of the 1980's. Of course more massive famine may be avoided if other events cause a prior rise in the human death rate.

Both worldwide plague and thermonuclear war are made more probable as population growth continues. These, along with famine, make up the trio of potential "death rate solutions" to the population problem—solutions in which the birth rate-death rate imbalance is redressed by a rise in the death rate rather than by a lowering of the birth rate. Make no mistake about it, *the imbalance will be redressed.* The shape of the population growth curve is one familiar to the biologist. It is the outbreak part of an outbreak-crash sequence. A population grows rapidly in the presence of abundant resources, finally runs out of food or some other necessity, and crashes to a low level or extinction. Man is not only running out of food, he is also destroying the life support systems of the Spaceship Earth. The situation was recently summarized very succinctly: "It is the top of the ninth inning. Man, always a threat at the plate, has been hitting Nature hard. It is important to remember, however, that NATURE BATS LAST."

—Paul Ehrlich

The first step in evaluating the adaptation of a discourse to an audience is to identify the audience. This discourse appeared in the magazine *Ramparts*, a liberal (some say radical) publication. The audience, then, is the readers of *Ramparts*. Perhaps the most obvious trait of this audience is a strongly liberal socio-political outlook. There may be a few conservatives or middle-of-the-roaders who read *Ramparts* in order to know what the other camp is doing, but it's likely that the great majority of this audience is liberal-left in its political and social views. The results of a survey of over 2,000 readers of *Ramparts*, given in the December 14-28 issue of 1968, showed that the average reader was 25-30 years old, married, two kids, a TV set, a Democrat, an apartment dweller, about $14,000 a year income, drove a VW or a Chevy, had traveled at least once outside the U.S., bought 20-30 books and about a dozen records a year, and, if employed, was a teacher or other educated professional.

Obviously this is not an extremely small, tightly-knit audience whose ideas and attitudes can be known with a great deal of certainty. But it's a far cry from the huge and unwieldy audience that is the general American public. Thus it will be difficult for the author to speak with intense directness, but much easier to fit his facts to this audience than to, say, the readers of *Life* magazine.

I think that the most striking aspect of the emotional appeals made here has to do with the form of the discourse. This is a rhetorical act that uses the historical or story-telling mode; there is an imaginary point of view set up in time, and we look backward from that point to the present. There is a science fiction quality that is achieved. And this mode of presentation has an immediate and enormously valuable function for this audience, though it might not work for others: it allows and/or entices them to behave like readers of a science fiction novel or short story, with the added lure of reading about their own future. This function is valuable because this audience is, in all probability, already familiar with all the major arguments against environmental pollution. And although their social and political beliefs will certainly make them support actions to curb pollution, the very fact of the familiarity of the argument will probably make it difficult to stir up strong feelings in them. That is, it would have been difficult if the rhetorician had chosen to address his readers in the usual fashion. But this one didn't. He put them into a dramatic situation in which they imaginatively acted out or felt the horrors that will result from continued pollution, and as a result this was a far more emotionally effective and intense discourse than it would otherwise have been. Ecological problems are so frightening that they are much like the problems authors of science fiction put into their works, and this writer has chosen a form of discourse that allows the reader to face those problems as science fiction before confronting them as scientific fact—or, better, that allows the reader to face those problems as science fiction *in order to confront them* as scientific fact.

Imagine how different the whole thing would have seemed if Dr. Ehrlich had started out like this: "I want to point out as emphatically as I can the dangers that lie ahead if we continue to pollute our planet." There's a completely different tone in those words. We are not caught up in this statement as dramatic participants, but are addressed in a very familiar fashion. And even though we may have felt strongly about the problem of pollution in the past, we are less likely to respond emotionally to this sort of discourse.

More specifically, this rhetorician uses a great many scientific and scientific-sounding labels, most of which he does not define, for he can safely assume that this audience will understand them. But it's a question of a good deal more than that. Most of us, especially the readers of *Ramparts* and similar publications, are aware that science invents its own terms in order to make statements neatly and precisely, *and* we have very probably come to assume that such scientific terminology is used to state truths that are, for the most part, unquestionable and unassailable. This author tells his story dramatically and uses a great amount of this sort of language, so that the audience is led to accept what is stated as SCIENTIFIC TRUTH, in capitol letters. There is no hullabaloo, no fanfare, no passionate pleading. And none are needed. For the calm recital of "facts," put in the implacable words of SCIENCE, is quietly convincing. The whole thing is really an understatement; consider, for instance, this sentence:

> Apparently it was a combination of ecosystem destabilization, sunlight re-duction, and a rapid escalation in chlorinated hydrocarbon pollution from massive Thanordrin applications which triggered the ultimate catastrophe.

There is no shriek of protest here; it is simply and effectively put. But within the dramatic framework signaled by the opening line, "The end of the ocean came late in the summer of 1979 . . . ," this use of invincibly impersonal scientific terms is most persuasive. *For this audience* that is. There are audiences, I'm sure, who would react with little understanding or belief.

Once the readers are caught up in the dramatic form and chilled by the apparently incontestable statements of science, the discourse achieves another effect: a sense of inevitable doom, a feeling that one event leads to the next and that the sequence of disasters cannot be halted. Along with this goes the feeling of helplessness, of being a puny and powerless individual. This effect is created by a mixture of two things: the unyielding statements of science and interlaced with them, the descriptions of the ugliness, the weakness, and the corruption of men. And the two work together so that it is entirely believable that these events should *or will* occur. Again, it is believable *for this audience.* Those who still cling to faith in America's supremacy on all fronts may be little affected by this discourse; indeed there may even be the old cry of "communist" and "Russian agent," despite the fact that the discourse indicts *both* the U.S.A. and the U.S.S.R. However, the readers of *Ramparts* are not likely to believe in the Christian purity of American industry, so *for them* this picture of human weakness that leads to scientific folly, that leads to further scientific abuse of the planet, and that is unchecked by rational thought is believable and persuasive.

Then there is the last section of the discourse. The author takes us to the actual beginning of the final convulsion in, "On October 13, Chinese armies attacked Russia on a broad front. . . . " Abruptly he turns back to the usual form of rhetorical address. He points out events in his science fiction horror story that are not fiction but that have already occurred, and he adds that the others will probably occur as well. Several of the statements in this section are icily effective, as, "Most of the people who are going to die in the greatest cataclysm in the history of man already have been born," and, "Make no mistake about it, *the* (birth rate—death rate) *imbalance will be redressed,*" and the earlier reference to the sale of Azodrin that is going on now.

Still, I think it must be said that this final section is less rhetorically effective than the preceding parts. It's just a bit anticlimactic. It seems to me that what was needed here was coldly impersonal understatement—understatement carried to the point of flat, colorless indications of those incidents that had already occurred. That, plus a final paragraph that remarked casually, as an afterthought, that "Of course, plague or thermonuclear war *could* reduce the population enough to avoid the disasters described here." And a last sentence to the effect that "Obviously, one or the other will occur." As it stands, the discourse strikes such a high level of rhetorical intensity, is so dramatically taut, that the final section lets us down a little.

However, *for its audience,* an audience aware of social issues and already informed about the dangers of pollution, this discourse is, I believe, unquestionably effective. Audience adaptation takes the major form of a dramatic science fiction narration in which those terms and events already familiar to the readers become threatening and fearsome. As a result the author does not have to persuade his audience once again to think and to feel indignant about the destruction of their own habitat; instead he places them in a dramatic situation in which they react to horrors that they have already felt or imagined, but that are newly formed and newly frightening. At the same time he uses science and the language of science to present coldly and clinically the most terrifying face of the future. Rhetorically, it's an emotionally effective and persuasive discourse.

I don't wish to imply that this work is more emotionally effective than other great discourses. In fact many of the things I've said are relevant to this rhetorical event only. And that is always and importantly the case. The measure of the emotional proofs in a discourse is, in a very real sense, the measure of its uniqueness; to the extent that a particular speaker or writer adapts his particular ideas to a particular audience, the discourse involved can be said to function emotionally. And to that same extent, of course, the discourse is unique, is particular. Evaluation of the *pathos* of a work, then, necessarily means that the critic must "get inside" the material, must start with what is said, must develop his critical approach from the discourse itself, rather than apply preconceived notions or standards of what should or should not constitute emotional proofs. (The idea of the uniqueness of discourses will be treated more fully in the section on Style later in this chapter.)

### Logical Proofs

As stated earlier, reason is the most important element in neo-Aristotelian Rhetoric. A few writers have come close to the view that *only* rational discourse is rhetorical. [33] Traditionally, the rationality, i.e., the logical proofs, of a discourse has been thought to consist of *evidence* and *argument*. "Evidence" is the "raw material used to establish proof," [34] and "argument" is the way evidence is "woven into a complete pattern." [35]

*Evidence* includes the following logical and linguistic devices: *authoritative testimony, examples, statistics, analogies,* and that class of statements loosely called "facts." Surprisingly, considering the importance of evidence in a rationally based Rhetoric, these evidential forms are quite simple in nature. "Authoritative testimony" is the statement of a person or source possessed of expertise on the subject in question; "examples" are instances of actual or imagined occurrences of the object or event being discussed; "statistics" are numerical methods of dealing with large numbers of examples; "analogies" are comparisons in which a particular likeness between two items is presumed to exist because of the existence of many other significant likenesses between the same items. "Facts" are the most complicated of the lot, as might be expected from what I've already said. (The first four kinds of evidence are themselves factual; so I'm using "facts" here as a term for kinds of evidence *other* than the four specific types.) In rhetorical terms facts are a far cry from the notion of "directly verifiable data" that most of us are used to. On the one hand, a fact is whatever the audience accepts as fact; on the other, a fact is whatever the ethical position of the speaker/writer allows him to present as factual, and that position will normally include a marked concern for the findings of independent qualified investigators; combining the two (a process that is necessary if you are to avoid the pitfalls in either approach taken singly), a fact is whatever the audience believes to be fact and that is also consistent with the ethical attitude of the rhetorician.

Rather than the *nature* of the types of evidence, it is their *function* that is rhetorically significant and that is, in some cases, complex. There are *no inherent values* in these forms of evidence. Their importance is entirely rhetorical, i.e., is to be found in the ways they affect audiences.

Authoritative testimony works one or both of the following effects on its hearers or readers: *logically,* it provides a context within which statements that are otherwise partially or wholly meaningless may be understood; *psychologically,* it offers a model, a chance to imitate the actions or attitudes of someone who knows. The context within which understanding may occur is simply the expertise of the particular authority. If I argue that education in America does in fact discriminate against the majority of students who are far above average in intelligence, that proposition may well seem meaningless, or nearly so, to many readers. But if I cite the testimony of several psychologists who have found that, while there are a great many kinds of intelligence, only a few are rewarded by our present educational

---

[33] A summary of the degrees of emphasis theorists place on rationality is found in Lester Thonssen and A. Craig Baird, *Speech Criticism* (New York: The Ronald Press Company, 1948), p. 332. The most interesting extreme view of the need for a solely rational basis of language is, I think, Jonathan Bennett's *Rationality* (London: Routledge & Kegan Paul, 1964).

[34] Thonssen and Baird, p. 341.

[35] Thonssen and Baird, p. 344.

system, I've provided a framework within which the proposition can be understood. Of course, the understanding and agreement of the audience will depend on the clarity and credibility with which I explain the authorities' ideas about intelligence, their reasons for considering that there are many kinds, etc. If, in addition, these authorities are persons or types of persons who are respected or admired by my audience, I may have gone a long way toward proving my case by using this form of evidence. Authoritative testimony will be most effective when its impact is *both* logical and psychological. And although the logical effect alone may be a strong one, notice that the psychological effect alone is rationally valueless, for it urges the audience to believe or behave in a certain fashion *because* someone else does, but it doesn't tell *why* that person acts in that manner.

It's worth stressing that a great deal of the evidence used in rhetorical discourse is likely to be authoritative testimony, for audiences are nearly always asking some form of the question, "How do *you* know?" and the answer will very probably involve testimony of authority, for the answer will very likely demonstrate the rhetorician's expertise.

Examples are a rhetorical means of making an idea concrete. In effect, examples tell an audience that something *really* happened or that something happened to *real* people, and the frequent implication is that those real happenings and real people could well involve or be the audience. If I make the statement that few presidents of the United States have had what is usually called an outstanding or even particularly good education, and I then list the names and educational backgrounds of ten or more presidents, I have made my point in very concrete terms. (Assuming, of course, that I have set up a clear and reasonable definition of "good education.") Or if I argue that dozens of people have been executed for crimes they did not commit, and I describe several of them in such a way as to make clear the fact that they were perfectly ordinary human beings, I have made my point concrete by demonstrating that such ugly and useless deaths really occurred and that real people died.

Examples are conventionally called "real" and "hypothetical," but those labels are misleading, for *both* "real" and "hypothetical" examples have the effect of making issues or concepts seem *real.* If I say that members of even the upper middle class can no longer afford the cost of serious illness, and then add, "Imagine a man who makes $35,000 a year, and who becomes seriously ill . . ." I have used a hypothetical example, for I have not referred to an actual person. But if I fill in the details vividly, the length and cost of the illness, etc., the effect of that hypothetical example is to make the audience realize that that sort of thing can *really* happen, or that it can happen to people like themselves, i.e., to *real* people. I may refer to a hypothetical Mr. X or to a real person, but the effect is the same.

Statistical statements provide a way of handling large numbers of examples. If I say that very few college professors earn more than $20,000 a year, it becomes an impossibly cumbersome job to cite individual instances of those who do and those who don't by saying, "For example, John Smith earns . . ." etc. But I can say concisely and precisely (if I use statistics with care) that only 1.7%, or whatever the figure may be, of U.S. college professors receive salaries above $20,000. For the rhetorician the great value of statistics is just the preciseness and conciseness that I have mentioned. For the audience statistics have the effect of saying that something happens very frequently or infrequently, often with the implication that that something may well happen, or not happen, to them or to persons close to them. The statement that over 60,000 people will be told that they have lung cancer this year and that 75% of them will be dead within twelve months of diagnosis may easily mean to an audience of smokers that the odds are getting worse every day.

"Analogy" is often misunderstood to mean simply "a comparison," whereas it is a comparison of the following very special sort: if two items are shown to be alike in many significant ways, it can be assumed that they will be similar in a further, particular aspect. Analogies may be literal or figurative—literal if the items being compared belong to the same category or group, figurative if they do not. The effect on the audience of a figurative analogy is to suggest that what may seem to be strange, unknown, and foreign can be understood and dealt with because it is like something that is familiar. "The Chinese dragon breathes no fire" is a figurative statement that might be used to offer analogical evidence that China is not nearly as great a threat to the U.S. as has been supposed. If that analogy is to work, the ways in which China is figuratively like a dragon that does not breathe fire, i.e., that is peaceful, must be pointed out clearly and precisely, and the more such resemblances there are, the better.

Literal analogies can be used for their predictive value. A literal analogy might compare two cities, say, Los Angeles and Chicago, and if it were demonstrated that the two were alike in many important respects, it might then be assumed that in one particular respect, say, civil rights demonstrations, Los Angeles will follow the pattern set by Chicago. The more the resemblances and the more important those resemblances, the greater the strength of the prediction.

I've already talked about facts in terms of their pluralistic and relativistic nature and their emotional impact on the specific audiences to which they are adapted. In addition, facts have a deeper and more generalized effect on audiences. This effect is due to the "fact" that ours is a scientifically oriented society in which the entire range of analytic investigations usually called "science" is respected. This has led to what can be rightly called an ethic. It is the ethic of realism, of objectivity, the idea that facts are the only acceptable basis for belief. It may be that this is merely a continuation of Aristotle's faith in the morality of reason and that we have added little that is new. However, it feels to me as if we are in the midst of what is at least a new emphasis on this life style. We hear constantly of applications of advanced technology to areas and problems such as housing, food shortages, war, urban renewal, international relations, etc. And very often the assumption is that the technology or science can do what other approaches have been unable to do. Thus, it has become possible to believe that such problems are essentially technical in nature. And given that belief, facts become extremely valuable commodities.

Obviously you can quarrel with this point of view on philosophical grounds, and I will certainly do so in pages to come. Nevertheless, it's a matter of rhetorical significance that for audiences facts are charged with the values that the society reads into them.

Insofar as the nature of facts is concerned, I think it's important to point out that these four categories or kinds of evidence are not neatly and mutually exclusive, and that one reason for setting up the category called "facts" is the simple difficulty of fitting all evidence into the first four classes. For instance, in Roosevelt's declaration of war speech there were several short statements about Japanese military forces attacking targets in the Pacific. They weren't examples, or statistics, or analogies. They might be called testimony of authority, for you might say that the audience believed them only because the president asserted that they were facts. But that seems to me too broad an interpretation of authoritative testimony, for as I said earlier, in *that* sense every statement is testimony of authority, because every statement must somehow or other answer the question, "How do you know?" I don't think that the American public believed that Guam had been attacked simply because the president said so. Rather, it was one of the group of statements that we accept as true either because it seems reasonable to do so or even for no very good reason at all. For instance, we read a newspaper account of a murder and accept the essentials of the story as fact even though we have no reason to admire that particular paper for its objective and accurate reporting. Indeed we often accept statements as factual simply because we can't think of any reason not to. So in one sense facts are whatever cannot easily be thought of as examples, statistics, authoritative testimony, or analogies. The short excerpt from President Kennedy's Inaugural Address that I quoted at the very beginning of this chapter stated that a "new generation of Americans" had taken over the reins of government. Was that a fact? Well yes, if only because it wasn't anything else. On the other hand, near the end of his essay about the death of the oceans, Dr. Ehrlich makes the statement that Robert Finch, Secretary of the Department of Health, Education, and Welfare, has expressed concern over the problems of pollution. We are likely to consider that sort of statement a fact, not just because it isn't authoritative testimony, example, statistic, or analogy, but because it seems reasonable; it strikes us as believable; it doesn't contradict what we already know or believe; *in sum,* there is apparently no reason to disbelieve it, so we say that it is a fact.

All this in no way constitutes a precise definition of the term "fact." We are, I'm afraid, left with the definition or description I gave earlier: a fact is whatever the audience will accept as fact *and* whatever the ethical position of the speaker/writer will allow him to present as fact. The nature of facts then is at best rather vague. They are statements that we accept, for whatever reasons, as true or valid. And they affect us emotionally both because they can be especially meaningful to us and because ours is a social order that puts special values on them. For scientists it may *seem* feasible to say simply that a fact is an empirical observation capable of verification by independent qualified observers, but in rhetorical discourse facts are not nearly so clean-edged and precise. (And it will develop later that there are some strangely subjective elements in even the most objective and scientific statements of fact.)

As an illustration of these forms of evidence, here is a discourse of my own that includes all five of them. I have, quite obviously, structured this essay so that the forms of evidence are part of the subject as well as techniques for justifying points of view. In that sense it's a discourse within a discourse, for it's about evidence on one level and about a social problem on another.

The most dangerous of our offspring are our Ideas, for they have rare powers to harm or tear those whom they touch, and those powers are too little respected. An idea that is heavily flawed but that is widely believed can turn on those who bear it and distort not only their lives but the lives of the community or the nation.

Some such ideas have become famous by being exposed. Or perhaps infamous is a better term. We have seen, in retrospect, the hurt that we have inflicted on ourselves by using them. The notion of racial superiority, for instance, is a concept that causes damage today, and that was used as an instrument of genocide against the Jews in Germany and the Indians in the United States. We are beginning at last to see the malignancy of that idea.

Still others of these ideas are as yet unmasked. We continue to accept them as fact, as truth. Indeed it does not even occur to us to question them in some cases. It is one such idea, and the manner in which I discarded it, that is the subject of this essay.

For a good many years I had heard from many sources the statement that the crime rate in the United States was rising. It was asserted that the rates for various crimes were rising at various speeds, that the rates in certain areas were rising faster than others. But many sources, conservative and liberal, agreed that in over-all terms there had been a significant and even frightening increase in the number of crimes committed in the country in the last ten to fifteen years.

I had accepted this idea as a valid one. I often disagreed with suggested remedies, for all too frequently they seemed to me to ignore the causes of the problem. Thus I never understood the wisdom of beating, shooting, and gassing our own children for the "crime" of campus demonstration. Still, I assumed that the fact of a nationwide increase (and a sizable one) in the crime rate was unquestionable. Of course I had heard it said that part of the increase was simply due to more efficient methods of crime reporting. But it seemed to me that that would still leave the bulk of the increase as a real and ominous problem that had to be dealt with.

And then I read the section entitled "Perspective on Crime in the United States" in *The History of Violence in America.*

I no longer believe the simple assertion that the crime rate is, or has been, rising. And my inability to believe in that idea affects my ability to believe in others. So I have had to rearrange the cluster of concepts about our society that I am willing to accept. It's been rather like the "domino theory" on a personal and psychological scale—a toppling of one concept by another.

My disbelief began with a belief—a belief in the book, *The History of Violence in America.* I was impressed by several things: first, by the fact that the Eisenhower Commission, the group (appointed by President Johnson to study the causes and prevention of violence) to which this report was submitted, was even more middle-of-the-road, white, and middle-class than the previous Kerner Commission—certainly, there is far more reason to call this Commission conservative than liberal; second, by the fact that the

Commission was able to "find no significant work on violence in America, much less any that would relate it to that in other countries,"[36]—apparently we had ignored this part of our national character; third, by the fact that, when they realized there were no significant data already assembled, the Commission used the resources of many fields, employing scholars from sociology, history, political science, psychology, psychiatry, anthropology, law, and industrial relations; and fourth, by the fact that the report was put in what seemed to me to be direct, honest language—one summarizing statement saying bluntly that "illegal, collective violence is so much a part of our culture, so much used by virtually all interest groups, including the government from time to time, that it has become reinforced in our society, and it is high time we faced up to this fact and quit fooling ourselves."[37] In a word, the work itself, *The History of Violence in America*, became for me an authoritative testimony; I was quite willing to accept it as having been done in good faith and meriting the most careful thought, with the benefit of the doubt, if any, being accorded it.

My disbelief grew as I read that at least until 1967 or 1968 the most respected criminologists in the country refused to accept official crime statistics as valid or trustworthy and were emphatic in *denying that there was an increase in crime rates.* [38] People such as Thornstein Sellin, the most eminent of American criminal statisticians, Robert M. Cipes, attorney and consultant to the President's Commission on Crime in the District of Columbia, Dr. Karl Menninger of the famed psychiatric clinic, and Attorney General Ramsey Clark were united in saying "that a crime scare was being launched on the basis of questionable conclusions drawn from unreliable statistics" or simply that there was no crime wave in America. [39] What validity there was to the reported higher crime rates was explained in a very simple manner: either more sophisticated statistical procedures and different methods of categorizing crimes resulted in the inclusion of many previously unreported infractions, or there was deliberate misrepresentation of the facts, as when property or nonviolent crimes were included in the category of violent or major crimes in 1961. [40]

My disbelief leaped as I read of the FBI's manipulation of criminal statistics. It is the FBI's crime index that "has been widely accepted by politicians, policemen, and editorial writers as the official barometer of crime." [41] Yet it is this same crime index that deliberately eliminates the years in which the crime rate declines and uses only the years in which the rate rises so that, in graph form, statistics "seem to bear out its claim of 'record highs' in crime, even in mild years." [42] It is this same crime index that is itself dependent on the reports of local police departments and that

[36] *The History of Violence in America: A Report to the National Commission on the Causes and Prevention of Violence*, ed. Hugh Davis Graham and Ted Robert Gurr (New York: Bantam Books, Inc., 1969), p. xv.
[37] *Ibid.*, p. xvi.
[38] *Ibid.*, p. 466.
[39] *Ibid.*, p. 466 and p. 488.
[40] *Ibid.*, pp. 490-94.
[41] *Ibid.*, p. 487.
[42] *Ibid.*, p. 491.

interprets those reports as it sees fit: "For years the police of Chicago reported many times more robberies than the city of New York, which has more than twice as many people (in one year, Chicago reported eight times as many robberies. Finally, in 1949, the FBI stopped including New York's statistics *because it did not believe them*"[43] (italics mine)—and although New York has since been reinstated, the whole matter of why one set of figures was accepted and another rejected was not reported openly or honestly to the public. And it is this same crime index that is the work of an organization that is far from objective about the incidence of crime, but that has "a vested interest in magnifying the magnitude of criminal activity in order to substantiate its bureaucratic demands for increased appropriations."[44]

And my disbelief became complete when I read of the ugly and callous use of statistical devices that deliberately created the false impressions that the FBI wished the country to believe. The worst example of these was the "crime clock" that was published yearly and that purported to show that the "average interval" between the occurrence of various crimes was growing smaller and smaller. Thus in 1966 the "crime clock" showed that "An American woman is raped every 12 minutes. A house in the United States is burglarized every 27 seconds. Someone is robbed every 4½ minutes in this nation."[45] Of course, this is a disreputable form of statistical evidence. It demonstrated literally nothing, although it is quite clear that it can "have no purpose other than sheer terror,"[46] for it is evident that the public will understand these figures to mean that their personal danger is constantly increasing. Had the FBI been interested in the public welfare, they might have reported that the individual's risk from willful homicide in any particular year is about 1 in 20,000 (and 75% of murders are committed by friends or family members), that the risk of being attacked by a stranger and hurt at all seriously is 1 in 4,500 (and much lower in many areas), or, "as Ramsey Clark used to put it, the average individual's chance of being the victim of a crime of violence is once in 400 years, and Clark added that if one wished to improve his odds he could avoid his relatives and associates—since they are statistically the most likely to do him harm."[47] Or as another observer indicated, "rather than publishing the fact that some unfortunate individual is murdered every 48 minutes, the FBI could have told the country that the average citizen's chances of becoming a murder victim on any given day are about 1 in 2 million, and that then he might well have been willing to brave those odds without hedging on personal freedom of movement or the country's traditional scheme of personal rights."[48]

So I arrived at the point at which I rejected the bald, unqualified statement that the crime rate is rising. As I now understand it, the techniques used in spreading that idea have been manipulative and propagandistic in the worst

43 *Ibid.*, p. 497.
44 *Ibid.*, pp. 466-67.
45 *Ibid.*, p. 501.
46 *Ibid.*, p. 500.
47 *Ibid.*, p. 501.
48 *Ibid.*

sense of both terms. When issues of political power are added to the picture, issues such as the breast-beating cry for "law and order" in the 1968 political campaigns, the ugly uses to which such distorted statistical statements can be put is abundantly clear.

But the matter is not quite as simple as rejecting a previously accepted idea and leaving it at that. For it is pointed out in these same pages that beginning in 1967 or 1968 there *has been* an increase in the over-all crime rate and particularly in the crime of robbery, which many theorists believe to be an important indicator since it is a crime that occurs between strangers and always involves force or the threat of force. Suddenly, after years of misleading reports, it seemed that the FBI's ominous warnings might be borne out! It was almost as if the bad guys had suddenly become the good guys—a very unsettling sort of change. But there are at least three important and, to me, frightening observations that have been made about this increase. First, there is the matter of the population explosion, which we seem to believe is occurring only in such safely exotic lands as India; "each year since 1961 an additional 1 million youths have reached the age of 15 years *than did the year before,*" [49] (italics mine) and, of course, these are the young men who, under certain conditions, are most likely to resort to crime. Second, there is the matter of the generation gap which is directly involved in the problem of crime; not only are there more young men, but they are more frustrated, more tightly squeezed into ghettos, more contemptuous of the society that oppresses them, and more alienated from their elders. And third, there is the matter of racial tensions; this problem is interlaced with the two preceding ones, for it is White racism that is responsible for the existence of the ghetto and the pressures that push many Blacks toward crime.

In addition to these, there is a matter I think warrants discussion— a notion that is partially my own and partially derived from the materials on crime that I have already discussed. It can be stated simply: we have cried wolf so often that we have created one. By constantly proclaiming that crime was on the increase, that our streets were unsafe, that the "crime clock" was ticking away, we have helped to bring about the very increase that has been so frequently reported falsely. "The FBI's statistical image of a rising national crime rate has been translated into a personal threat in the minds of many Americans. . . ." [50] There has been created in this country "a persuasive 'fear of strangers,' " [51] and once that fear began to grow it fed on events such as the TV coverage of one particular crime, using such events to justify itself. Without a belief in lawlessness and the lurking danger at each dark corner, these individual crimes (the Boston Strangler, for instance) would be just that; but falling on fearful ground, they sprout quickly into new fears, "I told you so's," "see, another one," and the new dangers are seen crowding in from all sides. Preparations are made for defense. I myself live in a large apartment building that has a doorman, an attendant in the lobby, and an armed guard at night, yet a third or more of the tenants have special locks installed in addition to those already on the doors. And who knows how

[49] *Ibid.*, p. 504.
[50] *Ibid.*, p. 495.
[51] *Ibid.*

many guns are kept ready in drawers and closets. But the thing that scares me most is this: if upper middle class Whites are this frightened and edgy despite the infrequency with which crime touches them, how is it for the poor, the insecure, the Black, the ghetto victim—all those who feel the results of crime directly and heavily! How much more tension must they feel and how much more frustration and willingness to fight for survival or for revenge on a society that doesn't seem to care!

I think we have created the spiral of despair in which we are now struggling largely by intoning piously the heightened rates at which the various "they's" are breaking "our" laws. We make ourselves fearful without reason; because of those fears and because of the prejudices, the racism inherent in the society, we fasten on the minority groups and the young as the source of our danger; we apply at least symbolic pressures (in the form of our clearly stated disapproval) to keep the dangerous ones at bay; the pressures are felt, the enmity perceived and understood as a very real threat for which defenses must be found; counterpressures are exerted; we intensify our symbolic pressures, adding some overt and physical elements to be sure the "they's" are kept at bay; "they" react to defend themselves and intensify their pressures, adding. . . . And on and on.

And where will it end? I don't know. I am not hopeful. But I no longer accept the bare statement that the crime rate is rising. I think that is a fact that distorts fact. It is like the business of the San Francisco vote; it was not enough to say one third for or two thirds against, for part of that fact was the surprising size of the vote for that time. And part of the fact about crime rates is the population explosion, the generation gap, the racial tensions, and the ways in which we have acted to bring about the increases in those rates. None of these can be eliminated without distorting the whole picture, the whole fact. Only together do these items constitute a fact that is meaningful.

I do not believe that the crime rate is rising; I believe that, after a great many false and manipulative reports about crime, and as part of the fears and distrust that exist between young and old and black and white, acts of violence are now increasing in this country. Put simply, I believe that *the fact is* that the very recent rise in the crime rate is a direct outgrowth of the problems of population explosion, the generation gap, White racism, and the deliberate distortion of crime statistics. That, I think, is a fact.

Whether we can do much about that fact or not, I don't know. I firmly empty and misshapen "fact" that the crime rate is rising.

This is an example of a discourse within a discourse. On one level I was talking about a change in my attitude, my belief concerning the crime rate, and I was implicitly urging acceptance of my new outlook. On another level I was talking about the functions of different sorts of evidence, and I constructed the discourse so that it demonstrated those functions.

When I said "My disbelief began with a belief — a belief in the book, *The History of Violence in America,*" I was dealing with authoritative testimony. In this case the authority was a work rather than a person. The book seemed to me to merit belief. This is a common form of testimony of authority, for readers find all sorts of publications to be dependable and authoritative. For me *The Annals of the American Academy of Political and Social Science*, *The Center Magazine*, and *The Occasional Papers* of the Center for the Study of Democratic Institutions are as authoritative as the works of any individual, if not more so.

More importantly, the authority of this particular book provided a context within which a statement that was previously largely meaningless acquired meaning. Looking backward, I suppose I'd have explained my belief that the crime rate was rising by some sort of vague reference to the size of our society. I might have talked about quantitative changes becoming qualitative changes, but that talk would have explained the fact in question poorly and nonspecifically, if at all. By comparison, the ideas that the FBI had deliberately manipulated crime statistics, that until recently there was no actual rise in the crime rate, and that the present rise is a direct result of other basic social problems constitute a context that has great explanatory power. That power rests in large part on my belief in the reality and importance of the other social problems — the population explosion, the generation gap, and the problem of White racism. For those persons who believe that these problems do not exist or that they are of little importance, the book will have little or no authoritative value.

I used examples frequently. In talking of my acceptance of the book as an authoritative work, I employed as examples elements or aspects of the book, the Commission that was responsible for the book, and the apparently direct and honest language used in the book; all these items were the bases of my belief. In talking of people who denied the validity of the FBI's statistics, I cited four names as examples. In talking of the specific abuses of statistical evidence, I used the example of the "crime clock." These examples worked for me in that I accepted them as real occurrences or instances of the item in question. By implication, I intended them to function similarly for you.

Statistical evidence was referred to a great many times, but I think the most important statistical evidence was in the fairly long paragraph beginning with my statement that the FBI had made "ugly and callous use of statistical devices that deliberately create false impressions. . . . " In that paragraph the effect of the statistical "crime clock" was discussed explicitly. Further, alternative statistical statements that the FBI might have made, but chose to ignore, were quoted at some length. The result was (hopefully) that both the statistical evidence that the FBI *actually* used and the evidence that *could* have been used was treated in terms of the effects that *were* or *might have been* created. Those effects were the individual citizen's fears that the statistics represented crimes that were likely to really and directly involve him. Thus the statistics were described as meaningful in terms of the well-being of those exposed to them—a notion I had already advanced and that I wished you to accept as demonstrated in this discourse.

Near the end I set up an analogy between the "fact" of the increase in the crime rate and the earlier discussion of the anti-Vietnam vote in San Francisco. I clearly hoped that the two would be accepted as similar, that you would have agreed with my earlier talk about the San Francisco vote, and that therefore any strangeness or unfamiliarity you might find in my assertions about the crime rate would be made understandable by reference to the anti-war vote. It's apparent that those who disagreed with my views about the facticity of the San Francisco vote would find no analogy at all, and at least as far as this particular bit of evidence was concerned, would be unlikely to agree with my idea of what the fact of the matter was regarding the crime rate.

Facts were everywhere for some, and, I suppose, scattered sparsely for some. I assume that everyone, or nearly everyone, accepted it as fact that I did read those chapters in *The History of Violence in America* and that the quotes and paraphrases I used are, in fact, to be found in those pages. Some will agree that it is a fact that the most respected criminologists disagreed with the FBI's statistics, a few may not. Some will accept the fact that the FBI manipulated its statistics in an indefensible fashion, some will not. But most important is the fact that *the very recent rise in the crime rate is a direct outgrowth of the problems of the population explosion, the generation gap, White racism, and the deliberate distortion of crime statistics,* and the corollary fact that "the crime rate is rising" is an incomplete and misleading statement. I accept this last fact; some of you will, some will not.


*Argument* must be understood to mean *reasoning* as well as *contention*. The word "argument" is often used to mean a direct exchange between opposing points of view, as a debate or verbal competition. Such forms of argument are *contentions* in a very specific sense, but there is a broader and more basic sort of contention that exists in argument. Every statement, every assertion that I make is chosen from the group of statements I might have made; thus, *by virtue of having been chosen,* every statement or assertion is a contention that it is the preferred, the most worthy one and that the others are of less value. We use the word *contention* in this sense when we say "I *contend* that the important issues here are such-and-such" or "he *contended* that there was no valid approach but the one he advocated." Used in this way, "contention" means "reasoning" or "reasoned," for there need not be two or more explicitly stated, conflicting viewpoints—it is enough that a statement by its very existence and utterance amounts to a contention that it is the most profitable, the most sensible, the most *reasonable* of the statements that are possible in that context. The process of reasoning also occurs when one explains, illustrates, or defends the statements he has made. Thus argument is the act of reasoning—an act that sometimes involves contention in the narrow sense of outright verbal conflict, but that always involves contention in the broad sense of affirming, by the process of choosing to say what one does say, that one's utterances are of a high degree of merit and denying, by that same choice, that other possible utterances are of equally high, or higher, merit.

Having stated this preliminary description of argument, I must warn that I am about to take a somewhat unusual view of the whole matter of the *logical* nature and structure of argument. Most rhetorical theorists, most philosophers, and of course most logicians have taken the position that argument is a process that is primarily or wholly logical.[52] Logic has been considered as *the* method of reasoning, and dictionaries define logic as "the basic principles of reasoning." Although it would be utter foolishness to contend that argument should *not* be logical, a problem arises when theorists go on (and they usually do) to define logic as "the science involving the principles of valid reasoning, *either inductive or deductive*" (italics mine). The problem is simply that *if* you consider that the logical patterns or structures of argument are of either the deductive or inductive variety, you are forced to say that a great many rhetorical discourses, including some of the finest, *are not logical.* Considering the discourses I have used so far in these pages, what were the deductive and inductive logical structures in President Roosevelt's "Declaration of War Address," in Professor Mayer's essay, "The Children's Crusade," in Dr. Ehrlich's "Eco-Catastrophe," and in my own discourse on the crime rate? It seems to me that the great bulk of those, and other discourses, must be discussed in terms of something other than the familiar inductive and deductive logical structures, for I can find very few such structures in those, and other, discourses. Therefore I shall define argument as consisting of three processes: *deduction, induction,* and the most frequently used process, *definition.*

*Deduction* is probably most familiarly described as a process of reasoning from the general to the specific. In addition, the path from the general to the specific is marked out in complete detail. That path is called a "syllogism," which consists of two propositions "so formulated and laid down that a third proposition necessarily follows."[53] The first proposition is called the major premise, the second the minor premise, and the third the conclusion. The classical example is:

All men are mortal. (Major premise)
Socrates is a man. (Minor premise)
Socrates is mortal. (Conclusion)

Such formal syllogisms can be discussed at great length; they can be divided into categorical, hypothetical, and disjunctive syllogisms; the treatment of the terms that make up the propositions (in the above example, "men" or "man," "mortal," and "Socrates") can be finely detailed. And all this may be of much interest to the logician. The rhetorician and the philosopher, however, must be extremely wary of one severely limiting characteristic of formal syllogisms, namely that they can deal *only* with matters of *certainty.* The first proposition, the major premise, constitutes the problem for it can concern only the certain. *All men are mortal* is a fine major premise. The difficulty is that there are extraordinarily few arguments that are worth making, or that involve matters that men find urgent, that can be put forth in syllogistic form. I do not remember any example of a rhetorical discourse in which there is a significant argument that is framed as a full, formal syllogism.

There is, however, a type of deductive argument that sometimes appears in

[52] Compare the space texts devote to logical matters with the amount spent discussing emotional or stylistic affairs. Thonssen and Baird reflect this emphasis in Chapter 11.

[53] Aristotle. *Prior Analytics.* i. 1.

rhetorical discourses, which is similar to a syllogism. This form of argument is called an "enthymeme," and it is, just possibly, the most widely disagreed upon rhetorical technique that exists. [54] Various definitions of the enthymeme have been suggested, but the one I find most significant, is Professor Lloyd Bitzer's idea that the enthymeme is a syllogism based on beliefs or opinions rather than certainties (an idea put forth by various writers) *and* that its "construction is accomplished through the joint efforts of speaker and audience."[55] Bitzer's view is that there is a sort of silent dialogue that goes on between the rhetorician and his listeners or readers, and that the speaker/writer creates his arguments on the basis of his assumptions about the opinions that the audience holds. For example, if I'm addressing a group of college professors who have been attacked by the legislature (as is quite often the case today), I may assume with some safety that they believe in the notion of autonomy for their schools, at least to the extent of being free to hire faculty, institute courses, invite visiting speakers to their campus, and so on. With this audience I may use as a major premise, "A great deal of autonomy is desirable for colleges and universities." That premise does not deal with certainties, and I may *never utter* those exact words or any words very like them. But if I've assumed correctly that my hearers or readers do favor such autonomy, I may then go on to urge a specific act, say, voting for a candidate, *because* it is likely to increase the amount of autonomy of institutions of higher education. The whole argument *could* be written out in something like syllogistic form:

> A great deal of autonomy for colleges is desirable.
> Candidate X is likely to increase the colleges' autonomy.
> Therefore, candidate X should be supported.

The key elements are the lack of certainty ("great deal" and "likely" are very vague terms) and, more important, the contribution that the audience makes to this argumentative form (in this case the major premise).

Enthymematic structures *can be read into* almost any discourse that you encounter, and precisely therein lies their weakness. For instance, you may say that Dr. Ehrlich was arguing enthymematically. You could insist that his assumed major premise was the audience's belief that "Planetary pollution is undesirable." He actually argued the issue, "We are doing things that seriously pollute our planet." And he surely advocated the conclusion, "The things we are doing to pollute the planet are undesirable." These propositions do form an enthymematic structure. The difficulty is that that major premise is too obvious, too much a matter of "common sense." It would be grotesque to argue that planetary pollution is desirable; no one would take such a view. But that is to say that that first proposition is not an opinion, but is entirely self-evident. It is not a matter of *belief* in the ordinary sense of that term, for opinions or beliefs must always be faced by counter-opinions, and to hold that pollution is *desirable* would simply be an absurdity. Therefore the major premise as

<hr />

[54] For contrasting discussions of the enthymeme, see Lloyd F. Bitzer, "Aristotle's Enthymeme Revisited," *Quarterly Journal of Speech* XLV, 4: 399-408 and Daniel J. Goulding, "Aristotle's Concept of the Enthymeme," *Journal of the American Forensic Association* II, 3: 104-8.

[55] Bitzer, p. 408.

such must be eliminated, leaving an argument that works perfectly well when it consists solely of the propositions that we are polluting the planet and that we must stop doing so. To insist that broad, universally accepted notions be considered as major premises of arguments is to force our statements into a deductive pattern which they rarely fit.

Enthymemes occur in rhetorical discourse, but they must be founded on opinions, opinions that differ from or conflict with other opinions. Many people believe income should not be tied to work; many others believe that the two should continue to be directly related. So it's possible to use either of these opinions as an assumed major premise and to construct an enthymeme that follows from it. But you cannot say that people hold the *opinion* that cancer is undesirable; that usage makes a mockery of the word "opinion." And as a result you cannot build enthymemes that start from such pervasive premises.

What happens when "pollution" or "lung cancer" is argued as an issue is that the *value* of preventing one or the other is contrasted with the *value* of economic gain or the *value* of smoking. So it's not enough to point out the foolishness of saying that either pollution or lung cancer is desirable. You must add the conflict that stems from two or more incompatible values. Otherwise you imply a simple two-valued analysis: all good or all bad. That analysis is quite correct on one limited level, i.e., the unqualified notion that pollution, cancer, war, or poverty is completely undesirable; but on that level it's impossible to argue at all. So when arguments do occur it means that there is a conflict in values. And such conflicts make it even more difficult to use enthymematic forms, for the importance of dealing with a particular problem must be compared with the importance of some other process that would be disrupted by solving the initial problem. "It's more important to end environmental pollution than it is to maintain our present levels of production" is a fine basis for argument. It's also extremely difficult to create an enthymeme that begins with that notion.

As I warned, my opinion of the logical structure of argument is somewhat unusual, partly due to my belief that deductive logic plays a small and unimportant role in rhetorical discourse. Syllogisms occur with extreme rarity; enthymemes are found somewhat more frequently, but the enthymematic structure crumbles when the major premise is discarded or when there is a conflict in values.

*Inductive* logic is most familiarly described as a process of going from the specific or particular to the general. The logician, however, will not be satisfied to say that deductive arguments move from the general to the particular, inductive in the opposite direction; he will add that formal deductive arguments deal with certainties and that, therefore, their conclusions are necessary but contain no new information, while inductive arguments deal with probabilities, and their conclusions are not necessary but do contain new information. An example of inductive argument that can be contrasted with the classical syllogism given earlier is the following:

Philbus is mortal.

Aeneas is mortal.
Canius is mortal.
Romanius is mortal.
Omeras is mortal.
Scanateus is mortal.
Therefore, it seems probable that all men are mortal.

It must be immediately emphasized, however, that this sort of inductive argument is fully as rare in actual discourse as the formal syllogism. The rarity is probably due to the fact that such an argument would be enormously dull. Imagine listening to a recital of such specific instances.

Inductive arguments, as they actually appear in rhetorical discourse, do not consist simply of a list of items, all of a kind; rather, they are formed of evidence in all its diversity. My discourse on the crime rate was in a certain general sense an inductive argument. I cited instance after instance of my increasing dissatisfaction with and disbelief in the statement that the crime rate is rising; each of the instances was some sort of evidence—statistics, analogy, examples, authoritative testimony, or facts. Finally I arrived at the generalization—my belief that crime rates are the direct result of other problems, including the problem of the FBI's manipulation of crime statistics. Dr. Ehrlich's discourse on pollution was an inductive process (*not* an enthymematic one); he presented a great deal of evidence indicating that we are already polluting our planet dangerously and that the present pollution is going to continue and to grow much worse unless we do something about it. Given the evidence, the conclusion is that pollution is highly significant and that it will continue to grow worse. But we (the audience) may also furnish a kind of added conclusion—that we must do something about this problem.

In the sense in which the above examples constitute inductive arguments, logical structure appears with some frequency and has some importance in rhetorical acts. Writers/speakers do attempt to get their audiences to make inferences or inductive leaps based on the evidence presented. Those inferences are wisely or unwisely made depending on the evidence offered, on whether a sufficient number of instances has been cited, and on whether they are representative enough to warrant the conclusion that is drawn.

But by far the most frequently used and most important logical process in argument, the most frequently used and important *form* of argument, is the one that I shall call simply *definition.* "Definition"—*the act of creating meaning, the act of determining outlines or limits, the act of making clear, of explaining.* This is argument as we most frequently engage in it, logic as we most frequently employ it. There is an important difference between this argumentative form and the previous two, deduction and induction. Whereas there's a certain roughness, a certain indeterminate quality to the notion of definition, the idea of deduction or induction seems to be one that is, or can become, exact, precise, sometimes even mathematical. And that is indeed a difference, for it means that definition is an act that is carried on in natural languages, while induction and, especially, deduction are processes that can and do occur in artificial languages. [Natural languages are

Chinese, English, Italian, etc., artificial languages, codes and symbol systems such as mathematics, music, Morse code, Fortran, etc.] It's precisely this use of inductive and deductive logic in artificial languages that is sometimes thought to be its strength, for degrees of clarity can be achieved in this manner that are otherwise impossible. Natural languages are full of the emotional, connotative, and idiosyncratic values in which we find the richness and the juice of language. But these values also blur edges and hamper precision and accuracy. So logicians have used artificial languages as contexts in which to display various argumentative structures. For instance, the syllogistic *form* can be handled easily in an artificial language, as:

A is B.
C is A.
Therefore, C is B.

Or, a slightly different manner:

If A, then B.
A.
B.

These are absolutely precise forms of argument. The problem is that when you attempt to translate them into natural language, they nearly always stop being precise or they stop being arguments. The one about Socrates' mortality is precise, of course, but what possible occasion could arise when anyone would argue that Socrates was *not* mortal! And without the possibility of a counter-argument, how can there be an argument? Or as I've pointed out, if you make this argumentative form meaningful (if you turn it into an enthymeme), it loses its precision, its certainty.

The whole business of using artificial languages (and they are *languages* only in a figurative sense) for *any* purpose, and *certainly* as a context for forms of argument, is subject to a simple but severe handicap: *to talk about artificial language, you must use natural language;* and if you don't talk about it, that artificial language remains peculiarly distant from the affairs of men. This seems to me an especially important point, for we live in a scientistic culture in which those processes that are exact or mathematical are likely, for that very reason, to be revered. I'm not interested in abolishing the sciences or mathematics; I am interested in putting things into some sort of appropriate perspective, for I believe that we have too long and too highly emphasized the sciences, or rather the "purity" of the sciences. And I think the facts are that no man has ever written a poem, or found a way through a lonely night, or told of his love, or moved the multitudes to a course of honor, or inquired into the ways of his own heart—except by using and being used by the language that is natural to the human state. I will not say that artificial languages are paltry things, for in them one may accomplish useful matters, although such accomplishments often carry with them a certain symbolic danger, [56] but neither will I place them on the same level as the

[56] For a description of the innate dangers of science, see Theodore Roszak, *The Making of a Counter Culture* (New York: Doubleday & Company, Inc., 1969), especially Chapters 7 and 8, and the Appendix.

natural languages, nor will I call them *languages* in the full and humane sense of that word.

Clearly, my bias is anti-deduction/induction and pro-definition. Definition seems to me to constitute the most important part of rhetorical discourse, and the very definition of "definition" shows why. By defining we give meaning and make meaning clear, we mark out the limits of an idea, and we create truth. Kenneth Burke, who perhaps has worked more tenderly with language than anyone else, has said that "as definition is a symbolic act, it must begin by explicitly recognizing its formal grounding in the *principle* of definition as an act."[57] That is to say, the very act of defining is a human act that by its simple existence defines man as the defining animal. And the defining process is no mere matter of substituting one label for another, but is, again in Burke's words, "the critic's equivalent of a lyric or of an aria in opera."[58] Here Burke is describing the definitional process in its finest or fullest form. But whether we define gracefully or shoddily, clearly or furtively, we *always* define. To use language is to define, and to use language rhetorically is to emphasize the importance of defining. The finest Rhetoric is that in which both rhetorician and audience are clearly aware of the definitions stated or implied and are led to realize that these definitions do not contradict each other but develop inevitably, each leading to the next.

On April 30, 1970, President Nixon delivered his "Cambodia Address," the televised speech in which he announced that U.S. and South Vietnamese troops were attacking communist *sanctuaries* in Cambodia. The word "sanctuary" was used many times in the speech, and the basic argument was that these *sanctuaries* threatened U.S. forces in South Vietnam and that that threat could no longer be tolerated. Now, what is a *sanctuary?* Originally the word referred to a church or other religious edifice in which one could find safety. But surely there was no religious significance to the term as Nixon used it. In his speech it meant simply a place of safety, a place where enemy forces found refuge. And Nixon saw such areas as threatening. At this point there was a profound contradiction involved in this rhetorical act: the U.S. enjoyed (and enjoys) *exactly the same sort of sanctuaries* that Nixon refused to allow the enemy. Our bombers take off from Okinawa and Thailand—areas that are safe from enemy attack, areas that are *sanctuaries*. Earlier in the war, U.S. warships shelled North Vietnam from equally safe offshore positions. Obviously these strategies were not accidental. Airfields, for example, were constructed in certain places precisely because they afforded safety, *because they were sanctuaries*. Nixon's basic definition (unintended, of course) was that *our* sanctuaries were permissible but that theirs were not—a definition that completely contradicts itself. (And as of this writing, Mr. Nixon has decided to attack *sanctuaries* in Laos. One wonders when Chinese or Russian *sanctuaries* will be targets.)

The rhetorician must avoid such contradictions. The essence of argument by definition is consistency. Definitions must imply each other; one must lead directly to the next without conflict or contradiction.

Possibly the greatest strength of clear and honest definition as a form of

[57] Burke, *Language as Symbolic Action*, p. 14.
[58] *Ibid.*, p. 3.

argument is the ease with which audiences can be involved. Defining is a matter of opening up ideas and issues so that their implications, manifestations, and consequences can be seen clearly. It is a process in which the rhetorician says in effect, "See, this is what is involved here," and that is a statement that can be made even to hostile audiences. For example, there's a brief bit of Rhetoric that has been repeated hundreds and hundreds of times since "the riots" began in 1964, and it goes like this: "No matter how legitimate their grievances, minority groups must not resort to lawlessness and violence." Those very words, or others much like them, have been uttered over and over in this era of righteous concern for Law and Order. Of course, given the student demonstrations, the word "minority" has been understood to include all sorts of minorities—social, political, and intellectual, as well as ethnic. But what is involved in these words? What would a definition of them disclose? Well, that first phrase says "no matter *how legitimate* their grievances"—no matter how legitimate, how well-founded, how reasonable. In other words, no limits are imposed. It isn't a question of minor or medium-sized grievances only. *All* grievances, *no matter how legitimate,* are included. And it seems to me that the statement clearly emphasizes the *most severe* grievances, for it would make little sense to utter such a statement and then to add something like, "Now, what I'm really talking about is the everyday, ordinary sort of problem that results in some grievance." That is *not* what is being talked about, of course, for if that were the case, a simple demonstration that certain grievances were of enormous importance would largely invalidate the statement. So, "no matter how legitimate" must mean not only "no matter *how legitimate,*" but must refer primarily to those grievances that are *most legitimate.* And what is likely to create the most legitimate and well-founded and reasonable grievances? Not some vague and intermittent disregard for the well-being of a particular group, but direct, consistent, and ugly oppression of that group. And such oppression can be reasonably assumed to involve lawlessness and violence.

In other words, clearly implicit in the statement, "No matter how legitimate their grievances, minority groups must not resort to lawlessness and violence" is the statement that "No matter to what extent the legitimate grievances of minority groups are *caused* by the lawlessness and violence of other groups, those minority groups must not resort to lawlessness and violence." This second statement is the definition directly implied by the first statement. And nowhere was that implied definition clearer than when, following the lawless and violent murder of Dr. Martin Luther King, Jr., we said that Black Americans "must not resort to lawlessness and violence."

Definition is just this process of pointing out and making clear hidden assumptions, unnoticed implications, and unforeseen consequences. It is the process of bringing about awareness of meanings that may have been ignored. The act of defining can clarify or change the ways people think and use language: it can do so by clarifying the assumptions with which they start, the meanings with which they operate, and the consequences to which they are led.

Here are two discourses, the first an example of argument based on an enthymeme, the second an example of argument by definition. The first is a shortened version of a speech by William Pitt, Earl of Chatham, delivered in the House of Commons on January 14, 1766. Pitt believed passionately in the authority of the British crown over the American colonies and, at the same time, in the right of the colonies to use their own monies as they saw fit. If Pitt's views had prevailed, the course of history would have changed.

It is my opinion that this kingdom has no right to lay a tax upon the colonies. At the same time, I assert the authority of this kingdom over the colonies to be sovereign and supreme, in every circumstance of government and legislation whatsoever. They are the subjects of this kingdom; equally entitled with yourselves to all the natural rights of mankind and the peculiar privileges of Englishmen; equally bound by its laws, and equally participating in the constitution of this free country. The Americans are the sons, not the bastards of England! Taxation is no part of the governing or legislative power. The taxes are a voluntary gift and grant of the Commons alone. In legislation the three estates of the realm are alike concerned; but the concurrence of the peers and the Crown to a tax is only necessary to clothe it with the form of a law. The gift and grant is of the Commons alone. In ancient days, the Crown, the barons, and the clergy possessed the lands. In those days, the barons and the clergy gave and granted to the Crown. They gave and granted what was their own! At present, since the discovery of America, and other circumstances permitting, the Commons are become the proprietors of the land. The Church (God bless it!) has but a pittance. The property of the lords, compared with that of the Commons, is as a drop of water in the ocean; and this House represents those Commons, the proprietors of the lands; and those proprietors virtually represent the rest of the inhabitants. When, therefore, in this House, we give and grant, we give and grant what is our own. But in an American tax, what do we do? "We, your Majesty's Commons for Great Britain, give and grant to your Majesty"—what? Our own property! No!! "We give and grant to your Majesty" the property of your Majesty's Commons of America! It is an absurdity in terms. The distinction between legislation and taxation is essentially necessary to liberty. The Crown and the peers are equally legislative powers with the Commons. If taxation be a part of simple legislation, the Crown and the peers have rights in taxation as well as yourselves; rights which they will claim, which they will exercise, whenever the principle can be supported by power.

There is an idea in some that the colonies are virtually represented in the House. I would fain know by whom an American is represented here. Is he represented by any knight of the shire, in any county in this Kingdom? Would to God that respectable representation was augmented to a greater number! Or will you tell him that he is represented by any representative of a borough? a borough which, perhaps, its own representatives never saw! This is what is called the rotten part of the constitution. It cannot continue a century. If it does not drop, it must be amputated. The idea of a virtual representation of America in this House is the most contemptible idea that ever entered into the head of a man. It does not deserve serious refutation.

The Commons of America, represented in their several assemblies, have ever been in possession of the exercise of this, their constitutional right, of giving and granting their own money. They would have been slaves if they had not enjoyed it! At the same time, this kingdom, as the supreme governing and legislative power, has always bound the colonies by her laws, by her regulations, and restrictions in trade, in navigation, in manufactures, in everything, except that of taking their money out of their pockets without their consent.

Gentlemen, sir, have been charged with giving birth to sedition in America. They have spoken their sentiments with freedom against this unhappy act, and that freedom has become their crime. Sorry I am to hear the liberty of speech in this House imputed as a crime. But the imputation shall not discourage me. It is a liberty I mean to exercise. No gentleman ought to be afraid to exercise it. It is a liberty by which the gentleman who calumniates it might have profited. He ought to have desisted from his project. The gentleman tells us that America is obstinate; America is almost in open rebellion. I rejoice that America has resisted. Three millions of people, so dead to all the feelings of liberty as voluntarily to submit to be slaves, would have been fit instruments to make slaves of the rest.

Pitt's speech is closely reasoned, and his basic line of argument is clear and forcible: the power to effect the "gift and grant" of a tax is a power that is reserved for the Commons; the Commons can tax only those lands whose proprietors are represented in that House; the American colonists are not represented in the House of Commons; therefore, the Commons has no power to tax the American colonies. This argument can easily be put into the form of an enthymeme:

The Commons has no right to tax lands whose proprietors are not represented in that House.
The American colonies are not represented in that House.
Therefore, the Commons has no right to tax the American colonies.

(It's interesting to note that because Pitt failed to persuade his audience to agree with him, his enthymeme might be considered faulty in that he did not use a widely held audience opinion as one of his premises.)

Along with the enthymematic argument, there is an argument by definition—an argument that defines "tax" and "representation." But the enthymematic form is the major one. It is buttressed by eloquent and elegant language, by a formal and even fluid style, but it is the tightly knit reasoning that makes this an outstanding discourse.

This second example is a very different matter. It is a discourse that argues by definition, and it defines an issue, an idea that is part of the problem that seems likely to destroy the West. The problem is White racism, and the idea defined in this discourse is the infamous "White Man's Burden." That idea is defined by its ugly origin and development and by the actual burden that now rests on Black and White shoulders.

# Black Man's Burden[59]

The "Negro Problem" and the "White Man's Burden" are historical misnomers—logical inversions. The Problem never was "Negro." The Problem is, and ever was, Caucasian-Anglo-Saxon-European-white. And now today, this very moment, the problem facing most of the races of mankind is: "What are we going to do about these Europeans? How are we going to get them off our backs, and how are we going to undo the centuries of deliberate dehumanization? And having liberated ourselves from them, politically, economically, socially, psychologically, culturally, how are we going to integrate them into the New World of Humanity, where racial prejudice will be obsolete, where the whiteness of their skin will not be held against them, but at the same time, will not afford them any special privileges? How are we going to teach them the meaning of some of the terms they themselves claim to have invented, but never practiced, as far as we were concerned; such terms as "democracy," "human dignity," and the "brotherhood of man"? This is the enormous black man's burden today. There never was a white man's burden, in this context, unless it was his guilty conscience, assuming that he had a conscience, where black men were concerned.

The Black Man's Burden was, simply stated, slavery and colonialism.

Once upon a time, not too many centuries ago, in time and space, men-of-little-pigmentation, who dwelt in the midget-sized countries of Europe, embarked on a bloody venture of empire. American aborigines dubbed these people "palefaces," a designation far more accurate than the one they chose for themselves. They preferred to look upon themselves as "white men." The "Pale-faces" came from many and various tribes, who, not very long before, had lived in holes in the earth and had waged internecine wars and had worn no clothes save the skin of an animal which was thrown over the shoulders, and fastened at the breast by a thorn or a sharp pointed stick. A few centuries later, this pale-faced barbaric people had become the "Master Race."

One of the most important things the Pale-Faced Ones did in those times was to discover America. A man named Christopher Columbus got the credit for it. Now obviously Columbus did not discover America, since there were people there when he arrived. The kindest thing you can say for old Christopher is: "He stumbled upon the place and cased the joint for Isabella." It was the same the world over. You did not exist until the great Pale-Faced Ones discovered you. You just waited in a kind of limbo. You just stood on some exotic piece of real estate in that vast continuing "jungle" that stretched from America to Africa to Asia to the islands of the mighty oceans, and you "noble savage" you, you just waited to be "discovered," to be "civilized" and "Christianized," or annihilated. You had no alternatives.

Having "discovered" America, the Pale-Faced Ones stole black men from the continent of Africa and dubbed them "niggers" and brought them across the Atlantic Ocean in the holds of ships, stacked together like cordwood, men, women, and children. Thousands of African villages were depopulated. Some still are to this very day. There is no problem of population explosion on the great continent. Peaceful villages were devastated. Chiefs and kings were corrupted, and many of the indigenes, who worked hand in glove with the "nigger catchers," were in their own turn made captives. . . .

More than sixty million people lost their lives on the high seas, known in those days as the Middle Passage. Most of the ships were death traps, floating plagues and epidemics. Wherever you were stacked at the beginning of the voyage, was where you spent the entire trip. You ate, you moved your bowels, you vomited, you urinated, you lived and slept in your own defecation. You got sick and you died all in your allotted spot. In the last stages of this lucrative trade, if you were one of the lucky ones, and a British ship spotted your outlaw ship on the high seas, your captain would throw the whole load of you overboard, chained to one another, and you would be spared the slow death of the ocean voyage and the even slower death that awaited you at the journey's end.

Most of the unfortunate survivors of the trip were sold into slavery in America, that haven for all men who cherished freedom. And thus evolved the cruelest irony in history. The Sweet Land of Liberty, the brave New World, this New Hope for mankind, became the stage upon which was enacted the most inhuman story in the entire history of man's brutality to man. By comparison with American slavery and the slave trade, the era of the Nazi bestiality was an exercise in tiddlywinks. The prime reasons the civilized world (meaning those who had fire power) did not rise up in protest, was that the victims were of a "pagan" and a "savage" race of people, and were indeed lucky to be brought to America under whatever conditions, to be "civilized" and "Christianized." But the blacks did not believe in their good fortune. Many leapt into the sea en masse; many others mutinied; every kind of method of committing suicide was attempted. The blacks were truly an ungrateful lot.

Having invented the Negro, to justify slavery, the Negro Invention was used as an apologia for the colonialization of three-quarters of the world's people. Asia and Africa and the Islands became the objects and the victims of these civilizing missions. Thus there evolved two kinds of people on this earth, men and non-men, white folks and "niggers," Christians and heathens, masters and slaves. On the one hand was the Master Race, on the other hand the Chosen People. From one-quarter of the earth's populations came the Men and the exploiters. They came from the Master Race—naturally. The rest of humanity were the Chosen People, chosen for exploitation and to live out their lives as non-humans. It is a peculiar thing the way Western man evinced such great shock at Der Fuhrer's theory of the Master Race, when, for centuries, men of the West had taken this theory for granted in relation to the darker races who were the great majority of the people of the world.

But now we live at a moment when time is catching up with history. Throughout most of the earth, Time and History have entered into a conspiracy to put an end to the domination of the Pale-Faced Ones, to bring the bottom to the top, to make the prophecy of the Elders come true; to wit, that "the stone the builders rejected shall become the head of the corner."

For our purpose in this dialogue, we will arbitrarily define the West as all of Europe, which means to us Europe, Canada, the U.S.A., New Zealand and

Australia. And the Republic of South Africa. When we speak of the West, we mean the western and eastern part of Western civilization. The Cold War division of the world into Eastern and Western camps is but another example of the exaggerated self-importance with which the European looks upon himself. What he really means is Eastern and Western white people, and he demands that the rest of humanity join one camp or the other. "You're either with me or against me!" both camps proclaim self-righteously.

But now, the people of this nation must make a grave decision. "To be or not to be." Whether to die along with the rest of the aging West, or to live in freedom and in dignity with the New World of the colored peoples. Put the question another way: "Is America too young to die of old age?"

Australia has to answer similar questions. "Are we Australians ready to live in equality with the races of mankind? Can we forego the prerogatives that historically accrued to the very fact of our whiteness? There is Australia, a vast continent with a smaller population than the city of New York, and instead of reaching out her hands to most of mankind residing on her doorsteps, she stares ten thousand miles away toward white men in the dying Western World. The two-thirds of humanity in her front yard are invisible to her. It seems to me that young Israel must also wipe the West out of her eyes and turn them toward the New World, which she must be a part of if she is to live and freely prosper, the New World which is neither East nor West, as we understand those Cold War terms, but somewhere in between where the twain is meeting, Rudyard Kipling notwithstanding.

At a time when a revolutionary and creative spirit was raging in the West, it gave the world great human values, such as the Common Law and habeas corpus, but the lid was clamped down on this spirit a long, long time ago. In the true context of time and space, this spirit died a-borning. And now in the middle of this century, the West is jaded, disillusioned, cynical. What more convincing evidence of the decadence of the West than the fact that they have now succeeded in achieving the means of mankind's total destruction? Eureka! It is the disgrace of the Western World that people are starving throughout the world, young folks in the bloom of life are dying of cancer and other "incurable" diseases, while governments of super-affluent nations spent billions on destruction and men in space and moon trips, and all in the name of progressive civilization. This is an obvious perversion of human energies and values. The hope of all humanity is for the New World to give mankind a new dialogue—a brand new set of values.

One has only to look at the map of the world as it was in 1945, and then compare it with the map as it is today, to get some idea of the decline of Western power and influence. There was a time just two decades ago when Englishmen could rightfully boast that the sun never set on the British Empire. It was the same time when France ruled great hunks of Africa and Asia. Colored peoples throughout the world were dominated by the pale-faced men of that medium-sized continent called Europe. Sir Winston Churchill must have had prescience of the future already becoming the present, when he proclaimed, with forced bravado, that he had not taken over the reins of Her Majesty's government to preside over the dissolvement of the British Empire.

That this civilization is at death's door, some Western sages will admit, and this is disquieting enough. But the suspicion, indeed the growing evidence, that the rest of the world will not voluntarily lie down and die along with the West is nothing short of terrifying to most of the Western wise men. And there is the rub; that the deadly germ killing the West is not irresistible, that three-quarters of the earth's people will fight off the germ, Genet and his avant-garde notwithstanding; that black and brown men will survive and write the West's obituary. Can you imagine the slave master living with the fear that his liberated slave will preach his, the master's funeral? Western man lives with a built-in nightmare that the disinherited will soon and finally inherit the earth and rewrite the history of the last five hundred years, and that "niggers" everywhere will be vindicated, from Birmingham to Johannesburg, which means that mankind, no matter the color, will at long last be vindicated.

Alain Albert was right when he said (in *Presence Africaine*) that one of the cruelest things Western man had done was to "build a fence between man and man." It should be obvious that Western man meant to fence three-quarters of mankind out, but what he succeeded notably in doing, is to fence himself in. And so in the middle of the Twentieth Century, the West finds itself in a self-constructed isolation ward. The hope of America, indeed its sole salvation, is that the Freedom Movement will tear the fences down and bring this country into the family of mankind. This is a part of the black man's burden. But instead of tearing the fences down, the West seeks to extend the fences to enclose the entire world. At this late date, it wants everyone within the Pale.

—John O. Killens

For many the first response to this discourse will, I imagine, have to do with the "we-they" groups that are set up. "We," you quickly discover, is defined as Black; "they," White. If you yourself are White, you are likely to feel oddly placed in relation to this discourse; is it directed to you, or is it merely about you? Whites are not used to being talked to, or about, by Blacks in this manner, though White discourses constantly define Black problems, Black solutions, Black needs, and Black people. Apparently, most Whites are totally blind to the profound importance of the assumption that they somehow have the right to talk about, to describe, to define Black needs and attitudes. If you are Black, these words may well be a welcome relief from the usual White discourses. That is not to say that you will necessarily agree with what is said here simply because you are Black; you may, for example, feel that a far more vigorous or violent approach is indicated.

If you had not considered it before, you might now be led to think of the title more closely. Since a new "we-they" grouping has been set up, does the same reversal operate in some way in the title? Oh, indeed! And it operates with definitional and symbolic force that is brilliant. The phrase "the White man's burden" has been used for several centuries to mean that the White man has had the difficult duty of bringing civilization, and Christianity, and democracy, and all other good things to his backward brothers, the Brown, Yellow, Red, and Black people of the earth. It is a burden that the White man shouldered out of the goodness of his spirit, and out of the deep knowledge that God had placed him on this planet to turn others into replicas, slightly flawed perhaps, but replicas, of himself. But there was a problem involved in carrying this "burden"—the problem that other Gods might not have agreed that Whites were to bring enlightenment to other peoples. The solution, of course, was to extend the idea of race into theology, to make the White's God *the* God and non-White deities merely gods. The idea that Black, or Brown, or Yellow gods might not have accepted the "White man's burden" was easily disposed of once the notion of Whiteness was extended into religious areas. God, Jesus Christ, Mary, etc., were White. So Black or Brown gods were simply not *the* God. They were small-g gods; the White, a big-G God.

This discourse brands "the White man's burden" as a label that has tried to hide the filth, the disease, the death, the endless cruelties, and the constant symbolic dehumanization that Whites have heaped, and still heap, on the Black, Brown, Yellow, and Red peoples of the world. Here, then, is the opposite of that phrase—the *Black* man's burden. And how is *it* defined? "The Black Man's Burden was, simply stated, slavery and colonialism." Those symbols glow with a fierce honesty. They strip the hypocritical coverings crusted with the deceits of the years from the human behaviors that shame us all. The reference to our moanings about Hitler's cruelties when we have practiced those same cruelties is perhaps the strongest instance of this uncovering of the truth, no matter how repulsive and incriminating that truth may be. Here is definition indeed. Definition that sears.

Throughout the discourse, this process of revealing new meanings and new motivations allows us to perceive newly, if we have the faith to look. The notion of "discovery" would be hilarious if it were not so ugly; the very idea that people from one place could say that they had *discovered* another place although that other place was already inhabited is shocking. The ability to use the word "discovery" in that context rests on the deeper ability to define the act of discovering in terms of race; if a White man lives in a country, that country is already known, already discovered—the Romans did not *discover* the British Isles, for instance—while if a Black man lives in a country, it is unknown territory.

Notice also the metaphorical definitions with which this discourse ends: the references to "the deadly germ killing the West," "the slave master living with the fear that his liberated slave will preach his, the master's, funeral," and "the disinherited will soon and finally inherit the earth." The fact of metaphor is itself defining here, but the cross references in the last example are particularly important. There are many works in which inheritance and disinheritance figure: the biblical "the meek shall inherit the earth," and (a particular favorite of mine) Edwin Markham's lines from "The Man With the Hoe," in which he might well be describing Blacks—"humanity betrayed,/Plundered, profaned, and disinherited." Some of the flavor of these other statements is brought into this one by defining with such cross references.

There is at least potential violence in this discourse: the description of Black men and women dying in their own vomit and defecation could well have led to open violence or calls for such violence. I wonder that it did not. But the fact is that there was no call for destructive violence; instead there was a call to Black Americans and to the Freedom Movement to tear down the fences that the Whites have built up. This is a profoundly important element of definition. Frightened White voices cry from all sides that Black militants are going too far and too fast, that they have no right to disrupt the educational or social order, and that Black studies departments restricted solely or largely to Blacks are a form of racism that will not be tolerated, though hundreds of White departments (racist in terms of staffing and curriculum) are placidly ignored. Yet here is a call to join together. There is not the slightest hint that vengeance will be taken, though the White mind may fear just that vengeance. Rather there is the direct and powerful definition that abolishes all "we's" and "they's" and that urges human beings to refuse to violate each other's human-ness. How strange, how bitterly strange that this discourse that defines us as *one* should strike fear in White hearts. And how constructive the violence that is called for.

In summary, Invention is a process of readying the persuasive elements and techniques that are to be used. Among these elements are *ethical proofs*—the ways in which the character of the speaker/writer is revealed by his attitudes toward his subject and his audience. The directness and honesty of the rhetorician is often dependent on two-sided persuasion—the exposure of negative as well as positive aspects of the proposition or subject. Also included in the elements of persuasion are *emotional proofs*—the ways in which the discourse is adapted to its audience. Here it's important to discard the pejorative view of emotional appeals, and to recognize that the most logical or factual statements are also emotional. Finally, *logical proofs* are involved, and they include *evidence* and *argument*. Evidence consists of authoritative testimony, examples, statistics, analogies, and facts; all these forms of evidence are important because of the ways in which they affect audiences. Argument means reasoning, a process that involves contention at least indirectly, but that is not limited to overt debate. The basic argumentative structures are those of *deduction, induction,* and *definition.* In their formal sense, deductive arguments are found very rarely in rhetorical discourse, though the *enthymeme,* an allied form, does occur; inductive arguments are used more frequently, for they are more appropriate to discussions of human affairs; most common and most important in rhetorical discourse are definitional arguments, those that open out and make plain the assumptions behind, the meanings in, and the consequences of ideas and attitudes.

## Disposition

As Invention is the process of readying, of discovering, and developing the persuasive materials to be used in a discourse, *Disposition* is the process of arranging those materials in an effective sequence or pattern. The word that comes most readily to mind as a synonym for Disposition is *organization,* and two things must be said about this process at once: it is far simpler (less complex, not easier) than

Invention, and it cannot really be separated from Invention. The second statement is particularly important, for although it may seem that you *first* invent the persuasive materials and *then* organize them in some fashion, it quickly becomes apparent that the process of Invention includes organization and that without some *appropriate* organizational pattern there is little likelihood that *persuasive* materials will be invented. Invention is not a matter of discovering *unpersuasive* materials, and an unorganized group of statements that bear little relationship to each other, that form no sequence, that build to no climax will in all probability do little to persuade an audience. So it's entirely for the convenience of discussion that Invention and Disposition are treated separately; in rhetorical reality they are interdependent and inseparable, for the materials that are invented must be persuasive, and to be persuasive they must be organized.

Disposition is traditionally viewed as the process of beginning with the smallest units of the discourse and organizing them into larger units, arranging those into still larger ones, and so on until the major sections of the discourse have been created. It's a matter of creating a structure out of "building blocks." Of course it's easy to view this process in a prescriptive fashion, to consider that some particular arrangement or formula is good *per se,* but, so far as I know, there is no reason at all to assume that any particular organizational device is to be preferred over another in absolute terms.[60] Various organizational schemes have been proposed: the Roman rhetorician Quintilian suggested an eight-part formula—*Proem, Narratio, Digressio, Propositio, Divisio, Confirmatio, Refutatio, Peroratio;* Aristotle thought that there should be no more than four parts—Introduction, Statement, Argument, Epilogue—and that only the statement and argument were indispensable[61]; the widely taught Introduction, Body, Conclusion formula can be traced to Plato, who wrote, "Well, there is one point at least which I think you will admit, namely that any discourse ought to be constructed like a living creature, with its own body, as it were; it must not lack either head or feet; it must have a middle and extremities so composed as to suit each other and the whole work."[62] Probably the most important aspects of any pattern of organization are its flexibility and ease of handling, and on these counts the three-part pattern may well rank near the top—not because of inherent qualities that will affect the audience in some desired manner, but simply because it is easier for the writer or speaker to use.

Along with the ill-advised notion that some method of organizing a discourse is *the* best one goes another dangerous idea: it is that the parts that are combined to form wholes remain parts and are readily discernible as such. That is a vastly misleading notion. Certainly there are cases in which the parts remain clear, as in this example:

[60] Evidence for this point of view is provided by Wayne N. Thompson, *Quantitative Research in Public Address and Communication* (New York: Random House, 1967), pp. 65-72.

[61] Aristotle *Rhetorica.* iii. 13. 1414b. 8-9.

[62] Plato *Phaedrus,* trans. R. Backforth, *Plato: The Collected Dialogues,* ed. Edith Hamilton and Huntington Cairns, Bollingen Series LXXI (New York: Pantheon Books, 1961), 264. c. 510.

I advocate the establishment of completely autonomous universities, and I do so for four reasons. First, the present system of political control of the universities seems to me to oppose the very goals of those universities. Second, it can be easily determined that the controlled university produces graduates of a lower quality, as witness the comparisons between our state colleges and church-dominated private colleges, the relatively free schools such as Harvard and the University of Wisconsin, and those schools that enjoy maximum amounts of freedom such as Oxford and the University of Mexico. Third, those scholars who have concerned themselves with the problems of the universities have almost unanimously supported the idea of autonomy, as indicated by Dr. Robert M. Hutchins' statement, "If the university is to be a beacon, there must be some principle of selection among its activities. It can't simply respond to any demand. The definition of purpose is decisive. And my definition of purpose is that a university is an autonomous intellectual community thinking together about matters both speculative and practical."[63] And fourth, our society is becoming more and more monolithic, and thus exhibits an ever-increasing need for a pluralism of structures and forces—a pluralism that could be initiated by a free university.

In this chunk of language parts remain parts. The first unit is the opening statement, and it's followed by four units that are reasons for, or supports of, that opening statement. The relationship between the statement and its supports is clear; you may agree with none of what is said here, but you couldn't possibly assume that the opening sentence supported, say, the sentence about political control being in opposition to the goals of the university. Further, absolute qualities are obvious in each unit: only the opening sentence can function independently; all the supports are clearly dependent on some statement by virtue of their content and of the simple fact that they begin with "first," "second," etc.

But language does not always remain so analytically and organizationally clear. Consider this example:

We are, of course, lost. We are breeding turned-off, tuned-out, closed-up, unfeeling creatures. And it's not that we are especially evil or especially cursed. It's simply that, the more open, the more outgoing, the more in touch with your feelings you are, the more difficult it is to survive. Imagine an astronaut who not only felt, but expressed his feelings; clearly, he couldn't function as an astronaut. And the same is true of the engineers, the accountants, the lawyers—all those who must function with precision and accuracy in situations of stress. Worse, the same is true of all of us, for the stresses increase everywhere as we live with too much deceit, too much pollution, too many people. And since we cannot tolerate those continued stresses, we tune them out, we stop feeling. It is the last tragic link in a chain that perhaps began when some creature wriggled out of the sea for a few painful moments and was able to stand the pain because he felt it less. Ever since then, the feeling, the warm, the tender man has been penalized, and the man who was least aware of his own feelings has had the best hope of, first, survival, second, success. What is and has always been prized is schizophrenia.

[63] Robert M. Hutchins, "University Beacon or Mirror?" *The Center Magazine* II, 5:18.

This is a very different matter from the previous example. It seems to me that the *only* parts that can be seen here *as parts* with any clarity at all are the two sentences about astronauts, engineers, accountants, and lawyers, which are examples supporting the earlier statement about the difficulty of surviving with emotional openness. These relationships are not nearly as precisely etched as the ones in the first example, but I think they are recognizable. The rest of the sentences in this mini-discourse do not fall into analytic patterns or groups; instead they form a whole in which parts are (for the most part) indistinguishable as parts. Most of the sentences are statements that are related to, but that do not directly support, other statements. The last sentence is the key one; but so is the first one; and so is the one that begins "It's simply that, the more open. . . ." They fuse to form a discourse that proceeds by definition, by unfolding an idea.

In light of all this, in view of the intertwining of Invention and Disposition, the lack of evidence to support the primacy of any organizational pattern or method, and the frequent fusion of parts into wholes, I must return to an earlier statement. You remember I said that "without some appropriate organizational pattern there is little likelihood that the materials used will be persuasive." That statement is frequently understood to mean that materials are organized by the speaker/writer into some pattern, that that pattern has an objective existence and reality, that that pattern will, as a matter of course, be perceived by the audience, and that without such a deliberate pattern language events are *disorganized*. That understanding, that rather complicated assumption, is unfortunate in several respects, chief among which is the notion that unless the rhetorician organizes the material the audience will perceive it as disorganized. Nearly all recent thought emphasizes the importance of patterns, of patterning in human behavior, and especially language behavior[64]; it appears that perceiving in patterns, drawing relationships between items is a process that is part of the human organism and that could not be discarded even if we wished to. Toss two or three somethings into the area of my awareness, and I will instantly connect them[65]: three words that I choose at random—cannon, exposure, northward—become, in the very act of choosing, related to each other; I imagine soldiers exposed to a bitter wind as they crouch behind their cannon that faces northward, or more simply, the soldiers' exposure to a cannon that points northward. The organization is not *in* those words; I read it into them. Similarly, audiences will organize discourses in the very act of perceiving them. But that changes things mightily. It's not a question of organizing language because disorganization must be avoided; if the language is coherent enough to express thought, the audience will organize it with or without help from the writer/speaker. The problem is whether the audience's pattern will match that of the rhetorician, or better, whether the audience will perceive the pattern that the rhetorician does. And why should the two coincide? Because Disposition is inseparable from Invention; to change an organizational pattern is to

[64] Lenneberg, p. 212.
[65] Thompson, pp. 33-36.

change the emphasis of the discourse, to stress one thing rather than another, indeed to *say* one thing rather than another.

*Emphasis* can work as the key term here. As I organize a discourse differently, I emphasize different things. I may stress chronological relationships or logical ones; I may divide the subject into arbitrary but sensible categories or I may wish to create a discourse that is one unit, seamless, indivisible. But no matter what my organizational approach is, I use it to present to the audience my view of the matter. Not because they will see no pattern unless I provide it for them (they will assuredly find meaningful patterns of their own), but because it is precisely *my pattern* that I wish to present and to emphasize.

Here are some of the organizational techniques I may use to emphasize one or another aspect of a discourse. I've already talked of *statements* and *supports*, and that is where organization begins. Let's say my basic idea is that the concept of America as a melting-pot is sheer myth. At once I must decide to make various statements about that myth. I cannot simply "talk about it" if I am to offer any meaningful insights to an audience. I must have some specific ideas I want to present: say, the fact that it *is* a myth, that this society is made up of groups that have remained separate in most senses; or the idea that this is a dangerous myth because it constitutes a sort of cultural blindness to the ills that are increasingly disruptive; or the concept that it is by using this myth, by manipulating the very groups that have not *melted*, that political power is attained. To create a discourse of any significance, I must make some assertions, observations, declarations—some statements about my subject. If, as is usually the case, the essay or speech is fairly short, I shall have time for only a few statements; in a discourse such as this book, I make a good many.

The first matter of organizational importance is that those statements must be related to each other in such a way as to emphasize the aspects of the subject that seem to me to be important. If the changes in past attitudes toward the notion of a melting-pot society are what I consider important, I may make statements that are chronologically related, as: "In the seventeenth century, this notion simply did not exist," "in the eighteenth century, there were the beginnings of the myth," "in the nineteenth century, the myth was proclaimed fervently by all sorts of people," and "in the twentieth century, the myth attained full status and was accepted as a completely obvious fact, despite the overwhelming evidence to the contrary." If I present such statements to an audience, I urge them to consider the chronological dimension of the subject. Similarly, I may use statements that are logically related, as: "The myth of the melting-pot was caused by a hypocrisy that was essentially religious—the stern puritan belief in one's own goodness, despite the entirely tangible signs of evil," and "the myth has resulted in a peculiar cultural schizophrenia in which the culture sees in itself what it wants to see, not what is so abundantly and clearly there." By using statements that are related in this cause-effect manner, I invite the audience to consider that the cause and effect of the myth are of particular importance. Or I may divide my subject into categories or topics, as: "This myth has profoundly altered our view of history," "this myth has limited the intellectual and academic life of the country," and "this myth has been a major factor in shaping the political processes of the nation." This sort of organization is usually called "topical," and if I use it, I say in effect to my audience that these are the important aspects or parts of the subject.

Once I've chosen the statements I'm going to use, I must support them. A statement is just that—my (or your) assertion that such-and-such is true, false, exists, should be changed, is dangerous, etc. Considered alone, there is no basis on which a statement can be accepted or rejected other than one's immediate liking or dislike of it (a factor that is sometimes of considerable importance). Certainly there's nothing that could be called a logical reason for belief or disbelief; no reasons have been given that can be examined and found to be convincing or unconvincing. To give such reasons is to provide supports for the statements made, supports that take the form of evidence or argument. For example, I may make the statement that the myth of the melting-pot is one of the elements that sustains White racism in America, and I may then support that statement by quoting the authoritative testimony of a leading sociologist who agrees with me, or by advancing an argument that defines and explains the myth as one of the means used to avoid facing the social ugliness that we have created.

I said earlier that in most discourses there would be only a few statements. That's so because the great majority of the discourse consists of supports. It would be foolish to say the more supports the better, but it's surely true that a single support is almost never enough to adequately justify a statement and that a goodly number of varied supports is nearly always needed for each statement. The exception to this general tendency (I don't want to present it as a "rule") is support by argument; a single argument *can* be lengthy and involved, and it *can* have enough impact to support a statement quite satisfactorily. But whether I use many different kinds of evidence or a single, lengthy argument, I am still devoting most of the discourse to supports that explain, justify, and lend power to the statements.

In many discourses Disposition is a matter of choosing statements that are related in the desired fashion, finding supports for those statements, and then creating a beginning and an end for what has already been formed as the middle part or Body. The beginning, the Introduction, usually brings together the writer/speaker, the audience, and the subject. It says, implicitly or explicitly, "Here's what I'm going to talk about, here's why I think this is important and why I chose this subject, and here's why I think you will find it significant and interesting." The ending, the Conclusion, usually summarizes what has been said and stresses its value or importance for that audience. As I mentioned, there's nothing in this three-part scheme that should be interpreted as prescriptive. But it does work, it's easy to use, and it fits a great many different discourses and situations.

I've already briefly illustrated the discourse that is seamless, that doesn't break up into parts. One further word on that process. Again it's a matter of presenting a particular emphasis to the audience, in this case the *singleness* of the subject. Once in a while the speaker or writer and the subject may fit so closely and so well that there are no statement-support units; instead the discourse develops smoothly and organically, one idea shading into another, one issue leading to

*Rhetoric:*

another, so that the whole is a single unit. It's my feeling that the rhetorician must have an enormous amount of knowledge of, and experience in, the subject for such a pattern to work. When it does work, the result may be extraordinarily effective, and I'm inclined to think that such discourses are likely to be all or nothing affairs, exceedingly good or exceptionally bad, rather than the many grades from terrible to magnificent that are possible with more ordinary speeches or essays.

Although the preceding paragraph is about those discourses in which parts are most thoroughly and obviously transcended, in which parts disappear almost entirely, *all* discourses involve some transcendance and transformation of parts. A discourse is never a simple adding up of statements and supports, for the very fact that these units occur in the *same* essay or speech means that they affect each other. Obvious examples: use a great many statistical supports and you achieve a sense of precision, accuracy, scientific detachment (and, if you're not careful, dullness); use much authoritative testimony and you may give the impression of being widely read (or of having nothing of your own to say); depend primarily on argument and you will perhaps be seen as independent, a careful thinker; put your statements in similar grammatical and stylistic form (all short and terse, or smoothly involved) and you may give the effect of having sculpted or shaped the discourse with care.

Probably the most clear-cut illustration of the way parts dissolve, partially or wholly (that pun is intended), is to be found in the nature of the language forms called "outline" and "prose." A great many rhetoricians find it useful to make outlines in the early stages of the preparation of discourses. These outlines are valuable in that they preserve the separateness of parts; there is no blending or mixing together. Outline form, by its nature, points out each separate part of the discourse and indicates the relationships between it and every other part of the discourse. Consider this example:

I.    The idea that there is a need for a responsible and intelligent
conservative view of matters in this society is a contradiction in terms.
    A.    By definition, conservative ideas cannot be stated intelligently
and responsibility.
        1.    The belief that property is more valuable than people can
only be muttered, it cannot be put forward in responsible
and intelligent terms.
        2.    The belief that White racism either does not exist or has
been foolishly exaggerated by liberal bleeding hearts can
only be grunted out, it cannot be put responsibly and
intelligently.
        3.    The belief that pollution is necessary to the welfare of
business can only be mouthed, it cannot be set down
responsibly and intelligently.
        4.    The belief that students must be beaten into obedience or
insensibility can only be gritted menacingly, it cannot be
stated responsibly and intelligently.
        5.    The belief that it is moral to save money when the nation's
cities are falling to pieces can only be blurted out in anger,

it cannot be formulated responsibly and intelligently.
6. The belief that this country should go on killing its own young and the old and young of Vietnam rather than lose face can only be repeated endlessly, it cannot be entertained by responsible and intelligent beings.

B. The conservative position is one that opposes those very changes that the country needs most.
1. The country needs massive federal expenditures to eradicate ghettos and rebuild cities, and the conservatives oppose such action.
2. The country needs strictly enforced civil rights laws in the South and the North, and the conservatives oppose such action.
3. The country needs laws that provide harsh penalties for continued environmental pollution, and the conservatives oppose such action.
4. The country needs a basic change in its tax structure, and the conservatives oppose such action.
5. The country needs an immediate and unconditional end to the horror of Vietnam, and the conservatives oppose such action.

Here is a piece of language that is the framework or skeleton for a discourse. Each part is clearly labeled, and the label defines its relationship to other parts. Part I is a statement that is directly supported by parts A and B. A and B are both supports and statements; they support I, and they are supported by their respective 1, 2, 3's, etc. All this is immediately apparent from the nature of outline form—the system of indentation and labeling.

Outline form may be helpful or necessary in creating discourses. But discourses are never spoken or written in outline form. The finished discourse always occurs in the connected, flowing language form we call prose. The above outline might be turned into prose as follows:

We have for many years been told that, as a society, we need a responsible and intelligent conservative opinion or outlook in order to temper and balance our socio-political system. Of course, in *relative* terms, there will always be some viewpoints that are more conservative than others, but I think that is not the sense in which the word "conservative" is used; I think that "conservative" is used to mean a group of opinions and attitudes that are clearly identifiable as conservative and that change quite slowly. Conservatives, for instance, usually oppose restrictions on corporate and business activities, and they have opposed those restrictions for a good many years.

Many of us have fallen prey to this doctrine and have accepted it as simple and sensible. Unfortunately, it is neither simple nor sensible; it is an outright contradiction in terms. We do not need a responsible and intelligent conservative view of matters in this country because the notions that make up the conservative position *cannot be advanced responsibly or intelligently.* That, of course, is an extreme sounding statement. But consider some examples: certainly the great majority of conservatives put more emphasis on property rights than on human rights, and there is nothing there to articulate responsibly, for the humanistic tradition has been discarded; conservatives either deny the existence of white racism or claim that the tender-hearted liberals have grossly exaggerated this problem, and this defensive stand is not one to be framed intelligently or responsibly; conservatives believe that pollution, while unfortunate, is necessary to the welfare of business, and this idea, uttered while the environment deteriorates, is surely incapable of being stated intelligently; conservatives have made clear their belief that education is a process of learning to fit into society and that students will be forced by whatever means are necessary to accept that process—a belief that seems entirely alien to a mind capable of responsible and intelligent thought; with their constant emphasis on fiscal respectability, conservatives have proclaimed the money-morality of thrift, a morality that can be put only in the most flaccid terms, never intelligent ones; and, finally, the conservatives are clearly unwilling to bring to an end the war in Vietnam, an ugly and militaristic outlook that has in every instance failed to be put honestly or convincingly or decently or intelligently or responsibly.

These are some of the notions that make up the conservative position, and it seems to me laughable to think of any one of them being put forward neatly or with grace. But there are other evidences that indicate the self-contradictory nature of the idea that an intelligent and responsible statement of the conservative position is needed in this country. Those evidences concern the problems that constitute, for a great many observers, the most pressing needs of the society. For instance, although all authorities agree that massive federal expenditures will be needed if the ghettos are to be wiped out and our decaying cities are to be rebuilt, the conservatives oppose such action; and although strict enforcement of civil rights laws is necessary if the widespread racism in the North and South is to be lessened, the conservatives oppose such action; and although it is evident that harsh penalties will be required to force industry to stop environmental pollution, the conservatives oppose such action; and although profound changes are patently necessary if the glaring inequities of our present tax structure are to be eliminated, the conservatives oppose such action; and although, for the most childishly obvious political, social, economic, psychological, and moral reasons, we desperately need an end to the seemingly endless horror of Vietnam, the conservatives oppose such action.

These are some of the needs of our nation. Faced with such needs, what room is there for the *conflicting* need for a responsible and intelligent statement of the conservative position? None, I say. None, because that position is one that opposes, that prevents the enactment of solutions and satisfactions of these needs. And, none, because that position is one that cannot be taken or defended intelligently or responsibly.

Now, look at some of the differences between these two forms. First, the prose is longer than the outline; fillers were added, transitions and restatements put in. Whereas the outline is a group of discrete items, the prose passage is just that—a passage—a movement from one item to the next. These differences are apparent at the very beginning of the two examples: the outline begins with statement I followed by support A; the prose begins with the same statement but explains it, qualifies it a bit, stresses the way in which the word "conservative" is used, points out that what may seem sensible is really dangerous, and ends by repeating the statement emphatically. In other words, the prose does considerably more, functions in a great many more ways, than does the outline. The outline is clear-cut, even-edged, precisely structured; the prose is smoother, the edges are blurred, and the structure is softer, gentler, less angular.

More important than the above differences are the matters of stress, of shading, of innuendo, of passion, if you will, that are possible in prose, impossible in outline. I wrote the outline in sentences that were not only complete, but were somewhat unusually lengthy and involved. Thus as outlines go, there's a goodly amount of punch to many of the points. Still the prose is far richer, far more varied. Look at these examples:

A.   By definition, conservative ideas cannot be stated intelligently and
     responsibly.
     6.   The belief that this country should go on killing its own
          young and the old and young of Vietnam rather than
          lose face can only be repeated mindlessly, it cannot be
          entertained by responsible and intelligent beings.
and:

Many of us have fallen prey to this doctrine and have accepted it as simple and sensible. Unfortunately, it is neither simple nor sensible; it is an outright contradiction in terms. We do not need a responsible and intelligent conservative view of matters in this country because the notions that make up the conservative position *cannot be advanced responsibly and intelligently.*

Although, for the most childishly obvious political, social, economic, psychological and moral reasons, we desperately need an end to the seemingly endless horror of Vietnam, the conservations oppose such an action.

Notice that the excerpt from the outline is a static one, two—a simple pairing of items. The prose excerpt, short as it is, builds to a small climax; it begins, warns of a danger, proclaims that a contradiction is present, and then refutes the need for the conservative view by saying with some heat that that view *cannot be* reponsible or intelligent. This sort of difference is exceedingly important. It means that prose is the language of discourse, of Rhetoric. It's in prose that we make statements, reflect on them, amend them, voice misgivings about them, etc. An outline is the bare bones of a discourse; it must be fleshed out in prose. Think of an entire speech or essay in outline form; it's a ludicrous notion, for the thousands of small ways of playing with language, of making it a personal creation, are difficult-to-impossible in an outline.

Put differently, prose is the whole, the outline is the series of parts. Those parts may be profitably specified and nailed down in outline form when you are preparing a discourse, but they will always dim and fuse together, to some extent, in the prose of the actual discourse.

Here are two discourses that display widely disparate forms of Disposition. The first is fairly analytic: there are parts that are easily recognizable as such; and the relationships between many of these parts are quite clear. This is a speech that was delivered by Susan B. Anthony, perhaps the most noted advocate of the right of women to vote. Miss Anthony was arrested in 1872 for the crime of having voted in the presidential election. She was judged guilty and was fined $100.00. She refused to pay the fine, and in fact never did pay it.

### On Woman's Right To Suffrage

Friends and fellow Citizens, I stand before you tonight under indictment for the alleged crime of having voted at the last presidential election, without having a lawful right to vote. It shall be my work this evening to prove to you that in thus voting, I not only committed no crime, but, instead, simply exercised my *citizen's rights,* guaranteed to me and all United States citizens by the National Constitution, beyond the power of any State to deny.

The preamble of the Federal Constitution says:

"We, the people of the United States, in order to form a more perfect union, establish justice, insure *domestic* tranquility, provide for the common defense, promote the general welfare, and secure the blessings of liberty to ourselves and our posterity, do ordain and establish this Constitution for the United States of America."

It was we, the people; not we, the white male citizens; nor yet we, the male citizens; but we, the whole people, who formed the Union. And we formed it, not to give the blessings of liberty, but to secure them; not to the half of ourselves and the half of our posterity, but to the whole people, women as well as men. And it is a downright mockery to talk to women of their enjoyment of the blessings of liberty while they are denied the use of the only means of securing them provided by this democratic-republican government—the ballot.

For any State to make sex a qualification that must ever result in the disfranchisement of one entire half of the people is to pass a bill of attainder, or an *ex post facto* law, and is therefore a violation of the supreme law of the land. By it the blessings of liberty are for ever withheld from women and their female posterity. To them this government has no just powers derived from the consent of the governed. To them this government is not a democracy. It is not a republic. It is an odious aristocracy; a hateful oligarchy of sex; the most hateful aristocracy ever established on the face of the globe. An oligarchy of wealth, where the rich govern the poor, an oligarchy of learning, where the educated govern the ignorant, or even an oligarchy of race, where the Saxon rule the African, might be endured; but this oligarchy of sex, which makes father, brothers, husband, sons, the oligarchs over the mother and sisters, the wife and daughters of every household—which ordains all men sovereigns, all women subjects, carries dissension, discord and rebellion into every home of the nation.

Webster, Worcester and Bouvier all define a citizen to be a person in the United States, entitled to vote and hold office.

The only question left to be settled now is: Are women persons? And I hardly believe any of our opponents will have the hardihood to say they are not. Being persons, then, women are citizens; and no State has a right to make any law, or to enforce any old law, that shall abridge their privileges or immunities. Hence, every discrimination against women in the constitutions and laws of the several States is today null and void, precisely as is everyone against negroes.

—Susan B. Anthony

The organizational pattern, the Disposition of this discourse, is clear and analytic. She begins by introducing her subject; indeed she announces it with precision and emphasis. Her experiences and her leadership of the suffrage movement make her part of that subject and lend a dramatic quality to her belief that she was guilty of no crime, but had merely exercised her right as a citizen.

Then she brings in constitutional evidence for her position, and in stressing that the "people" referred to was the *whole* people she creates an analogy between race prejudice and sex prejudice. She goes on to explore the results of "disfranchisement" for both the victims and the government that disfranchises.

She ends by defining the term "citizen," remarks defiantly that even her opponents could hardly deny that women are persons, and refers again to the similarity between the discrimination based on sex and that based on race.

This is reasoned discourse based on enthymematic argument, and the bases on which the speaker's views may be found to be valid or invalid are set out neatly and precisely.

Compare it with what follows. I shall say nothing except that this is a very different sort of Rhetoric.

### The Figure A Poem Makes[66]

Abstraction is an old story with the philosophers, but it has been like a new toy in the hands of the artists of our day. Why can't we have any one quality of poetry we choose by itself? We can have in thought. Then it will go hard if we can't in practice. Our lives for it.

Granted no one but a humanist much cares how sound a poem is if it is only *a* sound. The sound is the gold in the ore. Then we will have the sound out alone and dispense with the inessential. We do till we make the discovery that the object in writing poetry is to make all poems sound as different as possible from each other, and the resources for that of vowels, consonants, punctuation, syntax, words, sentences, meter are not enough. We need the help of context—meaning—subject matter. That is the greatest help towards variety. All that can be done with words is soon told. So also with meters—particularly in our language where there are virtually but two, strict iambic and loose iambic. The ancients with many were still poor if they depended on meters for all tune. It is painful to watch our sprung-rhythmists straining at the point of omitting one short from a foot for relief from monotony. The possibilities for tune from the dramatic tones of meaning struck across the rigidity of a limited meter are endless. And we are back in poetry as merely one more art of having something to say, sound or unsound. Probably better if sound, because deeper and from wider experience.

Then there is this wildness whereof it is spoken. Granted again that it has an equal claim with sound to being a poem's better half. If it is a wild tune, it is a poem. Our problem then is, as modern abstractionists, to have the wildness pure; to be wild with nothing to be wild about. We bring up as aberrationists, giving way to undirected associations and kicking ourselves from one chance suggestion to another in all directions as of a hot afternoon in the life of a grasshopper. Theme alone can steady us down. Just as the first mystery was how a poem could have a tune in such a straightness as meter, so the second mystery is how a poem can have wildness and at the same time a subject that shall be fulfilled.

It should be of the pleasure of a poem itself to tell how it can. The figure a poem makes. It begins in delight and ends in wisdom. The figure is the same as for love. No one can really hold that the ecstasy should be static and stand still in one place. It begins in delight, it inclines to the impulse, it assumes direction with the first line laid down, it runs a course of lucky events, and ends in a clarification of life—not necessarily a great clarification, such as sects and cults are founded on, but in a momentary stay against confusion. It has denouement. It has an outcome that though unforeseen was predestined from the first image of the original mood—and indeed from the very mood. It is but a trick poem and no poem at all if the best of it was thought of first and saved for the last. It finds its own name as it goes and discovers the best waiting for it in some final phrase at once wise and sad—the happy-sad blend of the drinking song.

No tears in the writer, no tears in the reader. No surprise for the writer, no surprise for the reader. For me the initial delight is in the surprise of remembering something I didn't know I knew. I am in a place, in a situation, as if I had materialized from cloud or risen out of the ground. There is a glad recognition of the long lost and the rest follows. Step by step the wonder of unexpected supply keeps growing. The impressions most useful to my purpose seem always those I was unaware of and so made no note of at the time when taken, and the conclusion is come to that like giants we are always hurling experience ahead of us to pave the future with against the day when we may want to strike a line of purpose across it for somewhere. The line will have the more charm for not being mechanically straight. We enjoy the straight crookedness of a good walking stick. Modern instruments of precision are being used to make things crooked as if by eye and hand in the old days.

I tell how there may be a better wildness of logic than of inconsequence. But the logic is backward, in retrospect, after the act. It must be more felt than seen ahead like prophecy. It must be a revelation, or a series of revelations, as much for the poet as for the reader. For it to be that there must have been the greatest freedom of the material to move about in it and to establish relations in it regardless of time and space, previous relation, and everything but affinity. We prate of freedom. We call our schools free because we are not free to stay away from them till we are sixteen years of age. I have given up my democratic prejudices and now willingly set the lower classes free to be completely taken care of by the upper classes. Political freedom is nothing to me. I bestow it right and left. All I would keep for myself is the freedom of my material—the condition of body and mind now and then to summon aptly from the vast chaos of all I have lived through.

Scholars and artists thrown together are often annoyed at the puzzle of where they differ. Both work from knowledge; but I suspect they differ most importantly in the way their knowledge is come by. Scholars get theirs with conscientious thoroughness along projected lines of logic; poets theirs cavalierly and as it happens in and out of books. They stick to nothing deliberately, but let what will stick to them like burrs where they walk in the fields. No acquirement is on assignment, or even self-assignment. Knowledge of the second kind is much more available in the wild free ways of wit and art. A schoolboy may be defined as one who can tell you what he knows in the order in which he learned it. The artist must value himself as he snatches a thing from some previous order in time and space into a new order with not so much as a ligature clinging to it of the old place where it was organic.

More than once I should have lost my soul to radicalism if it had been the originality it was mistaken for by its young converts. Originality and initiative are what I ask for my country. For myself the originality need be no more than the freshness of a poem run in the way I have described: from delight to wisdom. The figure is the same as for love. Like a piece of ice on a hot stove the poem must ride on its own melting. A poem may be worked over once it is in being, but may not be worried into being. Its most precious quality will remain its having run itself and carried away the poet with it. Read it a hundred times: it will forever keep its freshness as a metal keeps its fragrance. It can never lose its sense of a meaning that once unfolded by surprise as it went.

—Robert Frost

Here is a magnificence. I am caught in these words as surely as on a thousand tiny fishhooks.

I suppose I must begin by saying that this is Rhetoric, if only because this sort of discourse is not usually dealt with by rhetoricians. It's Rhetoric because it attempts to persuade, and it does so by reasoned discourse based on the process of definition. The writer is urging a point of view toward poetry and poets, toward the value of subjective knowing, and even toward the sort of society in which poets and poetry can flourish. More specifically, he denies the worth of poetry based primarily on technical effects, on contrived rhythmical and syntactical structures; he denies, too, the freedom or "wildness" of poetry in any absolute sense. Instead he underscores the need for language rich in meaning, for theme, for content in poetry—not an arid, objective, logical content, but a content of feeling.

But what of the Disposition? Well, it's not much like Miss Anthony's speech, for there's little that fits *any* formal pattern. Frost's own words may well describe the pattern of this discourse: "like giants we are always hurling experience ahead of us to pave the future with against the day when we may want to strike a line of purpose across it for somewhere. The line will have the more charm for not being mechanically straight." That's what Frost has done here—tossed ideas ahead of himself as he proceeded from one to the next, leaving the reader to fill in the details. Consider the words just quoted and those that immediately follow:

... like giants we are always hurling experience ahead of us to pave the future with against the day when we may want to strike a line of purpose across it for somewhere. [Granted, when we proceed in this fashion it will be crookedly, but] the line will have the more charm for not being mechanically straight. [Pure straightness is a bad thing; we want crookedness mixed in, as when] We enjoy the straight crookedness of a good walking stick. [and that sort of enjoyment is so needed that we see on all sides that] Modern instruments of precision are being used to make things crooked as if by hand and eye in the old days.

The words in the brackets were not written, but they (or others much like them) will be "read," for Frost stepped easily from the important part of one idea to the important part of the next without concern for detail. So to read this discourse is to put in the words that Frost left out. Interestingly, as a poet Frost labeled himself a synecdochist—one who used parts to stand for wholes—and he does something quite similar as a rhetorician.

Throughout the work it's the same thing, as witness this example:

All that can be done with words is soon told. So also with meters—particularly in our language where there are virtually but two, strict iambic and loose iambic. The ancients with many were still poor if they depended on meter for all tune. [And as for the moderns] It is painful to watch our sprung-rhythmists straining at the point of omitting one short from a foot for relief from monotony. [By contrast] The possibilities for tune from the dramatic tones of meaning struck across the rigidity of a limited meter are endless. [So, since it is meaning that is the critical factor, we are forced to discard the notion that poetic virtue rests in the manipulation of technical or metrical complexities; we must avoid too much emphasis on manner.] And [if we do] we are back in poetry as merely one more art of having something to say, sound or unsound.

And this:

The figure a poem makes. [I use "figure" to mean movement, growth, a magical passage from one thing to another. And a poem *is* a figure in this sense.] It begins in delight and ends in wisdom. The figure is the same as for love. [The two are similar, for there is ecstasy in both, and] No one can really hold that the ecstasy should be static and stand still in one place.

With but a few exceptions it's this hurling ahead of ideas that is the organization of this discourse. The first three paragraphs are a bit more analytic: the first introduces the subject, though obliquely; the second treats the technical matters of verse; the third deals with the emotional abundance, the "wildness" of poetry. But from there on the pattern of this discourse consists of notions, the hearts of which are hurled ahead so that they acquire new contexts, new dimensions; then the step is made to that renewed thought, and from there another related chunk of idea is tossed forward; another step, not in a mechanically straight line, but the more charming because of the natural crookedness.

Stepping stones. Each is related to the one before, and the relationships are reasonable and can be spelled out. They are not, however, formally logical. Wildly logical, rather, a logic of feeling.

Thus, an organizational pattern that's far from the conventional sort. And it's one of many, of infinitely many. For this sort of organic development grows from the discourse, so that there are as many possible patterns as there are discourses. No one is better or worse in absolute terms; they may work poorly or not at all, or they may be ideal for the discourse that holds them, as this one is.

### Style

Some pages ago I talked about emotional proofs as a measure of the uniqueness of a discourse, as an indication of the degree to which a particular speaker found particular ways to present his particular idea to a particular audience. That very particularity, I suggested, is the emotionality of the discourse. At that time I was considering the particularity or uniqueness of discourses from a limited viewpoint, that of the audience. Emotional proofs are felt by the audience, and it was their impact on hearers or readers that I was concerned with. I want to use now a much broader approach to the uniqueness of rhetorical discourses, an approach that will include the views of the audience, the writer/speaker, and the critic who may be part of or removed from the immediate rhetorical situation. That broad approach can be labeled simply "Style"—the *style* of the discourse.

Like Invention and Disposition, Style is one of the classical canons of Rhetoric that were conceived during the Greek and Roman periods. I shall use the term to include both oral and written style, though the two have been separated and continue to be treated singly by some writers (a problem I'll discuss a little later).

Style has very often been thought of as ornamentation, as the decorative aspects of language. Even more frequently, it has been assumed that Style refers to the ways in which you state ideas, ways that can be changed without changing the ideas themselves. Here are two brief quotations:

> And of course it is understood that mere variation of style is made not to alter the substance or content of what is expressed but only the way of expressing it; underlying the very notion of style is a postulate of *independence of matter from manner.*[67]

> Euphemisms are logically indefensible, but socially unavoidable. They are illogical because, as Juliet says, "a rose by any other name would smell as sweet." It is the thing which is good or bad, not its name. What is unpleasant to contemplate is not the word *die*, but the fact of death. Changing the word but keeping the message intact is like using a code, but who is taken in? *Love child* or *illegitimate child* carry the same social stigma as *bastard*. It is the idea

[67] Rulon Wells, "Nominal and Verbal Style," in *Selected Readings in Public Speaking*, ed. Jane Blankenship and Robert Wilhoit (Belmont, Calif.: Dickenson Publishing Company, Inc., 1966), p. 126.

of illegitimacy which society has found censurable, not the sound used to express it.[68]

The above statements were made by contemporary writers, but they are representative of a view that is centuries old. I quote contemporaries to show that this approach is still taken: indeed it's still popular. And it's an approach with which I disagree violently.

Evidence that directly contradicts this approach is abundant. For instance, it has been shown that verbal labeling or indexing affects perception very significantly, that all sorts of word changes can and do determine the ways in which we see our world and ourselves.[69] But let me give a single example that will, I think, demonstrate the point; it's from a work by Kenneth Burke, who represents a viewpoint absolutely opposed to the one I'm attacking. Burke is discussing the power of symbols, and he writes:

A merely funny example concerns an anecdote told by the anthropologist, Franz Boas. He had gone to a feast being given by Esquimaux. As a good anthropologist, he would establish rapport by eating what they ate. But there was a pot full of what he took to be blubber. He dutifully took some, and felt sick. He went outside the igloo to recover. There he met an Esquimau woman, who was scandalized when she heard that they were serving blubber. For they hadn't told her! She rushed in—but came out soon after in great disgust. It wasn't blubber at all, it was simply dumplings. Had the good savant only known, he could have taken dumplings in his stride. But it was a battle indeed for him to hold them down when he thought of them as blubber![70]

By other names, not only do roses *not* smell as sweet, but food is *not* as savory, art works *not* as desirable, personalities *not* as pleasant, and societies *not* as comfortably structured. Your own examples will come readily to mind. Mine include the absurd fights waged over the words "socialism" and "communism" in this country, even when there was not the slightest evidence that socialistic or communistic behavior was involved; the problem of horse meat during World War II, and those who ate it happily, bravely, protestingly, unknowingly, or not at all; the contemporary preoccupation with four-letter words; and the mysterious transformation of that federal agency, the War Department, into the Department of Defense. "Who is taken in" by this sort of change? A great many people, I think. All of us!

It's hard for me to understand how one can say that "it is the thing that is good or bad, not its name," when legal action can be and *is* taken against some who prefer the shorter alternatives to "sexual intercourse" or "human excrement." And

[68] Richard E. Hughes and P. Albert Duhamel, "Rhetorical Qualities of Words," *ibid.*, p. 137.

[69] Percy H. Tannenbaum, "The Indexing Process in Communication," in *Communication and Culture*, ed. Alfred G. Smith (New York: Holt, Rinehart and Winston, 1966), pp. 480–88.

[70] Burke, *Language as Symbolic Action*, p. 7.

in philosophical terms it's hard for me to understand the "independence of matter from manner," for that would seem to require that we have ideas or thoughts that we are able to think or express in *no* Style at all, and, on the other hand, that we be able to use various Styles (ornate, simple, etc.) to express *nothing*. How can that be? How can I utter anything except by uttering it in *some* manner or Style? And how can I use, say, a bombastic or gentle or sarcastic Style without using it to say *something*?

I can't, of course. But that means that changes in Style are also changes in meaning. Neither matter nor manner is independent of the other. I cannot say the "same thing" in "different words." When I use different words I say different things. The difference may be great or small, but it *is* a difference. "Hell no!" is not the same thing as "certainly not!" "You are an utterly stupid man" is not the same thing as "Good lord, you're dumb." And even the slightest changes make a difference: "The man entered the room slowly looking straight ahead" is not quite the same as "The man came into the room slowly staring straight ahead." Even this sort of difference *is* a difference—in Style *and* content. What specifically is this difference? Well, "enter" means "come in" in one sense, but "enter" is, first, a slightly more formal verb—there are few colloquial expressions that include enter—and, second, a verb that implies nothing at all about its user, about the observer. "Come in" means "enter" in one sense, but it's more informal—many slang expressions involve "come," as "to come across," "to come at," "a come down," "to come off," "to come out with," etc.—and it can easily imply that the person described as "coming in" is nearing the observer, for one meaning of the single word "come" is "to move toward the speaker, to draw near, to approach." Then, "looking" is a rather simple and straightforward sort of word that means "using the sense of sight" or "turning one's eyes in a certain direction so as to see." By contrast, "staring" is a far stronger word; its major meaning is "to gaze in a fixed manner, often with the eyes opened wide, as if from fear, surprise, or admiration."

Even with differences as slight as "entered—came in" and "staring—looking" general tendencies are apparent. "Come in" is an Anglo-Saxonate expression, "enter," a Latinate term. Generally, when you choose Latinate terms you choose the more formal, more precise, more scholarly, more pedantic forms; when you choose Anglo-Saxon derivatives you choose the somewhat more informal, more colloquial, more ambiguous, more ordinary forms. So much for "enter" and "come in." "Looking" and "staring" are both derived from the Old English, so the above tendency doesn't operate here. But one of these words is most frequently used in a relatively unemotional sense, while the other is most frequently used in a sense that involves emotional loading. And even when a particular context contradicts these degrees of emotionality, "look" will probably be perceived as emotionally weaker or more neutral than "stare."

Let me be clear. I am talking about small differences indeed. The "entered — came in" difference seems to me to be about as small as can reasonably be discussed. Yet it is a difference—a difference in what is said and in how it is said. The two can't possibly be separated.

So it will not do at all, this matter versus manner approach to Style. For it assumes that language exists (since concepts, ideas, thoughts exist) apart from Style, and Style apart from language. And to say that is, essentially, to dehumanize language, for if there is language without Style that must include Style of the idiosyncratic sort that I, and you, and all individual users of language, bring to it; and that means that there is language without those individual users of language—language without people. And that, as I argued in the Introduction, is the ultimate contradiction in terms. To be human is to use language, and to use language is to be human. If you assume that language exists without people, you are doomed to one of two evil ends: you must commit the philosophical foolishness of defining language in such a way that you cannot yourself use language, since it is language without you that you must discuss; or you must stumble into the empirical absurdity of arguing that language can exist without emotional or connotational values, without personal or attitudinal bias, and you cannot argue that view without using in your own language the same personal and attitudinal qualities that you are opposing.

An entirely different approach must be found. And it has been. A long time ago. The Roman rhetorician Quintilian said that Style was a matter of the function of language, not of the presumed existence of certain traits in language. Following Quintilian's lead, Hugh Blair said in the eighteenth century that Style is "the peculiar manner in which a man expresses his conceptions, by means of language."[71] The immediate effect of such statements is to fuse language and Style, to make clear that the two cannot be separated under any circumstances. Style of one sort or another is evident in every language event; and with every language act the choice is between this or that Style, never between Style or no Style. In sum, language *is* Style in the simple sense that the various discernible Styles are the various functions of language as man uses it to conduct transactions between himself and the universe, between the selves of his own being, and between himself and others.

Because Style is so integral a part of language, and because language is basic to, or *is* the human condition, it seems to me that Style must first be considered as the sense in which every user of language is individual and every discourse unique. Then, because I am still concerned with Rhetoric, Style must be discussed as the ways or means by which individuals function rhetorically. The two go together of course, but I shall use the headings "Individual Style" and "Rhetorical Style," emphasizing their interrelatedness as I go.

*Individual Style*

In the same sense in which we are unique as individuals, our discourses are unique. To use language is to be human. As I use language, verbal and nonverbal, in certain ways, I am Paul Campbell, you are . . ., and you, and you. Since language cannot be separated from people, it follows that the uniqueness of the individual cannot be separated from his language, but must be apparent in that language.

[71] Hugh Blair, *Lectures on Rhetoric and Belles Lettres* (London, 1783), p. 103.

Individual style seems to me most easily understood by talking about the notion of *constitutive language acts*.[72] Most frequently, philosophers, rhetoricians, and even language theorists have tended to assume that the fundamental form of language is an interpersonal and communicative one. Certainly language is frequently used in interpersonal contexts and for purposes of communication, but that is not to say that the most important use of language can be so labeled or that the most basic form of language is either communicative or interpersonal.

At certain times we speak aloud when no one else is present and when there is not even the communicative need to talk to ourselves. We yell "Damn!" on missing an easy golf putt, or dropping a heavy weight on a bare toe; we exclaim "Gorgeous!" or "Oh, wow!" on seeing a lovely sunset or a sensuous woman; we cheer the athlete on TV and curse the traffic jam ahead of us. In none of these cases are we talking *to* anyone, even ourselves. Rather, the words we utter are *part of* the frustration or admiration or intense concentration that we are experiencing. The words *constitute* part (and often a large part) of the psychological state in which we find ourselves. That is, they are not merely outward manifestations or reflections of such inner states as anger, admiration, irritation; they are ways of *being* angry, admiring, irritated. The "Damn!" and the "Gorgeous!" are *constituents* of passing or permanent states of being. By uttering those words in the ways that we utter them, we act, we behave irritatedly or admiringly.

The idea is perhaps clearest in oral language, but it's just as true in silent language. After all, our "Damns!" may be silent or oral, but in both cases they are ways of *being*. We curse or mutter joyously both silently and aloud, and the silent statement *constitutes* part of our frustration or delight just as the oral one does.

But that brings a whole new category of *constitutive* language acts into view. As we habitually use language sloppily, or wittily, or tenderly, or sarcastically, or sullenly, we are engaged in constitutive language acts. To say that a certain use of language is *habitual* is to say that it does not depend on the communicative factors in a given situation, but that it is characteristic of the user, that it constitutes part of the user's personality. Almost all the ways in which we utter words, silently or aloud, are constitutive in this sense, but so are a great many of the words themselves. For instance, as you will have noticed, I have a habit of using several (most frequently two or three) adjectives or descriptive phrases. Clearly there are times when one would do perfectly well. I often use words like "clearly," "certainly," "surely," and "indeed" to begin sentences. I may achieve a sort of emphasis in this fashion, but that emphasis occurs too frequently to be simply a communicative technique. It is a constitutive language act.

And from here on the realm of constitutive language behaviors is easily extended. A large or a small vocabulary is a constitutive element; so is a thorough awareness, or only a limited one, of grammatical niceties; so are all idiosyncratic acts, from regional accents, to matters of voice, gesture, and facial expression, and to attitudes of pedantry, pomposity, gentleness, disdain, and warm acceptance.

[72] Most of what follows in this section is based on Alexander Sesonske's article, "Saying, Being, and Freedom of Speech," *Philosophy and Rhetoric* I, 1: 25–36, and on my own article, "Language as Intrapersonal and Poetic Process," *Philosophy and Rhetoric* II, 4: 200–212.

And the final step is the obvious and simple one. *All language is constitutive*—constitutive in the sense that language constitutes the human condition and in the sense that the aggregate of an individual's language behaviors *constitutes* that individual. The most basic symbolic process—perceiving ugliness and beauty in and into the world —constitutes part of the state called humanity. And the tiniest personal mannerism, say, a tendency to draw away from people, constitutes part of the individual being.

All these are matters of Style. As language is constitutive, it is stylistic—it is the symbolic style of the individual and of the race. When language becomes communicative *it does not stop being constitutive*. All language is constitutive. It may be communicative as well—the communicative function may simply be added to the constitutive one.

But there's a problem in all this. I'm arguing that it's language in the broadest and deepest sense that makes me human and that makes me Paul Campbell. I'm arguing that my language *is* my Style, that I *am* my Style. Fine. That certainly removes any possibility of the Style-as-frosting-on-the-cake notion. But it does nothing, it says nothing about any changes in Style that may occur or that may be desired. It seems to leave open the possibility that I simply *am* my Style, that you are yours, and that we are stuck with it. And that clearly won't do, for we do change the Style of our language in a great many ways. I don't write and talk now the way I did 20 years ago; I talk to my wife differently than I do to my students; even in this book I write differently in various places.

One part of the answer to this problem is quite simple. All language is constitutive, but when it becomes communicative as well, that very fact will elicit different kinds of Style. The communicative demands of a situation usually make it fairly clear that formality or informality, brusqueness or gentleness, direct confrontation or indirect testing, etc., are the appropriate language traits. This sort of Style is, of course, deliberately and purposefully employed.

But there's another part of the answer. I talked earlier of language being personal, attitudinal, "sermonic." Language always consists of preachments; it always reveals, to some extent, the person or the position of the user. It must follow then that those preachments, those revelations are made with neatness, or grace, or even splendor, depending on the tension with which we shape our discourses. If language is personal, biased, constitutive, the simple fact of self-awareness must force us to speak with whatever degree of eloquence we can muster. It cannot be that we make those preachments, that we reveal ourselves, and that we do so impersonally, unfeelingly, objectively. To say that would be to set up the most basic contradiction in symbolic terms imaginable. Language carries in it an aesthetic, a drive for the pleasurable, a need for Ritual. And that element is one of the major determinants of the various Styles we use in various situations.

### Rhetorical Style

As individuals we obviously differ stylistically. Equally obvious are the differences between our rhetorical and our ritualistic language acts.

The oldest view of rhetorical Style divided it into three types: high, middle, and low. High Style was extremely ornate, florid, full of metaphors and literary allusions; middle Style was moderately formal and ornate and moderately plain; low Style was plain, uncluttered, and simple. Despite its age, this approach has not proved to be an exciting and profitable one. For one thing, almost all discourses of worth appear to fall into the middle or low Styles, for high Style seems pretentious and overdone. For another, differences between degrees of ornateness or formality are often exceedingly difficult to pin down. (For example, how do "The Black Man's Burden" and "On Woman's Right to Suffrage" differ?)

Northrop Frye, the outstanding literary critic, has suggested an approach to Style that I find stimulating and rewarding. Professor Frye retains the terms high, middle, and low, but he defines them quite differently. *Middle* Style, he says, is

> the ordinary speaking style of the articulate person, and its basis is a relaxed and informal prose. [To fully understand this definition, you must know that Frye has already said that prose "is not ordinary speech, but ordinary speech on its best behavior, in its Sunday clothes, aware of an audience and with its relation to that audience prepared beforehand. It is the habitual language only of fully articulate people who have mastered its difficult idiom."[73] ] It is the language of what ordinarily passes for thought and rational discussion, or for feelings that are communicable and in proportion to their objects.[74]

*Low* Style Frye describes as "a colloquial or familiar style."[75] He adds that "with all its anti-grammatical forms, it has its own vocabulary, its own syntax, its own rhythm, its own imagery and humor."[76]

Most impressively, Professor Frye says that *high* Style

> emerges whenever the middle style rises from communication to community, and achieves a vision of society which draws speaker and hearer together into a closer bond. It is the voice of the genuine individual reminding us of our genuine selves, and of our role as members of a society, in contrast to a mob. Such style has a peculiar quality of penetration about it: it elicits a shock of recognition, as it is called, which is the proof of the genuineness. High style in this sense is emphatically not the high-flown style: all ornate language in rhetoric belongs to the middle style, the language of society engaged in routine verbal ritual. Genuine high style is ordinary style, or even low style, in an exceptional situation which gives it exceptional authority.... High style in ordinary speech is heard whenever a speaker is honestly struggling to express what his society, as a society, is trying to be and do. It is even more unmistakably heard, as we should expect, in the voice of an individual facing a mob, or some incarnation of the mob spirit, in the death speech of Vanzetti, in Joseph Welch's annihilating rebuke of McCarthy during the McCarthy hearings, in the dignity with which a New Orleans mother explained her reasons for sending her white child to an unsegregated school.

[73] Northrop Frye, *The Well-Tempered Critic* (Bloomington, Ind.: Indiana University Press, 1963), p. 18.
[74] *Ibid.*, p. 40.
[75] *Ibid.*, p. 41.
[76] *Ibid.*

All these represent in different ways the authority of high style in action, moving, not on the middle level of thought, but on the higher level of imagination and social vision.[77]

Frye's description of Style clearly includes situational factors as well as language characteristics. To my mind, the most basic words in the above quotation are "aware of an audience, and with its relation to that audience prepared beforehand." This is a characteristic of prose. And at a different point Frye distinguishes between bastard speech, or the voice of the ego, and prose by saying that the former

is concerned mainly with self-expression. Whether from immaturity, preoccupation, or the absence of a hearer, it is imperfectly aware of an audience. *Full awareness of an audience makes speech rhetorical* [emphasis mine].[78]

By his stress on situational factors (the dramatic situations in which high Style occurs and the rhetorician-audience situations of all Rhetoric), Frye seems to put the primary and proper emphasis on Rhetoric as discourse, as language addressed to an audience. He describes Rhetoric as language in which the writer/speaker appeals *directly* to his audience, and this is the most important aspect of rhetorical Style.

Put differently, rhetorical Style brings the rhetorician into direct contact with his audience. There is an I—you relationship involved (as there is in this book). I don't mean that the rhetorician must come into physical contact with his audience. (Although, who knows, there may well be a rhetorical element there too.) I mean that the writer or speaker who behaves rhetorically presents *himself* to his audience. He stands before them figuratively or physically, wearing no mask, hiding behind no facade. Except, I must hurry to add, the masks and facades we all use in the various roles we play; however, we have no difficulty in calling these roles our "real" selves. The furthest extreme from Rhetoric is the performer who spends his life reading Hamlet's lines, or Lear's, or Othello's, and who may never disclose himself to his audiences in any meaningful fashion. His listeners may never know him. Indeed there is a sense in which he is his own and only audience. The rhetorician, on the other hand, is constantly disclosing himself to his audience. We say, almost instinctively, that the rhetorician who hides behind words, behind platitudes, behind the easy, glib phrase is unreal, a phony.

Rhetoric requires awareness of an audience. The more honest the Rhetoric, the fuller that awareness. Conversely, as Frye has said, awareness of an audience makes language rhetorical. In its simplest terms, if I talk or write *to* someone, I am behaving rhetorically. And in doing so I am dealing in direct address—discourse in which I offer myself to an audience, a specific audience.

So, Styles differ in Rhetoric depending on the degree of directness of address and on the nature of the rhetorical contact. The rhetorician who cannot or will not

[77] *Ibid.*, pp. 44—46.
[78] *Ibid.*, p. 21.

fully disclose himself to his audience is only partly a rhetorician. But even when disclosure is direct and fairly complete, there are differences in the nature of the rhetorical contact. A speaker/writer may look and talk down to his audience; he may present himself as an authority figure, one who is superior to his hearers/readers. Or, a rhetorician may plead, he may be a suppliant; he may present himself as the audience's inferior. Or, of course, the contact may take place between equals. Then, the rhetorician may view the audience as the enemy, as unknowns who must be approached cautiously, as rather unpredictable types who need some careful treatment, as people who may well be amicable if given a chance, or simply as friends. And the way the rhetorician looks at his audience (and of course himself, for individual Style is involved, too) will determine, will constitute his rhetorical Style. If he is afraid of the audience and tries to hide his fear behind sound and fury, we are likely to call him bombastic, pretentious, overblown. Stylistic terms, all. If he is assured and gentle, and seems to welcome the presence or the existence of his audience, we say he is warm, relaxed, easy. Again, stylistic words. Robert Frost's discourse seems to me to be of this sort. I have the feeling that he is enjoying the rhetorical act, that he is pleased to write to his readers. Or, if the rhetorician disapproves of or is disdainful of his audience, we may call him cold, aggressive, or peremptory. Once more, labels of Styles. And in Frye's terms, if the rhetorician sounds a call for understanding and acceptance, particularly in the face of intolerance or bigotry, we call him honorable, a moral man. These, too, are words that describe Style—the high and humane Style. Pitt's speech to the Commons is of this sort; he calls his audience to duties above their personal and narrow interests. Killen's essay, "The Black Man's Burden," belongs to this category, for he faces Whites and tells them the unpleasant truth about themselves. Even Miss Anthony's short speech on woman's suffrage is of this type, for she faces down the men who defined themselves as superior. And Mayer's "The Children's Crusade" certainly falls into this area, for he confronts himself and his peers as well as his audience.

To conclude this section, I want to talk about the stylistic qualities of two discourses. The first is Abraham Lincoln's Second Inaugural Address. Reading it, it's important to keep these facts in mind: these words were spoken on March 4, 1865; Richmond surrendered on April 3, 1865; General Lee conceded defeat on April 9, 1865; in the lower South, General Forrest was defeated on April 2, 1865; and General Johnston asked for an armistice on April 11, 1865. The armistice was delayed by Lincoln's assassination on April 14, and Johnston finally surrendered on April 26, 1865. In other words, when Lincoln delivered this discourse the war was almost over, and that fact was perfectly obvious to all. By the time of the inauguration, General Lee's army had been drastically weakened by defeats and desertions, and General Johnston's troops were mustered in a highly disorganized, helter-skelter fashion to meet the threat of Sherman's forces. There was simply no chance that the Confederacy would triumph, and the imminence of the collapse of all Southern resistance was inescapably clear.

And yet Lincoln said:

Fellow Countrymen: At this second appearing to take the oath of the Presidential office, there is less occasion for an extended address than there was at the first. Then a statement, somewhat in detail, of a course to be pursued, seemed fitting and proper. Now, at the expiration of four years, during which public declarations have been constantly called forth on every point and phase of the great contest, which still absorbs the attention and engrosses the energies of the nation, little that is new could be presented. The progress of our arms, upon which all else chiefly depends, is as well known to the public as to myself; and it is, I trust, reasonably satisfactory and encouraging to all. With high hope for the future, no prediction in regard to it is ventured.

On the occasion corresponding to this four years ago all thoughts were anxiously directed to an impending civil war. All dreaded it—all sought to avert it. While the inaugural address was being delivered from this place, devoted altogether to saving the Union without war, insurgent agents were in the city seeking to destroy it without war—seeking to dissolve the Union, and divide effects, by negotiation. Both parties deprecated war; but one of them would make war rather than let the nation survive; and the other would accept war rather than let it perish. And the war came.

One eighth of the whole population were colored slaves, not distributed generally over the Union, but localized in the southern part of it. These slaves constituted a peculiar and powerful interest. All knew that this interest was, somehow, the cause of the war. To strengthen, perpetuate, and extend this interest was the object for which insurgents would rend the Union, even by war; while the government claimed no right to do more than to restrict the territorial enlargement of it.

Neither party expected for the war the magnitude or the duration which it has already attained. Neither anticipated that the cause of the conflict might cease with, or even before, the conflict itself should cease. Each looked for an easier triumph, and a result less fundamental and astounding. Both read the same Bible, and pray to the same God; and each invokes his aid against the other. It may seem strange that any men should dare to ask a just God's assistance in wringing their bread from the sweat of other men's faces; but let us judge not, that we be not judged. The prayers of both could not be answered—that of neither has been answered fully.

The Almighty has his own purposes. "Woe unto the world because of offenses! for it must needs be that offenses come; but woe to that man by whom the offense cometh." If we shall suppose that American slavery is one of those offenses which, in the providence of God, must needs come, but which, having continued through His appointed time, He now wills to remove, and that He gives to both, North and South, this terrible war, as the woe due to those by whom the offense came, shall we discern therein any departure from those divine attributes which the believers in a living God always ascribe to Him? Fondly do we hope—fervently do we pray—that this mighty scourge of war may speedily pass away. Yet, if God wills that it continue until all the wealth piled by the bondsman's two hundred and fifty years of unrequited toil shall be sunk, and until every drop of blood drawn with the lash shall be paid by another drawn with the sword, as was said three thousand years ago, so still it must be said, "The judgments of the Lord are true and righteous altogether."

With malice toward none; with charity for all; with firmness in the right,
as God gives us to see the right, let us strive on to finish the work
we are in; to bind up the nation's wounds; to care for him who shall have
borne the battle, and for his widow and his orphan—to do all which may
achieve and cherish a just and lasting peace among ourselves and with
all nations.

Knowing that sure victory was just ahead, what did Lincoln say? Two things, basically. After a short introduction, he gave a brief, cuttingly honest summary of the history of the war, and then, incredibly, he refused to use even the word "victory," but instead *joined* the North and South in the assigned blame for the war and in the need to suffer because of past wrongs. It is a stupendous rhetorical act. The president of a nation that has put down an enormously dangerous armed revolt not only refuses to talk of victory, but insists that the whole nation is to share in the blame. What makes the discourse masterful is the combination of the knife-edged honesty in the first part and the refusal to evade Northern blame in the second. If Lincoln had started out by saying that both North and South were well-meaning and that war had come upon the nation despite its best efforts to keep the peace, the discourse would have been terribly weakened. As it was, Lincoln told the brutal truth: the South made war "rather than let the nation survive," the South's efforts to extend and make permanent the institution of slavery did in fact "rend the Union," and the South asked for the blessing of God in her efforts to dehumanize one eighth of the population.

And then, having directly and bluntly told of the South's actions in making the war inevitable, and *knowing* that the South's military efforts were *at that very time* hopelessly ineffectual, Lincoln said, "Let us judge not, that we be not judged." He refused to take the so obvious next step—indeed the obviousness is such that you can imagine the very words:

We must press on to assure the final victory of our cause, which, indeed,
almighty God himself has seen as just. We must make our nation whole, even
though our efforts include the destruction of that part that would itself have
destroyed us. We must eliminate forever the spectre of man owning man, and,
looking to God for His Truth and His Vengeance against the agents that
warred to bring disunion to this land, work fervently to blot from our
country the very names of those who would thus have disgraced and debased
us!

Words such as these *might* have been said. And Lincoln said, "Let us judge not, that we be not judged." And he added that the living God "gives to *both, North and South,* this terrible war, *as the woe due to those by whom the offense came*" [emphasis mine]. Clarifying even further the North's deep share of the guilt, he said that even if God willed that the war continue for many years and result in enormous additional bloodshed, both Northern and Southern, still "the judgments of the Lord are true and righteous altogether."

And then, finally, he ended with an entreaty, a plea for all Americans to avoid malice, to display charity, to unite the country, and to care for those, *all* those, who had suffered in the battle. And all of this during the very last days of a war that the North was winning. In sum, Lincoln spoke for and to the nation, not merely the North. He began by honestly exposing Southern actions, and ended by uniting North and South, confronting whatever vengeful feelings existed in the audience, the North, or in himself, and transcending them.

Perhaps the most incredible aspect of this discourse is that the stylistic frame of reference Lincoln adopted would have been particularly suitable to a call for complete victory, for the elimination of the enemy, even for savage revenge. That frame of reference was, of course, a religious one. After a brief history of the civil conflict, Lincoln turned at once to religious concepts and noted that both sides (strangely) prayed to the same god and read the same bible. From that point on, the discourse used religious or biblical criteria to evaluate the past and the future. And those very criteria could have been used so easily to "prove" that right lay with the North. My own words-that-might-have-been indicate something of this. Throughout history men have found it exceedingly easy to demonstrate that god wished them to murder their enemies efficiently and quickly. The western, the Judeo-Christian notions of god are especially suitable to war, for that god is wrathful, vengeful, fierce; he punishes those who follow him simply to test them; he smites his enemies, etc. Yet armed with what can almost be called the perfect stylistic weapon, the weapon with which he could have pictured the North as the Ally of the Almighty and the South as the Disciple of the Devil, Lincoln spoke of peace, of *shared* blame, of the need to heal. The Style of the speech was so honest, so understanding, so compassionate, that it seems almost that the speaker was himself superhuman. Certainly he fell prey to none of the thoroughly human needs for revenge, for self-vindication, for preening; rather, he so transcended the immediate reality that the Style of the discourse rose "from communication to community."

The second example is from an essay that appeared in *The Annals of the American Academy of Political and Social Science*. It is an essay that opened up new perceptions and ideas for me. I hope that it may for you.

### from "The Generation Gap"[79]

> . . . conflict between the generations is less a consequence of the ways in which old and young perceive, or misperceive, each other than of structurally created, genuine conflicts of interest. In this, as in other relationships, ideology follows self-interest: we impute to other people and social groups characteristics that justify the use we plan to make of them and the control over them that use requires. The subordinate group, in turn, often develops these very characteristics in response to the conditions that were imposed on them. Slaves, slum-dwellers, "teenagers," and enlisted men do, indeed, often display a defensive stupidity and irresponsibility, which quickly abates in situations which they feel to be free of officious interference, with which they can deal, by means of their own institutions, in their own way.

[79] Reprinted from *The Annals of the American Academy of Political and Social Science* (March 1969) by permission of the publisher and the author.

For American youth, these occasions are few, and have grown relatively fewer with the escalation of the war in Vietnam. The Dominican intervention, the scale and permanence of our military investment in Southeast Asia, and the hunch that our economic system requires the engagement of its youth at low pay, or none, in a vast military-academic complex, in order to avoid disastrously widespread unemployment—even under present circumstances far greater among youth than among older persons—suggest to thoughtful young people that their bondage may be fundamental to the American political system and incapable of solution within its terms.

That bondage is remarkably complete—and so gross, in comparison to the way in which other members of the society are treated, that I find it difficult to accept the good faith of most adults who declare their sympathy with "the problems of youth" while remaining content to operate within the limits of the coercive system that deals with them, in any official capacity. To search for explanations of the problems of youth in America in primarily psychological terms while suggesting ways of easing the tension between them and the rest of society is rather like approaching the problem of "the American turkey in late autumn" with the same benign attitude. Turkeys would have no problem, except for the use we make of them, though I can imagine clearly enough the arguments that a cadre of specialists in poultry-relations might advance in defense of Thanksgiving, all of them true enough as far as they went: that wild turkeys could not support themselves under the demanding conditions of modern life; that there are now more turkeys than ever before and their general health and nutritional status, if not their life expectancy, is much more favorable than in the past; that a turkey ought to have a chance to fulfill its obligations and realize the meaning of its life as a responsible member of society; that, despite the sentimental outcries of reformers, most turkeys seem contented with their lot—those that are not content being best treated by individual clinical means, and, if necessary, an accelerated program; and that the discontented are not the fattest, anyway, only the brightest.

Young men in America, like most Negroes, are excluded from any opportunity to hold the kind of job or to earn the kind of money without which members of this society committed to affluence are treated with gross contempt. In a sense, the plight of youth is more oppressive, for the means by which they are constrained are held to be lawful, while discrimination against Negroes is now proscribed by law and what remains, though very serious indeed, is the massive toxic residue of past practice rather than current public policy.

Students are not paid for attending school; they are held to be investing in their future—though if, in fact, they invested as capital the difference between the normal wage of an employed adult high school graduate for four to seven years and what little they may have received as stipends during their academic careers for the same length of time, the return accrued to them might easily exceed the increment a degree will bring. But, of course, they have not got it to invest, and are not permitted to get it to live on. The draft siphons off working-class youth, while middle-class youth are constrained to remain in college to avoid it. If there were no draft, their impact on the economy would probably be ruinous. Trade-union restrictions and child-labor laws, in any case, prevent their gaining the kind of experience, prior to the age of eighteen—even as part of a high school program—that would qualify them for employment as adults by the time they reach their legal majority, though young workers could be protected by laws relating to working conditions, hours, and wage rates, if this protection were indeed the intent of restrictive legislation, without eliminating the opportunity for employment.

Even the concept of a legal majority is itself a social artifact, defining the time at which the social structure is ready to concede a measure of equality to those of its members whom youthfulness has kept powerless, without reference to their real qualifications, which, where relevant, could be directly tested. Nature knows no such sharp break in competence associated with maturation, except in the sexual sphere; and comparatively little of our economic and political behaviour is overtly sexual. Perhaps if more were, we would be more forthright and less spiteful. Nor is there any general maturational factor, gradual but portentous in its cumulative effect, which is relative to society's demands.

Neither wisdom nor emotional stability is particularly characteristic of American adults, as compared to the young; and where, in this country, would the electoral process become less rational if children were permitted to vote: southern California? Washington, D. C.? If there should be any age limitation on voting, it ought to apply, surely, to those so old that they may reasonably expect to escape the consequences of their political decisions, rather than to those who will be burdened and perhaps destroyed by them. Certainly, the disfranchisement of youth is impossible to square, morally, with the Selective Service Act—though politically, there is no inconsistency: the second implies the first. But the draft is pure exploitation, in a classical Marxian sense. The question of the need for an army is not the issue. A volunteer army could be raised, according to the conservative economist Milton Friedman,[80] for from four to twenty billion dollars per year; and to argue that even the larger sum is more than the nation can afford is merely to insist that draftees support the nation by paying, in kind, a tax rate several times greater than the average paid by civilian taxpayers in money, instead of being compensated for their loss in liberty and added risk. To argue that military service is a duty owed to one's country seems quite beside the point: it is not owed more by a young man than by the old or the middle-aged. And, at a time when a large proportion of enlisted military assignments are in clerical and technical specialties identical with those for which civilians are highly paid, the draft seems merely a form of involuntary servitude.

Without a doubt, the Selective Service Act has done more than any other factor not only to exacerbate the conflict between generations, but to make clear that it is a real conflict of interest. The draft makes those subject to it formally second-class citizens in a way to which no race is subjected any longer. The arrogance and inaccessibility of Selective Service officials, who are neither elected nor appointed for fixed terms subject to review; the fact that it has been necessary to take court action even to make public the names of draft-board members in some communities; the fact that registrants are specifically denied representation by counsel during their dealings with the Selective Service System and can only appeal to the courts after risking

[80] Quoted in *Newsweek*, December 19, 1966, p. 100.

prosecution for the felony of refusing induction—all this is without parallel in the American legal process.

But the laws of the land are, after all, what define youth as a discriminated-against class. In fact, it is their discrimination that gives the term "youth" the only operational meaning it has: that of a person who, by reason of age, becomes subject to special constraint and penalties visited upon no other member of the commonwealth—for whom, by reason of age, certain conduct, otherwise lawful, is defined as criminal and to whom special administrative procedures, applicable to no other member of the commonwealth, are applied. The special characteristics of "youth culture" are derived from these disabilities rather than from any inherent age-graded characteristics. "Youth culture" is composed of individuals whose time is pre-empted by compulsory school attendance or the threat of induction into the Armed Service, who, regardless of their skills, cannot get and hold jobs that will pay enough to permit them to marry and build homes, and who are subject to surveillance at home and in school dormitories if they are detected in any form of sexual activity whatever. Youth and prisoners are the only people in America for whom *all* forms of sexual behavior are defined as illicit. It is absurd to scrutinize people who are forced to live under such extraordinary disabilities for psychological explanations of their resistance or bizarre conduct, except insofar as their state of mind can be related to their real situation.

In their relationship to the legal structure, youth operate under peculiar disabilities. The educational codes of the several states provide for considerably more restraint even than the compulsory attendance provisions provide—and that provision would be regarded as confiscatory, and hence doubtless unconstitutional, if applied to any member of the commonwealth old enough to be respected as having the right to dispose of his own time. Soldiers are at least paid *something*. But the code does more than pre-empt the students' time. It is usually interpreted by school authorities as giving them the power to set standards of dress and grooming—some of which, like those pertaining to hair length, of a kind that cannot be set aside while the student is not in school. It becomes the basis for indoctrination with the values of a petty, clerical social subclass. Regulations on dress, speech, and conduct in school are justified by this subclass as being necessary because school is supposed to be businesslike; it is where you learn to behave like a businessman. This leaves the young with the alternative of becoming little-league businessmen or juvenile delinquents, for refusal to obey school regulations leads to charges of delinquency—which seems a rather narrow choice among the possibilities of youthful life.

But I have written so much more elsewhere about education as a social sanction that it seems inappropriate to devote more space to the functioning of the school as such. I have introduced the topic here simply to point out that the educational code, from the viewpoint of those subject to it, constitutes the most pervasive *legal* constraints of the movements and behavior of youth. It is not, however, from the viewpoint of legal theory, the most fundamental. The juvenile code and the juvenile court system provide even more direct contradistinctions to the standard of due process afforded adults in American courts.

For the juvenile court is, ostensibly, not a criminal court. It is technically a court of chancery before which a respondent is brought as a presumptive ward—not as an adversary, but as a dependent. It is assumed—the language is preserved in the legal documentation used in preparing juvenile court cases—that the authorities intervene *on behalf of the minor*, and with the purpose of setting up, where necessary, a regime designed to correct his wayward tendencies. The court may restrict; it may, as a condition of probation, insist that a respondent submit to a public spanking; it may detain and incarcerate in a reformatory indistinguishable from a prison for a period of years—but it may not punish. It is authorized only to correct.

Because action in juvenile court is not, therefore, regarded as an adversary proceeding, the juvenile courts provide few of the legal safeguards of a criminal court. There is considerable public misunderstanding about this, because the effect of recent Supreme Court decisions on the juvenile court process has been widely exaggerated, both by people who endorse and by people who deplore what the Court has done. What it *has* done, in effect, is to require the juvenile court to provide the usual safeguards if its actions are ever to become part of an adversary proceeding in a regular criminal court. Since the state may at its discretion, try as adults rather than as juveniles youngsters over a certain minimum age who are accused of actions that violate the criminal code, and since the more serious offenses are usually committed by older adolescents, it may choose to provide these accused with the safeguards granted adults from the time of arrest rather than impair its chances for subsequent successful prosecution. It is, therefore, becoming usual, for example, to provide counsel for juveniles in serious cases; to exclude, in the event of a subsequent criminal prosecution, statements taken by probation officers or youth-squad members in a legally improper manner; and to permit juvenile respondents to summon and cross-examine witnesses— procedures which have not been part of juvenile court in the past.

These are improvements, but they leave untouched the much vaster potential for intergenerational conflict afforded by the summary treatment of casual offenders, and, particularly, of those youngsters of whose behavior the law could take no cognizance if they were older; for example, truants, loiterers, runaways, curfew violators, and twenty-year-olds who buy beer in a tavern. For such as these, there is no question of compromising future prosecution in a formal court, and their treatment has been affected very little, if at all, by high-court decisions. The law still presumes that its intervention in their lives is beneficial *per se*, and they have few enforceable civil rights with respect to it. If young people are "troublemakers," they are punished for it—that is all. Step out of line, and the police "take you away," as the Buffalo Springfield described it—on the occasion of a Los Angeles police roundup of the youngsters strolling on the Sunset Strip in the autumn of 1968—in the song, "For What It's Worth," that gained them a national reputation among teenagers.

It is quite clear that one's moral judgment of the legal position of youth in American society depends very largely on the degree to which one shares the fundamental assumption on which juvenile proceedings are based: that they are designed to help; that the adults who carry them out will, by and large, have the wisdom and the resources, and the intent to help rather than to punish. Legal authorities have caviled at this assumption for some time. Thus, Paul W. Alexander writes in a paper on "Constitutional Rights in Juvenile Court":

> In the area of the child's constitutional rights the last decade has seen a minor but interesting revolt on the part of some highly distinguished judges. So repellent were some of the juvenile court practices that the judges were moved to repudiate the widely held majority rule that a delinquency hearing in a juvenile court is a civil, not a criminal action. . . . This doctrine appeared so distasteful to a California appellate court that the following language appeared in the opinion: "While the juvenile court law provides that adjudication of a minor to be a ward of the court should not be deemed to be a conviction of crime, nevertheless, for all practical purposes, this is a legal fiction, presenting a challenge to credulity and doing violence to reason." (Included in Margaret K. Rosenheim (ed.), *Justice for the Child* [New York: Free Press of Glencoe, 1962], p. 83).

The kind of legal structure which youth face would appear to be, of itself, sufficient to explain why young people are often inclined to be skeptical rather than enthusiastic about law and order—and about those of their number who are enthusiasts for law, as student leaders and prominent athletes tend to be. Yet, the hostile relations that develop between youth and law-enforcement agencies are, even so, probably more attributable to the way in which police generally respond to young people than to the oppressive character of the legal system itself—though the two factors are, of course, causally related, because the fact that youth have few rights and many liabilities before the law also makes it possible for law-enforcement agencies to behave more oppressively.

With respect to youth, law-enforcement agencies assume the role of enforcers of morals and proper social attitudes, as well as of the law, and—having few rights—there is not much the young can do about it. Police forces, moreover, provide a manpower-pool by "moonlighting," while off duty, as members of private enforcement squads hired to keep young people from getting out of hand, a task which they often try to perform by making themselves as conspicuous as possible in order to keep the young people from starting anything—exactly what police would *not* do in monitoring a group of orderly adults in a public place.

My own observations at folk-rock concerts and dances, for example, which are among the best places for learning how young people express themselves and communicate with one another, confirm that surveillance on these occasions is characteristically officious and oppressive. It often expresses a real contempt for the customs of the youngsters, even when these are appropriate to the occasion. Police, clubs in hand, will rush onstage or into the pit at any sign that the performers are about to mingle with the dancers or audience—if a soloist jumps down from the stage, say, or if members of the audience attempt to mount it; or they will have the lights turned up to interrupt a jam session or freakout that has gone on too long, or with too great intensity, for their taste; or insist on ruining a carefully designed and well-equipped light show by requiring that the house lights be kept bright. All this is done smirkingly, as if the youngsters at the concert knew that they were "getting out of line" in behaving differently from a philharmonic audience. It should be borne in mind, considering the fiscal basis for rights in our culture, that tickets for the Beach Boys or Jefferson Airplane are now likely to cost more than tickets for a symphony concert, and the youngsters are poorer than symphony subscribers, but they rarely enjoy the same right to listen to their music in their own way, unmolested.

The music itself provides some of the best evidence of the response of the "further-out" youngsters to police action, which, indeed, sometimes inflicts on them more serious damage than the annoyance of having a concert ruined. In Watts, San Francisco, and Memphis, the civil disorders associated with each city in recent years were triggered by the slaying of a Negro youth by a police officer. "Pot busts" are directed primarily against young people, among whom the use of marijuana has become something of a moral principle evoked by the destructive hostility of the legal means used to suppress it: thirty students at the State University of New York at Stony Brook, for example, were handcuffed and herded from their dormitories before dawn last winter, before the lenses of television cameras manned by news agencies which the Suffolk County police had thoughtfully notified of the impending raid. (*The New York Times*, Jan. 18, 1968). Rock artists, speaking to, and to some degree for, youth, respond to the social climate which such incidents, often repeated, have established. I have already cited the Buffalo Springfield's song "For What It's Worth." The Mothers of Invention are even more direct in their new album, "We're Only In It for the Money," where they represent the typical parent as believing that police brutality is justified toward teen-agers who look "too weird" and make "some noise." (Copyright by Frank Zappa Music Company, Inc., a subsidiary of Third Story Music, Inc. BMI.)

Finally, exacerbating the confrontations between youth and adults is the fact that the control of youth has largely been entrusted to lower-status elements of the society. Custodial and control functions usually are so entrusted, for those in subjection have even lower status themselves, and do not command the services of the higher grades of personnel that their society affords. Having low status, moreover, prevents their being taken seriously as moral human beings. Society tends to assume that the moral demands made on the criminal, the mad, and the young by their respective wardens are for their own good and to reinforce those demands while limiting the subjects' opportunities for redress to those situations in which the grossest violations of the most fundamental human rights have occurred. The reader's moral evaluation of the conflict that I have described will, therefore, depend very largely, I believe, on the degree to which he shares society's assumption.

As has surely been obvious, I do not share it. The process by which youth is brought into line in American society is almost wholly destructive of the dignity and creative potential of the young, and the condition of the middle-aged and the old in America seems to me, on the whole, to make this proposition quite plausible. Nevertheless, the violation of the young in the process of socialization fulfills an essential function in making our society cohesive. And curiously—and rather perversely—this function depends on the fact that custody and indoctrination—education is not, after all, a very precise term for it—are lower-status functions.

American democracy depends, I believe, on the systematic humiliation of potential elites to keep it going. There is, perhaps, no other way in which an increasingly educated middle class, whose technical services cannot be spared, can be induced to acquiesce in the political demands of a deracinated and invidious populace, reluctant to accept any measure of social improvement, however generally advantageous, which might bring any segment of the society slightly more benefits than would accrue to it. Teachers, police, and parents in America are jointly in the business of rearing the young to be frightened of the vast majority who have been too scarred and embittered by the losses and compromises which they have endured in the process of becoming respectable to be treated in a way that would enrage them. Anything generous—or perhaps merely civil, like welcoming a Negro family into a previously white community, or letting your neighbor "blow a little grass" in peace—does enrage them, and so severely as to threaten the fabric of society. A conference of recent American leaders associated with a greater measure of generosity toward the deprived—John and Robert Kennedy, Martin Luther King, Jr., and Malcolm X, for a start—might, perhaps, agree, if it could be convened.

Many of today's middle-class youth, however—having been spared, by the prevailing affluence, the deprivations that make intimidation more effective in later life—are talking back; and some are even finding support, rather than betrayal, in their elders—the spectacle of older folks helping their radical sons to adjust their identifying armbands during the spring protests at Columbia University is said to have been both moving and fairly common. The protest, in any case, continues and mounts. So does the rage against the young. If the confrontation between the generations does pose, as many portentous civic leaders and upper-case "Educators" fear, a lethal threat to the integrity of the American social system, that threat may perhaps be accepted with graceful irony. Is there, after all, so much to lose? The American social system has never been noted for its integrity. In fact, it would be rather like depriving the Swiss of their surfing.[81]

—Edgar Z. Friedenberg

This discourse is surgingly, even violently, rhetorical. The author plays no games with neutral, impartial language. He presents a point of view—one that is not frequently heard. And he presents it with reason, with force, and with passion. It seems unlikely to me that you will read this discourse without reacting quite strongly. There is no requirement that you agree—indeed the speaker does not even call for agreement—he voices his own feelings, but leaves choices to you.

An important part of the Style of this discourse lies in the "new" look at an oft-discussed problem. It is almost the sort of newness that makes for Ritual. The very notion of widespread legal discrimination against youth—a discrimination that is a basic part of our society—is a jolting, jarring, blasting loose of old, unquestioned

[81] Notice that, although *The Annals of the American Academy of Political and Social Science* is an extremely reputable and prestigious scholarly journal, this discourse has none of the dry fusty qualities so often associated with scholarly writing.

attitudes about the superiority of adulthood. The disclosure of the frustrations and humiliations heaped on youth in the name of age-knows-best is a sobering picture. And it is fitting that the irony is repeated and sometimes savage. The comparison of the treatment of youth and the treatment of turkeys is a biting and a bitter one. There is humor at work here, but the humor is thrusting and bleak. The final likening of the importance of integrity in our society to the importance of surfing to the Swiss is the culminating statement that weds merciless honesty and stinging satire.

Unlike Lincoln in his Second Inaugural, this writer is distinctly human. He does not transcend the situation. Rather, his Style is the sharp observation, the sharp comment. The entire discourse has a quality of pointedness. Professor Friedenberg points out the similar treatment accorded "slaves, slum-dwellers, 'teenagers,' and enlisted men." He points out the social, psychological, and legal bondage of the young. He points out the inconsistencies and hypocrisies in the elders' view of youth. He points out the strange illogic of the Selective Service Act. He points out the likeness between the attitudes toward prisoners and youth, particularly as regards sexual behavior. And he points out the legal schizophrenia with which America has burdened itself in oppressing the young.

Consistently, this discourse probes deeply into the social myths of America. It's not a process of flailing away at, or bludgeoning, the Establishment; it's a pointed, a sharply pointed probing beneath the crusts of hypocrisy. Always there seems to be a comment that cuts a bit deeper, at a slightly different angle than I am used to. And the over-all effect is of rapier strokes that thrust home, that pierce our fraudulent piety. This author's style is incisive, and that pun is most intended. He writes cuttingly, with control—there is no ranting here. But the cut is always made.

It is worth noting that though this was a written rhetorical event and Lincoln's address an oral one, there is little to be said about oral versus written Style. In fact despite the sizable number of descriptions of the difference between oral and written Style, there appears to be little reason to assume that they are *any significant* differences between them.[82] One writer puts it: "What rhetoricians have called an 'oral' style appears to be approximately the same as the written style termed 'easy,' or 'readable' by the inventors of readability indices."[83] So I shall not assume that these, or any, discourses can be meaningfully contrasted stylistically simply in terms of written versus oral language.

The two preceding discourses differ a great deal in terms of individual Style. The first is marked by a calm strength, a point of view that unites warring factions. The second is characterized by a relentless and penetrating keenness of observation and comment. There are differences in rhetorical Style, too. Lincoln's outlook was so much larger than that of either North or South that he was, in effect, talking to them from a superior position. Though he spoke simply, almost humbly, he spoke from "above" his audience in the sense that he avoided most of their limitations. Friedenberg's viewpoint was that of sharp-eyed adversary. He was not superior to his audience, despite the fact that he saw more clearly and deeply. He was an equal

[82] Thompson, pp. 73–75.
[83] *Ibid.* p. 73.

who disclosed himself even as he stripped away the ugly deceits of those he was addressing.

## Summary

I've talked about one of the two major language processes, Rhetoric. It is a process that pervades all language, for language is a personal, attitudinal (i. e., rhetorical) symbolic process. Traditionally, Rhetoric has been considered to be reasoned discource that attempts to persuade, and I've changed that definition but slightly: Rhetoric is the theory and practice of persuasion by reasoned discourse. Traditionally, too, Rhetoric has been thought to consist of the elements of Invention (the discovery and development of the materials of persuasion), Disposition (the arrangement or organization of those materials), and Style (the measure of the uniqueness of discourses from the viewpoints of the rhetorician, the audience, and the critic). I've used these classical concepts (canons), and have discussed Invention in terms of ethical proofs, emotional proofs, and logical proofs, Disposition in terms of the emphasis with which the rhetorician wishes his audience to perceive the subject and the degree to which language falls into analytic patterns or transcends those patterns, and Style in terms of the inseparability of manner and matter, the disclosure of the individual, and the nature of the rhetorical contact that is made.

I hope that I've made clear the notion that there is no such thing as "mere Rhetoric." Rhetoric is the reality within which we spend most of our lives. It's the stuff of deciding to fight, or vote, or listen further, or even deciding not to decide. Men and nations depend on their rhetorical efforts for survival, and very often their Rhetoric is more powerful and more lasting than their weapons of war. I've heard Neapolitans say with their own fierce tenderness that Naples is the oldest continuously inhabited city in the world. It's a good statement, true or not. Who remembers now the Neapolitan kings? Their wars and terrors are gone. But the songs of Naples, the hyperbole and heartbreak and gypsy freedom of its people—the Neapolitan Rhetoric—these remain.

In the last chapter I talked of the traditional view of Rhetoric. Or to put it more accurately, I did the best I could to present what can be called the traditional view in such a way as to make it believable, vital, workable. That "best I could" involved breaking with tradition at some points, as I indicated at the time, but it seems to me that the last chapter can fairly be called traditional. Certainly it would have been possible to write *more* traditionally, but in my opinion that would also have meant taking a position that was less convincing, less justifiable. For instance, I might have argued that the processes of informing and persuading were separate ones, that the foundation of Rhetoric was formal logic, that a particular organizational pattern was best, etc. It could be maintained that those arguments

# 2

# *Rhetoric:*

## *An Anti-Thesis*

*all ignorance toboggans into know*
*and trudges up to ignorance again*
*—E. E. Cummings*

would have been more conventional, but it's my belief that they would also have been less provocative and profitable. So, I said what I said.

The problem now is that what I said is not enough. It's not that the last chapter, or any part of it, is simply wrong or inaccurate. Everything I said is true—in *some situations. But not in others.* It's not a matter of throwing out all or any of what I wrote; rather, it's a matter of identifying the shortcomings and the limitations, and then finding a broader context within which enlarged and revised notions of Rhetoric can function.

In this chapter I propose to point out the problems. The business of solving them will have to wait a bit, for reasons that will, I think, become clear.

The difficulties with the traditional view as presented in the last chapter can be quickly separated into minor and major ones, and I shall tackle them in that order.

## Minor Problems in the Neo-Aristotelian View of Rhetoric

First of all, despite the fact that I warned of overlapping, the very use of the separate canons—Invention, Disposition, Style—seems to me to encourage the notion of independent elements. For example, it can reasonably be argued that a large part of Disposition is simply the use of logical proofs, and that element is considered to be part of Invention. You make a statement, and then you support it in some way. And what are the supports? Simply the materials of logical proofs—evidence and argument. You cite examples, use statistics, refer to authoritative testimony, or offer "facts." In talking of Disposition, these items are called supports; in discussing Invention, they are termed evidence and argument. So, it seems to me that the implied separateness of the three canons is markedly misleading.

And not only is the implied separateness misleading, there is a change in the order of importance that is, I believe, indicated. It should be stressed that Style is the most basic, even the most important, of the canons. No matter what aspect of Disposition or Invention may concern you, Style will also be involved for the utterly simple reason that language is always a stylistic process regardless of its other dimensions. I may argue illogically, or create discourses that seem disorganized, or behave in rhetorically unethical ways, but I can no more use language without Style than I can talk without words. Style is instantly evident in each of my language acts. So, in my judgment, we need a reordering in which it is made clear that Style occupies the most basic position in the hierarchy of language dimensions or characteristics.

Finally, in the reordering I've just mentioned, I think the point that I made in the last chapter about the relative unimportance of formal logic in Rhetoric should be given major status. When you consider the fact that you can find no trace of formal logic in many rhetorical masterpieces, it becomes apparent that we need to officially demote logic, as we have used that notion, to a lesser position. I don't wish to argue that Rhetoric is, or should be, illogical or nonlogical, but that it often uses a logic of its own, a "wildness of logic" that, like Frost's poetry, must often "be more felt than seen ahead like prophecy."

Without this sort of demotion, without this sort of "felt" logic, we have far too little to say of discourses such as this:

### The Gettysburg Address

Four score and seven years ago our fathers brought forth on this continent a new nation, conceived in Liberty, and dedicated to the proposition that all men are created equal.

Now we are engaged in a great civil war, testing whether that nation, or any nation so conceived and so dedicated can long endure. We are met on a great battlefield of that war. We have come to dedicate a portion of that field as a final resting place for those who here gave their lives that that nation might live. It is altogether fitting and proper that we should do this.

But, in a larger sense, we cannot dedicate, we cannot consecrate, we cannot hallow this ground. The brave men, living and dead, who struggled here, have consecrated it far above our poor power to add or detract. The world will little note nor long remember what we say here; but it can never forget what they did here. It is for us the living, rather, to be dedicated here to the unfinished work which they who fought here have thus far so nobly advanced. It is rather for us to be here dedicated to the great task remaining before us: that from these honored dead we take increased devotion to that cause for which they gave the last full measure of devotion; that we here highly resolve that these dead shall not have died in vain; that this nation, under God, shall have a new birth of freedom; and that government of the people, by the people, and for the people, shall not perish from the earth.

—Abraham Lincoln

If we cling to neo-Aristotelian orthodoxy, we are forced to say that this discourse consisted of statements that were almost entirely without supports. There are no examples, no statistics, and no authoritative testimonies here. Facts, yes, but they are of the sort that could be called completely self-evident. It was a fact that President Lincoln and his audience were "met on a great battlefield," for example, but was the facticity of that remark of some particular significance? I think not.

And what of the reasoning in this reasoned discourse? It seems painfully simple, even obvious, even weak. "We are gathered here to dedicate part of this field as a cemetery; in fact, the dedication, the consecration has been performed by those who died here; so, for us, the need is to dedicate ourselves to the completion of the war and the preservation of the country." That's the reasoning as I see it. I won't argue that it's *not* reasoning, but it seems to me most important to recognize that what is worthy here is a matter of tone, of quiet dignity, of rhythm, of syntax, of metaphor, *not* of syllogistic or enthymematic or inductive logic.

I've talked of the process of definition as an opening up of an idea or attitude, and that notion might be used with this speech, but I believe it must be made far more prominent in our rhetorical scheme of things. For it is such notions, such processes that are necessary if we are to talk meaningfully of many rhetorical works—the speeches of Churchill, of a large number of European orators from Mazzini and Garibaldi to Napoleon and Robespierre, to Clemenceau and Zola, to Mussolini and Hitler, and the essays or writings of men from Marcus Aurelius to Bacon, to Locke, to Montaigne, to Emerson, to Lin Yu-t'ang. All these are rhetorical discourses that are important in various ways. Indeed they can all be called outstanding rhetorical events, and an approach to Rhetoric that makes it difficult or impossible to deal with such discourses is too limited.

I call these minor problems, not in the sense that they are unimportant, but in the sense that they can very probably be dealt with by rearranging, reemphasizing, reordering the aspects of Rhetoric that I discussed in the last chapter.

It's significant that these problems all derive from a too strict notion of *reason*. And the broadening, the loosening of that notion (probably in Frost's sense) might well solve these problems.

But there are others.

## Major Problems in the Neo-Aristotelian View of Rhetoric

Those others derive from a too analytic notion of persuasion or of the communicative process itself. The major problems in the ideas I dealt with in the last chapter can be listed as the forms of alienation implied by neo-Aristotelianism and the philosophical and ethical difficulties in using and evaluating neo-Aristotelian procedures.

The clear implication behind almost every page of the last chapter was that separate discourses, rhetoricians, and audiences do in fact exist. I talked about individual rhetorical acts and individual rhetoricians. There is a sense, of course, in which it is perfectly proper to do so; this book, for example, is a separate and discrete rhetorical act in the simple sense that it begins and ends—before you began reading it, it did not exist for you, and after you finish with it, it will no longer exist, at least in the active sense in which it was part of your behavior during the reading. Similarly, I am an individual rhetorician, separate and separated from the creators of the various discourses I quoted in the last chapter. Fine.

But there is a very important sense in which all this separateness is misleading and distorting. Consider this simple example: you go to a physician because you feel sick; he examines you, tells you to do such-and-such to get well. That might seem to be an example of an individual rhetorical act, but I think that's too simple a judgment. Surely you will have responded to the physician's statements, presumably by following his directions, but that is not to say that your response was *determined by*, or was a response *to* those statements *alone*. Probably you had been to that physician before or had heard him recommended by someone. You were, in other words, already conditioned to some extent, either by previous visits or by the praise of the person who gave the recommendation. In addition, you went to him with certain ideas about physicians; you had preformed attitudes that you brought with you. Surely you do not listen to the Rhetoric of the physician and the politician with the same ears. There is a sort of unquestioning, uncritical acceptance of the medicine man that many of us develop. (I fight to overcome mine.) But whatever your attitudes toward physicians, they affected your response to that particular physician. Or, put the other way round, the rhetorical event in question did not begin with this M.D.'s advice to do this-and-that, but started with the first attitudes toward physicians that you began to develop. This discourse, in other words, had one of its beginnings long before you ever saw this rhetorician; as a discourse it can be traced back to your earliest experiences with physicians.

Exactly the same thing must be said of all other speakers/writers. There is one sense in which they are separate, another in which they are not. I suppose that most of you are students, since this book is being published by a company that puts out textbooks. That means that your perception of me will be affected by whatever attitudes you have developed toward writers of textbooks (even though I am trying to make this an untexty book). And that means that there is a sense in which I am *not* separate from those other textbook writers that you have experienced.

Similarly, rhetoricians are not quite as separate from, or independent of their discourses as the last chapter implied. The notion that rhetorical events affect only audiences is not, I think, a justifiable one. There is a very important sense in which I affect myself with this book. In fact there is a sense in which I am always my primary audience. (I'll have much more to say on that point later on.) By saying what I did in the last chapter I made some choices that clearly affected what I say in this one. By saying what I do in this book I limit, I determine to some extent what I shall say in the next one. Rhetoricians affect themselves with their own discourses.

Then there is the obvious sense in which we affect each other both as rhetoricians and as members of audiences. There are standards, appropriate forms of behavior that we will flout or follow as audiences or as writers/speakers. It's a far more violent act to boo a speaker or performer in this country than it is in some others. We usually confine our disapproval to such acts as not listening, refusing to read further, etc. And as rhetoricians we are subject to similar pressures. If we play the scholarly role, we are supposed to cite authorities, to footnote, to maintain a certain personal aloofness. Too much passion is suspect. Or if we adopt a "scientific" attitude, we are supposed to stay pretty cool, unemotional, uninvolved. We exist in a culture in which emotions and "science" are presumed to be incompatible. And all these roles, all these cultural pressures affect all of us and in one sense unite us.

The separateness is simply overdone in the neo-Aristotelian scheme of things. Granted, there is one level on which the separateness of rhetoricians, discourses and audiences is perfectly valid; but there is another level on which there are strong and clear relationships between all of these seemingly separate elements. It is that second level that, to my mind, is either unrecognized or underemphasized.

But even more important than these forms of alienation are the ethical and philosophical problems inherent in the notions I presented in the last chapter. Throughout that chapter I implied a *one-directional* process, a speaker-speech-audience process. The simplest view of the process is usually stated these days as the sender-message-receiver model of communication. The assumption is that rhetoricians are capable of persuading audiences, and that they do so by sending out messages that have an effect on those audiences. In schematic form the model is:

The alienation implied by those separate boxes I've already discussed. It's the one-directionality of the model, indicated by those little arrows, that I think is the real villain of the piece. I understand this model to mean that the sender, the rhetorician, is the active agent who puts out a message, a discourse, while the receiver, the listener or reader, is the passive element that takes in the other's message. It's basically a one-way street, from sender to receiver. Of course, the model can be made more complicated, but the complications do little to change the one-directionality of the process. The major attempt to make this sort of model two-directional, or multi-directional, consists of the addition of a "feedback loop." In simple form, it looks like this:

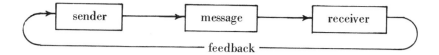

The feedback loop simply means that the receiver gets the message and reacts in some fashion, and that that reaction is a message of its own that can be received and reacted to by the sender. Applied to a two-person conversation, the sender says something, the listener reacts, and by judging the reaction the sender may then modify his message to achieve the desired result. The process remains one-directional, first one way then the other.

The whole thing remains unsatisfactory. The assumption is still that the sender is the actor, the receiver the acted on. The sender's job is to get the receiver to believe or behave in a certain manner, and the very clear implication is that the sender can do just that if he creates his message carefully and judges the receiver's reactions shrewdly.

One of my objections to all this can be put in philosophical terms. If I postulate a persuasive or communicative process in which I have the *power* to persuade, to communicate something to another person, I have defined a process in which I am powerful and my listeners or readers are powerless. And that is to say that I have dehumanized first my audience, then myself. It's this level of one-directionality that disturbs me most. It seems to eliminate the element of freedom of choice in regard to audiences. And it will not do to merely qualify the matter by saying that *I* have the power to persuade *you* so long as you are not distracted by outside forces, or are not too tired or depressed, etc., to hear me. Those elements are external in that they are not actions that you may freely choose to take.

In this sense communication becomes a manipulative process. I am communicating well or successfully when I get you to do what I want. But that is precisely the "salesmanship" approach to which I have already objected on other grounds. If it is indeed possible for me to sell you an idea, or a belief, or an attitude in anything like a simple, direct sense, then I am your master and you become a puppet. If I can persuade you of anything at all—if I can communicate anything at all to you *without* your active cooperation, I become de(super)human, and you de(sub)human.

I am perhaps belaboring this point, and I do so because I find it to be extraordinarily important. It's been my experience that the most usual views of persuasion rest on just the manipulative process that I've described. For instance, I've found that it's frequently believed that the advertising industry is capable of all sorts of sneaky things that affect us regardless of our intentions or choices. Too often we assume that the ad-makers can put something so subtly, can bring such strange pressures to bear on us, that *without even knowing that we've been persuaded* we buy some cereal, or car, or candidate. I think that's a terrible notion, for it deprives me of the ability to exercise free choice; it reduces me to a blob that is jerked here and there by the crafty manipulators who somehow know what it takes to get me to do as they wish.

Particularly in relation to feelings, to emotional needs, is this a dangerous idea. If there is someone who can figure out my most basic drives, and who can plug into the appropriate ones at the appropriate times, that someone will rule me, perhaps without my knowing that I'm being ruled. But that is to make of communication a sort of switchboard activity; you calculate the component elements of your audience; you plug into the one that suits your purpose; and, presto, you've activated them in the desired way or direction.

I am not a switchboard operator. Nor are you a switchboard. Communication is not this sort of hypodermic-needle activity whereby I shoot you with a load of persuasion $x_3$, and you go trotting off to vote, or buy, or believe. Philosophically, such a notion is dehumanizing for both rhetoricians and audiences.

Further, this one-directional, manipulative process contradicts some very basic and important ideas about language. As I've said, language has to do with meaning, and meaning is experientially based. That is, the meanings that I perceive in words, sentences, etc., are based on *my* experiences, the meanings that you perceive, on *your* experiences. There can be no simple, direct ties between words and chunks of the real world, for if that were the case we would all mean the same things by the language we used. We would employ language as a *signalling* system to refer to aspects of the outer world that impinged on our consciousness. Clearly that is *not* the case. I have written what I have written in this book, but all readers will not find the same meanings here. As your experiences differ from mine, your use of "the" language in these pages will differ from mine. Put simply, a word is not a symbol for a thing, as I stated in the Introduction. Rather a word is a symbol for my, or your, experiences with the thing. We all use what we call the "same" words, but the meanings of those words vary with each user. The variations are often slight, and often serious, but they always exist.

Now look what happens with this sender-message-receiver notion of communication. With it we imply that the sender uses language in which meanings are based on his own experiences. He is the active agent who creates the message; in fact it is "his" message. But we imply that the receiver's job is to pick up his, *the sender's,* message, and that means that the receiver must use the sender's language and the sender's meanings. Actually, it seems to me that we often imply that the passive receiver has no language of his own, but that he takes on or uses the other's language.

Surely these ideas run counter to the very nature of language. Surely we must give the receiver the same right to base his meanings on his experiences that we give the sender. And when we do that, surely we must assign to the receiver an *active*, an entirely active role in the rhetorical event. At that point, however, we have radically changed the notion of persuasion or communication. In addition to persuasive writing and speaking, rhetorical discourse must include persuasive listening and reading. The very terms ring oddly, do they not? Persuasive speaking *sounds* right; persuasive listening *sounds* off-balance. And I think that's because we are so used to the idea of passive audiences. Yet the very idea of passivity does violence to basic concepts of language and of meaning.

I've put all this strongly, and I rather feel that a period of calming down is indicated. But there's more to come, for I have another major objection to the implications of the last chapter.

The ethical dimension of the traditional notions of Rhetoric is, I believe, far too weak and elusive. In fact there are instances in which it simply ceases to exist. The problem begins with the results of the rhetorical act and how they shall be judged. What makes a discourse a success or a failure? Well, the implication of everything I said in Chapter 1 was that if you do in fact persuade an audience of such-and-such, you've succeeded; if you don't persuade them, you've failed. This approach can seem reasonable enough, for it's obvious that we do try to persuade others in all sorts of ways. I would like you to agree with the ideas I'm presenting right now, for example. But if I make success, in the usual sense of that word, the basis on which I judge Rhetoric and rhetoricians, I'm in immediate trouble. The discourse I quoted earlier by Pitt on the rights of the American colonists did not result in the adoption of Pitt's view by the British government. In other words, that rhetorical act was a failure. Socrates' funeral oration did not result in the removal of his death sentence, so despite the fact that that discourse has been admired for many centuries, it must be called a failure. On the other hand, there is every reason to believe that a great many of Adolf Hitler's discourses were successful in that the German people supported him. And there are used-car dealers and politicians who must be called successful because they make the sales and get the votes, even though their Rhetoric is distinctly unsavory.

Then there are the discourses that we call successful, even though we cannot demonstrate that they caused a particular effect. President Roosevelt's war speech "resulted" in the Congress declaring war. Or did it? Is there any way that we can show that cause-effect relationship? Might not almost *any* speech have had the same result?

And last, there are discourses that do not have identifiable results. What were the effects of the "Gettysburg Address"? One writer says, "Lincoln spoke with a small voice and was heard by few in the great gathering. His speech passed almost unnoticed in the newspapers the next day."[84] Another states that

> testimony can be brought to bear to prove that the speech was received with prolonged applause, or with perfunctory applause, or with no applause at all. Evidence can be adduced to prove that the speech was read, that it was spoken without the use of a manuscript, or that it was delivered with slight reference to a manuscript. Witnesses attest variously that the speech received close attention, or that the hearers had just begun to follow the speech when they were astonished to discover that the speaker had concluded. The reports and editorial judgments that appeared in the newspapers following the speech are similarly inconclusive.[85]

There appears to be remarkably little agreement as to what did happen after the

[84] George W. Hibbitt, ed., *The Dolphin Book of Speeches* (Garden City, N.Y.: Doubleday & Company, Inc., 1965), p. 16.
[85] Bower Aly and Lucile Folse Aly, *American Short Speeches* (New York: The Macmillan Company, 1968), pp. 30-31.

"Gettysburg Address." And it would seem to follow that, because we cannot identify results, we should withhold judgment as to the success or failure of the discourse.

And the above discourse is far from unique. I think it would be just as difficult to identify the results of Frost's "The Figure A Poem Makes." In fact most written discourse probably creates serious problems for the seeker of effects because, although oral Rhetoric is often confined to a specific time and place, written Rhetoric can so easily reach audiences that are widely scattered, spatially and chronologically. And obviously, if we can't specify the audience we can't measure effects, for we're talking about effects *on* an audience.

It's quite apparent that we don't use the results criterion in the ways I've just described, even though they would seem to be logical. We don't call Hitler a great rhetorician; we don't call discourses such as Pitt's and Socrates' failures; and we don't refuse to evaluate rhetorical acts such as those by Lincoln and Frost. What we *do* is to switch from one criterion to another. We switch from the *results* criterion to an *artistic* or *ethical* criterion when it suits our purposes. Almost all critics of Nazi Rhetoric, of the Rhetoric of Southern pre-Civil War leaders, and of contemporary figures such as George Wallace condemn those rhetorical acts, *not* because of the lack of results, but because the statements made are objectionable. Those rhetoricians did, or do, achieve results that were significant and noteworthy. Yet they are criticized. The following is a typical example of the criticism of ante-bellum Rhetoric:

> The tragedy is that they were saddled with a cause of such moral perversion that they could win the verdict neither from the nation nor in the depths of their own hearts. . . . Nor is there cause to doubt that it was a cancer which ate into the manhood of the very men who were its most ardent defenders.[86]

It appears to me that what is very clearly implied here is that these rhetoricians are called failures because their cause was unjust, and that they would be called failures no matter how many followers they found. I think there's a deep inconsistency involved in this: for one thing, it's not really fair to single out the Southern rhetoricians for not winning "the verdict" from the nation, since Northern rhetoricians also failed to get national approval; for another and more important item, we usually do *not* say that the success or failure of the Rhetoric of Richard Nixon, or Hubert Humphrey, or Eugene McCarthy should be determined by the moral acceptability of their discourses—in those cases it's results that count.

Of course some of us do object to the Rhetoric of the right or left on moral or ethical grounds. My point is simply that the whole notion of ethics is often ignored when we emphasize results and that, at best, we are inconsistent in switching from one criterion to another.

Let me deal with an example or two. Suppose that a rhetorician tries to persuade an audience to discard certain racist behaviors, knowing full well that that audience is most unlikely to follow his suggestions. It seems obvious that the odds

---

[86] Robert T. Oliver, *History of Public Speaking in America* (Boston: Allyn & Bacon, Inc., 1965), p. 190.

are very high that that speaker/writer will achieve no practical success. In fact it may be quite clear from the outset that the rhetorician cannot possibly win. What shall we say then? All such rhetorical efforts are failures? And because the probability of failure was easily predictable, should not the rhetoricians have *avoided* such situations? The essay, "The Generation Gap," that I used in the last chapter seems destined for this sort of failure; the chances that this society will reorganize and reshape itself as a result of this article seem slim indeed. Do we say then that the discourse is a failure, that that failure could have been predicted, and therefore should have been avoided?

Or turn again to the political Rhetoric of 1968. Who was successful and who failed? Which discourses achieved the desired results and which did not? Well, as between the Democratic contenders for the presidential nomination, it might seem that Humphrey won and that McCarthy and McGovern lost. Yet long after the battle at Chicago one commentator wrote:

> The uniqueness, the importance of the McCarthy-for-President movement was its proof of the power of popular participation, given a popular issue. The consequences are with us in the Vietnam Moratorium, in the McGovern Commission's efforts to pry the Democratic party open, and in the renewing of local Democratic organizations; in brief—"The New Politics."[87]

That sounds rather like McCarthy affected this country very directly and importantly. It's tempting but probably futile to try to set up some sort of comparison with Humphrey. How did his campaign, his Rhetoric, affect us? Then of course, the Democrat who apparently gained the most during the election campaign was Senator Muskie, yet he and Humphrey lost to Nixon. So seemingly, the winner in the whole business was Richard Nixon. He got the votes. Yet looking back on that turbulent period, which are the discourses that are remembered? What, for example, did Nixon say during the campaign? Law and order? If you had to single out the discourses that produced specific results, would you say that Nixon's pleas for law and order were the most successful rhetorical acts of that year? How do they compare with McCarthy's quiet pleas that seem largely responsible for the "New Politics?" Or with the Rhetoric of other campaigns—John F. Kennedy's call for national movement, for example?

In my opinion, there is some extremely important ingredient missing in all this. We should not have to change criteria to evaluate rhetorical events. After all, if the neo-Aristotelian view of Rhetoric is really workable, there is no room for anything but the results criterion. I say that because the very notion that Rhetoric is persuasion by reasoned discourse will, if followed strictly, eliminate from the realm of Rhetoric those discourses that persuade by means *other* than reason, and will make the act of reasoning itself the artistic dimension of Rhetoric. It appears absurd to so define Rhetoric and then to say that although large numbers of people were convinced by what was for them the reasoning of a particular speaker/writer, there was a rhetorical failure. Yet if we do use the results criterion consistently, we end

[87] Gilbert A. Harrison, "McCarthy on His Campaign," *The New Republic* (Oct. 25, 1969): 21.

up in the embarrassing position of having to acclaim Hitler, Wallace, Roosevelt, Nixon, Churchill, etc., with equal fervor. If we switch to an artistic standard, we run the risk of simply defining those rhetoricians who do not agree with us as failures, regardless of the results.

Finally, the business of stressing results seems to imply that though Rhetoric is a language process, what counts as results are "real" actions. And that amounts to saying that language, that Rhetoric doesn't really matter. You've heard the phrase, "mere Rhetoric." I think that label is based on the idea that symbolic or language acts are one thing and "real" acts another. This problem has been discussed by a rhetorical theorist who put it this way:

> We have talked, psychologists and people in speech, as if words are not really important, as if what we really were interested in was *other* kinds of behavior. Why is it that we study William Jennings Bryan? Why is it that we study Roosevelt or Churchill or any of the other great speakers? In the final analysis we sort of retreat to the position that the language is really not important, except in the sense that it moves men; and that when we say "it moves men" what we mean is that it gets things done. People go out and build dams; they set up complex economic systems; they raise teachers' salaries, and so on. These are the things we really are interested in, and the words are only a means to that end. Language in itself is really nothing except as it influences behavior. This, I say, is the kind of attitude under which we have been operating in the past.
>
> I wonder if this is really true. I wonder if, much of the time, we don't make speeches just in order to get people to talk a certain way—in other words, if the object of the speech is not, in many instances, *to change the verbal behavior* of our respondents, to make them say certain things or stop saying certain things, or deal with people in a certain way—on a purely verbal level. If you look for the effects of a really great single public speech, one which produces, apparently, a powerful and immediate effect, you'll find that these are rare. . . .
>
> How is it that a typical speech does produce its effect, then? It produces it, I think, through secondary communication. It gets people talking in a certain way. As a result of people talking in a certain way, an atmosphere of a certain kind develops, and that atmosphere is what produces the effect.[88]

I agree entirely with this author's notion that language is the thing that's important. He deals only with speech, with oral discourse, but I think his comments can easily apply to all Rhetoric, written and oral. (I note, though, a one-directional movement from speaker to audience implied by the above discourse.)

Add this to the other problems and the resulting picture seems to emerge: (1)

[88] *An Informed Colloquium on Trends in Speech Communication Research with Dr. Theodore Clevenger, Jr., Director, Communication Research Laboratory, Department of Speech and Theatre Arts, University of Pittsburgh, Visiting Consultant* (sponsored by The Speech Communication Division of the Department of Speech and Drama and The Communication Research Center, The University of Kansas, Lawrence, Kansas, August 7, 1965), pp. 23-24.

Rhetoric cannot be judged by its effects, partly because audiences may be difficult to identify, partly because effects may be largely verbal and therefore impossible to specify, and partly because it may have been impossible for the rhetorician to achieve the results he desired; (2) the business of switching back and forth from a results criterion to an artistic or ethical criterion is unsatisfactory, partly because of the inconsistency, partly because the artistic criterion is itself included in the notion that Rhetoric is reasoned discourse, and partly because we can so easily find ourselves in the position of arbitrarily defining as failures those rhetorical events with which we disagree.

Put in the simplest terms, I want Rhetoric to be evaluated on the basis of what is said, not merely on the results that may follow. But I do not want to say that if I choose to disapprove of a particular discourse, I may legitimately brand it a failure. From these two statements, it seems to me that it necessarily follows that what I want is a somewhat different *definition* of persuasion—one that *forces* me, as a critic, to deal with discourses in ethical terms. Assuming that cigarettes, or war, or politicians, or ideas can be sold by a Rhetoric that ignores the well-being of those who buy (a very shaky assumption, I think), I do not wish to have to pretend that that Rhetoric is successful.[89]

When I say that I want Rhetoric to be evaluated on the basis of what is said, I am not implying any distinction between what is said and how it is said. The two are one, and the "what" includes the neatness or savagery of the statement; indeed it starts with the neatness or savagery. And that is to say that it is just those aesthetic language elements that must be considered most basic. However, I can't simply stop there. I can't simply define language as a process that is basically aesthetic or artistic, for that leaves me in the position of having equated Rhetoric and Ritual, Rhetoric and imaginative or creative language. *It is perfectly true that language is, at its deepest levels, an aesthetic or artistic process.* But I am committed to the notion that there are two major currents of language, the rhetorical and the ritualistic. And that means that I must distinguish between them, must define Rhetoric in such a way as to make possible its practice and evaluation without confusion with Ritual.

At this point, I can offer only hints of what is to come. I'm quite aware that I haven't defined or described fully what I mean by artistic or aesthetic language, or by Ritual itself. I haven't talked of the interrelationships between Rhetoric and Ritual, or of the senses in which they can be separate forms. I can say, with no meaningful explanation, that it is a fusion of *the aesthetic and the ethical* that I require in Rhetoric—that all that I said in Chapter 1 must be encased in a larger view that rests on this aesthetic-ethical rhetorical base.

These statements are necessarily vague, I'm afraid. And I can't do much to clarify matters until I've talked about the ritualistic dimension of language and its relationship to Rhetoric. Chapter 1 amounts to an incomplete statement, and in

[89] A valuable discussion of this moral-rhetorical problem is found in Parke G. Burgess, "The Rhetoric of Moral Conflict: Two Critical Dimensions," *Quarterly Journal of Speech* LVI, 2: 120-130.

this chapter I've tried to point out the ways in which, and the reasons for which I find it incomplete. But the completion of that statement will require a large amount of new material, a large number of new concepts. I'm going to suggest much of that material, of those concepts, in the next chapter. However, it will turn out that the next chapter, like the last one, will be incomplete. I'll try to indicate *its* shortcomings in Chapter 4, and after that I'll be ready to attempt to tie it all together.

It's as if Chapter 1 were an initial and important movement of some sort into new territory; Chapter 2 discloses obstacles that require some modifications of that initial movement—modifications that can't be made without further knowledge; Chapter 3 will constitute another important movement into this new territory, but from a *different direction;* there too, obstacles will be found that, as indicated in Chapter 4, will require some modifying and rearranging. At that point, I will have made two basic statements, two basic movements, and will then have sharply qualified each. The next step, Chapter 5, will be either a total disaster or a method of completing each of the movements and tying them together by a pincer action into a single language structure.

All this may seem strange. I can only ask for patience and perhaps offer a clue to what lies ahead. Let me go back to Lincoln's "Gettysburg Address." I've pointed out that the results criterion doesn't work and that the reasoning is overly simple. Obviously I need a new view of such language acts. Briefly, the view that I shall eventually offer is that, although there is an element of Rhetoric here, the work is primarily Ritual. If I had to evaluate these words solely *as Rhetoric,* I'd call them weak, unimportant, a failure. I think the "Gettysburg Address" is very poor Rhetoric, but is very good and very important Ritual.

And now—to that process.

*Part II*

*RITUAL*

Throughout recorded history man has used language to please himself. Somehow he has found endless joy in the artistic or aesthetic effects that he could produce by a witty joining of words. And somehow he has delighted in hearing or reading time after time others' joinings that seemed especially taut. The wonder is not that man has been able to work magic with words—indeed what is more magical than words? —but that that magic seems to endure in so many instances. That so many men in so many places at so many times should agree that a particular line or story or play brings rapture or release appears to be irrefutable evidence that magic exists and endures in the Ritual of language.

# 3

# *Ritual:*
## *A Thesis*

*Sometimes in its box of
sky lavender and cornerless, the
moon rattles like a fragment of angry candy*

—*E. E. Cummings*

Somewhere around the fifth century B.C., Confucius chose from much earlier collections some odes which he called the "Shi King." Here are words written more than twenty-five centuries ago:

### Maytime

Deep in the grass there lies a dead gazelle,
The tall white grass enwraps her where she fell.
With sweet thoughts natural to spring,
A pretty girl goes wandering
With lover that would lead astray.

The little dwarf oaks hide a leafy dell,
Far in the wilds there lies a dead gazelle;
The tall white grass enwraps her  where she fell,
And beauty, like a gem, doth fling
Bright radiance through the blinds of spring.
"Ah, gently! do not disarray
My kerchief! gently, pray!
Nor make the watch-dog bark
Under my lattice dark."

—translated by L. Cranmer-Byng

Here is the beginning of a short story written in the fifteenth century. It is from a group of stories called "The Lights of Canopus."

### from "Poor Cat, Rich Cat"

In former times there was an old woman in a state of extreme debility. She possessed a cot more narrow than the heart of the ignorant and darker than the miser's grave; and a Cat was her companion which had never seen even in the mirror of imagination the face of a loaf nor had heard from friend or stranger the name of meat. It was content if occasionally it smelt the odour of a mouse from its hole or saw the print of the foot of one on the surface of a board. And if on some rare occasion, by the aid of good fortune, and the assistance of happy destiny, one fell into its claws,

> Like a poor wretch who finds out
> buried gold,

its cheek lighted up with joy, and it consumed its past sorrow with the flame of its natural heat, and a whole week, more or less, it subsisted on that amount of food, and used to say:

> "In slumber see I this, my God! or
> with my waking eyes?
> Myself in plenty such as this, after
> such agonies?"

—translated by Edward B. Eastwick

In the seventh century, the Japanese poet Kakinomoto no Hitomaro wrote:

> O Boy cutting grass
> On that hill,
> Do not cut like that!
> Just as it is
> I want it to be grass for the honourable horse
> Of my Lord who is going to deign to come.

—translated by Arthur Waley

About fifteen hundred B. C., these Sanskrit verses were written:

### from "Indra, the Supreme God"

> Highest of Immortals bright,
> God of gods by lofty might,
> He, before whose prowess high
> Tremble earth and upper sky,
> He is,—mortals, hear my verse,—
> Indra, Lord of Universe!

*A Thesis*

He, who fixed the staggering earth,
Shaped the mountains at their birth,
Sky's blue vault held up and bent,
Measured out the firmament,
He is,—listen to my verse,—
Indra, Lord of Universe!

—translated by Romesh Dutt

The Arabian poet Ibn Kolthúm composed these lines in the sixth century:

from "Pour Us Wine"

By herself she is fearless
And gives her arms to the air,
The limbs of a long camel that has not borne.

She gives the air her breasts,
Unfingered ivory.

She gives the air her long self and her curved self,
And hips so round and heavy that they are tired.

All these noble abundances of girlhood
Make the doorways divinely narrow and myself insane.

—translated by E. Powys Mathers

These words, now part of our own culture, were written in the eleventh century by Omar Khayyám:

The Moving Finger writes; and, having writ,
Moves on: nor all thy Piety nor Wit
        Shall lure it back to cancel half a Line.
Nor all thy Tears wash out a word of it.

—translated by Edward FitzGerald

And these, an even more important part of our culture, were written some four hundred years ago by William Shakespeare. Here is sheer foolery as Falstaff and the young prince take turns abusing each other as they pretend to be the King, Henry IV.

from *Henry IV, Part I*
(Act II, Scene iv)

PRINCE:    Do thou stand for my father, and examine me upon the
        particulars of my life.
FALSTAFF:  Shall I? Content. This chair shall be my state,
        this dagger my scepter, and this cushion my crown.
PRINCE:    Thy state is taken for a joined stool, thy golden
        scepter for a leaden dagger, and thy precious
        rich crown for a pitiful bald crown!

FALSTAFF: Well, and the fire of grace be not quite out of
thee, now shalt thou be moved. Give me a
cup of sack to make my eyes look red, that
it may be thought I have wept; for I must speak
in passion, and I will do it in King Cambyses'
vein.
PRINCE: Well, here is my leg.
FALSTAFF: And here is my speech. Stand aside, nobility.
HOSTESS: Oh Jesu, this is excellent spot, i' faith.
FALSTAFF: For God's sake, lords, convey my tristful queen,
For tears do stop the floodgates of her eyes.
HOSTESS: Oh Jesu, he doth it as like one of these harlotry
Players as ever I see!
FALSTAFF: Peace, good pintpot: peace, good ticklebrain.
Harry, I do not only marvel where thou spendest
thy time, but also how thou art accompanied.
For though the camomile, the more it is trodden
on, the faster it grows, yet youth, the more
it is wasted, the faster it wears. That thou
art my son, I have partly thy mother's word,
partly my own opinion, but chiefly a villainous
trick of thine eye, and a foolish hanging of
thy nether lip, that doth warrant me. If then
thou be son to me, here lies the point; why,
being son to me, art thou so pointed at? Shall
the blessed sun of heaven prove a micher and
eat blackberries? A question not to be asked.
Shall the son of England prove a thief and
take purses? A question to be asked. There
is a thing, Harry, which thou hast often
heard of, and it is known to many in our land
by the name of pitch. This pitch, as ancient
writers do report, doth defile; so doth the
company thou keepest. For, Harry, now I do
not speak to thee in drink but in tears, not in
pleasure but in passion, not in words only,
but in woes also. And yet there is a virtuous
man whom I have often noted in thy company,
but I know not his name.
PRINCE: What manner of man, an it like your majesty?
FALSTAFF: A goodly portly man, i' faith, and a corpulent;
of a cheerful look, a pleasing eye, and a most
noble carriage. And, as I think, his age
some fifty, or, by 'r Lady, inclining to three-
score. And now I remember me, his name is
Falstaff. If that man should be lewdly given,
he deceiveth me, for, Harry, I see virtue in
his looks. If then the tree may be known by the
fruit as the fruit is by the tree, then, peremptorily

I speak it, there is virtue in that
Falstaff. Him keep with, the rest banish. And
tell me now, thou naughty valet, tell me, where
hast thou been this month?

PRINCE: Dost thou speak like a king? Do thou stand for me,
and I'll play my father.

FALSTAFF: Depose me? If thou dost it half so gravely, so
majestically, both in word and matter, hang me
up by the heels for a rabbit-sucker or a
poulter's hare.

PRINCE: Well here I am set.

FALSTAFF: And here I stand. Judge, my masters.

PRINCE: Now, Harry, whence come you?

FALSTAFF: From Eastcheap.

PRINCE: The complaints I hear of thee are grievous.

FALSTAFF: 'Sblood, my lord, they are false. Nay, I'll tickle
ye for a young Prince, i' faith.

PRINCE: Swearest thou, ungracious boy? Henceforth ne'er look
on me. Thou art violently carried away from
grace. There is a devil haunts thee in the
likeness of an old fat man, a tun of man is
thy companion. Why dost thou converse with that
trunk of humors, that holting hutch of beastliness,
that swollen parcel of dropsies, that
huge bombard of sack, that stuffed cloak bag of
guts, that roasted Manningtree ox with the
pudding in his belly, that reverend vice, that
gray iniquity, that father ruffian, that
vanity in years? Wherein is he good, but to
taste sack and drink it? Wherein neat and
cleanly, but to carve a capon and eat it? Wherein
cunning, but in craft? Wherein crafty, but in
villainy? Wherein villainous, but in all things?
Wherein worthy, but in nothing?

FALSTAFF: I would your Grace would take me with you. Whom
means your Grace?

PRINCE: That villainous abominable misleader of youth,
Falstaff, that old white-bearded Satan.

FALSTAFF: My lord, the man I know.

PRINCE: I know thou dost.

FALSTAFF: But to say I know more harm in him than in myself
were to say more than I know. That he is old,
the more the pity, his white hairs do witness
it; but that he is, saving your reverence, a
whoremaster, that I utterly deny. If sack and
sugar be a fault, God help the wicked! If to
be old and merry be a sin, then many an old host
that I know is damned. If to be fat be to be
hated, then Pharoah's lean kine are to be loved.

No, my good lord. Banish Peto, banish Bardolph,
banish Poins. But for sweet Jack Falstaff, kind
Jack Falstaff, true Jack Falstaff, valiant Jack
Falstaff, and therefore more valiant, being,
as he is, old Jack Falstaff, banish not him thy
Harry's company, banish not him thy Harry's
company. Banish plump Jack, and banish all the
world.

Somewhere between twenty-five hundred and thirty-five hundred years ago, a
Hebrew poet(s) wrote this:

### from "The Song of Solomon"

How beautiful are they feet with shoes, O prince's daughter!
the joints of thy thighs are like jewels, the work of the hands
of a cunning workman.
Thy navel is like a round goblet, which wanteth not
liquor; thy belly is like a heap of wheat set about with lilies.
Thy two breasts are like two young roes that are twins.
Thy neck is a tower of ivory; thine eyes like the
fishpools in Heshbon, by the gate of Bathrabbim; thy nose
is as the tower of Lebanon which looketh toward Damascus.
Thine head upon thee is like Carmel, and the hair of thine
head like purple; the king is held in the galleries.
How fair and how pleasant art thou, O love, for delights!
This thy stature is like to a palm tree, and thy breasts
to clusters of grapes.
I said, I will go up to the palm tree, I will take hold
of the boughs thereof; now also thy breasts shall be as clusters
of vine, and the smell of thy nose like apples;
And the roof of thy mouth like the best wine for my
beloved, that goeth down sweetly, causing the lips of those
that are asleep to speak
I am my beloved's, and his desire is toward me.

Incredibly, some six thousand years ago, Egyptian scribes set down verses
that had then been in existence for untold centuries; these verses constituted the
Egyptian religious and poetic work, *The Book of the Dead*. Here are words that
were ancient when Rome was born:

### from "The Dead Man Ariseth and Singeth a Hymn to the Sun"

Homage to thee, O Ra, at thy tremendous rising!
Thou risest! Thou shinest! the heavens are rolled aside!
Thou art the King of Gods, thou art the All-comprising,
From thee we come, in thee are deified.

Thy priests go forth at dawn; they wash their hearts with laughter;
Divine winds move in music across thy golden strings.

At sunset they embrace thee, as every cloudy rafter
Flames with colour from thy wings.

—translated by Robert Hillyer

In the sixth century B. C., Sappho, perhaps the foremost woman in the world of literature, wrote these lines:

### Mother, I Cannot Mind My Wheel

Mother, I cannot mind my wheel;
　　My fingers ache, my lips are dry;
Oh! if you felt the pain I feel!
But oh, who ever felt as I!

—translated by Walter Savage Landor

Caius Valerius Catullus, whom Tennyson called the tenderest of the Roman poets, composed these words in the first century B.C.

### My Sweetest Lesbia

My sweetest Lesbia, let us live and love,
And though the sager sort our deeds reprove,
Let us not weigh them. Heaven's great lamps do dive
Into their west, and straight again revive,
But, soon as once set is our little light,
Then must we sleep one ever-enduring night.

If all would lead their lives in love like me,
Then bloody swords and armour should not be;
No drum nor trumpet peaceful sleeps should move,
Unless alarm came from the camp of love:
But fools do live and waste their little light,
And seek with pain their ever-enduring night.

When timely death my life and fortune ends,
Let not my hearse be vext with mourning friends,
But let all lovers rich in triumph come
And with sweet pastimes grace my happy tomb:
And, Lesbia, close up thou my little light,
And drown with love my ever-enduring night.

—translated by Thomas Campion

That such words as these have been maintained over the centuries seems to me a matter for wonder. The devotion of men to these lines has been strong enough for them to have survived wars, neglect, and that period of western withdrawal, the Dark Ages. Other works have perished of course. And they may well have been superior to any that we have saved. And yet the very fact that a chain of humans stretching from the dim years of prehistory to the present should have passed down as many treasures as we now possess is testimony to the value of those treasures. Aristotle's *Poetics* proclaimed the value of words such as these 2500 years ago, and men of every era have found these words to be worthy. They have turned to these lines in times of love, of disaster, of loneliness, and of joy. And constantly, in spite of later wars and terrors, they have added to this Ritual, this storehouse of treasures. They are adding to it today with such as:

### The Resolution[90]

You broke Your teeth upon the question Why,
Sucking its acrid marrow dry,
Its taste of silence wry.

Like You, on quandaries ripened in the brain,
Dropped on the heart, I bruised in vain;
Poised on this point of pain.

We find no room, whether at odds like fencers,
We two, or in embrace like dancers,
For questions or for answers.

Except ourselves when, I in You, for once
The query rests in the response,
The candle in its sconce.

—Vassar Miller

I shall use the term "Ritual" in talking of this sort of language. The labels "literature" and "poetry" are more usual, but for reasons that I'll discuss later, and especially for the reason that we return over and over to these works, we repeat them again and again and find comfort and joy in the repetition, "Ritual" seems to me the most appropriate title for these symbolic actions.

In addition to the pleasure men have found in Ritual, the mysteries of its nature have occupied them at least since the earliest stages of recorded history. Some of the major academic endeavors of classical and modern times concern themselves directly with language like that of the above examples. Writers, artists, critics, philosophers, dramatists, psychologists, and language theorists continue to study Ritual intensely, sometimes almost fiercely. Predictably, contemporary writings are often more troublesome to deal with than are those of the past. The words of the artist safely dead for some centuries have been winnowed repeatedly by the winds of convention, of prudence, of disinterest, and of change. Our contemporaries are difficult to judge as artists partly because they intrude upon us as people—people who offend or soothe our personal senses of what is appropriate, who violate taboos with disarming or disconcerting candor, who force us to confront our own failings too directly. In 1968, the creator of a play about an American soldier caught in the tragedy of Vietnam faced not only the possibility of critical rejection, but the very real chance that attacks would be made upon his social and political views.

*A Thesis*

Yet the problems of the contemporary are simply clearer, more noticeable than the problems involved in studying the ancient. Ritual is language that functions as art, as an aesthetic act, as a pleasurable process, and that sort of language is difficult to study. We respond to Ritual in ways that are usually subjective, subtle, and diffuse. Rarely is there any simple, overt response to a ritualistic language event. Similarly, ritualistic acts vary in so many ways and in such delicate and intricate fashions that it is difficult to decide which differences are significant and which are not.

Despite the difficulties, however, the study of Ritual has proceeded with some order and some profit, and it has done so by using the concepts of *form* and *content*. The theme of a piece of Ritual is its content, the structure, its form. This approach can be called conventional, not in the sense that neo-Aristotelian rhetorical theory is conventional, but in the sense that it is, and has been for some years, the most familiar and widely used basis for the study of Ritual. It's this approach that I'm going to discuss in the rest of this chapter.

### The Forms of Ritual

The three basic forms, i.e., the three major areas of Ritual, are *poetry, prose,* and *drama.* You may be used to thinking of these as mutually exclusive forms. That they are not is indicated by the existence of works that are both drama and poetry, as is the case with plays in verse form, works that are both prose and drama, as is the case with most plays and some short stories and novels (in large parts of which the characters' words appear in dialogue form), and works that are both prose and poetry, as witness the common label "poetic prose." But though these forms are not distinct and mutually exclusive, there are qualities and characteristics of each that make for significant differences, and it is those differences that I want to talk about now.

*Poetic Form*

There are two aspects of the excerpts and examples of poetry quoted in the preceding pages that immediately claim the reader's attention. They are the rhythmic structures that are employed and the metaphorical language that is at work. To pick a single line, "let not my hearse be vext with mourning friends" differs from our ordinary speech in two fundamental ways: it's based on a consistent and perceptible rhythm, and it's centered on what is usually called a metaphor. These two aspects of poetry, rhythm and metaphorical language, have always seemed of prime importance. Historically, many rhythmic patterns used in particular times and places have later been discarded. And there have been what almost amounted to fashions in metaphor, in poetic diction—fashions that sometimes lasted, sometimes died out completely. But regardless of changes in particular rhythms or figures, or in the relative importance of either, it is, and always has been, these dimensions of poetry that have been considered fundamental to the art.

*Poetic Rhythm*     The rhythms of poetry differ enough to seem almost infinitely varied, but for convenience they can be grouped under two headings—the rhythms of *metrical verse* and those of *free verse.* As in all rhythm, poetic rhythms are based on the repetition of something. By definition, a *single* phenomenon, a shot, a musical note, or a syllable, cannot be rhythmical. The thing must be repeated. And therein lies the key to poetic rhythm; it is *what* is repeated, and how often or how regularly it is repeated, that determines the particular rhythm of poetry and that creates distinctions between metrical verse and free verse.

In metrical verse, groups of syllables are repeated from none to seven times. That is, a line of metrical verse will consist of anywhere from one to eight of these groups or clusters of syllables. The line can then be given a name, a label derived from the number of those clusters that it contains. The first part of the label indicates the number of syllable clusters; the last part is "meter." Thus, the possible metrical lines are *monometer, dimeter, trimeter, tetrameter, pentameter, hexameter, heptameter,* and *octameter.*

The line quoted above, "let not my hearse be vext with mourning friends," is pentameter—five groups of syllables. It's conventional to indicate such syllabic groups with' marks that indicate the relative volume, or stress, or emphasis that falls on the syllable. This line would be written:

$$\breve{~}\;\acute{~}\;\breve{~}\;\acute{~}\;\breve{~}\;\acute{~}\;\breve{~}\;\acute{~}\;\breve{~}\;\acute{~}$$
let not my hearse be vext with mourning friends.

˘ indicates an unstressed syllable, ´ a stressed syllable, and each of the unstressed syllables joins with a stressed syllable to form a pair, a unit. That is except in the most extreme cases, the line would not be read Dum! Dum! Dum! Dum! etc., with the syllables evenly spaced. Automatically and naturally the reading goes da-Dum, da-Dum, da-Dum, etc., with the syllables joined in pairs. Each of these pairs—each of the groups of syllables in any metrical verse—is called a *foot.* In this case, five feet per line—pentameter.

This line is tetrameter, though it is not as regular as the first one:

He, who fixed the staggering earth.

And here is a line of trimeter:

The candle in its sconce.

And one of dimeter:

Thundering like a God

Here is a long line—hexameter:

Falling from my dream into a night that has no end; and as I fall the world turns grey.

And this one is longer still—heptameter:

Down in the dark and the wet of the mine is he who will shriek for the daylight.

And this one, octameter, is the longest line found in ordinary English verse:

The man who will sing of the bird on the wing is a man who was born with a taste for pure corn.

Theoretically, there could be lines of nine, ten, or more feet, but they would be inconvenient because they would take up too much space on the page, and, more basically, they would be difficult to read with anything approaching normal breathing and phrasing patterns. In fact, hexameter, heptameter, and octameter sometimes cause problems when you read them aloud for just that reason. The visual line can be too long for the oral phrase, i. e., for a usual breath supply to last. Reading the above example of octameter may illustrate this difficulty.

In brief form, so much for the various meters of English verse. These are the rhythmical patterns that will be found in lines of metrical verse. Within those lines there are, of course, differing sorts of feet, as evidenced by the above examples.

Literary historians have found dozens of different feet that have been used by poets of the past. Today, however, there are only five feet that one will find with any regularity at all, plus another four that are found on infrequent occasions. The feet widely used are:

*iambic;* one unstressed and one stressed syllable, ˘ ′

*trochaic:* one stressed and one unstressed syllable, ′ ˘

*anapestic:* two unstressed and one stressed syllable, ˘ ˘ ′

*dactylic:* one stressed and two unstressed syllables, ′ ˘ ˘

*paeonic:* four syllables, any one of which may be stressed while the remaining three are unstressed—depending on the order of the syllables the foot is called first, second, third, or fourth paeonic, ′ ˘ ˘ ˘, ˘ ′ ˘ ˘, ˘ ˘ ′ ˘, ˘ ˘ ˘ ′

In addition to these commonly used feet, there is the *spondee* (two stressed syllables, ′ ′ ), the *pyrric* (two unstressed syllables, ˘ ˘ ), the *amphibrach* (one unstressed, one stressed, and a final unstressed syllable, ˘ ′ ˘), and the *tribrach* (three unstressed syllables, ˘ ˘ ˘ ).

The vast majority of English verse is usually described by joining a term from the vertical column at the left of the following chart to a term from the horizontal column running across the top of the chart.

Most readers find the study of verse forms a bit confusing, and I want to emphasize the idea that many of the difficulties in that study are more apparent than real. If you realize that metrical rhythms *normally vary* around a particular

*Ritual:*

|  | MONOMETER | DIMETER | TRIMETER | TETRAMETER | PENTAMETER | HEXAMETER | HEPTAMETER | OCTAMETER |
|---|---|---|---|---|---|---|---|---|
| **IAMBIC** | ∪/ | ∪/ | ∪/ | ∪/ | ∪/ | ∪/ | ∪/ | ∪/ |
| **TROCHAIC** | /∪ | /∪ | /∪ | /∪ | /∪ | /∪ | /∪ | /∪ |
| **ANAPESTIC** | ∪∪/ | ∪∪/ | ∪∪/ | ∪∪/ | ∪∪/ | ∪∪/ | ∪∪/ | ∪∪/ |
| **DACTYLIC** | /∪∪ | /∪∪ | /∪∪ | /∪∪ | /∪∪ | /∪∪ | /∪∪ | /∪∪ |
| **PAEONIC (FIRST)** | /∪∪∪ | /∪∪∪ | /∪∪∪ | /∪∪∪ | /∪∪∪ | /∪∪∪ | /∪∪∪ | /∪∪∪ |
| **(SECOND)** | ∪/∪∪ | ∪/∪∪ | ∪/∪∪ | ∪/∪∪ | ∪/∪∪ | ∪/∪∪ | ∪/∪∪ | ∪/∪∪ |
| **(THIRD)** | ∪∪/∪ | ∪∪/∪ | ∪∪/∪ | ∪∪/∪ | ∪∪/∪ | ∪∪/∪ | ∪∪/∪ | ∪∪/∪ |
| **(FOURTH)** | ∪∪∪/ | ∪∪∪/ | ∪∪∪/ | ∪∪∪/ | ∪∪∪/ | ∪∪∪/ | ∪∪∪/ | ∪∪∪/ |

metrical norm, and if you neither expect to find nor are disappointed by the absence of metrical regularity, the entire process of dealing with verse becomes much easier.

Whereas metrical verse consists of groups of syllables that are repeated to create a rhythmical pattern, there is another verse form that's less strict or rigid in defining the phenomena to be repeated. The rhythmic patterns of that form are created by phrases or groups of words of approximately equal length, and the form is called, appropriately enough, "free verse."

Unlike metrical verse, free verse doesn't lay before you a host of rhythmical structures and sub-structures. While the phrase that is repeated may vary in length from verse to verse, or even within the same selection, there's nothing in free verse that is analogous to the various feet or the various meters in metrical verse. For most of us, the single difficulty of free verse lies in its freeness, for although there's some free verse that's clearly and easily recognizable as such and in which the phrases are quickly and surely discernible, most free verse is complicated by its closeness to prose.

Here's an example of free verse that's quite obviously both "free" and "verse." There's an undeniable rhythm here, and that rhythm is based on word groupings, not syllabic groups. (Groupings are indicated by diagonals.)

# Pub[91]

The glasses are raised,/the voices drift into laughter,/
The clock hands have stopped,/the beer in the hands of the soldiers
Is blond,/the faces are calm/and the fingers can feel
The wet touch of glasses,/the glasses print rings on the table./
The smoke rings curl and go up/and dissolve near the ceiling,/
    This moment exists and is real./

What is reality?/Do not ask that./At this moment/
Look at the butterfly eyes of the girls,/watch the barmaid's
Precision in pouring a Scotch,/and remember this day,/
This day at this moment/you were no longer an island,/
People were friendly,/the clock in the hands of the soldiers/
    For this moment/had nothing to say./

And nothing to say/and the glasses are raised,/we are happy
Drinking through time,/and a world that is gentle and helpless
Survives in the pub/and goes up in the smoke of our breath,/
The regulars doze in the corner,/the talkers are fluent:/
Look now in the faces of those you love/and remember
    That you are not thinking of death./

But thinking of death/as the lights go out/and the glasses
Are lowered,/the people go out/and the evening,
Goes out,/ah, goes out like a light/and leaves you alone,/
As the heart goes out,/the door opens out into darkness,/
The foot takes a step,/and the moment of falling
    Is here,/you go down like a stone./

Are you able to meet the disaster,/able to meet the
Cold air of the street/and the touch of corruption,/the rotting
Fingers that murder your own/in the grip of love?/
Can you bear to find hateful/the faces you once thought were lovely,/
Can you bear to find comfort alone/in the evil and stunted,/
    Can you bear to abandon the dove?/

The houses are shut/and the people go home,/we are left in
Our island of pain,/the clocks start to move/and the powerful
To act,/there is nothing now,/nothing at all
To be done:/for the trouble is real:/and the verdict is final
Against us./The clocks go round faster and faster./And fast as confetti/
    The days are beginning to fall./

                            —Julian Symons

---

[91] Reprinted by permission of Julian Symons.

The diagonals indicating the phrasing are placed where I feel that they're most appropriate. Others will place them somewhat differently. That this is a rhythmic form, a verse form, will be clear, however, to all readers if a simple comparison is made with prose such as this paragraph. The selection consists, in the main, of relatively short phrases of approximately equal length. At several places phrase lengths vary considerably, but in only two or three instances is it possible to create phrases as long as the phrases and clauses that abound in prose—the preceding part of this sentence, for instance.

Notice that the phrase markings don't match the punctuation. There are seventeen instances in which phrase endings are not indicated by punctuation marks of any sort. Obviously there's some relationship between punctuation and phrasing in free verse, for punctuation is a major means of setting off groups of words. Clearly though, it's not simply a one-to-one relationship.

Notice, too, that phrase endings sometimes correspond to line endings, but that frequently the two differ. To go to the extreme of pausing, of ending a phrase at the end of every line would destroy much of the meaning, as in the following two examples:

the beers in the hands of the soldiers/
Is blond/
able to meet the/
Cold air of the street/

Perhaps unfortunately, the above selection is not representative of the body of poetry commonly known as free verse. It's far more regular in its rhythmic structure than is most such verse. By contrast, here is a selection with a freer and looser rhythmical base—one that is closer to prose, that is therefore more difficult to handle rhythmically, and that is much more typical of free verse as a form.

The Language[92]

Locate *I*
*Love you* some-
where in

teeth and
eyes, bite
it but

take care not
to hurt, you
want so

much so
little. Words
say everything,

[92] "The Language" (Copyright ©1964 Robert Creeley) is reprinted with the permission of Charles Scribner's Sons from *Words* by Robert Creeley. "The Language" first appeared in *Poetry* (©1964 The Modern Poetry Association) and is also reprinted with the permission of the Editor of *Poetry*.

*I*
*love you*
again,

then what
is emptiness
for. To

fill, fill.
I heard words
and words full

of holes
aching. Speech
is a mouth.

— Robert Creeley

A part of the rhythm of this selection, and of most free verse, consists of the visual arrangement of the words on the page. Suppose these words were printed in prose form, margin to margin. It would look, and feel, like this:

Locate *I love you* somewhere in teeth and eyes, bite it but take care not to hurt, you want so much so little. Words say everything, *I love you* again, then what is emptiness for. To fill, fill. I heard words and words full of holes aching. Speech is a mouth.

Rhythmically, this is not quite the same selection as the one printed in lines of arbitrary length. The very fact of the typography of the original version tends toward rhythm. You tend, to some extent, to perceive the lines as rhythmical units simply because you tend to read line by line. The importance of the visual or typographical element of rhythm in free verse has led some authors to define free verse as that form that sounds like prose but looks like verse.[93] If lines such as those in this selection are read aloud, they will probably not be perceived as lines by the hearer. Thus such material may well sound like prose. For me a visually based definition of free verse is unnecessarily narrow. Much free verse certainly owes part of its rhythmical structure to visual patterning, but as I've said, there is some free verse that's made up of clearly perceptible rhythms built on the chronologically based repetition of phrases, regardless of typographical patterns. Both the chronological and visual dimensions of free verse rhythms can be included if you define that form as *verse based on the repetition of phrases—the repetitions being indicated by temporal and/or typographical techniques.*

*Metaphorical Language in Poetry*        Rhythm is the first ingredient of poetry. The second is metaphorical language. It's possible to think of metaphors or figures of speech as a kind of poetic afterthought, a frosting applied to the "real"

[93] See, for example, Charles W. Cooper, *Preface to Poetry* (New York: Harcourt, Brace and Company, 1946), p. 126.

poetic cake. This notion is emphatically and entirely false. Figurative language is not *applied to* poetry in some way; figurative language *is* poetry. This sentence, for instance, contains no figurative language, and it is not the kind of statement one would find in poetry. If the figurative or metaphorical language were to be removed from poetry, there would be no poetry left; it's the metaphor that, mixed with the rhythmical pattern, *makes* the poetry.

Now it's possible to talk about metaphorical language by simply defining the various kinds that exist. The word "metaphor," for example, can be used broadly (as I've used it) to mean all sorts of figurative language; it can also be used narrowly to mean a direct comparison of unlike items not involving the words "as" or "like": "He was a lion of a man," "the mouldering ruins of her face" are examples. Similarly, there are the familiar figures *simile*, a comparison using "like" or "as"—"he was as charming as a used dress-shield," *synecdoche*, the use of a part to stand for a whole—"the circling eyes tightened around him," and *hyperbole*, an elegant exaggeration or straining of the truth—"his wit was drier than the Sahara, deadlier than the asp, and as relentless as the tradewinds." In addition to these there are a good many others; their very names indicate something of their exotic nature: *onomatopoeia, litotes, metonomy, autonomasia, paranomasia, ellipsis, asyndeton, polysyndeton, anaphora, anadiplosis, aphaeresis, syncope, apocope, prothesis, paragoge, mimesis, metathesis*, etc. And there are more—many more.

A problem arises with all these figures. They may well be of interest and importance in some situations, but as the list grows longer the risk grows greater that the poetic values of many or all these items are being ignored while the differences between them are being stressed. For instance, *ellipsis* means the omission of words or phrases in order to achieve terseness and emphasis, as "From my friends, cries of joy are music—from my enemies, of pain!" This specific technique need not be part of poetry at all; in fact it is just as likely to be found in Rhetoric as in Ritual. Or, *metonomy* and *autonomasia* both deal with names, metonomy with names that stand for the object ("Washington fears the unknown," where "Washington" stands for the federal government) and autonomasia with names that stand for activities or conditions ("Cupid had made him a pincushion," where "Cupid" stands for love). The difference here seems slight, and the question arises as to whether it's poetically significant.

So instead of tracking down the possible figures of speech, [94] I want to talk about the qualities that make figures poetic, that make them metaphorical. In other words, I want to continue using the term "metaphor" broadly.

Metaphorical uses of language are metaphorical because they are literally untrue. They're untrue, *not* in the sense of being merely *false*, but in the sense of being or seeming *impossible*. If you watch someone run rapidly *into* a building, and you say, "he ran *out of* the building," that's false but it's not a metaphor; but if you say, "he flew into the building," that's the beginning of a metaphor. "He

[94] For those interested in truly extensive lists of figures, see Gilbert Austin, *Chironomia; or a Treatise on (Rhetorical) Delivery: Comprehending Many Precepts Both Ancient and Modern, for the Proper Regulation of the Voice, the Countenance and Gesture* (London, 1806), and John Bulwer, *Chirologia ... Chironomia* (London, 1644).

bulldozed his way through the crowd," "her mouth was a velvet and vicious trap," "a voice as bitter as gall," and "he moved like a thick fluid oozing through cracks in ice" are all metaphors because they are literal untruths, impossible truths. A man may shove others out of the way, but he cannot literally act like a bulldozer; a woman's mouth can't be a literal trap, either vicious or velvet; voices are not literally bitter, as gall or anything else; and no man can literally move like a fluid, thick or thin, oozing, dribbling, or gushing through cracks in ice, granite, or linoleum.

Here's an interlinked series of metaphors that results in poetry, and it's the impossible and literal untruth of these statements that is the basis of the poetry.

### Song

Goe, and catche a falling starre,
    Get with child a mandrake roote,
Tell me, where all past years are,
    Or who cleft the devil's foot,
Teach me to heare Mermaides singing,
Or to keep off envies stinging,
        And finde
        What winde
Serves to advance an honest minde.

If thou be'st borne to strange sights,
    Things invisible to see,
Ride ten thousand daies and nights,
    Till age snow white haires on thee
Thou, when thou return'st, will tell mee
All strange wonders that befell thee,
        And sweare
        No where
Lives a woman true, and faire.

If thou findst one, let me know,
    Such a Pilgrimage were sweet;
Yet doe not, I would not goe,
    Though at next doore wee might meet,
Though shee were true, when you met her,
And last, till you write your letter,
        Yet shee
        Will bee
False, ere I come, to two, or three.

              —John Donne

    I use this work as an example of metaphorical language because it's one long string of interwoven metaphors, and because it's the nature of the metaphors that is a vital part of the poem. It's not just that "Teach me to heare Mermaides singing" is a metaphor because one cannot literally hear Mermaides who literally neither exist nor sing, but that it's the very impossibility of hearing Mermaides singing that makes this metaphor, and the others, work *here*. The character of the piece asks totally impossible things of his friend, and it's that impossibility that is part of the metaphor *and* of the meaning of the selection.

At this point I have crossed, or erased, the dividing line between form and content. Metaphor as a series of techniques may be called form, but metaphor as literal untruth is as much a part of meaning, of content, as it is of form. In this selection, the metaphors used can be called aspects of form, but they are part of the content as well; and the same thing is true of all poetry. The metaphor may be viewed as a formal technique, as in these lines from "The Song of Solomon":

> . . . the joints of thy thighs are like jewels, the work of the hands
> of a cunning workman.

The comparison of a lovely woman's body to beautifully wrought gems is, on one level, a formalistic device, but on another level it's a matter of meaning. The comparison *is* with magnificent jewels, not with something else. And that is to say that the loved one's body is as fair *as* those jewels, rather than as fair as sunlight, or music, or birds' song.

Metaphorical statements compare things that are not literally comparable. They combine objects, ideas, or events that have not previously been combined, at least not frequently. If I say "Unwritten books are like unpaid debts—after a certain time it becomes impossible to do anything about them," I have made a mild metaphor. Unwritten books are not really or literally like unpaid debts, but there is something in the way I feel about the one that is like something in the way I feel about the other. And that something becomes the similarity between them. If I have chosen well from experiences that are familiar to you, it may be that this metaphor will create a new view, idea, or attitude toward unwritten books—the idea that there is something debt-like about them. What's important, even with such modest metaphors, is the *newness*. "Books," written and unwritten, are familiar, known, commonplace; so are "debts," paid or unpaid. It's the combination that's important. The elements, the materials of metaphor may be entirely ordinary, but if the joining is new enough the result is priceless.

Here is one of the great metaphors:

> Now is the winter of our discontent
> Made glorious summer by this sun of York.

These are the opening lines of *Richard III*. "Winter" and "discontent" are unremarkable, taken singly. But "winter of our discontent" is electrically new. It suggests that "discontent" is the cold, frozen season of the emotions; it implies that discontent is a recurrent, a cyclical state, as is winter; and it may include the notion that a specific part, the coldest part, of the season of discontent is at hand. The metaphor fuses parts into a whole that is, in the most profound sense, new. [95] And

[95] I. A. Richards, *The Philosophy of Rhetoric* (New York: Oxford University Press, 1965), pp. 89-138.

it's this quality of newness that makes poetry so important. It's in poetry that you can say things that are otherwise unsayable. It's in poetry that new attitudes, new feelings, new ideas can be formulated; the newness comes from the combination of previously uncombined and apparently incompatible elements. [96]

(I want to point out that, though I have crossed the form-content boundary in talking about metaphor, the discussion of content is mostly to come. In other words, this section is necessarily incomplete and will remain so until the treatment of meaning, of content is added to it.)

*Prose Form*

Since I used the term "prose" in talking about Rhetoric, the first thing I must do here is to point out the difference between rhetorical prose and ritualistic prose.

In one sense prose form is the same no matter whether it occurs in Rhetoric or Ritual. In both it's a periodic form based on the recurrent unit, the sentence, and governed by the syntactical relationship between subject and predicate. The words, "He looked at her" could occur in both Rhetoric and Ritual, and in each case those words would constitute a sentence.

In another sense prose differs greatly depending on its grounding in Rhetoric or Ritual. The three general types (i.e., functions) of prose are *exposition*, *description*, and *narration*; the first is a language process that is primarily rhetorical, the second a process that can be either rhetorical or ritualistic, and the third a process that is largely ritualistic. Expository prose expounds, presents an idea, sets forth a viewpoint; it is the sort of language I described in the first chapter as attitudinal and biased. Exposition may occur in Ritual but it is not one of the distinguishing characteristics of that current of language. Descriptive prose presents the characteristics of objects or events; the form is rhetorical when the emphasis is on the reality of the items described, ritualistic when what is emphasized is a feeling about reality. Narrative prose tells a tale, unfolds a story; such prose may be found in Rhetoric, but its more important and more usual home is Ritual.

Another way to distinguish between rhetorical and ritualistic prose is to say that the former is nonfiction, the latter fiction. The fiction-nonfiction dichotomy is suggested especially by the nature of description, a language act that is rhetorical or ritualistic depending on what is described. (All these are preliminary distinctions; they will be developed further in the coming pages.)

*Exposition*    Here is an example of exposition by the Arabian author Ibn Khaldún who wrote these words in the fourteenth century, and whom Hugh Trevor-Roper described as follows:

> . . . the profoundest, most exciting historical writer between Antiquity and the Renaissance, who wrote his monumental work of philosophy and history in the late fourteenth century in a castle in Algeria, surrounded by desolation and barbarians. . . .[97]

[96] Koestler, pp. 320-21.

[97] Hugh Trevor-Roper, *The Rise of Christian Europe* (New York: Harcourt, Brace & World, Inc., 1965), p. 12.

### from "Observations on History"

Know that the science of History is noble in its conception, abounding in instruction, and exalted in its aim. It acquaints us with the characteristics of the ancient peoples, the ways of life followed by the prophets, and the dynasties and government of kings, so that those who wish may draw valuable lessons for their guidance in religious and worldly affairs. The student of History, however, requires numerous sources of information and a great variety of knowledge; he must consider well and examine carefully in order to arrive at the truth and avoid errors and pitfalls. If he rely on bare tradition, without having thoroughly grasped the principles of common experience, the institutes of government, the nature of civilization, and the circumstances of human society, and without judging what is past and invisible by the light of what is present before his eyes, then he will often be in danger of stumbling and slipping and losing the right road. Many errors committed by historians, commentators, and leading traditionists in their narrative of events have been caused by their reliance on mere tradition, which they have accepted without regard to its (instrinsic) worth, neglecting to refer it to its general principles, judge it by its analogies, and test it by the standard of wisdom, knowledge of the natures of things, and exact historical criticism. Thus they have wandered in the desert of imagination and error.

—translated by Reynold A. Nicholson

Two things are immediately apparent in this short excerpt. First, the author is propounding a point of view. His primary aim is a rhetorical one: to expound an idea, to put forth a proposition. He is *not* primarily concerned with fanciful description or imaginative narration; he is not engaged in setting up unreal situations and characters. He deals with the most profitable, the most realistic view of history that he knows. And he makes clear to the reader by his first two sentences that his subject is the value of the study of history. At once, however, he sets up qualifications; the study of history is valuable only in light of the present. And he goes to considerable lengths to illustrate what he means. He succeeds in stating his meaning clearly and accurately because of the care that he exercises and because of the lengths to which he goes.

Second, though this *is* an example of Rhetoric, of expository writing, it includes a Ritualistic dimension. The richness of the language, the rhythmic repetition of short phrases, and the scattered but effective metaphors ("wandered in the desert of imagination and error") make it obvious that the author meant for his words to be read, re-read, and savored, not simply milked of their rhetorical content.

*Description* Unlike exposition, with which the writer of fiction, of *Ritual,* is only indirectly concerned, description is one of the two major tools of the ritualist. Descriptive skills are basic for any author, and the writer who cannot describe people and events so as to plague and please us is unlikely to hold our attention for long.

As I've said, description in Ritual is based on imaginative attitudes toward reality, not on reality itself, and the foundation of imaginative description is *imagery.* It's through the use of imagery that sensory responses are elicited from the reader. It's in his reactions to the images presented that the reader conjures up in his mind sights, sounds, tastes, smells, etc. Thus an image is any word or group of words that makes possible a sensation, a sensory response.

Since images appeal to the senses, it's convenient to classify them accordingly: visual imagery—appeals to the sense of sight; auditory imagery—sense of hearing; tactile imagery—sense of touch; gustatory imagery—taste; olfactory imagery—smell; thermal imagery—heat or cold; kinetic imagery—motion external to one's own body; and kinaesthetic imagery—motion within one's body.

Imagery can range from the simplest sort of language—"the rough, pitted surface of the rock"—to complicated metaphorical statements—"her face was like an empty camp in which a band of wandering gypsies had stayed and laughed and sung briefly, but very long ago."

Here is an instance of fairly complex imagery:

### Apostrophe[98]

Ah, Russia, Russia, from my beautiful home in a strange land I still can see you! In you everything is poor and disordered and unhomely; in you the eye is neither cheered nor dismayed by temerities of nature which a yet more temerarious art has conquered; in you one beholds no cities with lofty, many-windowed mansions, lofty as crags, no picturesque trees, no ivy-clad ruins, no waterfalls with their everlasting spray and roar, no beetling precipices which confuse the brain with their stony immensity, no vistas of vines and ivy and millions of wild rosea and ageless lines of blue hills which look almost unreal against the clear, silvery background of the sky. In you everything is flat and open; your towns project like points or signals from smooth levels of plain, and nothing whatsoever enchants or deludes the eye. Yet what secret, what invincible force draws me to you? Why does there ceaselessly echo and re-echo in my ears the sad song which hovers throughout the length and the breadth of your borders? What is the burden of that song? Why does it wail and sob and catch at my heart? What say the notes which thus, painfully caress and embrace my soul, and flit, uttering their lamentations, around me? What is it you seek of me, O Russia? What is the hidden bond which subsists between us? Why do you regard me as you do? Why does everything within you turn upon me eyes full of yearning? Even at this moment, as I stand dumbly, fixedly, perplexedly contemplating your vastness, a menacing cloud, charged with gathering rain, seems to overshadow my head. What is it that your boundless expanses presage? Do they not presage that one day there will arise in you ideas as boundless as yourself? Do they not presage that one day you too will know no limits? Do they not presage that one day, when again you shall have room for their exploits, there will spring to life the heroes of old? How the power of your immensity enfolds me, and reverberates through all my being with a wild, strange spell, and flashes in my eyes with an almost supernatural radiance! Yes, a strange brilliant unearthly vista indeed do you disclose, O Russia, country of mine!

—Nikolai Gogol
(translated by D. J. Hogarth)

[98] From *Dead Souls* by Nikolai Gogol, translated by C. J. Hogarth, the Everyman's Library edition. Reprinted by permission of E. P. Dutton & Company and J. M. Dent & Sons, Ltd.

*Ritual:*

Although almost every sort of image is found in this selection, there are two sequences of images that are particularly notable—the chain of visual images in the second and third sentences, and the shorter series of auditory images that cluster around the word "song." In the first sequence, "lofty, many-windowed mansions," "ivy-clad ruins," "beetling precipices," and "ageless lines of blue hills" are samples of visual imagery. These are negatives, of course; the author states that none of these things exists. But by describing them he forces us to visualize them even though they are examples of what is not. In the auditory sequence that describes the song, "wail and sob and catch at my heart" and "notes which thus painfully caress and embrace my soul" are especially effective.

Most imagery is "mixed." Some images are entirely visual, or tactile, etc., but more often several sensory appeals are involved. For instance, in this selection "the notes which thus painfully caress and embrace my soul, and flit, uttering their lamentations" includes auditory, tactile, kinaesthetic, and kinetic elements: "notes," and all words that describe that term, exert an auditory appeal; "painfully caress and embrace my soul" is a tactile appeal; "embrace my soul" involves a kinaesthetic appeal, an internal movement of some figurative sort; finally, notes which "flit . . . around me" adds a kinetic element, a description of movement outside the self.

Another example, the sentence "Even at this moment, as I stand dumbly, fixedly, perplexedly contemplating your vastness, a menacing cloud, charged with gathering rain, seems to overshadow my head," includes kinaesthetic, visual and auditory imagery. "As I stand *dumbly*," is an auditory appeal; "stand *dumbly*, *fixedly*, *perplexedly* contemplating" seems to involve internal tension—a kinaesthetic appeal—as does "a *menacing* cloud, *charged* with *gathering* rain"; and "*contemplating* your *vastness*," "*menacing cloud*," and "*overshadows* my head" are all instances of visual imagery.

The descriptive values of this selection rest squarely on the imagery. Certain characteristics of the land are described in images that evoke responses in us. The sense of tension, of shadowy forces drawing the character to his native land is a direct result of the imagery employed. The selection allows us to see Russia through this character's mind's eye, to hear her through his mind's ear, and to feel her pull and strain through his mind's nerves and muscles.

Even more than the above selection, the following lines contain extremely complex and involved images. This is a description of what is probably the finest, the most famous, and the most beautiful university in the world.

## from "The Pilgrim in Oxford" [99]

Of that extraordinary place I shall not attempt to speak with any order or indeed with any coherence. It must ever remain one of the supreme gratifications of travel for any American aware of the ancient pieties of race. The impression it produces, the emotions it kindles in the mind of such a visitor, are too rich and various to be expressed in the halting rhythm of

[99] Reprinted from Henry James, *A Passionate Pilgrim and Other Tales* by permission of Houghton Mifflin Company.

prose. Passing through the small oblique streets in which the long grey battered public face of the colleges seems to watch jealously for sounds that may break upon the stillness of study, you feel it the most dignified and most educated of cities. Over and through it all the great corporate fact of the University slowly throbs after the fashion of some steady bass in a concerted piece or that of the medieval mystical presence of the Empire in the old States of Germany. The plain perpendicular of the so mildly conventional fronts, masking blest seraglios of culture and leisure, irritates the imagination scarce less than the harem-walls of Eastern towns. Within their arching portals, however, you discover more sacred and sunless courts, and the dark verdure soothing and cooling to bookish eyes. The grey-green quadrangles stand forever open with a trustful hospitality. The seat of the humanities is stronger in her own good manners than in a marshalled host of wardens and beadles.

—Henry James

Oxford—"the seat of the humanities." Imagery is laced throughout this excerpt in a network of word-magic that creates as it describes. Consider that lovely and convoluted sentence: "Over and through it all the great corporate fact of the University slowly throbs after the fashion of some steady bass in a concerted piece or that of the medieval mystical presence of the Empire in the old States of Germany." Here is a tangled skein of imagery that is lustrous with sensory appeals. There's a basic kinaesthetic response to the opening words—"Over and through it all the great corporate fact of the University slowly throbs." The key word seems to be "throbs," but it's the combination of that term with "over and through it all" and "great corporate fact" that suggests an internal pulsing, an enormous heartbeat that sets up the rhythm of human existence. Then there's an auditory response involved with the words "after the fashion of some steady bass in a concerted piece." And there's an oddly mixed appeal, and response, in the words "or that of the medieval mystical presence of the Empire in the old States of Germany." "Medieval mystical presence of the Empire" suggests somehow ghost-like whispers of fog and mist, movements that are felt rather than seen, influences that are almost other-wordly; there can easily be both inner stirrings, kinaesthetic responses, and prickles on the back of the neck, tactile responses, as reactions to this volatile chunk of descriptive material. By comparison, the simple but extremely effective imagery in "sacred and sunless courts, and the dark verdure soothing and cooling to bookish eyes" is almost totally visual. There's a nonsensory element introduced by "sacred," and "soothing and cooling" add thermal and perhaps tactile appeals, but the main sensory channel that is activated here is the visual. Another highly complex cluster of images occurs in "The plain perpendicular of the so mildly conventual fronts, masking blest seraglios of culture and leisure, irritates the imagination scarce less than the harem-walls of Eastern towns." There's a feeling of weight and strength and solidity in "plain perpendicular" that masks and hides inner riches and resembles "harem-walls of Eastern towns," a feeling that stirs the interior sense of slow movement that is the kinaesthetic response. And "irritates the imagination" contributes a tactile dimension, though "irritates" is here used in the sense of "to stimulate." Also, the double comparison with the sexual—"seraglios" and "harem-walls"—gives to the word "irritates" a sensual overtone. Visual appeals are felt at several places in this sentence—"plain perpendicular," "mildly conventual fronts," and "harem-walls."

As is evident in these two short selections, imagery is a major element of prose fiction. Such prose is not concerned with objective or impersonal description, but with description that awakens the senses and that enables us to visualize the scene or the action being described. The imagery employed may be the most simple, ordinary sort that stimulates only one of the senses, or it may be the complicated rich type that elicits multiple sensory responses, but in every case it's the involvement of the senses that is the goal.

*Narration*     To narrate means to tell a story. The term discloses at once the heart of narrative form—the plot, the story line. Narratives arrange events into sequences that engage and hold us. Of course the characters involved in the story are "other selves" with which we identify. But since characterization is a major formal element of drama, I'm going to define narrative prose as the process of creating a story line, leaving characterization to be treated in the following section.

What happens, what events occur, is the essence of any narrative, and the point of view from which those events are described is a basic and important narrative technique. Both the events and the technique may be defined as *"directness"* (a term used, you remember, in discussing Rhetoric).

Stories that move forward in time and that have only one plot (no secondary plots) are one of the most direct sorts. The following short story is an example of a somewhat less direct narrative approach. Consider especially the backward-forward chronological movement.

Of An Old Passion

"The party's over,
It's time to call it a day. . . ."

He listened to the lyrics of the song and thought how strange it was that song writers so consistently dealt with unhappiness. Most of the time it was innocuous enough. When they sang the songs the crooners even smiled, in a half-pained way that was meant to be sexy.

When he'd heard this one for the first time, with Betty, the sadness had had a sort of remote attractiveness. Now it was a real and endless hurt.

He looked for the bartender, carefully avoiding the eyes of the woman sitting at the end of the bar. There were only four people in the room. Another man who was drinking beer with a Germanic thoroughness, the bartender, the woman, and himself.

The bartender put his drink on a little paper napkin that had a picture of a naked girl with enormous breasts sitting in a huge martini glass. Underneath it said, "Better than a little old olive, isn't it?"

He poked at an ice cube with one finger, remembering how Betty had teased him. "Cognac on the rocks . . . tell the truth darling . . . it sounds interesting when you order it . . . something different." He studied the drink for a second, relaxing, letting the memories flow past. Then he grunted to himself, "Fine, here we go again . . . the tragedy of the man at the bar . . .

French Foreign Legion, modern style."

The bartender helped him back to reality by turning on a radio beneath the shelf of glasses. It was a newscaster giving the ball scores.

"Damn! How about them Dodgers!"

"Yeah." He nodded, thinking instantly and helplessly of the time he'd taken Betty to a ball game. She'd loved the color, the movement, without for a second pretending to understand the intricacies of the game, or having to shower him with the usual questions.

He tried to catch himself again because he'd learned that there were times when it was just no good remembering. The emptiness was too deep.

"It would have been different," he thought, "if we'd been married."

A broken marriage was something that could be dealt with. Friends would rally round taking one side or the other. Willing listeners aplenty . . . people wanting to help. But an affair, he'd found, was something else. Especially for a man. When an affair ended it was assumed that there was nothing involved that the man couldn't handle. Certainly the picture of the male broken heart was near-ridiculous today.

True, there'd been a kind of token-sympathy offered. But basically there was the belief that without the legal sanctity of marriage a true union was impossible, and that therefore true pain was impossible on separation.

He and Betty had had almost five years of being as emotionally married as was possible. And the fact that they hadn't been actually married, and hadn't even lived together, except for occasional weekends, or trips out of town now and then, had made them even closer in many ways. Perhaps because they'd never had the little daily problems of marriage. Sharing the bathroom, doing the shopping, cleaning house. When they'd done these things it had been a special event, almost a party. Never drudgery.

"All right, then," the thought, worn and familiar, was there for the thousandth time, "what happened? Why didn't you get married?"

Why? He almost smiled.

"For all the obvious reasons. All the obvious wrong reasons."

. . . He and Betty had each been married before. They wanted to be careful this time. No more mistakes. So, five years of avoiding another mistake.

. . . Then, too, it was so simple the way it was. Why change things? Why take the chance of ruining a lovely affair? What he'd really meant by that was why take on the responsibilities of marriage when there was no need to.

. . . And there was a money problem. Betty liked gracious living. She was not at all opposed to Cadillacs, or swimming pools, or mink coats. And he'd gone along with her, pretending that by saving for a few years they'd be able to afford all that. Never saying, "Look, sweetheart, it'd be nice to have all those things, and if we can we will. But right now we're going to get married." Never saying that.

He swallowed half his drink, deliberately looking straight ahead, and followed the pattern to its known frightening end.

Next question. His mind presented it with deadly smoothness. "Why not stay together, then? You didn't have to get married. All your friends had quit expecting it. They accepted you the way you were. Why break it up?"

"A very good question, sir. One deserving of an honest answer. Now . . . ."

Sometimes humor helped. Sometimes he could laugh himself out of it. But not now. The "why" hammered at him.

He remembered the first time their hands had touched and the air had suddenly filled with magic. Later, when he'd kissed her, with the sand of the beach cool to their bare feet, and the moon painting a streamer across the sea, it had seemed that they were inside one skin . . . that nothing at all separated them . . . or ever could.

They'd gone home and made love that same night. The first night. And their lovemaking was perfect and natural and inevitable. Holding her, afterwards, his hands had slowly traced the loveliness of the full proud breasts, the absurdly tiny waist, and the silken thighs. He remembered thinking that that was as close to godliness as a human being was likely to get.

And, strangest of all, it had stayed that way. Their bodies had been filled with passion and tenderness that seemed to grow every time they touched. Almost five years of feeling so wild with oneness that even the thought of another woman was an alien impossible thing.

"Then why . . . why. . . ."

Wearily he began the answer.

"Incredibly, because she was so lovely."

Because every time he saw her he had to touch her. Because they made endless plans to read together, or listen to music, or go to the ballet, but most of the time forgot their plans and spent endless hours making love. And finally, his own background, and friends' remarks, even though made in warmth, and the culture that he was a part of, had combined to push him into the terrible, the evil trap of thinking that there was one thing called sex and another thing called love, and that the two could never be one.

And he'd begun to wonder if he had the one but not the other. If he and Betty were really in love, even though they were perfectly matched sexually. And wondering had led to doubting. And that had been like opening a door to destruction.

When he'd looked for faults he'd found them. She spent money like it was going out of style. Sometimes her dresses were too extreme, too tight, too low-cut. She lied about her age, even to him. She wasn't his intellectual equal.

Then he smiled.

All these things were true. But they merely covered the deep raw wound of his own fear. Fear of loving, of being loved.

Since they weren't married it'd been easy, in a way. There'd been no social barriers to hurdle. He often wondered, now, if the main value of marriage wasn't the simple fact that it made it difficult to leave the other person.

And so he'd left Betty. Or rather, the relationship had slowly crumbled, and he'd made no real effort to build it up, to keep them together. It had been almost a year now since he'd seen her.

At first it hadn't been too bad. There'd been the excitement of new women, and since he'd decided that he needed sex and love there was always the anticipation that perhaps this was the one. He found, though, that the combination he was looking for was apparently pretty rare. He found, too, that no one made him feel the electricity, the softness and the ecstasy that Betty had been able to awaken just by walking into a room.

And five years had made a difference. At thirty-five he'd been young, but at forty he was an indeterminate age, neither young nor old. Perhaps it was because of that that the chase no longer thrilled him. It was too easy to predict now.

Then he'd realized that friends weren't calling as often. It wasn't hard to figure out why. For them it would have been easier if he and Betty had been married. They could have placed their loyalties with one person or the other, and it would have been quite simple. This way there were no sides, no right or wrong, no one at fault, so friends had to divide their time between the two of them or else wash their hands of the whole thing. And some of them did just that.

After that the basic routine of living had begun to seem strange. While it had been new, the newness had occupied him. He'd moved to another apartment. But then, after he'd furnished it, it seemed too big, too empty. And meals were a problem. He hated cooking for himself, yet going to restaurants alone was almost as bad. So he ended up at coffee shops and hamburger stands.

But the worst thing of all was time. . . evenings especially. During the week they could be managed, but weekends were unending deserts of loneliness unless he deliberately made plans to fill every minute.

He remembered Christmas vacation. By then it had been nearly seven months since he'd seen Betty, and the thought of calling her was beginning to haunt him . . . till he heard that she was engaged. The holidays had seemed designed to emphasize his loneliness. Christmas eve had been a session of terror, shut out of the brightly lit houses, drenched with the commercial warmth of TV and radio carols, feeling totally alone in the universe, unable to resist the raw acid of self-pity. It was in April that he'd gotten the news that Betty had married. And it was then that he knew he had to build a defense against the memories that constantly flooded over him. So, methodically, he created patterns that left him very little time to remember.

He moved again. This time to an apartment in the center of town, surrounded by lights, people, movement. He joined a club, went to the dances, worked on committees. He took on more work at his office, welcoming the overtime required.

Even the tiny things. He discovered that by turning on the TV as soon as he got home, even though he seldom watched it, he could make the rooms seem less empty. He started working out at a gym every other evening because sleep came more easily with fatigue. He made rituals of shopping, of taking out the cleaning, rather than having things delivered, simply because it was another activity that used up time.

And on the whole he managed rather well. Without racing from one thing to another, he kept going at a steady self-perpetuating pace that, if not pleasant, was at least therapeutic in its steadiness. Planning, of course, was the secret. And he planned well. But there were times when the plans failed, when the unexpected happened. Like this weekend.

He'd been supposed to go fishing with a friend, although he was totally uninterested in fishing. But that morning the phone had rung. A sick wife. And the trip was off.

He'd made some phone calls, but evidently everyone else had planned well for this weekend. No parties, not even a movie partner.

So he faced the enemy. More than forty-eight hours with nothing to keep him from thinking. Unless he got drunk. But it was difficult for him to stay drunk for more than a few hours. Nature had given him too weak a stomach.

And that left only one thing. . . that would end in emptiness without even the pain of frustration . . . but that would at least protect him from. . . .

Hopelessly, he looked up and met the bright beckoning eyes of the woman. . . .

—Jeffrey Paull

This narrative begins in the present, but then alternates between the present and the past, making some fourteen time changes in all. And beyond the simple present-past changes there are changes to the immediate past, the intermediate past, and the distant past. The leading character jumps back and forth imaginatively over some six years of time. And yet the story line is quite simple; the treatment is chronologically indirect, but logically direct. There are many time changes, but the focus is always on the man and his affair with Betty. The only element other than the affair and the resulting pain he experiences is the briefly implied relationship with the woman at the bar, and even that is a consequence of his loneliness.

In addition to the chronological order of narratives, their directness must be seen in terms of the narrative *point of view.* The most direct point of view is the sort from which the author writes as if he were a central character in the story. The first person is used: "I went into the building," instead of "he entered the building," or "she looked at me for a long instant" instead of "she looked at him for a long moment." Less direct are those narratives in which the author writes as though he knew the thoughts and feelings of one or all of his characters; in such narration the author may make one of the characters his "favorite," may color the story and give it a bias by implicitly endorsing the values and actions of that character, or he may describe the feelings of all the characters in an impartial fashion. Still less direct is that kind of narration in which the author is an observer who relates the behavior of the characters but does not enter into their minds and emotions.

The selection that follows is one in which the author's point of view is the second one described above. He writes as if he knew the leading character's thoughts.

The Vulnerable One

David Matthews was not a homosexual. He felt none of the extreme anger or embarrassment in the presence of homosexuals that so often indicates hidden sexual fears; and he was prey to none of the fascinated curiosity that can lead to homosexual practices.

Nevertheless, every since his late teens David had frequently been labelled a homosexual.

Seated now in his office in the big western university, David felt the sort of freedom he'd dreamed of for years. A brand new Ph.D., even his title seemed reassuring.

"Dr. Matthews," he repeated it aloud, "assistant professor of modern languages." It vibrated with safety, with connotations of scholarship, of ideas, of learning, of security. What a far cry, he thought to himself, from the considered cruelty of his college mates, from the circle of homosexuals into which he'd been forced in his months as a writer in New York, from the cold unfriendliness of the big advertising agency where he'd sought anonymity.

Here he was protected by all the traditions, the bulwarks of the academic world.

David leaned back and stretched relaxedly. He was a slight man, five-eight or so, about a hundred and fifty pounds, blond hair, and light gray eyes. There was a kind of physical refinement, of fineness about him that suggested delicacy. The small bones of his wrists, the carefully manicured nails, the extreme neatness of dress.

The clock on his desk showed ten minutes to the hour. Ten minutes until his beginning class in French. He thought of the many trips through Europe with his formidable mother. It had never occurred to her that he might not enjoy traveling, and it had certainly never occurred to him to question her decisions. He smiled faintly at the thought of how unexpectedly valuable those trips had become. His French was fluently perfect, his Italian and Spanish the same.

David stood up and walked over to the window. He watched a few early students wander toward the classroom, talking casually of girls, exams. Even their voices seemed young and healthy to his ears.

The world had begun to seem to David a very wonderful place indeed. Possibilities of peace, of friends, even of marriage and family flitted through his rosy thoughts of the future.

He sighed happily and turned to gather up some books for the class.

Students appeared now in groups of two and three, beginning to hurry a little. David almost laughed aloud for joy as one of them asked a friend, just as they passed beneath his window, how the past indefinite of "être" and "avoir" went.

Before he left his office, he went to the window for one last look at the loveliness of the campus.

Two stragglers were just hurrying past. One of them, expensively dressed, the assurance of the best fraternity and his father's money in his movements, was talking.

"No, I tell ya,' he's a fairy. You watch his face today when I ask him the French word for homosexual."

David stood for a moment, then turned and went out of the office, very carefully closing the door behind him.

—John Reynolds

In this story, the author has written the thoughts and feelings of the central character, and, in addition, he's narrated in such a way as to side with, to sympathize with that character. It is an understated sort of bias; the author doesn't explicitly praise David or condemn the student, but the events are slanted unmistakably in David's favor. There's little doubt that the reader's awareness will be centered on David in a positive, if not a sympathetic manner.

By contrast, here is the most direct, the most immediate and involved narrative point of view.

## from "My Mother's Death"[100]

Here begin my misfortunes.

But I am putting off too long a necessary statement, one of the two or three which will perhaps make me throw these Memoirs into the fire.

My mother, Madame Henriette Gagnon, was a charming woman, and I was in love with her.

I hasten to add that I lost her when I was seven years old.

In loving her at the age of, perhaps, six (1789), I had exactly the same character as when, in 1828, I loved Alberthe de Rubempré with a mad passion. My way of starting on the quest for happiness had not changed at all in essentials, with this sole exception: that in what constitutes the physical side of love, I was what Caesar would be, if he came back to earth, with regard to the use of cannon and small arms. I should soon have learnt, and it would have changed nothing essential in my tactics.

I wanted to cover my mother with kisses, and for her to have no clothes on. She loved me passionately and often kissed me; I returned her kisses with such ardour that she was often obliged to go away. I abhorred my father when he came and interrupted our kisses. I always wanted to give them to her on her bosom. Be so good as to remember that I lost her, in childbed, when I was barely seven.

She was plump, and of an exquisite freshness; she was very pretty, and I think she was only rather short. She had an expression of perfect nobility and serenity; she was dark, vivacious, and surrounded by a regular court; she often forgot to give the orders to her three maid-servants; and to conclude, she used often to read in the original the *Divine Comedy* of Dante, of which I found long afterwards five or six different editions in her apartments, which had remained shut up since her death.

She perished in the flower of her youth and beauty; in 1790 she might have been twenty-eight or thirty years old.

Here begins my moral life.

—Marie Henri Beyle Stendhal
(translated by Catherine Alison Phillips)

Here the author is part of the story. He narrates events and describes people as seen through his own eyes. In a sense the author *is* the story. In comparison with the previous selection, the directness of this narrative is easily measured. In the earlier story the author related events from the viewpoint of one who knew the thoughts of the main character. In this example the author acts as central character, and in the description of his mother, a first person point of view.

Finally, here is a narrative in which the author writes from the impartial, objective viewpoint I've described.

[100] From *The Life of Henri Brulard*, by Stendhal, translated by Catherine Alison Phillips. Copyright 1925 and renewed 1953 by Alfred A. Knopf, Inc. Reprinted by permission.

## from "The Way The World Goes"[101]

Among the genii who preside over the empires of the world, Ithuriel holds one of the first places, and has the province of Upper Asia. He came down one morning, entered the dwelling of Babouc, a Scythian who lived on the banks of the Oxus, and addressed him thus:

"Babouc, the follies and disorders of the Persians have drawn down upon them our wrath. An assembly of the genii of Upper Asia was held yesterday to consider whether Persepolis should be punished or utterly destroyed. Go thither, and make full investigation; on thy return inform me faithfully of all, and I will decide according to thy report either to chastise the city or to root it out."

"But, my lord," said Babouc humbly, "I have never been in Persia, and know no one there."

"So much the better," said the angel, "thou wilt be the more impartial. Heaven has given thee discernment, and I add the gift of winning confidence. Go, look, listen, observe, and fear nothing, thou shalt be well received everywhere."

Babouc mounted his camel, and set out with his servants. After some days, on approaching the plains of Sennah, he fell in with the Persian army which was going to fight with the army of India. He first accosted a soldier whom he found at a distance from the camp, and asked him what was the cause of the war.

"By all the gods," said the soldier, "I know nothing about it; it is no business of mine; my trade is to kill and be killed to get a living. It makes no odds to me whom I serve. I have a great mind to pass over tomorrow into the Indian camp, for I hear that they are giving their men half a copper drachma a day more than we get in this cursed service of Persia. If you want to know why we are fighting, speak to my captain."

Babouc gave the soldier a small present, and entered the camp. He soon made the captain's acquaintance, and asked him the cause of the war.

"How should I know?" said he, "such grand matters are no concern of mine. I live two hundred leagues away from Persepolis; I hear it said that war has been declared; I immediately forsake my family, and go, according to our custom, to make my fortune or to die, since I have nothing else to do."

"But surely," said Babouc, "your comrades are a little better informed than yourself?"

"No," replied the officer, "hardly anybody except our chief satraps has any very clear notion why we are cutting each other's throats."

Babouc, astonished at this, introduced himself to the generals, and they were soon on intimate terms. At last one of them said to him:

"The cause of this War, which has laid Asia waste for the last twenty years, originally sprang out of a quarrel between a eunuch belonging to one of the wives of the great King of Persia, and a customhouse clerk in the service of the Great King of India. The matter in dispute was a duty amounting to very nearly the thirtieth part of a daric. The Indian and Persian prime ministers worthily supported their masters' rights. The quarrel grew hot. They

[101] Reprinted from *The Way the World Goes* by Voltaire, translated by R. B. Boswell, by permission of G. Bell & Sons, Ltd.

*Ritual:*

sent into the field on both sides an army of a million troops. This army has to be recruited every year with more than 400,000 men. Massacres, conflagrations, ruin, and devastation multiply; the whole world suffers, and their fury still continues. Our own as well as the Indian prime minister often protest that they are acting solely for the happiness of the human race; and at each protestation some towns are always destroyed and some province ravaged."

The next day, on a report being spread that peace was about to be concluded, the Persian and Indian generals hastened to give battle; and a bloody one it was. Babouc saw all its mistakes and all its abominations; he witnessed stratagems carried on by the chief satraps, who did all they could to cause their commander to be defeated; he saw officers slain by their own troops; he saw soldiers despatching their dying comrades in order to strip them of a few bloodstained rags, torn and covered with mud. He entered the hospitals to which they were carrying the wounded, most of whom died through the inhuman negligence of those very men whom the King of Persia paid handsomely to relieve them.

"Are these creatures men," cried Babouc, "or wild beasts? Ah! I see plainly that Persepolis will be destroyed."

Occupied with this thought, he passed into the camp of the Indians, and found there as favourable a reception as in that of the Persians, just as he had been led to expect; but he beheld there all the same abuses that had already filled him with horror.

"Ah!" said he to himself, "if the angel Ithuriel resolves to exterminate the Persians, then the angel of India must destroy the Indians as well."

Being afterwards more particularly informed of all that went on in both camps, he was made acquainted with acts of generosity, magnanimity, and humanity that moved him with astonishment and delight.

"Unintelligible mortals!" he exclaimed, "how is it that you can combine so much meanness with so much greatness, such virtues with such crimes?"

Meanwhile peace was declared. The commanders of both armies, neither of whom gained the victory, but who had caused the blood of so many of their fellow-men to flow, only to promote their own interests, began to solicit rewards in their respective courts. The peace was extolled in public proclamations which announced nothing less than the return of virtue and happiness to earth.

—François Marie Arouet de Voltaire
(translated by Robert Bruce Boswell)

In this case, though there's some emphasis on the interpretations of Baboue, the author is largely impartial. He uses the character of Babouc to disclose the horrors of the two societies, but there's very little subjective identification with Babouc as a person. The reader may respond *through* Babouc *to* the evils of Persia and India, but he's likely to respond *to* Babouc himself. Thus the author has avoided any major emphasis on a single character's thoughts and feelings, and has described in a psychologically unbiased fashion the events and personages in his story. Other than the use of the central character to stress the follies of the two cultures, the author's point of view is impersonal.

*Prose: A Combined Form*     Although description and narration have been discussed separately, I want to say most emphatically that these elements do not ordinarily occur separately. I don't know of a single prose work that is a pure example of either of these; in every case prose presents some combination of description and narration, often with one or the other predominant, but a combination nevertheless.

Here's an example that's perfectly representative. It's primarily descriptive but it has very important narrative elements. Indeed the narrative elements are descriptive, and the descriptive elements narrative.

## The Enemy

He was a slight man. Everything about him was neat. His nails were not so much freshly manicured as naturally clean. It was not that he seemed to have just finished shaving, but rather that his beard grew slowly. When he turned the pages of the book he was reading, he did it with one neat motion — the finger raising the page corner, sliding under it, and smoothly lifting up and over.

The careful absorption with which he read did not disturb the even arrangement of his features. And when he looked up from the book, savoring a cleverly made point, his enjoyment was indicated by a faint creasing of the eyes, as if the tiny muscles there had not yet learned the self-control of the rest of his body.

The afternoon sun crept across the desk in front of him until it touched the edge of the leather-backed blotter-ink-stand-letter-holder-clock. It was a handsome desk ornament, smooth, dark leather, the two pens black with gold bands, and the neat Roman numerals on the clock face. There was nothing else on the desk.

The room itself was small, books lining the two side walls, the frosted glass door and filing cabinets facing the desk, and behind it the window looking out on the three o'clock quiet of the campus. A leather armchair sat in front of the desk, and a straight-backed wooden chair at one corner, offering the visitor his choice of attentiveness or comfort.

The clock chimed three times, mildly, and he closed the book at once, slipping a leather placemarker between the pages. It was as if the new hour brought new duties that needed immediate attention.

He moved the chair back from the desk, turning sideways in one efficient movement, got up and took the book to the wall furthest from the desk, and neatly replaced it among its fellows. These were non-academic works. Seated again, he turned to the bookshelves only an arm's length from the desk and selected a text. The arrangement suggested that duty lay with the shelves nearby, while the books on the far wall might better be kept out of reach.

He put the book on the desk, took a small, leather-covered notebook from a drawer, opened both, and began to go over his notes for the coming class, refreshing his memory on points where he felt the text was inadequate and needed further details, correlating statements with those of other authorities. He worked carefully and efficiently, and when he finished he knew precisely, to the word, what he was going to say in his lecture.

Looking at the clock he saw that he had twenty minutes before the class began. Pleased, he leaned back in his chair and relaxed. He liked to be ready well before his classes began. Usually he was able to do nothing, literally nothing, not even to think, during most of these minutes, but today something pushed weightlessly at his mind. Instead of his regular period of stillness, he turned his chair and looked out across the campus.

Here and there students moved along the walks, secure in their belief that, when the exams were finished, the semesters over, the grades recorded, the future would begin.

He thought vaguely of his own undergraduate days. Then the brief attempt at writing, the job in the publishing house, things that made up a sort of token try at the outside before he returned to the academic fold. He remembered how secure and leisurely and alluring the professor's life had seemed to him during his graduate career. When he'd received his Ph.D. he'd thought of his future as a long succession of safe, golden years. Years in which he would become wise and respected. Years marked by classes of students who would look at him with, well reverence was perhaps overdoing it, but certainly with warmth and appreciation.

Twenty-five years. He'd seen twenty-five senior classes graduate. He was a full professor, only five years from retirement. He sighed silently.

The clock said ten minutes to four when it began.

He closed his eyes for a second, almost as though he were greeting an old friend. The thing was so familiar by now that it was as much a part of him as the trees, the buildings, the faculty meetings. He nearly smiled when he thought of how he'd once regarded it as the nervousness normal for a new teacher. He'd long ago recognized it for what it was.

Fear.

At first it had been so bad that he'd had to clench his hands and pace the classroom to keep the trembling from being apparent. Now, thankfully, it was completely controllable.

It always began the same way. The tiny coldness inside. The slow visceral tension. The slight dryness of the mouth.

And the voices.

They began now. The same questions. Always unanswerable.

"Suppose you forget? Suppose you simply forget what you were going to say? What will you do then? Just stand there? Or suppose one of them asks something you can't answer? And suppose he sneers at your stupidity? Or suppose you, somehow or other, do something wrong, something terribly wrong, and ugly? And they laugh at you? Mock you?"

He answered because, as always, he had to answer.

"I will not forget. I have never forgotten. That's why I know every word I'm going to say. And if I did forget, I'd simply look at my notes. It's all written down. And the odds are a thousand to one against any of them asking me anything I can't answer. That's why I've read everything written in this field. And if I couldn't answer it would be impossible to sneer at me because I've made the situation forbiddingly formal. And I'm not going to do anything wrong or ugly or embarrassing. I always check myself first, and besides, I'd always have time to leave the room."

He knew that his answers were correct and complete and convincing and that there was always the chance, however slight, that he was wrong and that the voices were right.

It was five minutes to the hour. He stood up. He never liked to be late. It seemed unfair. He picked up the text and the notebook, put two pencils in his pocket, and went toward the door.

As he walked, he changed slightly. A veil of deadness slid down over his eyes.

He went out of the room and closed the door neatly behind him.

— Jeffrey Paull

The first four paragraphs are largely descriptive. In the fifth paragraph narration enters significantly with the words "and he closed the book at once." The rest of the selection is a mixture of description and narration; each paragraph describes and also relates present or past feelings and actions. The last seven paragraphs, in which the internal dialogue takes place, are somewhat more obviously narrative, but there too description plays a major part.

You may wish to analyze prose works in relation to only one of these elements, and such analyses are often valuable, but you must be aware that prose itself is a combined form, a fusion of description and narration.

### Dramatic Form

Drama is literature intended for performance. Again, there's some overlap between drama and narrative prose. The defining characteristic of narration is the story line or plot; the defining elements of drama are characterization and conflict. The fact that plot and characterization are important in both dramatic and narrative forms need not be confusing if you remember that the elements most central to each form are those used as bases for the discussions offered here.

Drama is literature *intended* for performance, and dramatic works *can be* performed because the actors have something to act. In other words, dramatic works are written so that they provide actors with action, with behavior. Put a bit differently, a piece of drama gives the actor someone to *be,* some character to create. Drama without people, without characters, is a contradiction in terms; characterization is basic to drama.

The earliest and one of the most important dramatic theorists was Aristotle. The characters in drama he described as "men in action." [102] Nowhere in the *Poetics* does Aristotle suggest that impersonal, or objective, or detached observations of human beings constitute drama. Those human beings must be "in action," and he makes it quite clear that action means stress, strain, success, failure, effort—in a word, conflict. You may disagree with some of Aristotle's pronouncements on the nature of drama, but the idea that characters acting out their destinies in the turmoil of intense conflict is the very heart of the dramatic form cannot be denied. Any other approach leads to a view of drama as a static description of persons who do not change, or who change easily and effortlessly and without pain.

[102] Aristotle *Poetics*, trans S.H. Butcher, *Aristotle's Poetics* (New York: Hill and Wang, 1961), ii. 2. 52.

Thus, although characterization and conflict are the two elements most important to drama, the two must be considered together. Characters without conflict are totally undramatic, and conflict without characters is an impossibility. Many years ago, I heard the following description of drama:

> The batter hits the ball sharply. It is a clean single. So far, there may have been some excitement, but there has been no drama. The batter stands on first base; the pitcher, who has one of the smoothest pick-off throws in the game, looks at the batter, then glances over his shoulder at the runner. Still no drama. The runner moves off the bag; he takes a short lead toward second. There is no drama present. The pitcher glances at him again. He increases his lead, making little threatening moves with his body. Now he is far enough off the bag so that he may have trouble getting back. And now, suddenly and electrically, the scene *is dramatic!*[103]

This drama may depend on a chunk of rather blatant Americana, but the central thought that drama exists only where there is some threat, or danger, or conflict is an idea that is of absolutely primary importance.

As an example, here is a scene from a play that is full of a very different sort of conflict. Here we are in the midst of high romance. Not romance in the sense of boy-meets-gets-loses-gets-girl, but romance in the sense that the characters, particularly the major ones, are larger than life-size, more flamboyant, more daring, and more tender.

Cyrano has just duelled with a noble fop who has dared to make light of his nose. He has defeated Valvert in what must be the most magnificent bit of swordplay in history. As he fought, he composed and recited a ballade, and on the final line, "Then, as I end the refrain, thrust home!" he dispatched his opponent with perfect grace before a theater full of onlookers. Now, after all the others have gone, his old friend Captain Le Bret is trying to point out to Cyrano that he is making too many enemies by his independent and unbending adherence to rigid principles.

from Cyrano de Bergerac[104]

LE BRET: These fatheads with the bellicose grand airs
    Will have you ruined if you listen to them;
    Talk to a man of sense and hear how all
    Your swagger impresses him.
CYRANO: (*finishes his macaroon*) Enormously.
LE BRET: The Cardinal —
CYRANO: (*beaming*) Was he there?
LE BRET: He must have thought you —

---

[103] This is my recollection of a description of the nature of drama given by Professor Frank Baxter in a course on Shakespearean drama at the University of Southern California. I do not, of course, imply that Professor Baxter limited himself to such simplistic descriptions in dealing with dramatic theory.

[104] From *Cyrano de Bergerac* by Edmond Rostand, Brian Hooker Translation. Copyright 1923 by Holt, Rinehart and Winston, Inc. Copyright 1951 by Doris C. Hooker. Reprinted by permission of Holt, Rinehart and Winston, Inc.

CYRANO: Original.

LE BRET: Well, but. . . .

CYRANO: He is himself a playwright. He will not be
too displeased that I have closed another
author's play.

LE BRET: But look at all the enemies you have made!

CYRANO: *(begins on the grape)* How many — do you think?

LE BRET: Just forty-eight
Without the women.

CYRANO: Count them.

LE BRET: Montfleury,
Baron de Guiche, the Vicomte, the Old Man,
All the Academy —

CYRANO: Enough! You make me
Happy!

LE BRET: But where is all this leading you?
What is your plan?

CYRANO: I have been wandering —
Wasting my force upon too many plans.
Now I have chosen one.

LE BRET: What one?

CYRANO: The simplest —
To make myself in all things admirable!

LE BRET: Hmph! Well, then, the real reason why you hate
Montfleury — Come, the truth now!

CYRANO: *(rises)* That Silenus,
Who cannot hold his belly in his arms,
Still dreams of being sweetly dangerous
Among the women — sighs and languishes,
Making sheeps' eyes out of his great frog's face—
I hate him ever since one day he dared
Smile upon—
Oh, my friend, I seemed to see
Over some flower a great snail crawling!

LE BRET: *(amazed)* How,
What? Is it possible . . . ?

CYRANO: *(with a bitter smile)* For me to love?
*(changing his tone; seriously)*
I love.

LE BRET: May I know? You have never said—

CYRANO: Whom I love? Think a moment. Think of me—
Me, whom the plainest woman would despise—
Me, with this nose of mine that marches on
Before me by a quarter of an hour!
Whom should I love? Why—of course—it must be
The woman in the world most beautiful.

LE BRET: Most beautiful?

CYRANO: In all this world—most sweet;
Also most wise; most witty; and most fair!

LE BRET: Who and what is this woman?

CYRANO: Dangerous.
Mortally, without meaning; exquisite
Without imagining. Nature's own snare
To allure manhood. A white rose wherein
Love lies in ambush for his natural prey.
Who knows her smile has known a perfect thing.
She creates grace in her own image, brings
Heaven to earth in one movement of her hand—
Nor thou, O Venus! balancing thy shell
Over the Mediterranean blue, nor thou,
Diana! marching through broad, blossoming woods,
Art so divine as when she mounts her chair,
And goes abroad through Paris!

LE BRET: Oh, well—of course,
That makes everything clear!

CYRANO: Transparently.

LE BRET: Madeleine Robin—your cousin?

CYRANO: Yes, Roxane.

LE BRET: And why not? If you love her, tell her so!
You have covered yourself with glory in her eyes
This very day.

CYRANO: My old friend—look at me,
And tell me how much hope remains for me
With this protuberance! Oh I have no more
Illusions! Now and then—bah! I may grow
Tender, walking alone in the blue cool
Of evening, through some garden fresh with flowers
After the benediction of the rain;
My poor big devil of a nose inhales
April . . .and so I follow with my eyes
Where some boy, with a girl upon his arm,
Passes a patch of silver . . . and I feel
Somehow, I wish I had a woman too,
Walking with little steps under the moon,
And holding my arm so, and smiling. Then
I dream—and I forget. . . .
And then I see
The shadow of my profile on the wall!

LE BRET: My friend!

CYRANO: My friend, I have my bitter days,
Knowing myself so ugly, so alone.

LE BRET: You weep?

CYRANO: *(quickly)* Oh, not that ever! No,
That would be too grotesque—tears trickling down
All the long way along this nose of mine?
I will not so profane the dignity
Of sorrow. Never any tears for me!
Why, there is nothing more sublime than tears,

Nothing! Shall I make them ridiculous
In my poor person?

—Edmond Rostand
(translated by Brian Hooker)

The matter of importance in this scene is that the conflict is almost entirely internal. In other parts of the play there are conflicts between characters, but here the conflicts are between Cyrano's desires. He is the proudest of men, and he would suffer a thousand lonely deaths rather than be ridiculed by a woman for his great grotesque nose. But he is a man, and an endlessly romantic one. He adores beauty, and in particular, beauty in the person of Roxane. The conflict is the fight between his constant need to confess his love to her and to receive her love, and his equally constant need to avoid humiliation at her hands. He is caught in a trap from which there is no escape. The conflict is profound and permanent, and it rages within him.

Again, it's in conflict that the character of Cyrano is revealed. He shows his tenderness and sensitivity, his fear of ridicule, and his iron determination to avoid feminine laughter—all in his own conflict-laden words.

As another example of dramatic form, here's a scene from Christopher Fry's brilliant *The Lady's Not For Burning.* The play is about Thomas, a young man who wants to be hanged because he finds it the only gesture fitting for a world filled with ugliness and horror, and about Jennet, a young woman who is accused of being a witch and is to be hung. The two escape their deaths by loving each other, but for much of the play Thomas fights valiantly against that love. In this scene he gives some of the reasons for which he resists Jennet.

### from *The Lady's Not For Burning*[105]

THOMAS: Don't entertain the mildest interest in me
    Or you'll have me die screaming.
JENNET: *(sits on bench)* Why should that be?
    If you're afraid of your shadow falling across
    Another life, shine less brightly upon yourself,
    Step back into the rank and file of men,
    Instead of preserving the magnetism of mystery
    And your curious passion for death. You are making yourself
    A breeding ground for love and must take the consequences.
    But what are you afraid of, since in a little
    While neither of us may exist? Either or both
    May be altogether transmuted into memory,
    And then the heart's obscure indeed . . .Richard
    There's a tear rolling out of your eye. What is it?
RICHARD: *(on floor C., looks up at JENNET)*
    Oh, that? I don't really know. I have things on my mind.
JENNET: Not us?
RICHARD: Not only.

[105] From *The Lady's Not for Burning*, by Christopher Fry, published by the Oxford University Press.

THOMAS: If it's a woman, Richard,
       Apply yourself to the scrubbing brush. It's all
       A trick of the light.
JENNET: The light of a fire.
*(RICHARD rises)*
THOMAS:                  And, Richard,
       Make this woman understand that I
       Am a figure of vice and crime . . .
JENNET: Guilty of . . .
THOMAS:                Guilty
       Of mankind. I have perpetrated human nature.
       My father and mother were accessories before the fact,
       But there'll be no accessories after the fact,
       By my virility there won't! Just see me
       As I am, me like a perambulating
       Vegetable, patched about with inconsequential
       Hair, looking out of two small jellies for the means
       To live, balanced on folding bones, my sex
       No beauty, but a blemish to be hidden
       Behind judicious rags, driven and scorched
       By boomerang rages and lunacies which never
       Touch the accommodating artichoke
       Or the seraphic strawberry beaming in its bed;
       I defend myself against pain and death by pain
       And death, and make the world go round, they tell me,
       By one of my less lethal appetites;
       Half this grotesque life I spend in a state
       Of slow decomposition, using
       The name of unconsidered God as a pedestal
       On which I stand and bray that I am best
       Of beasts, till under some patient
       Moon or other I fall to pieces, like
       A cake of dung.
       *(sits stool C.)*
       Is there a slut would hold
       This in her arms and put her lips against it?
JENNET: Sluts are only human. By a quirk
       Of unastonished nature, your obscene
       Decaying figure of vegetable fun
       Can drag upon a woman's heart, as though
       Heaven were dragging up the roots of hell.
       What is to be done? Something compels us into
       The terrible fallacy that man is desirable
       And there's no escaping into truth. Your crimes
       And cruelties leave us longing, and campaigning
       Love still pitches his tent of light among
       The suns and moons.
       *(THOMAS rises)*
       You may be decay and a platitude

Of the flesh, but I have no other such memory of life.
You may be corrupt as ancient apples, well then
Corruption is what I most willingly harvest.
You are Evil, Hell, the Father of Lies; if so
Hell is my home, and my days of good were a holiday;
Hell is my hill, and the world slopes away from it
Into insignificance. I have come suddenly
Upon my heart and where it is I see no help for.

There are two kinds of conflict here: conflict between the two main characters (Jennet is willing to love, Thomas unwilling to love or be loved— she will accept Thomas and the world as it is; he can accept neither) and conflict within Thomas. He strives to convince Jennet that he is evil and unworthy, and one cannot help feeling that he is convincing himself, too. In the conflicts within himself and between himself and Jennet he reveals his extreme sensitivity; he is a man who is deeply hurt by the pain that he sees around him. And in the conflict between the two of them Jennet reveals her deep, warm acceptance—her vibrant ability to love.

Once again, the characters are revealed through conflict, and the conflict occurs because of the characters. As in all drama, these two forces come together to create the nucleus of the dramatic form.

## The Content of Ritual

I've discussed various forms, or formal elements, of Ritual. In the following pages I'm going to talk about the content of these forms. The two concepts, form and content, make up a frame of reference within which most explorations of literature have been conducted.

Content, in its simplest sense, equals meaning. To ask "What are the contents of a poem, a play, a prose work?" is to ask "What does the work mean?" As with the discussions of form, I want to deal with the most general and important kinds of content, the ways in which Ritual exerts its meaning, rather than with the specific meaning of given works. So I'm going to explore two sorts of meaning: lexical-and-contextual meaning, and the universality of Ritual. These two kinds of meaning are common to all Ritual.

### Lexical and Contextual Meaning

Literature consists of words. Quite obviously then, you must understand and be familiar with those words if you're to appreciate the selection with which you're involved. Simple enough! Still, I've listened to many readings or performances in which it was painfully clear that certain words were simply unfamiliar to the reader. Such crimes are intolerable because, too often, they indicate an attitude that goes something like, "Well, the thing ought to be clear, and if it isn't, then it's the author's fault for using those strange words." Authors do have an obligation to make their works understandable, but *not* to the dolt who refuses to do the necessary work himself.

To know a word is to experience, usually vicariously, the object or event it symbolizes. Heine, in describing a young virgin, said: "Her face is like a palimpsest—beneath the gothic lettering of the monk's sacred text lurks the pagan poet's half-effaced erotic verse.[106] "Palimpsest" is a rarely heard word, and the reader who refuses to become familiar with it will never be able to fully enjoy these lines. The obvious inability to understand the excerpt is one thing, but worse still is the willingness to accept some murky idea of the word's meaning that may be furnished by the context. Never having heard the term, you could assume that it meant something about combining two images or qualities. But if you settle for that sort of "understanding" you're committing literary suicide. You must know the definition of that word. Without it you're lost. With it you can go on to deal with the excerpt in some detail. You can understand, for example, that the "earlier writings" in this case are the sexual or sensuous nature of the girl, that the "monk's sacred text" is the girl's religious training that has only partially covered over "the pagan poet's half-effaced erotic verse," and that the author here may be either praising the strong sensuality of the girl or condemning her because of her ever-present sexual nature.

Thus, though the purely lexical meaning of a word is entirely simple in the sense that you must become familiar with that meaning, such dictionary meanings are of basic importance to the larger meanings of the material.

Somewhat more complicated than lexical meanings, and of equal or greater importance, are the contextual meanings of Ritual. Two sorts of problems arise here. First, the context may exercise what can be called a "selective" function. That is, from a group of commonly understood meanings for a term, the context "chooses," "selects" an appropriate one. There's an Oriental proverb that says, "Lambs have the grace to suckle kneeling."[107] The key word here is "grace." Unlike "palimpsest," it's a commonly understood word. Any one of several meanings of "grace" will fit, at least approximately—"pleasing or smooth movements," for instance. The saying makes sense using that meaning. But there's another meaning that's an *exact*, not an approximate fit. It is "a sense of what is right." With that meaning the proverb attains a symbolic power that is impossible with any other; lambs are pictured as gentle creatures who have the grace to give thanks for their sustenance, to drink humbly. The context, then, has "selected" that meaning from the various available ones.

Quite often understanding a word in context requires a familiarity with word history. The history or derivation of a word may not be a part of the obvious meaning with which one normally deals, but it's frequently necessary for a full appreciation of a particular selection. Many times an awareness of word histories can make a seemingly dull and pedestrian selection into an exciting and pulsing work.

[106] Koestler, p. 89.
[107] Quoted in Wilma H. Grimes and Alethea Smith Mattingly, *Interpretation: Writer, Reader, Audience* (San Francisco: Wadsworth Publishing Co., Inc., 1961), p. 61.

Here's an example (far from pedestrian to begin with) that requires and
rewards a knowledge of word history:

## Blue Girls[108]

Twirling your blue skirts, traveling the sward
Under the towers of your seminary,
Go listen to your teachers old and contrary
Without believing a word.

Tie the white fillets then about your lustrous hair
And think no more of what will come to pass
Than bluebirds that go walking on the grass
And chattering on the air.

Practice your beauty, blue girls, before it fail:
And I will cry with my loud lips and publish
Beauty which all our power shall never establish,
It is so frail.

For I could tell you a story which is true:
I know a lady with a terrible tongue,
Blear eyes fallen from blue,
All her perfections tarnished—yet it is not long
Since she was lovelier than any of you.

— John Crowe Ransom

John Ciardi, in *How Does a Poem Mean?* discusses the word histories of some
of the terms used here.[109] He points out the use of "traveling" in line 1 and
"walking" in line 7. This is an especially rich example if you're a word-hungry
reader. Part of the history of the word "travel" includes "travail"—to labor. In
addition to the obvious meaning of going from one place to another, the blue girls
labor at the seminary. The bluebirds "walk," and part of the history of that word
includes "to roll, revolve," "a rolling motion." A highly appropriate term to
describe a bird's motion. But the important thing is the comparison that then
becomes possible. The bluebirds "walk," with a rolling or revolving motion, and the
blue girls "travel" (labor) but do so "twirling" their skirts—twirl, "to spin in a circular
or revolving motion." The actions of the girls and the birds involve the same sort of
movement.

Ciardi also points out the use of "practice" in line 9 and "perfections" in line
16, and says that since both terms derive from the root meaning "to do, to make,"
the girls (doing) and the woman (done), these word histories bring into being a new

[108] Copyright 1927 by Alfred A. Knopf, Inc. and renewed 1955 by John Crowe
Ransom. Reprinted from *Selected Poems*, revised edition, by John Crowe Ransom, by
permission of the publisher.
[109] John Ciardi, *How Does a Poem Mean?* (Boston: Houghton Mifflin Company, 1959),
pp. 802-3.

level of comparison between the girls and the woman. Interestingly, he does not refer to the background of the word "practice" that includes "to bring about, to try to get, to plan, to plot." On this level the girls are striving for their beauty, while the woman has lost hers. Or has she? The past of the word "tarnished" includes "hidden." In some sense the woman's past beauty is still present, although hidden. Also, the histories of the words "terrible" and "blear" include "to flee" and "to deceive, to hoodwink," respectively. Thus the woman has lost her friends or lovers because they have fled from her "terrible tongue" and deceiving "blear eyes."

The above selection may not seem particularly difficult on first look, and it is often surprising to find large numbers of hidden riches in such works. For instance, the following example is one that may well seem exceedingly simple. Certainly many of the words involved are far from unusual. But notice the unfolding and spreading of those words.

### Upon Julia's Clothes

When as in silks my Julia goes,
Then, then (methinks) how sweetly flowes
That liquefaction of her clothes.
Next, when I cast mine eyes and see
That brave Vibration each way free;
O,how that glittering taketh me!

—Robert Herrick

In these lines the recurrence of words that suggest or depend on liquidity or water-like movement is unmistakable. "Flowes" and "liquefaction" are examples. But if you look a bit deeper, other elements of meaning emerge. Julia's clothes *flowe*. That's the now obsolete spelling of "flow." "Flow" means "to move in a manner suggesting a fluid." It also means "to glide along smoothly, without harshness or asperity." And it means "to have or be in abundance, to abound." Lastly, one of the rare meanings of the word is "to express one's feelings." This context exerts an inclusive, rather than exclusive, influence; instead of choosing a single meaning, and excluding others, the context here includes all these meanings—all are appropriate and needed—all are involved in the simple word "flow." Julia's clothes move in a fluid manner, smoothly, suggesting a richness or abundance (of the clothes, or Julia, or both?), and perhaps expressing some smooth, fluid, sensual feelings. Such an expanded statement is the result of the influence of the context on the single word "flow" in this selection.

Further, Julia's clothes are of silk. Silk is a soft, flowing fabric that can visually resemble water, waves, wave-like motion, etc. And we're used to thinking of the word "silk" as a noun, but it's also a verb. As such, it means "to blossom." And what a perfect description of this Julia! She blossoms in silks, and the blossoming liquefies the silks.

"Liquefaction" is from the root word "liquid." In turn, "liquid" derives from Latin root terms meaning "extended," "prosperous," and "water." Julia is dressed in rich, lustrous silks, silks of a flowing design, and of quiet, watery colors.

In the next stanza "Vibration," with a capital V, is one of the key words. It means "to swing, to move to and fro." It also means "to pulse, to throb." And one of the unusual meanings of the verb "to vibrate" is "to throw or cast." Moving to and fro or pulsing and throbbing can suggest a wave-like motion. But it is a *brave* vibration. Why "brave?" Among the seldom-used meanings of this word are "superior, excellent, fine, making a fine show or display, and to adorn." All these are appropriate elements of meaning for this context. Julia's vibrations make a fine display indeed, and she is a rare adornment herself, in addition to being adorned with silks.

Julia's love looks at her. He *casts* his eyes. One of the meanings of vibrate is "to cast." An interesting sort of mutuality. And he is taken by the *glittering*. "Glitter" means "to shine lustrously, to gleam." Both silk and water can gleam. And more important, there are common elements of meaning between "glitter" and "flow" (each can be transformed into the other by using intervening water-terms) and between both of these and "brave" (the close ties between "glitter"—"to shine lustrously, to gleam"—and "brave"—"making a fine show or display," and between "flow"—"to have or be in abundance, to abound" and "brace"—"superior, excellent, find" are too numerous and apparent to be denied).

Finally, as an example of the sort of hidden meaning that word histories can turn up in even the most ordinary-seeming places, consider the word "goes." It means, for one thing, "self-originated movement," in contrast with more neutral verbs such as "move." Julia goes, and parts of Julia go, in a way that suggests independence, purpose. One of the root terms from which "go" is derived means "to reach, to overtake." Julia is in this sense a pursuer. She can, and seems entirely likely to, overtake her lover.

All meanings such as these are in no sense substitutes for more usual, everyday meanings of words. They are additions to those familiar meanings, additions that bring new dimensions, new and oblique riches to the material. And the more dimensions of this sort that you can find in the literature, the more exciting you make it for yourself.

The second of the two functions of the context referred to earlier is what I will call a "creative" function. In many cases one may search vainly for a commonly understood meaning of a term that will fit a context. There may be none. It may be that the context "creates" a new meaning. For instance, in the lines from *Richard III* quoted earlier, "Now is the winter of our discontent/Made glorious summer by this sun of York," there are several terms for which conventional meanings do not suffice. "Winter of our discontent," for example, is nonsense if one insists on a traditional meaning for "winter." This is, of course, metaphorical language, and as such it has been discussed earlier. It's in relation to such language that form and content meet; the form of the metaphor can be, and has been, discussed separately, but its content is a part of meaning, and that meaning is contextually created. First of all, "winter of our discontent" *has no* literal meaning; these words are literally untrue, as are all metaphorical statements. There is no actual "winter" of "discontent." But the phrase becomes meaningful, and powerfully so, because the context "creates" meaning by combining these terms in a new and special way, in a way that makes us aware that in this metaphorical sense there *is* something about "winter" that fits with something about "discontent."

Lexical and contextual meanings most frequently involve parts of the selection, words or phrases, but in addition to these there is the context that is the over-all meaning of the selection. Any piece of Ritual is *one* piece of Ritual, and there is something, some force that makes for that oneness. At least, that force exists in works that have some literary value.

The parts of a selection are interrelated in basic and important ways. The beginning is related to the ending, to the middle, and vice versa. For example, look at these lines from the poem "Bannockburn" by Robert Burns:

> Scots, wha hae wi' Wallace bled,
> Scots, ham Bruce hae aften led,
> Welcome tae your gory bed!
> Or, Tae victory!

Particularly if you know the tune to which these words have been set, it is all too easy to regard them as a simple sort of folk ballad, whereas the thing is obviously a war cry, a call to battle, as witnessed by the words, "Welcome tae your gory bed!" And it doesn't become a war cry somewhere in the middle or toward the end. It starts with the word, "Scots." That first word must be related to the later words, "Welcome tae your gory bed!" If that relationship is to exist, "Scots" must mean more than "you people living in the geographical area called Scotland." And it does. It means "you people, who live in the geographical area called Scotland, do not shame your proud heritage by cowardice," or something very similar to that. In other words, some hint of the "Welcome tae your gory bed!" meaning must be contained in, must be *predictable* form the word "Scots." If it's not, the unity, the oneness of the piece is destroyed.

The larger context, the over-all meaning requires that words, phrases, sentences must make sense in relation to preceding and following words, phrases, and sentences. There's nothing new about that statement, of course. But it may be useful to consider it from a point of view based on the concept of *predictability*.

We predict the future on the basis of present and past clues. We predict future words on the basis of preceding words. The important point is that there are ties between these words. They aren't separate little chunks of meaning. Rather, they constitute sequences. There are threads of meaning running through them. And those threads stretch *from the beginnings to the ends* of these sequences.

As an illustration, here's a fairly long and involved sequence. It is from Chapter 13 of Samuel Butler's *The Way of All Flesh*. A word of caution though: dealing with excerpts from novels is dangerous in that what is true of the excerpt need not be true of the novel as a whole. The safest approach is to regard the excerpt as a work in its own right, and to consider that assumptions based on the excerpt apply to the entire novel only very tentatively. The following selection can be treated fairly easily as an isolated work, but statements about it may or may not be applicable to the complete novel.

## from *The Way of All Flesh*

For some time the pair said nothing; what they must have felt during their
first half-hour, the reader must guess, for it is beyond my power to tell him;
at the end of that time, however, Theobald had rummaged up a conclusion
from some odd corner of his soul to the effect that now he and Christina
were married the sooner they fell into their future mutual relations the
better. If people who are in a difficulty will only do the first little reasonable
thing which they can clearly recognize as reasonable, they will always find the
next step more easy both to see and take. What, then, thought Theobald,
was here at this moment the first and most obvious matter to be considered,
and what would be an equitable view of his and Christina's relative positions
in respect to it? Clearly their first dinner was their first joint entry into the
duties and pleasures of married life. No less clearly it was Christina's duty to
order it, and his own to eat it and pay for it.

The arguments leading to this conclusion, and the conclusion itself,
flashed upon Theobald about three and a half miles after he had left
Crampsford on the road to Newmarket. He had breakfasted early, but his
usual appetite had failed him. They had left the vicarage at noon without
staying for the wedding breakfast. Theobald liked an early dinner; it dawned
upon him that he was beginning to be hungry; from this to the conclusion
stated in the preceding paragraph the steps had been easy. After a few
minutes further reflection he broached the matter to his bride, and thus the
ice was broken.

Mrs. Theobald was not prepared for so sudden an assumption of
importance. Her nerves, never of the strongest, had been strung to their
highest tension by the event of the morning. She wanted to escape
observation; she was conscious of looking a little older than she quite liked to
look as a bride who had been married that morning; she feared the landlady,
the chambermaid, the waiter—everybody and everything; her heart beat so
fast that she could hardly speak, much less go through the ordeal of ordering
dinner in a strange hotel with a strange landlady. She begged and prayed to be
let off. If Theobald would only order his dinner this once, she would order it
any day and every day in the future.

But the inexorable Theobald was not to be put off with such absurd
excuses. He was master now. Had not Christina less than two hours ago
promised solemnly to honour and obey him, and was she turning restive over
such a trifle as this? The loving smile departed from his face, and was
succeeded by a scowl which that old Turk, his father, might have envied.
"Stuff and nonsense, my dear Christina," he exclaimed mildly, and stamped
his foot upon the floor of the carriage. "It is a wife's duty to order her
husband's dinner; you are my wife, and I shall expect you to order mine."
Theobald was nothing if he was not logical.

The bride began to cry, and said he was unkind; whereon he said
nothing, but revolved unutterable things in his heart. Was this, then, the end
of his six years of unflagging devotion? Was it for this that when Christina
had offered to let him off he had stuck to his engagement? Was this the
outcome of her talks about duty and spiritual-mindedness—that now upon
the very day of her marriage she should fail to see that the first step in
obedience to God lay in obedience to himself? He would drive back to

Crampsford; he would complain to Mr. and Mrs. Allaby; he didn't mean to have married Christina; he hadn't married her; it was all a hideous dream; he would—But a voice kept ringing in his ears which said: "YOU CAN'T, CAN'T, CAN'T."

"CAN'T I?" screamed the unhappy creature to himself.

"NO," said the remorseless voice, "YOU CAN'T. YOU ARE A MARRIED MAN."

He rolled back in his corner of the carriage and for the first time felt how iniquitous were the marriage laws of England.

In this selection there's a smooth, steady progression from the neutral point of view in the first few phrases to the satirical and deeply sarcastic attitude expressed at the end. Probably the first clue comes with the words, "Theobald had rummaged up a conclusion from some odd corner of his soul." To "rummage up a conclusion" is not a particularly flattering description of a mental process, and "some odd corner of his soul" seems to indicate that Theobald's interior rather resembled a junk shop. The narrator is already letting us know that he does not think too highly of Mr. Theobald. But as yet we don't know why. However, the note of wry humor makes it quite clear that further developments and explanations are entirely predictable.

The next few lines picture Theobald as a logical man. It is a pedestrian, unimaginative sort of logic, and it is certainly a far cry from the tenderness and absorption in his bride that we might expect from a just-married man. Again, the "reasonableness" and "justice" of Theobald's views make the edge of irony unmistakable, and clearly indicate trouble of some sort ahead.

In the next paragraph there is a key sentence: "Theobald liked an early dinner; it dawned upon him that he was beginning to be hungry; from this to the conclusion stated in the preceding paragraph the steps had been easy." The narrator's thrusts are becoming a bit more vicious. He shows us Theobald reacting to his appetite, and reacting in an almost simian fashion—"it dawned upon him that he was beginning to be hungry"—almost as if he were discovering some significant concept in his own hunger. The sarcasm is beginning to drip a little. And we can predict pretty accurately at this point that Theobald is in for a bad time.

The focus then moves to Mrs. Theobald, and the attitude expressed is quite different. There is no sarcasm, no satire. She is shown as a nervous, uneasy, and perhaps slightly pathetic woman. And it is those very qualities, her extreme vulnerability, that make us dislike Theobald even more.

Then back to Theobald, a Theobald who is "not to be put off with such absurd excuses," absurd meaning anything that does not agree with his own ideas, and especially anything that is full of feeling instead of logic. By this time the narrator has made it quite clear that he is pitilessly dissecting Theobald. The tiny references to her ineffectual attempts to break the engagement—"when Christina had offered to let him off he had stuck to his engagement"—and to her efforts to find spiritual qualities to take the place of the romantic ones that were obviously missing—"her talks about duty and spiritual-mindedness"—give us quick looks at the bleak history of this relationship. By now we know that Theobald is the ugliest of men—an unfeeling, unkind, inconsiderate, and unintelligent person. We are prepared for the crowning satire that must follow. And follow it does! The world, the fates have wronged poor Theobald. This ungrateful woman denies him, thwarts him. That incredible, criminal blindness of hers—to "fail to see that the first step in obedience to God lay in obedience to himself!" And finally the realization of the terrible trap into which he had fallen—the iniquitous marriage laws of England.

The slight note of irony present in the early words, "Theobald had rummaged up a conclusion," has swelled to savage satire in the later words. Yet the later savagery was predictable, in at least an oblique sense, at the very beginning. It was predictable because a piece of Ritual is one work, and it functions as a whole, as a context that determines much of the meaning of its parts.

### The Universality of Ritual

Beyond the levels of lexical and contextual meaning lies the concept of the *kind* of meaning that is possible in ritualistic work. For many centuries writers have said that Ritual deals only with certain subjects or certain sorts of meaning. Aristotle wrote:

> It is, moreover, evident from what has been said that it is not the function of the poet to relate what has happened, but what may happen—what is possible according to the law of probability or necessity. The poet and the historian differ not by writing in verse or in prose. The work of Herodotus might be put into verse, and it would still be a species of history, with meter no less than without it. The true difference is that one relates what has happened, the other what may happen. Poetry, therefore, is a more philosophical and a higher thing than history: for poetry tends to express the universal, history the particular. [110]

This notion that literature should in some way deal with universals has been treated by many writers, most of whom have used the term to mean that quality that makes a work meaningful to many persons in many places at many times. Elizabeth Drew writes:

> We read poetry because the poets, like ourselves, have been haunted by the inescapable tyranny of time and death; have suffered the pain of loss, and the more wearing, continuous pain of frustration and failure; and have had moods of unlooked-for release and peace. They have known and watched in themselves and others what Hopkins calls "dear and dogged man" and what Yeats calls "passionate fragmentary man," and how he struggles to make himself whole, and to transcend his slavery to time by completion in something beyond his own ego—in love, in nature, in art, in religion— seeking eagerly a "still point in a turning world." Or how, in default of that, man has contented himself with a serene or a wry acceptance of "things as they are." [111]

[110] Aristotle *Poetics*, ix. 2. 68.
[111] Elizabeth Drew, *Poetry: A Modern Guide to Its Understanding and Enjoyment* (New York: Dell Publishing Company, Inc., 1959), pp. 102-3.

And in another book Miss Drew says that individual poets of talent and individual poems of quality deal with basic human feelings, and that,

> there is no common human emotion which is ever out of date, for though the emotions may be attached to ways of thought and schemes of belief in which we have no part, the human needs which call them forth remain the same.[112]

The point that these, and other authors make so strongly is that great poetry, great literature, indeed great art is necessarily rooted in the human condition. It is concerned with the hurts and healings that make up man's life. No matter how specific its subject matter may *seem* to be, if it is to survive the critical ravages of time and space, it must appeal to those desires and needs that we share as humans.

For instance, the selection "Upon Julia's Clothes" that I discussed a few pages ago is, on one level, a description of a man's feeling about the way a certain woman looks in certain clothes. But on a deeper and far more important level, it touches the way all men feel about the beauty and desirability of their women. It is a kind of meaning, a kind of content, that is universal.

In other words, literature should be addressed to all men, rather than to any specific man or group of men, and that is to say it should be addressed to no *one*. Insofar as a literary work limits itself to a certain audience, it limits itself as a literary work. Professor Don Geiger makes this statement:

> Even superior work which seems to "address" a particular audience—one recalls, for example, Pope's satires, the occasional poetry of Dryden, even some of the work of Shakespeare—is memorable, we think, because it was so well formed that it transcended its local purpose. Much of the worst of these—and other—writers' work is bad, we suppose, just because it was so particularly "addressed" to some particular audience. [113]

While it's surely impossible to set down a list of *specific* subjects suitable for Ritual, there's little doubt that the works of those who live by word-magic have for centuries fallen easily into the broad categories of love, death, the beauty or the terrors of nature, loneliness, and the ugliness or tenderness of the human creature. Nearly every ritualistic work that exists deals with one or more of these areas.

What strikes me as most important here is that these subjects *transcend particular situations*. They involve attitudes, feelings, desires that are shared by all men who have been able to rise above the problems of mere survival. These subjects are, in a very basic sense, characteristic of man, of his concerns and preoccupations. Whereas Rhetoric is *situationally* defined, Ritual must escape the limits of *situation*. Rhetoric is *discourse*—language addressed to an audience. Ritual, as Susanne Langer

---

[112] Elizabeth Drew, *Discovering Poetry: An Introduction to the Nature of Poetry and the Poetic Experience* (New York: W. W. Norton & Company, Inc., 1963), p. 182.

[113] Don Geiger, *The Sound, Sense, and Performance of Literature* (Chicago: Scott, Foresman and Company, 1963), p. 77.

repeatedly indicates, [114] is *not discourse.* It is language that is available to those who will take it, who will explore it, who will make it their own by repeating it. I said that Ritual seems to me an appropriate term because it indicates the pleasure of re-saying, of re-doing over and over again, and it is just there that one major difference between Rhetoric and Ritual lies. Ordinarily we do not repeat Rhetoric, and unless that Rhetoric includes important elements of Ritual (an issue that you will have already seen looming ahead), we do not repeat it for the simple pleasure of doing so. Repeatable language, language that catches and holds us with its silence or its song, is Ritual. Language that persuades, that exists because of the demands of a given situation, and that fulfills its function *within* that situation, is Rhetoric.

Thus the two great currents of language. One devoted to practical affairs, one to the matters that define us as men. One made up of discourses directed to audiences, one of works open to all those who can enter them. One a process that is, in the main, practical and that seeks aftereffects, the other a process that is, in the main, pleasurable, and that is its own reason for being.

## Summary

Throughout history man has used language to please, and tease, and sometimes taunt himself with bitter beauty. And throughout history man has been fascinated by and has studied those uses of language. He has studied their form and content. He has found the basic ritualistic forms to be poetry, prose, and drama. Poetry, he has said, consists of rhythmical patterns in which a group of syllables is repeated a certain number of times (metrical verse) or in which a group of words is repeated (free verse), and of metaphorical language from the simplest to the most exotic. Prose form in Ritual consists of description, the viewing of some segment of reality through the feelings of the author, and narration, the telling of a story. Description depends on imagery for its effects, and narration involves various kinds of directness that include the presence or absence of sub-plots, and the use of the immediately concerned point of view, the omniscient point of view, and the personal and detached point of view. Drama is Ritual intended for performance, and its key characteristics are characterization and conflict.

Content is equivalent to meaning; the contents of a selection are what that selection means. Content or meaning is usually studied on two levels: lexical and contextual meanings, and the universality of Ritual. Lexical meanings consist of dictionary meanings and word histories, contextual meanings of the selected lexical meaning and/or the created meaning (metaphorical), and of over-all meanings that relate words, phrases, and sentences to the words, phrases, and sentences that precede and follow in such a way as to create a single, unified work. Universality, the universal meaning of Ritual, is the quality of transcending situations.

In this chapter I've talked about word-magic. It's difficult to explain magic of

---

[114] Susanne K. Langer, *Feeling and Form* (New York: Charles Scribner's Sons, 1953), p. 211. This notion is also presented at many points in Professor Langer's *Philosophy in a New Key* and in her most recent work, *Mind: An Essay on Human Feeling,* vol. I (Baltimore: The Johns Hopkins Press, 1967).

any sort in a satisfactory fashion, and word-magic is no exception. Certainly it's necessary to start somewhere, to deal with one aspect of Ritual at a time. But even more important is the reassembly of those parts. The magic works only when everything is present and functioning smoothly, and Ritual works only when its various formal and semantic aspects come together. When they do, man experiences those moments that are enriching, ennobling, and sometimes terrifying. For Ritual can bring visions of the ultimate beauties and of the ultimate horrors, and apparently man needs both visions.

You know of course what I'll be up to in this chapter. So, to it at once. The last chapter doesn't quite work. None of it is false, and yet it's not true enough. Certainly it's true, and profoundly so, that man has amazed and pleased himself in his language for many centuries, and that he has determinedly studied those pleasurable uses and forms of language. It's true that over those centuries the forms of Ritual have slowly developed into the three I described—prose, poetry, and drama. It's true that the major characteristics or elements of poetry are metaphor and rhythm, of prose, description and narration, and of drama, character and conflict (though some reworking of those items is indicated, as I shall try to show in the next chapter).

# 4

# *Ritual:*

## *An Anti-Thesis*

the
*Rain is no respecter of persons*
*The snow doesn't give a soft white*
*damn Whom it touches*
                              —*E. E. Cummings*

There's only one important problem. Compared to the shortcoming of the conventional views of Rhetoric, the ritualistic situation is simple. One thing has been left out. People.

At least two-thirds of what I said in the last chapter implied that people and language exist independently of each other. Only in discussing drama did I talk about people; *characters* are imaginary people, and *conflict* is imaginary behavior. In talking of prose and poetry, the constant implication was that those ritualistic forms were significant, moving, meaningful *in themselves*. Throughout the chapter, I made such statements as "poetry *is* a metaphorical view of reality," "prose *is* based on imagery and description," "metrical verse *is* a tightly rhythmical form," "narration *is* the unfolding story line," etc. But all those "is's" work in an unfortunate fashion: they make the quality or characteristic described an integral part of the ritualistic form; they describe qualities that inhere in the form; they posit characteristics that are *formal* in the sense that they do not depend on behavior.

Perhaps I can make the point clearer by comparing poetry and prose with drama and Rhetoric. I've already said that drama is made up of people (characters) behaving in a certain way (in conflict). That means that when we describe a dramatic work we must describe the character and his behavior. And, of course, that's just what we do. After seeing the play *Hadrian, VII*, we talk of that great scene in which Hadrian confronts his college of cardinals and convulsively empties his soul; we say, if the scene was well done, "*He* was magnificent when he broke down at the end of that scene." The point here is that "he" does *not* refer simply to the actor who plays the part; the term refers also to the character. I saw Hume Cronyn in the role, and he did a brilliant job. But in responding to the play, I say "he" meaning Cronyn on one level and meaning the character Hadrian in a much more important sense. Or after the film *A Lion in Winter* we may talk of that rich moment when *the King* leans back and says, "God, how I love being King!" When *the King* says those words, not when Peter O'Toole says them. Or we may go over in our minds the lustrous Elinor of Aquitaine, *the Queen* in the same film; we may wonder at her strength when she watches her estranged husband embrace his lovely young mistress—her statement, "I am Elinor—I can look at anything," is the utter and final proclamation of her fierceness and pride; we may repeat for ourselves the moment when she faces her sons in her tower prison, the moment when she holds her husband's weeping mistress and comforts her, or the moment when she kneels beside the King who has tried (and failed) to kill his sons and once more offers love and safety to the man who has rejected and imprisoned her. All these thoughts and repeatings may, of course, lead us away from the film; for instance, I was led to consider that extraordinary woman, the real Elinor of Aquitaine who was first queen of France then queen of England, who bore two sons who became kings, who was a major element in determining the course of French and British history for most of a century, and who, at the age of 80, managed a military campaign against her grandson Arthur of Brittany that saved Mirabeau near Poitiers for her son John. In another direction, we may wonder at Katharine Hepburn, an actress who has fooled at least three generations into believing her a great performer. But both these directions are away from the Ritual; and so long as we wonder within its limits, it is neither Miss Hepburn nor Elinor of Aquitaine that exercises us, but *the Queen,* the character of the film.

In a very similar sense, Rhetoric is the language of people in action. Rhetoric is not drama; the two differ importantly. But they share the dynamic quality of being statements by people, and by people who are actively engaged in some pursuit. Rhetoric is the theory and practice of persuasion by reasoned discourse—that is to say Rhetoric necessarily involves a persuader, the attitudes and actions of that persuader, the one persuaded (the audience), and the attitudes and actions of that audience. I talked at some length of the notions of ethical appeals, emotional appeals, style, and of the active rhetorical roles played by both rhetorician and audience. It seems to me that those notions make it literally impossible, even ludicrous, to think of Rhetoric as a thing, an object, an impersonal event. Put simply, Rhetoric involves people.

In contrast, the traditional view of poetry and prose leads too easily to the belief that those forms exist apart from people, that they are objects. We say of a piece of poetry or prose, "It is"—good, bad, happy, sad, or whatever. And I'm afraid that that's not just an unfortunate phrase. We say "it" is such-and-such, meaning that the work itself, in itself, is effective, or depressing, or exhilarating, etc. In detailed terms we talk of rhythmical patterns, point of view, diction, style, and tone of the piece, always implying that these characteristics are somehow to be found in some objective sense *in* the work. When we go a step further, we define these ritualistic forms by listing such characteristics. And at that point we have in fact said that these forms of Ritual exist and perhaps have their worth apart from human beings.

One result of this impersonal attitude toward Ritual is the prescription, "thou shalt enjoy and admire this work," rather than the descriptive approach that evaluates the work and explains how it can be enjoyed. Of course no competent critic or teacher holds this sort of prescriptive attitude, but the point is that it is all too possible for the incompetent critic or teacher to do so. It would be strange indeed for even the dunce to urge us to admire a rhetorical discourse or a piece of dramatic literature simply by declaring that rhetoric or drama is *admirable*. We'd scoff because we insist that the rhetorical or dramatic language event *prove* its worth with audiences or with critics. But unfortunately we are sometimes told that literature in general should be read and appreciated because it is, *by definition*, an ennobling and elevating thing. Literature is good: it teaches wisdom, humility, respect for one's fellows, and love of god. That attitude obviously precludes any meaningful criticism.

Another result of the separation of man and Ritual, and one that is far more dangerous because it is far more widely held, has to do with specific critical comments. For instance, although rhythm is a characteristic of life forms, we are too accustomed to the idea that verse *is* rhythmical, that a particular rhythm exists *in* the verse itself. In the last chapter I used these lines,

> Why so pale and wan, fond lover,
>
> Prithee, why so pale?
>
> Will, when looking well can't move her,
>
> Looking ill prevail?
>
> Prithee, why so pale?

and I said that the first was tetrameter, the second trimeter, the third tetrameter, and the fourth and fifth trimeter. Now on one level that's quite true. As long as you think of rhythm as being *in* the work, as existing independently of the reader or hearer of the work, it's absolutely true that there are four beats in the first line, three in the second, four in the third, and three in the fourth and fifth. But when you read these lines, i.e., when the verse is behaved by a person, something very different happens. You put in an extra silent beat at the ends of lines two, four, and five. You read "Prithee, why so pale?" (pause), and "Looking ill prevail?" (pause). With these extra beats, all the lines are really tetrameter. Of course, you can argue that silent beats don't count, somehow, but that's an odd argument because we do count them in other rhythms. We hear the bass drummer beating out Dum! (pause) Dum! (pause) Dum! Dum! Dum! (pause) in a marching band, and we instantly react to a rhythm of *two's*—One, two, One, two, One, two, etc. We don't say that the silent beats make it a rhythm of one's, or three's. Why should we do so with verse?

Or you might wonder whether or not it's a matter of making all the lines even rhythmically. Two of the lines contain four beats, and you can't very well eliminate beats when you read, so perhaps it's a matter of adding beats so that they'll all come out tetrameter. Well, that's an idea that's easy to test. Just pick a work in which all the lines are trimeter, so-called, and see what happens. I think you'll find that you *always* add an extra silent beat to lines of trimeter. If you beat out the rhythm strongly and fairly regularly, waving an arm or tapping a foot, you find that trimeter is impossible in behavioral terms. We simply don't respond to three-beat lines.

And exactly the same thing is true of hexameter and heptameter; with six-beat lines we add two silent beats, one at the end of the line, one in the middle, and with seven-beat lines we add a silent beat at the end. We do it in all cases.

All this means that rhythm is one thing in visual terms and another in behavioral and chronological terms. As long as you think of rhythm as something that exists in the line of verse, trimeter, hexameter, heptameter, etc., are entirely real. But when you think of rhythm as behavior, visual reality and performance reality become rather different things. I'm not going to deal with rhythm at length in the next chapter because it's a matter complex enough for an entire book. I hope to point out, though, that rhythm, as well as other ritualistic qualities, must be behaved, must be seen as human action, and must be treated as part of a person. And when it is, rhythm must be viewed as the rhythm that the person imposes on the work. At that point, it becomes important to talk about *human* rhythms, the rhythms in which we are all steeped by virtue of the organisms that we are. Those organic rhythms are, I believe, always duple, always rhythms of two or even multiples of two, and that's a far cry from a visually based approach to verse patterns. [115]

Even more important than the rhythmic distortion is the semantic distortion that results from the separation of people and their Ritual. Rhetorical and dramatic events mean what they mean largely because of the actions of speakers, actors, and audiences. We may say that a particular discourse or a particular performance was poor because the speaker or actor didn't do justice to the subject or the character, but we surely wouldn't say that the meaning of a given discourse or performance had no relationship to the behavior of the actor or rhetorician. Yet that's just what we tend to say about prose and poetry. Because we separate people (readers, audiences) and Ritual, we tend to answer questions about meaning by referring to the author's *intent*. A poetic or prose work, we say, means what the author intended

[115] For an interesting presentation of this man-based approach to rhythm see John Dolman, Jr., *The Art of Reading Aloud* (New York: Harper & Brothers, 1956), pp. 70-110.

it to mean. Questions about the *real* meaning of a selection we answer by turning far too easily and quickly to the author.

There are various problems involved with this business of the author's intent, but before talking about them let me make it quite clear that I am not the discoverer of these difficulties. For a good many years this pitfall has been recognized; it has been discussed as the *intentional fallacy* by literary critics. [116] I am merely following those who have argued for a viewpoint that is still too widely ignored.

Some of the problems are almost comic: for instance, if the *real* meaning of a selection is to be determined by the intent of the author, we have little to say about works whose authors are anonymous. But many are quite serious. One of them involves the fact that, since very few authors seem to have the time or the inclination to make their intentions known, even with the most famous contemporary writers we usually have little knowledge of the intended meanings of their works. Further, the writing of most authors varies qualitatively, and it seems strange to expect, say, a poet to admit that a particular work is poor or limited in value. Yet we rather blithely accept the fact of authorship as an indication of both the nature and quality of a work, except in the rare instances when an author has in some sense disclaimed one of his creations. The view I'm arguing against makes it far too easy to think that a piece of Ritual is good simply because it was authored by Cummings, or Faulkner, or Camus.

Another reason for avoiding the split between human behavior and Ritual is the need to consider the behavior of audiences in evaluating ritualistic works, rather than having to ignore those responses. So long as we say that a work means what its author says it means, we are forced to ignore the reality of the pleasure and glinting insight, or the boredom and irritation, that audiences have felt when facing that work. So long as we decree that the author is supreme critic, supreme evaluator of his own work, we must shut our eyes to the joy, or wise delight, or impatient disgust that is the experiential fact of our commerce with that work.

By now I'm describing an extreme that is grotesque, but it is nevertheless true that the depersonalization of Ritual makes it perfectly possible to say that a given work or group of works is good or bad, regardless of the responses of audiences and critics, simply because the author of the work claims for it greatness or disgrace (usually greatness). Naturally few thinking beings are going to go that far. But an approach that makes that extreme possible seems suspect to me. And it's undoubtedly true that a good many of us take the first steps along this profitless path. We say, for example, that a ritualistic work is one in which the author tries to get the reader to feel as he does—and we are immediately in trouble, for we've said that the feeling, the emotional content, *is* what the author intends for us to experience. Or we say that we can't tell whether a work was successful or not unless we know what the author was trying to do—and once more we've stumbled, for if the poem *itself* succeeds we need no further evidence of intention, and if it does not, all further evidence is remarkably unimportant.

[116] The clearest description of this, and other, fallacies is, in my judgment, W. K. Wimsatt, Jr., *The Verbal Icon* (New York: The Noonday Press, 1958), especially pp. 3-18.

For me, the oddest and saddest part of the whole business of dehumanizing Ritual is that our attention is thereby drawn *away* from the work. It might seem that the very fact of postulating ritualistic events that existed and had value *in themselves* would mean that we would then be called upon to concentrate on the work itself. It doesn't turn out that way though. To the extent that we say meaning is determined by the author's intention, we are shunted away from the prose or poem and into historical or biographical areas that will inform us of the author's life, loves, moods, interests, etc. And to the extent that we define works by a prescriptive listing of characteristics, we are led into a sort of literary mechanics—we may measure meters, determine rhyme schemes, add up allusions to this or that, or even count adjectives, verbs, or commas. All these things have been done. My argument is simply that it is the Ritual itself that should concern us, and that, except in unusual cases, the matters described above are not central to the nature or worth of Ritual. All of these and other interests may be pursued with complete validity by literary historians, biographers, sociologists, and psychologists, but such persons are involved in matters that are primarily rhetorical. And our notions about Ritual should bring us ever closer to the ritualistic process, rather than luring us away from it.

We need a view of Ritual that will allow us, indeed will force us to talk of poems and prose works in terms as dynamic as those we use for drama and Rhetoric. We need something like the notion of the *characters* in plays that will let us describe all Ritual in living, in organic terms, not as a static and lifeless "it," nor as the psychobiographical product of an author.

I'll try to satisfy that need in the coming chapter.

# Part III

RHETORIC

The title of this chapter, which is the title of Part III of this book, and of the book itself, is unsayable. And that pleases me. It pleases me because it advances an idea that seems to me to be of great importance: language is a process that is dialectical, but that may involve the analytical. I made that point early in the book, but it needs further emphasis. There is a level on which many language acts are analytical: they can be broken down into parts, the parts can be described, labeled, manipulated, etc. This sentence, for instance, consists of words and groups of words that can be described as nouns, verbs, a dependent and an independent clause; such descriptions are valid. On another level however, this sentence and these clauses are indivisible wholes, for the quality of being a dependent or independent clause, the

*singing forever*
*a song made*
*of silent as stone silence of*
*song*
　　　　　　　　*—E. E. Cummings*

quality of being complex, and the quality of being a sentence are attributes of wholes but not of parts. There are no independent or dependent, or complex or compound, or declarative or interrogative words.

Many language acts are analytical on one level, dialectical on another. Many, but not all. Some are simply dialectical; they cannot be divided into parts. And so it is with the title of this chapter. The indivisibility of that title is indicated by the fact that you cannot say it. You may try "Rhetoric-Ritual" (that's the way I refer to the book discursively), "Ritual-Rhetoric," "Rhetoric superimposed on Ritual," "Ritual as the ground of Rhetoric," and perhaps other versions are possible. But they are all distortions. The title is what it is; it cannot be stated linearly or discursively, just as a picture cannot be stated in words.

The fact of the indivisibility and unsayability of the title is significant to me because I want to begin this chapter by arguing that in all natural language Ritual and Rhetoric are intertwined and inseparable, and the title is a symbolic act that demonstrates, that *is* that inseparability.

To start with, let me set forth the proposition in a form that is quite simple: there is no dividing line between Rhetoric and Ritual, no point at which one ends and the other begins. The notion that a language event can be totally rhetorical or totally ritualistic is untenable. Partial justification for this view is found in language acts that are clearly combinations of Rhetoric and Ritual. Here are two such acts. The first is a slightly condensed version of a speech delivered by Victor Hugo on the one-hundredth anniversary of the death of Voltaire.

A hundred years today a man died. He died immortal. He departed laden with years, laden with works, laden with the most illustrious and the most fearful of responsibilities, the responsibility of the human conscience informed and rectified. He went cursed and blessed, cursed by the past, blessed by the future; and these are the two superb forms of glory. On the death-bed he had, on the one hand, the acclaim of contemporaries and of posterity; on the other, that triumph of hooting and hate which the implacable past bestows upon those who have combatted it. He was more than a man; he was an age. He had exercised a function and fulfilled a mission. . . .

. . . The eighty-four years which this man lived span the interval between the Monarchy at its apogee and the Revolution at its dawn. When he was born, Louis XIV still reigned; when he died, Louis XVI already wore the crown; so that his cradle saw the last rays of the great throne, and his coffin the first gleams from the great abyss. . . .

. . . Before the Revolution the social structure was this:
    At the base, the people;
    Above the people, religion represented by the clergy;
    By the side of religion, justice represented by the magistracy.
    And, at that period of human society, what was the people? It was ignorance. What was religion? It was intolerance. And what was justice? It was injustice. Am I going too far in my words? Judge.
    I will confine myself to the citation of two facts, but decisive.
    At Toulouse, October 13, 1761, there was found in the lower story of a house a young man hanged. The crowd gathered, the clergy fulminated, the magistracy investigated. It was a suicide; they made of it an assassination. In what interest? In the interest of religion. And who was the accused? The father. He was a Huguenot, and he wished to hinder his son from becoming a Catholic. There was here a moral monstrosity and a material impossibility; no matter! This father had killed his son; this old man had hanged this young man. Justice travailed; and this was the result. In the month of March, 1762, a man with white hair, Jean Calas, was conducted to a public place, stripped naked, stretched upon a wheel, the members bound upon it, the head hanging. Three men are there upon a scaffold, a magistrate named David, charged to superintend the punishment, a priest to hold the crucifix, and the executioner with a bar of iron in his hand. The patient, stupefied and terrible, regards not the priest, and looks at the executioner. The executioner lifts the bar of iron, and breaks one of his arms. The victim groans and swoons. The magistrate comes forward; they make the condemned inhale salts; he returns to life. Then another stroke of the bar; another groan. Calas loses consciousness; they revive him and the executioner begins again; and, as each limb before being broken in two places receives two blows, that makes eight punishments. After the eighth swooning the priest offers him the crucifix to kiss; Calas turns away his head, and the executioner gives him the *coup de*

*grâce;* that is to say, crushes in his chest with the thick end of the bar of iron. So died Jean Calas.

That lasted two hours. After his death the evidence of the suicide came to light. But an assassination had been committed. By whom? By the judges.

Another fact. After the old man, the young man. Three years later, in 1765, at Abbeville, the day after a night of storm and high wind, there was found upon the pavement of a bridge an old crucifix of worm-eaten wood, which for three centuries had been fastened to the parapet. Who had thrown down this crucifix? Who committed this sacrilege? It is not known. Perhaps a passer-by. Perhaps the wind. Who is the guilty one? The Bishop of Amiens launches a *monitoire.* Note what a *monitoire* was: it was an order to all the faithful, on pain of hell, to declare what they knew or believed they knew of such a fact; a murderous injunction, when addressed by fanaticism to ignorance. The *monitoire* of the Bishop of Amiens does its work; the town gossip assumes the character of the crime charged. Justice discovers, or believes it discovers, that on the night when the crucifix was thrown down, two men, officers, one named La Barre, and the other D'Etallonde, passed over the bridge of Abbeville, that they were drunk, and that they sang a guard-room song.

The tribunal was the Seneschalcy of Abbeville. The Seneschalcy of Abbeville was equivalent to the Court of the Capitouls of Toulouse. It was not less just. Two orders for arrest were issued. D'Etallonde escaped, La Barre was taken. Him they delivered to judicial examination. He denied having crossed the bridge; he confessed to having sung the song. The Seneschalcy of Abbeville condemned him; he appealed to the Parliament of Paris. He was conducted to Paris; the sentence was found good and confirmed. He was conducted back to Abbeville in chains. I abridge. The monstrous hour arrives. They begin by subjecting the Chevalier de la Barre to the torture ordinary and extraordinary, to make him reveal his accomplices. Accomplices in what? In having crossed a bridge and sung a song. During the torture one of his knees was broken; his confessor, on hearing the bones crack, fainted away. The next day, June 5, 1766, La Barre was drawn to the great square of Abbeville, where flamed a penitential fire; the sentence was read to La Barre; then they cut off one of his hands, then they tore out his tongue with iron pincers; then, in mercy, his head was cut off and thrown into the fire. So died the Chevalier de la Barre. He was nineteen years of age.

Then, O Voltaire; thou didst utter a cry of horror, and it will be thine eternal glory!

Then didst thou enter upon the appalling trial of the past; thou didst plead, against tyrants and monsters, the cause of the human race, and thou didst gain it. Great man, blessed be thou forever!

. . . Voltaire alone, having before his eyes those united forces, the court, the nobility, capital; that unconscious power, the blind multitude; that terrible magistracy, so severe to subjects, so docile to the master, crushing and flattering, kneeling upon the people before the king; that clergy, vile *melange* of hypocrisy and fanaticism; Voltaire alone, I repeat, declared war against that coalition of all the social iniquities, against that enormous and terrible world, and he accepted battle with it. And what was his weapon? That which has the lightness of the wind and the power of the thunderbolt—a pen.

With that weapon he fought; with that weapon he conquered.
Let us salute that memory.

The second example is the first chapter of Charles Dickens' *A Tale of Two Cities:*

It was the best of times, it was the worst of times, it was the age of wisdom, it
was the age of foolishness, it was the epoch of belief, it was the epoch of
incredulity, it was the season of Light, it was the season of Darkness, it was
the spring of hope, it was the winter of despair, we had everything before us,
we had nothing before us, we were all going direct to Heaven, we were all
going direct the other way—in short, the period was so far like the present
period that some of its noisiest authorities insisted on its being received, for
good or evil, in the superlative degree of comparison only.

There were a king with a large jaw and a queen with a plain face on the
throne of England; there were a king with a large jaw and a queen with a fair
face on the throne of France. In both countries it was clearer than crystal to
the lords of the State preserves of loaves and fishes that things in general were
settled forever.

It was the year of Our Lord one thousand seven hundred and seventy-
five. Spiritual revelations were conceded to England at that favored period, as
at this. Mrs. Southcott had recently attained her five-and-twentieth blessed
birthday, of whom a prophetic private in the Life Guards had heralded the
sublime appearance by announcing that arrangements were made for the
swallowing up of London and Westminster. Even the Cock Lane ghost had
been laid only a round dozen years, after rapping out its messages, as the
spirits of this very year last past (supernaturally deficient in originality)
rapped out theirs. Mere messages in the earthly order of events had lately
come to the English Crown and people from a congress of British subjects in
America: which, strange to relate, have proved more important to the human
race than any communications yet received through any of the chickens of
the Cock Lane brood.

France, less favored on the whole as to matters spiritual than her sister
of the shield and trident, rolled with exceeding smoothness downhill, making
paper money and spending it. Under the guidance of her Christian pastors she
entertained herself, besides, with such humane achievements as sentencing a
youth to have his hands cut off, his tongue torn out with pincers, and his
body burned alive, because he had not kneeled down in the rain to do honor
to a dirty procession of monks which passed within his view at a distance of
some fifty or sixty yards. It is likely enough that, rooted in the woods of
France and Norway there were growing trees, when that sufferer was put to
death, already marked by the Woodman, Fate, to come down and be sawn
into boards, to make a certain movable framework with a sack and a knife in
it, terrible in history. It is likely enough that in the rough outhouses of some
tillers of the heavy lands adjacent to Paris, there were sheltered from the
weather that very day, rude carts, bespattered with rustic mire, snuffed about
by pigs, and roosted in by poultry, which the Farmer, Death, had already set
apart to be his tumbrils of the Revolution. But that Woodman and that Farmer, though they work unceasingly, work silently, and no one heard them as
they went about with muffled tread: the rather, forasmuch as to entertain
any suspicion that they were awake, was to be atheistical and traitorous.

In England there was scarcely an amount of order and protection to justify much national boasting. Daring burglaries by armed men, and highway robberies, took place in the capital itself every night; families were publicly cautioned not to go out of town without removing their furniture to upholsterers' warehouses of security; the highwayman in the dark was a City tradesman in the Light, and being stopped in his character of "the Captain," gallantly shot him through the head and rode away; the mail was waylaid by seven robbers and the guard shot three dead, and then got shot dead himself by the other four, "in consequence of the failure of his ammunition," after which the mail was robbed in peace; that magnificent potentate, the Lord Mayor of London, was made to stand and deliver on Turnham Green by one highwayman who despoiled the illustrious creature in sight of all his retinue; prisoners in London jails fought battles with their turnkeys, and the majesty of the law fired blunderbusses in among them, loaded with rounds of shot and ball; thieves snipped off diamond crosses from the necks of noble lords at Court drawing-rooms; musketeers went into St. Giles' to search for contraband goods, and the mob fired on the musketeers and the musketeers fired on the mob, and nobody thought any of these occurrences much out of the common way. In the midst of them, the hangman, ever busy and ever worse than useless, was in constant requisition; now stringing up long rows of miscellaneous criminals; now hanging a housebreaker on Saturday who had been taken on Tuesday; now burning people in the hand at Newgate by the dozen, and now burning pamphlets at the door of Westminster Hall; today taking the life of an atrocious murderer, and tomorrow of a wretched pilferer who had robbed a farmer's boy of sixpence.

All these things, and a thousand like them, came to pass in and close upon the dear old year one thousand seven hundred and seventy-five. Environed by them, while the Woodman and the Farmer worked unheeded, those two of the large jaws, and those other two of the plain and fair faces, trod with stir enough, and carried their divine rights with a high hand. Thus did the year one thousand seven hundred and seventy-five conduct their Greatnesses, and myriads of small creatures—the creatures of this chronicle among the rest—along the roads that lay before them.


These two selections are about the same period in history, the same geographical areas, and many of the same specific events. They are similar in that they look with disfavor on those events. They are similar too in that they are stylistically formal rather than casual, or idiomatic, or modern.

Both are rhetorical. The Hugo speech urges that Voltaire be honored; it gives reasons for that point of view; it argues that he merited and merits our profound respect. The Dickens chapter urges a point of view toward that period and also introduces the reader to the coming novel; it fulfills a double rhetorical function.

Both are ritualistic. There is drama and tension in Hugo's recital of the chilling deaths; and the passionate outcry, "Then, O Voltaire, thou didst utter a cry of horror, and it will be thine eternal glory!" is deeply ritualistic. Dickens' opening pages are more quietly dramatic; they draw a picture of evil and human suffering, but the drawing is done in a slightly detached, even an ironic fashion. The statement that the period described "was so far like the present period that some of its noisiest authorities insisted on its being received, for good or evil, in the superlative degree of comparison only" is surely a humanely vengeful stroke at the present as well as the past.

Further, both works set out their notions with ordered clarity. Dickens' famous first paragraph carefully stresses the ambiguity of that era; then descriptions of the rulers and the ruled follow in a straightforward sequence. Hugo begins by describing the ambiguity of society's view of Voltaire "cursed by the past, blessed by the future." And he then describes the life of that time and Voltaire's reaction to it in orderly progression.

The two works are similar in many ways. Very well. But the first is *primarily* rhetorical, the second *primarily* ritualistic. *And that is just what I shall mean from now on when I label any language act;* by Rhetoric I shall mean *primarily* rhetorical; by Ritual, *primarily* ritualistic. Always *primarily*, never *wholly*. Often, as with these examples, the secondary elements are exceedingly important. I think I'd say, if I had to play a numbers game, that these illustrations are about 55-45—55% Rhetoric, 45% Ritual, and *vice versa*. The Hugo speech has ritualistic elements that are of major importance, but it is still a piece of language whose primary function is to urge us to honor Voltaire. The Dickens chapter contains an extremely important rhetorical dimension, but it presents, first of all, an imaginative picture of a past era—a picture that leads us into a story that takes place in that era.

There may be blends of Rhetoric and Ritual that are still more even. In fact, I'm perfectly willing to accept the notion of works that are, for all practical purposes, half and half. The most likely candidates for a 50-50 split between Rhetoric and Ritual may well be plays, poems, songs, etc. that have obvious persuasive or propaganda values. The *Long Island Press* of May 18, 1969, described a series of plays that the District Attorney of Queens County, New York sponsored. The plays were put on for school audiences as part of an attempt to fight drug addiction in teenagers; the plots had to do with narcotics addiction among pupils. A dramatic project much like that one was undertaken in Los Angeles recently. In this case, the Inner City Cultural Center put on an agitprop theatrical venture that was, on one level, an outright argument for equal rights for Chicanos. The actors were Mexican farm workers using drama for obvious social purposes. Yet their work remained drama. According to a theatrical reviewer, the "rambunctious sketches go back to the very roots of theatre, and beautifully fulfill the twin tasks the medium has always set for itself: to delight and instruct."[117] And it is my own feeling that a very large amount of the poetry and music of the youth movement combines Rhetoric and Ritual about evenly. Indeed, I wonder whether some of the unsympathetic over-thirty responses to rock music aren't due to the attempt to hear Rhetoric as Ritual.

But my argument is incomplete. There may be some instances in which language is both rhetorical and ritualistic, even equally so, as with the examples I've mentioned. Still, that's no indication that *all* Rhetoric involves Ritual, and *vice versa*. To demonstrate that point, I must turn to natural language acts that are not

[117] *The Los Angeles Times*, September 27, 1969, part II, p. 9.

only not close to each other, as were the Hugo speech and the Dickens chapter, but that are as far apart as possible. If I can find Rhetoric in even the wildest Ritual and Ritual in even the most sedate Rhetoric, I think I'll have proved my point.

One extreme form of Rhetoric is the language of scholars, especially scholars who are attempting to be persuasive in a precise and controlled manner. Here's what seems to me to be a pretty good example of that sort of Rhetoric. It's from a doctoral dissertation, and one that is, in my judgment, exceedingly important. You will, if you garner the appropriate clues, discern here *two* major sources of many of the ideas in this book.

I'm going to quote at some length because the ritualistic dimension here is, as I've said, a narrow one, and a brief passage would make discussion difficult.

Because any theory of rhetoric must explain how men may be influenced, all such theories presuppose a theory of man. Each underlying ontology provides an explanation of human persuadability which locates the capacities, processes, and/or goals which the persuader may use in order to influence human behavior. Sartrean ontology has three major rhetorical implications. First, the ontology implies that all theories of rhetoric which proceed from essentialistic theories of man or deterministic views of human behavior will be indefensible and inconsistent. Sartre argues that if man acts at all, determinations to action or motives must also be actions, i.e., free choices. As essentialistic and deterministic doctrines argue that man is either internally or externally determined, Sartre contends that they preclude choice, freedom, and action. As a critique of presuppositions, Sartrean philosophy forces rhetorical theorists to confront this dilemma and decide whether or not persuasion, among the various means of influence, is to be defined as that means characterized by the exercise of free choice. If rhetorical theorists accept freedom and choice as basic characteristics of man, their theories of rhetoric will necessarily be based on language as a symbol system and man as a symbol-user. For only in this way can a theory of rhetoric be formed which will both evade the pitfalls of essentialism and determinism and be consistent with the natures of language, man, and freedom as the means, agent, and the goal in a process whereby self-disclosure and self-definition may occur.

Second, Sartrean ontology implies that all theories of rhetoric which proceed from rationalistic theories of man are incomplete, hence inadequate. The ontology argues that all human acts are intending, transcending, and negating, and that each act is a symbolic synthesis of the objective and subjective and of the cognitive and the evaluative. According to Sartre, rationalistic theories merely account for one possible choice of means toward ends which are pre-rationally chosen. They cannot account for the choice of ends or explain the synthetic character of man's symbolic acts. Sartrean ontology forces rhetorical theorists to question whether or not a rationalistic theory of man takes adequate account of all the elements of human behavior. If rhetorical theorists accept the notion that language is always evaluative and that all acts contain non-rational elements, a notion that is clearly indicated not only by Sartre's arguments but by recent experimentation in the field, they will necessarily create theories of rhetoric that include the rational and the non-rational, the logical and the emotional, the objective and the subjective. In a word, they will necessarily create theories of rhetoric based squarely on the nature of language as a symbol system and man as a symbol-user.

Third, Sartrean philosophy implies that the only adequate and viable onto-logical basis for a theory of rhetoric is one which explains human persuadability as a function of man's capacity for using symbols. If that capacity is to be consistent with the two previous implications of Sartrean ontology, it must exist in the ability of the individual to make choices for himself without in any way determining the choices of others. In other words, Sartre's ontology requires that the major focus of rhetoric be shifted from persuasion as an interpersonal use of language to self-persuasion as an intrapersonal use of language. It is via self-persuasion that the rhetorician makes choices for him-self and acts as a catalyst that allows, and perhaps facilitates, but in no way predetermines, the choices of others. In a rhetorical situation, self-persuasion or the intrapersonal use of language is a phenomenon to which an auditor may respond by initiating another self-suasory, intrapersonal process. There is an interpersonal element involved, but it is in no sense a controlling or a mani-pulative one. It exists, rather, in the fact that two self-persuasive, intra-personal uses of language are related to each other in terms of the rhetorical and social context in which they occur. One final point must be made in this description of Sartre's view of man and his language. It is that the self-persuasive or intrapersonal use of language is under no circumstances to be considered as mere self-expression or as a process that is empty, idle, or undemanding of the speaker. Indeed, Sartre's position is precisely the opposite. He sees self-persuasion as self-assertion, self-discovery, self-disclosure, and self-creation. He argues strongly that in the acts of assertion, discovery, disclosure, and creation, the self constantly faces risks, is constant-ly required to make commitments, and constantly undergoes transformations. These acts have the same demanding and even painful qualities for all partici-pants in the rhetorical situation. That is to say, the auditor who initiates his own self-persuasion will himself face the same risks, the same commitments, and the same transformations. The two processes, that of the rhetor and that of the auditor, are similar in that they both involve symbolic rigors and per-sonal risks. This similarity is the only interpersonal aspect of rhetorical dis-course and can be understood only in terms of the social and historical situa-tion in which it develops.[118]

Now that's a mouthful and a mindful, of course. If you got through it, it will have taken some effort. And that's one reason I chose it, for it's those language acts, rhetorical or ritualistic, that are a bit removed from us, that are a bit unfamiliar and a bit difficult that we are likely to judge most accurately. For example, you may have heard or said the pledge of allegiance to the flag a good many times, but I'd guess that you'd find some problems in dealing with it, as Rhetoric *or* Ritual, largely because it's too close, too known. Of course, language events that are too remote from our experiences and abilities cause other problems, but the fact that you've followed me this far makes me feel that the above excerpt is only difficult, not impossible.

[118] Karlyn Kohrs Campbell, "The Rhetorical Implications of the Philosophy of Jean-Paul Sartre" (unpublished doctoral dissertation, University of Minnesota, 1968), pp. 277-281.

It's Rhetoric, quite obviously. The major symbolic effort is devoted to a summation of the relationship between Sartre's theory of man and a workable theory of Rhetoric. But the manner in which the effort is expended betrays an element of Ritual. There's a force, a drive to this language. The parallelism of the structure of this discourse—the three implications of Sartre's thought, then the implications of each of those implications—adds to this drive. There's a sense of strong purpose here. It's not an overtly passionate or flamboyant statement, but it's language that is highly energized. The writer pursues a line of thought with determination; you get no feeling of looseness, of wandering around, of aimlessness. This language, and the thought within it, is taut, purposeful, sculpted.

In speaking of just this sort of language, Susanne Langer writes:

> Literal, logical thought has a characteristic form, which is known as "discursive," because it is the form of discourse. Language is the prime instrument of thought, and the product bears the stamp of the fashioning tool. A writer with literary imagination perceives even this familiar form as a vehicle of feeling—the feeling that naturally inheres in studious thinking, the growing intensity of a problem as it becomes more and more complex, and at the same time more definite and "thinkable," until the demand for the answer is urgent, touched with impatience; the holding back of assent as the explanation is prepared; the cadential feeling of solution, and the expanding of consciousness in new knowledge. If all these phases merge in one configured passage, the thought, however hard, is natural; and the height of discursive style is the embodiment of such a feeling pattern, modeled, word by word, on the progressing argument. The argument is the writer's motif, and absolutely nothing else may enter in.[119]

As with many of Professor Langer's observations, I am mightily impressed by these words. What a far cry this is from notions of neutral, impersonal, or informative discourse. Notice the sense of tension and cadence that is described in almost sensual terms. Sensual! For scholarly writing! The invitation to comedy is obvious, but look at the doors that are opened, the approaches that are possible to Rhetoric. No longer is rhetorical discourse basically nonemotional; no longer is that terrible division between thinking and feeling either necessary or justifiable, as Professor Langer makes very clear[120]; rather, *thinking is one form of feeling.* And discursive writing, scholarly writing is language that is laden with feeling.

Back to the example. Part of the force of this language comes from its density, its closely packed thought. The opening sentence will do as an illustration: "Because any theory of rhetoric must explain how man may be influenced, all such theories presuppose a theory of man." Here are the ideas that seem to me to be included in that sentence: (1) a theory of rhetoric is a theory about the ways that men persuade or influence men; (2) the persuasive abilities that one postulates will vary according to the underlying assumptions about man's nature; (3) any

---

[119] Langer, *Feeling and Form*, p. 302. I must add that Professor Langer does not call this kind of language "Rhetoric," but uses that term in quite a different fashion.

[120] *Ibid.*, pp. 378-79.

rhetorical theory that ignores the nature of man the persuader and the persuaded will be empty or incomplete; (4) thus every theory of rhetoric must also be a theory of man (ontology). Now it's not that it's particularly difficult to see those ideas in that opening sentence; in fact they're rather obvious. The point is that the sentence is densely constructed. The thought has been compacted, tamped down, till this sentence, like those that follow, has a mass that creates an impact when it meets the reader's mind. You find yourself involved very directly in this language; you must think as you read it. There's no possibility of skimming along the surface. The argument moves steadily onward *if*, and only if, you the reader make it move.

Here is language that is primarily rhetorical but that includes the qualities of strength, purposefulness, density, tightly worked reasoning, and a thrusting, driving, controlled feeling of opening up ideas. Those qualities I can only call ritualistic. And that means that even in so rhetorical a language act as this, I find an important dimension of Ritual.

If you compare the ritualistic dimension of this excerpt with that of Lincoln's "Gettysburg Address," it becomes clear, I think, that that address is *primarily* ritualistic. Consider the levels of Ritual that are involved. First, the very act of dedicating part of a battlefield as a home for the dead—Ritual of the most ancient sort. Second, the verbal act of honoring, of making heroes of those dead — equally ancient Ritual. Third, the admonition to complete the work the noble dead have started, i.e., to follow their course. Fourth, the rhythmic verbal Ritual — the short phrases that repeat themselves with greater or lesser variations, as "Our fathers brought forth on this continent," "Now we are engaged in a great civil war," "We are met on a great battlefield of that war," "We have come to dedicate a portion of that field," "conceived in liberty," "dedicated to the proposition," "so conceived," "so dedicated," "we cannot dedicate," "we cannot consecrate," "we cannot hallow," and many others, including of course, "of the people," "by the people," "for the people"—all these phrases make the address highly rhythmical and give it the quality of being almost intoned or chanted. Fifth, the formal, the almost biblical style—"Four score and seven years ago," "It is altogether fitting and proper that we should do this," "that we here highly resolve," "that from these honored dead we take increased devotion," etc. In sum, whatever function this discourse may have fulfilled initially, it is, I believe, predominantly ritualistic now.

And now for the other extreme. Here is a lyric poem, a form of Ritual that is quite distant from Rhetoric.

So, We'll Go No More A-Roving

So, we'll go no more a-roving
  So late into the night,
Though the heart be still as loving,
  And the moon be still as bright.

For the sword outwears its sheath,
  And the soul outwears the breast,
And the heart must pause to breathe,
  And love itself have rest.

Though the night was made for loving,
And the day returns too soon,
Yet we'll go no more a-roving
By the light of the moon.

—George Gordon, Lord Byron


Ritual, obviously. It's a song of sadness. The roving is over because of age (or death?). The heart is "still as loving," but the roving is done, beckon as the moon may. Clearly, this is not what we'd normally call persuasive discourse. Yet, is there an element of persuasion, a rhetorical dimension?

Yes. It seems clearest to me *in the change* between the first and second stanzas. In the first four lines, the point of view is that of one involved in the action: *we'll* rove no more. But the second stanza changes a bit: there the viewpoint is more nearly that of one outside the action. There an attitude is taken that covers more than this one case of roving no longer; general reasons are given as to why roving must end. In a word, the second stanza is more rhetorical. I overstate the case of course; it's actually a matter of degree, and very slight degree at that. But a change there is, and it's toward the rhetorical.

And even in the first and third stanzas there's more than a touch of rhetoric, for both those stanzas are *reasoned*. In the first stanza the statement is that we'll rove no more, "*Though* the heart be still as loving," and in the third, "*Though* the night was made for loving,/ And the day returns too soon,/Yet we'll go no more a-roving." There's an attitude expressed here that is essentially a reasoned one. Here's why we'll rove no more, to paraphrase it with rough simplicity.

So, Ritual, yes, but laced with Rhetoric, just as earlier the Rhetoric was veined with Ritual. And that concludes the opening argument of this final chapter. Rhetoric and Ritual are indivisible, for each exists in the other, whether on a level of equal importance, as secondary but still major elements, or as the thinnest edge of the persuasive in the ritualistic or the poetic in the rhetorical. There simply is no natural language event that can be imagined that is not both rhetorical and ritualistic (and that, of course, is the reason that Part III of this book consists of a *single* chapter).

Now, because it's quite a long one, a brief preview of the rest of this chapter. I've argued that Rhetoric and Ritual are inseparable. Next I'm going to propose the idea that the two are not of equal symbolic stature, but that Ritual is the ground of Rhetoric. Following that, a fairly short section on Rhetoric and Ritual as the limits of language, or the limits beyond which language begins to deteriorate. Then two major sections: the first proposing a view of Rhetoric that solves most of the problems pointed out in Chapter 2; the second, a view of Ritual that eliminates most of the defects mentioned in Chapter 4. And finally a concluding statement on the dialectical and dynamic relationship between Rhetoric and Ritual, and the sense in which that relationship explains many individual and social conditions and the symbolic stresses inherent in them.

## Ritual as the Ground of Rhetoric [121]

In talking about Style in Chapter 1, I pointed out that the majority of rhetorical and philosophical views of language rested on the assumption that the most basic and most important function of language was an interpersonal and a practical or communicative one. Then I argued that that assumption was not justifiable, but that language was *constitutive* before it was *communicative*, that we must constitute ourselves in and with our language before we can use that language to communicate. I want to continue that argument in this section, first by talking about language as intrapersonal behavior, then by discussing language as poetic behavior.

### Language as Intrapersonal Process

You remember that I talked about constitutive language acts that ranged from the simple shouted "Damn!" on pounding your thumb with a hammer, to singing in the shower, to the characteristic sloppiness or formality or warmth of our language behaviors. All these are constitutive language elements in the sense that they do not depend on the communicative demands of a particular situation, but are traits or characteristics of the individual user of language. For example, my tendency to use double or triple terms, as "traits or characteristics" in the previous sentence, is not limited to or dependent on requirements of a communicative situation, but is part of me, is an element of my symbolic being. Therefore such language processes are *intrapersonal* because their very existence constitutes the person, the individual, rather than depending on the relationship between persons. These processes are not instances of talking *to* others, or even of talking *to* ourselves, but are examples of *simply talking*. And as I emphasized in the Introduction, we are talking creatures, symbol-using animals. Take away our language, verbal and nonverbal, and you take away our humanity, for the two are one. There is no such thing as a *non*language-using human: to be human is to talk, silently or aloud, and not to talk *to* oneself or *to* others only but simply to talk.

But it's one thing to recognize the intrapersonal character of the "Damn!" when you pound your thumb, or the awed "o-o-o-h" on seeing a glorious sunset or a magnificent performance of *Hamlet* or *The Messiah*. That, I think, is fairly clear. We've all experienced that sort of language reality too frequently to mistake it for anything but what it is—an intrapersonal and constitutive use of language. It's quite another thing, though, to see the intrapersonal basis of such language events as a conversation between two people or a rhetorical discourse that is created by a writer or speaker and heard or read by an audience of many others. In those cases, the language act seems so clearly interpersonal. And, of course, on one level it obviously *is* interpersonal, for two or more people are involved. Yet even in those instances language is intrapersonal on its most basic level.

The argument for this intrapersonal basis of language rests on the idea of *listening*, and I use that term in a sense broad enough to include oral and silent

---

[121] Again, much of the material in this section first appeared as "Language as Intrapersonal and Poetic Process." *Philosophy and Rhetoric II*, 4: 200-212.

language. That is, you "listen" to a speech and also to essays, novels, etc.; you "listen" to oral utterances and to such language acts as this book. Auditors and readers are included in the group of symbol-users I call "listeners." Or, put in a slightly different manner, listeners are the *receivers* I talked about in Chapter 2; all those who receive messages, written or oral, I call *listeners*.

For a long time it's been assumed that three basic language acts were possible: talking to others, talking to yourself, and listening to the talk of others. The first two of these seem to me to cause no problems unless a sharp division between them is postulated. The familiar act of telling someone else of our own courage, or honesty, or candor, when in reality we are trying to persuade ourselves that we are courageous, or honest, or candid, appears to me to show quite clearly that we can and do talk to ourselves and to others at the same time.

It's the third notion, listening to the talk of others, that I find troublesome. It all seems simple enough, you talk and I listen *to* you, but I think it doesn't work that way. In Chapter 2, I indicated the idea of the passive nature of the listener which results from the usual notion of listening: the speaker or writer is the active agent, the listener the passive recipient of the other's words, the other's language. At this point I'm going to propose the idea that there is no simple or direct sense in which I can listen to you, or you to me, but that basically we must ever and always *listen to ourselves*. An extreme notion surely, but one that I think will prove workable.

Perhaps the simplest level of listening to oneself is indicated by the fact that congenitally deaf persons never develop anything like normal speech. It seems clear that the ability to acquire oral language depends on the ability to hear, to listen to oneself. Further, experimental tests in which people are prevented from listening normally to their own speech show that marked changes result; under such circumstances, people lose a significant amount of speech fluency.[122]

Of course this is a very basic level of language activity, almost a biological one. By itself it's unconvincing, for it can easily be argued that "hearing" and "listening" are quite different processes, that hearing is the simple ability to perceive sound, listening the ability to perceive *and interpret* language symbols. So further evidence is needed.

On a somewhat more complicated level, the science of phonetics seems to justify the idea that we listen to ourselves. A very few years ago phoneticians considered that speech consisted of actual acoustical events called *allophones* that were perceptually organized into groups called *phonemes* on the basis of distinctive and nondistinctive differences. That is, it was assumed that listeners to oral language responded to actual acoustical stimuli and that what they heard actually existed. Today the picture is much less simple. Recent thinking indicates that *actual* acoustical events, now called *phones*, bear nothing like a one-to-one relationship to *perceived* acoustical events, either on the grosser level of perceptual organization called *phonemic*, or the finer discriminatory level called *allophonic*.[123] In fact, for

[122] Hayes A. Newby, *Audiology* (New York: Appleton-Century-Crofts, 1958), p. 165.
[123] As early as 1943, however, this state of phonetic affairs was foreseen by Kenneth Pike, *Phonetics* (Ann Arbor: The University of Michigan Press, 1943), p. 115.

a significant amount of perceived acoustical reality, phonemic or allophonic, it can be instrumentally determined that there are *no* existent phones corresponding even indirectly to the sounds that are "heard." Apparently what is involved is a kind of pattern recognition in which a certain number of actual acoustical events prompts us to take over, to complete the pattern by assuming the existence of the remaining phones, and then to organize those events into phonemic structures which may have no objectively real counterparts at all. [124] These processes of taking over, filling in missing parts, and then organizing both real and filled-in parts into perceptual units are intrapersonal acts that seem to me to be fairly described as a species of listening to the self. I note especially that the filling-in and organizing transcends speech in that the filled-in items are not accoustical units but are part of internal or silent language. So even at this level *hearing* is not merely a matter of *perceiving* sound *per se*, but includes an *interpretative*, a filling-in element that must be called *listening*. Finally, the processes described appear to involve built-in activities or behaviors that are part of the listener, that inhere in his nature, rather than being some sort of response to external stimuli,[125] some sort of listening to another.

The argument remains inconclusive though. In addition to the somewhat technical nature of the ideas just described, it can be objected that they are still overly simple, that they concern our responses to sounds but say little about our responses to other persons.

Moving then to a much more sophisticated and personalized language act, it's my belief that the symbolic behaviors that make up the intimate and delicately convoluted language event known as psychotherapy constitute one of the most telling arguments for listening to oneself. It's a truism that the psychotherapist is worthless to his patient if he cannot identify with, cannot put himself in the situation of, cannot emphatically adopt the frame of reference of that patient.[126] I take this to mean that it's a waste of time for the therapist to sit and *listen to another person*, or to try to. Rather he must put himself in that person's emotional shoes so that he can see how it feels, so that he can tell himself, and as a result, *listen to himself*. For the patient the process is surprisingly similar, for the important point in therapy is reached, not when the patient perceives that the therapist is telling him something of emotional value, but when he begins to tell himself and to listen to himself. [127] In that regard it's significant and revealing that groups such as Alcoholics Anonymous nearly always require ritualistic behaviors in which one says, "I am an . . ." alcoholic, addict, etc. When that statement is listened to by the person who utters it, change is possible.

[124] To my knowledge, the most complete treatment of this issue occurs in William H. Perkins, *Speech Pathology: An Applied Behavioral Science* (St. Louis: The C. V. Mosby Company, 1971), Chapter 3.

[125] Alvin Liberman, *et al.*, "Perception of the Speech Code," *Psychological Review* LXXIV (1967): 431-36.

[126] Probably the most extreme view of this empathic process is taken by Carl R. Rogers, *Client-Centered Therapy* (Boston: Houghton Mifflin Company, 1951).

[127] A particularly vivid illustration of this self-telling and self-listening is found in Beulah Parker, *My Language Is Me* (New York: Basic Books, Inc., 1962).

The argument has developed, but it still seems to me to be of limited worth because I haven't talked of the most typical language acts that concern us. Let me move now to just those acts.

The facts of experience indicate unmistakably that in our ordinary daily conversations, written and oral, the other person very often listens so intently to himself that he doesn't hear what we say. He seems so clearly to listen to his own preformed statements, to hear what he wants to hear. (We don't recognize such actions on our own part, of course.) And in a very similar fashion, readers of this book (or of any written Rhetoric) are not "hearing" *me*. I've said what I've said, written what I've written, and if there were any direct link between my words and the readers' reactions, those reactions would be identical, or approximately so. They aren't, of course. And they aren't because, strictly speaking, readers don't read *my* words. They *see* squiggles on the page, but before *reading* can occur readers must interpret these squiggles, must translate them into *their own* words. And it is *their* words that they then read. The translations may bridge narrow crevices or gaping chasms; the change from another's statements to statements of your own may involve slight or drastic alterations. The translated versions of the message may resemble the original version of the message very closely or not at all, but in all cases it's the translated version, your own version, that you listen to.

Expanding this last point to include the comment on the nature of meaning that I made in the Introduction and Chapter 2, we listen to ourselves because meaning is experientially based. Words, or at least groups of words, are meaningful because they are symbols. But symbols for what? *Not* for objects or events, for that leads to the positivistic view that ties words directly to things and eliminates the possibility of connotative, emotional, subjective elements of meaning. If "cat," or "witch," or "fear" are labels for actual objects or events, it must follow that the only function of language, and of human beings, is to use those words to report on or describe objective reality. In such a view of meaning there's no room for the imaginative, the fanciful, or the poetic, for none of those processes need deal with outer reality at all. Necessarily then words are symbols, not for things, but for my or your *experiences* with those things. And because our experiences differ in many ways, including the emotional and the poetic, there's room in the meaning of words for highly subjective elements. "Book" means one thing to me partly because I know what it is to write books, something slightly different to the next person, partly because he has not written books and may not even read them. The point of it all is simply that, because meanings are based on experiences, and because experiences are subjective, are mine or yours, meanings too must be subjective, must be mine or yours. Our meanings will be similar to the extent that our experiences are similar, and our experiences are often very similar indeed. But they are never identical, and that means that no matter how great the similarity, I must always interpret or create meanings that are based on my experiences. I must always listen to myself. [128]

[128] I have, of course, put this argument strongly, if not bluntly. Those who feel I have overstated the case are referred to John Caffrey, "Auding," *Review of Educational Research* XXV (April 1955): 121-38, Richard H. Henneman, "Vision and Audition as

And that seems to me to complete the argument, or very nearly so. If, in language acts ranging all the way from the perception of the individual sounds that make up words to the use of emotionally significant or loaded language and to the ordinary business of reading and conversing, there's a basic subjective element that's present, the idea that we always listen to ourselves has been justified. But I said "or very nearly so" because of the question that still remains to be answered — What of the danger of solipsism? of ending up encased in private little worlds that float along never touching? of eternally listening to one's own voice and never hearing the voices from outside?

That danger exists but is avoidable. It is avoidable because language is an *active* process. Neither speaker/writer nor reader/listener is a passive participant in the act of language. Both are active agents. In Chapter 1, I spoke of Weaver's notion that language is "sermonic." All uses of language are *active* in that they disclose and affirm an attitude, a point of view. In that first chapter I was concerned with this notion because it indicated the persuasive dimension of language. Here I'm concerned with the same notion because it reveals the active and intrapersonal aspect of language. All my language acts are sermonic; they reveal my attitudes, i.e., my incipient or potential *actions*. That is to say, as rhetorician or audience I am constantly behaving persuasively. But beneath that persuasive act is an intrapersonal and an *active* one. Whether I speak or write to an audience of thousands or simply to myself, there is a level on which I am *acting* for myself, intrapersonally. Thus, in the most obviously interpersonal language event there is a basic symbolic reality that is intrapersonal and *active,* for no matter how many persons are involved, no matter how social the context, at bottom it is a matter of *each* individual *reaching out* empathically to the other(s). Each person is involved in the process of imaginatively transcending his symbolic boundaries. The transcendance is never total; two human beings can never touch in any utter, final sense, for to do so would destroy the symbolic nature of both the act and the actors. Still, each can transcend his usual limits, and the two can meet on an intermediate symbolic ground that is known to both but owned by neither. Just such a meeting may constitute this book: you may understand me, but you cannot think my thoughts, voice my arguments, or speak my words. The bridge between us can never be completed. We are forever limited to the intrapersonal reality of our own language, but in the shared act of attempting to touch we avoid the closed and meaningless isolation of separate and entirely private worlds.

Hugh Dalziel Duncan has written of just this process:

> If writers are to express what is of concern to the members of their society
> through conscious exploration of emotional stresses common to all, they
> must be able to explore their own emotions freely, to express these explora-·
> tions in their own symbolic forms, and, finally, to communicate the results of
> this exploration as they see fit. This is what writers mean by "autonomy."

Sensory Channels for Communication," *Quarterly Journal of Speech* XXXVIII, 2: 161-66, Charles M. Kelly, "Listening: Complex of Activities—and a Unitary Skill?" *Speech Monographs* XXXIV, 4: 455-65, and Giles W. Gray and Claude M. Wise, *The Bases of Speech,* third ed. (New York: Harper and Row, Publishers, Inc., 1959), pp. 60-65.

When the writer functions in this way, he is not trying to produce a preconceived emotional effect (as in advertising, propaganda, or liturgy) in his public but to explore his own emotions through imagination, for the purpose of creating forms of expression, which allow him to "understand" his emotions and, by communicating this process to a public, to enable individuals within this public to undertake a similar process and thus make similar discoveries about themselves. [129]

And in somewhat broader terms, the concept of communication has been described as follows:

We cannot actually and literally *communicate* or *transfer* meanings to others; all we can hope to do is *stir up* meanings in others. Therefore, the meanings which the reactor gets come not from the speaker but from himself. [130]

Finally, as is often the case, Kenneth Burke has perhaps said it best:

Only those voices from without are effective which can speak in the language of the voice within. [131]

So much for the intrapersonal basis of language. Now for a closely related notion.

### Language as Poetic Process

Several theorists have argued that the most fundamental aspects of language are not practical and instrumental, but are consummatory and poetic. That is, language is most basically a symbolic activity that is pleasurable and that is its own reason for being. David K. Berlo employs the term "instrumental" to mean acts whose values exist in the results they cause and "consummatory" to mean those acts that are pleasurable in themselves. [132]

I think the clearest evidence of the poetic basis of language is to be found in the beginnings of language, viewed both ontogenetically and phylogenetically— both in the human race and the human individual. Susanne Langer suggests that as a race we found poetic values in our symbolic acts before we turned those acts to practical purposes.

The first symbolic value of words is probably purely connotative, like that of ritual; a certain string of syllables, just like a rite, embodies a concept, as "hallelujah" embodies much of the concept expressed in the Easter service.

[129] Hugh Dalziel Duncan, *Language and Literature in Society* (Chicago: The University of Chicago Press, 1953), p. 9.

[130] Andrew T. Weaver, "What Is Speech? A Symposium," *Quarterly Journal of Speech* XLI, 2: 152.

[131] Burke, *A Rhetoric of Motives*, p. 563.

[132] David K. Berlo, *The Process of Communication: An Introduction to Theory and Practice* (New York: Holt, Rinehart and Winston, 1960), pp. 17-18.

But "hallelujah" is not the name of any thing, act, or property; it is neither noun, verb, adjective, nor any other syntactical part of speech. So long as articulate sound serves only in the capacity of "hallelujah" or "alack-a-day," it cannot fairly be called language; for although it has connotation, it has no denotation.[133]

Then Professor Langer explains the development of language, the change from poetic symbolic acts to those that are practical as well.

The utterance of conception-laden sounds, at the sight of things that exemplify one or another of the conceptions which those sounds carry, is first a purely expressive reaction; only long habit can fix an association so securely that the word and the object are felt to belong together, so that the one is always a reminder of the other. But when this point is reached, the humanoid creature will undoubtedly utter the sound in sport, and thus move the object into nearer and clearer prominence in his mind, until he may be said to *grasp* a conception of it by means of the sound; and *now the sound is a word.* [134]

These excerpts seem to me to make plain the idea that language began as sport, as play, as pleasurable symbolic acts. Those acts acquired communicative and practical dimensions later on, but I think it's exceedingly important to remember that they began as play, as poetry, and that we simply can't assume that their earlier nature vanished. Rather, that early poetic nature remained, remains still, and is to be found underneath the instrumental and communicative aspects of language.

Putting this issue in simpler but broader terms, Kenneth Burke writes:

As for poetics pure and simple: I would take this motivational dimension to involve the sheer exercise of "symbolicity" (or "symbolic action") for its own sake, purely for love of the art. If man is characteristically the symbol-using animal, then he should take pleasure in the use of his powers as a symbolizer, just as a bird presumably likes to fly or a fish to swim. [135]

Burke's comment points out the profundity of our poetic acts. We don't come to poetry as a kind of fanciful added-on window-dressing; instead we are *basically* poets because it is our nature to create and use symbols, and the exercise of that natural ability is pleasing, i.e., poetic.

Much the same thing happens in the individual. The notion that as infants we acquire language in order to communicate is contradicted by many things. First, if communication were the goal, it would be logical to assume that the child learned sounds, combined those sounds into words, the words into sentences, etc., in some sort of deliberate effort to affect his environment; but it's been pointed out that there are at least $10^{20}$ sentences 20 words long, and if the child set himself the task

---

[133] Susanne K. Langer, *Philosophy in a New Key*, pp. 118-19.
[134] *Ibid.*, p. 119.
[135] Burke, *Language as Symbolic Action*, p. 29.

of learning only these sentences it would take approximately 1,000 times the age of the earth just to listen to them. [136] Second, the symbolic behavior that directly precedes speech, the babbling stage, is markedly noncommunicative in nature, for the infant babbles endlessly and seemingly with much pleasure to nonspeaking objects such as toys, furniture, etc., and *most frequently of all when he's alone.* Third, infants succeed in communicating quite well before they've acquired any verbal language at all. They cry, gesture, throw tantrums, all very effectively, and these behaviors must be based on a sort of inner language that is nonverbal, possibly consisting of visual and kinaesthetic imagery. And fourth, the only theories that seem to fit the available evidence directly oppose the notion of communication as the goal of language learning: Mowrer's Autism Theory, for example, suggests that the infant experiences pleasure at the attentions paid him by the mother, attentions that include holding, caressing, and *talking;* that therefore the sound of the mother's voice becomes associated with pleasure; that the infant, unable to distinguish with any clarity between inner and outer reality, finds the same pleasure in hearing his own voice that he does in hearing the mother's; that slowly he develops the ability to distinguish between the sounds he produces and those his mother utters; and that in order to maintain the identification of his own speech with that of the mother (thereby continuing the pleasurable bond between the two) he must change his speech so that it approximates ever more closely that of the mother. [137] Finally of course, the infant produces words and experiences the reward that will eventually lead him to perfect his communicative abilities.

Professor Langer quotes another author on the development of language in the individual human being:

> "The primary function of language is generally said to be communication. . . .
> The autistic speech of children seems to show that the purely communicative aspect of language has been exaggerated. It is best to admit that language is primarily a vocal actualization of the tendency to see reality symbolically, that it is precisely this quality which renders it a fit instrument for communication, and that it is in the actual give and take of social intercourse that it has been complicated and refined into the form in which it is known today." [138]

And again we are led to the act of symbolization as the basis of language, an act that Burke has already said is pleasurable in itself, i.e., poetic.

Combining the processes of language development in the individual and the race, and at the same time moving to more specific comments about the poetic basis of language, here are two brief statements by Arthur Koestler:

> Thus rhythm and assonance, pun and rhyme are not artificially created ornaments of speech: the whole evidence indicates that their origins go back

[136] William H. Perkins, "Language and Articulation," *The Voice* XV, 2-3: 36.
[137] O. H. Mowrer, "Speech Development in the Young Child: 1. The Autism Theory of Speech Development and Some Clinical Applications," *Journal of Speech and Hearing Disorders* 17: 263-68.
[138] Langer, *Philosophy in a New Key,* p. 99.

to primitive—and infantile—forms of thought and utterance, in which sound and meaning are magically interwoven, and association by sound-affinities is as legitimate as association by other similarities. [139]

And just as rhythm is not an artificial embellishment of language but a form of expression which predates language, so visual images and symbols are not fanciful embroideries of concepts, but precursors of conceptual thought. The artist does not climb a ladder to stick ornaments on a facade of ideas—he is more like a pot-holer in search of underground rivers. [140]

With these two statements I want to change the level of the argument, to consider particular elements of what I'm calling poetic language. Koestler seems to me to agree with Langer and Burke in saying that poetry is the most basic level of language, but he has talked of that basic level in more specific terms, in terms of rhythm and imagery. I'm going to continue his line of thought and point out that the term "poetry" is used in two senses, one broad, one narrow. Broadly, poetry means all literature or all language notable for its imaginative and emotional qualities. It is in this sense that Langer and Burke have written of the basic act of language as a symbolic and poetic one. Narrowly, poetry has been defined in so many ways that it's unlikely that any one of them is widely accepted. There are, however, the two characteristics of poetry in this narrow sense that I described in Chapter 3 and that are commented on by all theorists with which I'm familiar—*rhythm* and *figurative* or *metaphorical language* (the latter term being one that I take to be broad enough to include Koestler's notion of imagery). So, I think it's fair to say that poetry in the narrow sense may not *mean* but certainly includes, and includes in an important and significant fashion, rhythm and metaphorical language. And these same elements are included in the same central and important manner in the basic consummatory and symbolic level of language, as I'll try to show now.

All language, silent and oral, verbal and nonverbal, is rhythmic in that it involves chronological patterning of one sort or another. Speech is the most obvious example, but thinking too is a process that begins, continues, and ends in time. Temporal relationships are thus basic to language, and that is to say that those relationships are not random, but are formed patterns. Eric Lenneberg, in his recent and extremely important work on the biology of language, has tentatively advanced the amazing thesis that language is not only chronologically patterned, but that the pattern is a specific rhythm that is made up of approximately six events per second and that is perceptible in the oral, silent, physiological, psychological, and neurological dimensions of language. [141]

But if all language is significantly rhythmical, some language behaviors are clearly more strongly rhythmical than others, and those behaviors seem to lie at the very base of language, at the very beginnings of our symbolic lives. Professor Langer conjectures that language began as the pleasurable vocal and physical chants and

[139] Koestler, p. 315.
[140] *Ibid.*, p. 325.
[141] Lenneberg, pp. 107-120.

gestures of social Ritual. It's clear that in the realm of literature highly rhythmical verse forms have predated those of prose, sometimes by many centuries. And in what I think I'll call "personal literature," i.e., the private, imaginative language processes in which we all engage, the babbling stage already mentioned is the extremely rhythmical activity from which more prosaic and prose-like forms develop. In other words, both as a race and as individuals we begin with consummatory and vividly rhythmical behaviors and move toward symbolic actions that are less impressively rhythmical. Our symbolic rhythms persist, however; they are perceptible in all language, and they become prominent in those forms that are consummatory rather than instrumental. Our dreams, our profanity, our dances, and of course, our poetry are drenched with rhythm.

Metaphor is quite as pervasive and as important as rhythm. One of the most valuable comments on metaphor, in my judgment, is this one by I. A. Richards:

> The processes of metaphor in language, the exchanges between the meanings of words which we study in explicit verbal metaphors, are superimposed upon a perceived world which is itself a product of earlier or unwitting metaphor, and we shall not deal with them justly if we forget that this is so. [142]

I understand Richards to be saying that language is metaphorical on its deepest symbolic levels, that we look out at the world through language, and that what we see is a metaphor, a mix, of the seen and the process of seeing. Further, there is the metaphor involved in the verbal-nonverbal matrices of language, for as Richards points out, words are transcended by their nonverbal sensory appeals and at the same time verbally transcend those appeals.[143] A word does not merely refer to something, but makes us feel things. We label imagery with the names of the senses (auditory, visual, etc.) because our sensory responses are part of the meaning a word has for us. Yet imagery, the sensory appeals of words, is not made up of direct copies of the outer world, but is in every case a sensory appeal that is summed up and surpassed by words which "are the meeting points at which regions of experience which can never combine in sensation or intuition, come together."[144]

That the most factual and literal statements can be quickly broken down into metaphor (as witness this sentence) has been widely noted. However, the metaphorical quality of language is clearest in those cases in which there is no assumption of factual or literal truth, where language is openly and avowedly consummatory rather than instrumental. Poetry, in the narrow sense, is such a case. So are dreams, in which metaphors blur the dividing lines between reality and unreality and ignore the demands of temporal and logical priority; Freud's processes of "over-determination" (the simultaneous presence of various meanings in one form), "condensation" (a fusion of forms that heightens awareness), and "presentability" (emotional and dramatic immediacy) are symbolic modes that are metaphorical in Richards' sense and that are prominent in both dreams and poetry.

[142] Richards, p. 109.
[143] Ibid., p. 130.
[144] Ibid., p. 131.

These processes are seen too in profanity, a form that is metaphorical in a creative and hortatory fashion. Indeed, under the spur of anger or fear, under *any* strong emotional impluse, we are very likely to turn to specific and overt metaphor.

Shakespeare's statement that "The lunatic, the lover and the poet/Are of imagination all compact" is an apt one, and can be taken to mean that when we are most pressed to use language in a manner that will determine our outer or inner reality, bring us closer to another solitary being, or create order of some private chaos, we must resort to metaphor.

Professor Langer points out that metaphor is not limited to poetry, but is the foundation of Rhetoric as well, for all novelty, all new thought, every new idea depends on metaphor. And she makes the sweeping comment:

> . . . if ritual is the cradle of language, metaphor is the law of its life. It is the force that makes it essentially *relational*, intellectual, forever showing up new, abstractable *forms* in reality, forever laying down a deposit of old, abstracted concepts in an increasing treasure of general works.[145]

To summarize this section, language that is intrapersonal and poetic is the sort of language I call Ritual. And that sort of language is not merely equal to or co-existent with Rhetoric, but is the foundation of Rhetoric, of all language. Language must be viewed as a symbolic process that is basically consummatory, that needs no reason for being other than itself, that is basically intrapersonal in that constitutive symbolic acts undergird those that are communicative, and that is poetic in the broad sense of being an imaginative and a pleasurable event and in the narrow sense of being a rhythmical and metaphorical one. (On this level "rhythm" and "metaphor" are used somewhat more broadly than they were in Chapter 3.)

We may turn frequently from this poetic and intrapersonal process to one that is interpersonal and practical, i.e., from Ritual to Rhetoric, but that is not to say that the Ritual, the intrapersonal, the poetic has disappeared. Just as communicative language acts are communicative in addition to being constitutive, practical language behaviors are practical in addition to being poetic. In a word, Ritual is the ground of Rhetoric. To argue otherwise is to make language an instrumental rather than a consummatory act, a practical rather than a poetic process, a communicative rather than a symbolic behavior—and finally, to remove man from his own words, to separate him from his language.

## Rhetoric and Ritual as the Limits of Language

In reading this book, I hope you've asked yourself from time to time whether or not I'm really talking about language—*all* language. Or am I dealing with certain specific and fairly narrow types of language? The question seems to me to be extremely important, for many of my statements may be only trivially true if I have defined language too narrowly. If I have simply constructed definitions that leave out

[145] Langer, *Philosophy in a New Key*, p. 125.

significant or major language forms and processes, what I have said may be both true and insignificant. On the other hand, if I have included all language in my considerations, what I've said must be significant if it's true.

Predictably, I want to argue that I *am* describing all language, and I'm going to make that argument by talking about what seem to me to be the limits of language. That there are limits we would quickly agree, for we are instantly disposed to say that the sound of a brick dropped on the sidewalk, the sight of a dent in a metal surface, and similar objects and events are beyond or outside of language.

So the problem seems to be to set the limits in some reasonable fashion and then find out what lies between them. And that problem is similar to the difficulty of looking at two mountains separated by a valley and determining where one mountain ends and the other begins, or where each mountain ends and the valley begins. One possibility is to say that each mountain ends precisely in the middle of the valley, simply because that's the midpoint between them; another possibility is to say that because it's impossible to determine any ending-point by other than arbitrary means, there is no valley between the two mountains; and between these extreme approaches there are various other possibilities.

The first notion to get clear, I think, is the idea that language doesn't end suddenly. We don't engage in language activities up to a particular point and then, bang, find ourselves outside of language. Rather there are tapering-off areas within language, areas in which language fades, loses more and more of its characteristics until it simply disappears.

In the section on Rhetoric and Ritual as inseparable processes, I gave examples of extremes in *natural* language—extreme Ritual in the form of a lyric, and extreme Rhetoric in the form of scholarly writing. To offer another example of such an extreme, here's a familiar Ritual in the form of a lyric statement:

from "Annabel Lee"

It was many and many a year ago,
In a kingdom by the sea,
That a maiden there lived whom you may know
By the name of Annabel Lee;—
And this maiden she lived with no other thought
Than to love and be loved by me.

—Edgar Allan Poe

I say that's extreme because it seems to me to be very largely ritualistic. Of course there's an element of Rhetoric, a necessary element, in the clarity and simple reasoning of the narrative, but the rhythm, the almost myth-like reference to a "kingdom by the sea," and the quietly tender description of the maid who "lived with no other thought" but love are ritualistic through and through.

But I do not mean by that that language ends with such Ritual, that there is no language beyond this. For example I sometimes sing in the shower, and when I do I very often forget the words and have to resort to "la-la-la." (Actually, I find "lo-lo-law" much better, much more singable.) Now, I'm certainly not willing to say that my "lo-lo-law's" are something *other* than language, despite their fragmented character. Similarly, the nonverbal Ritual of some pantomime and dance is impossible to call something *other* than language; and there are cases in which the semantic and emotional values of these forms can be translated easily into verbal language. Yet they are clearly not as fully linguistic as the types of Rhetoric and Ritual with which I've been dealing. Most important of all, there's a sort of literature, usually poetry, that seems to me to belong to the realm of partial or faded language. It's the sort that may be overly subjective, even to the point of gibberish. For example:

> The dark soul-like electric fire
> thrives the hate and anger through,
> and spewing filth that man no longer hides
> to seas wide death.
> Fortune will call and yet
> No one here alone and full of
> white-fear gut-song
> cries because of pain.

These lines are not beyond language, but they are language that has faded perhaps to the point of near meaninglessness. And there are a good many examples of similarly faded language to be found.

The important thing is that there is some Ritual of much value that lies squarely in the middle of this transitional area between language and non-language. I've already mentioned pantomime and dance which, when narrative in nature, are quite obviously language. But verbal Ritual of this sort is possible too. For instance,

> Aiaee! Ho-o-oh!
> Ah-la-a-ah!
> Aieaee! Ha-a-a-ah!
> Ah-lo-o-oh!

This group of sounds can in some sense be effective. It can be read to suggest a war-cry, or a mournful death-song. Of course the reader infuses the sounds with whatever meaning he finds "in them," but that is merely the act of assigning meaning that we all carry on all the time. The point is that even language as faded as this (and we would surely call this a very partial or limited form of language as compared with, say, a Shakespearean sonnet) can function, and can function effectively and with grace.

What do I mean then by "fading," by "faded language"? In the case of the ritualistic extreme, I mean language that is in the process of losing its rhetorical element. Simple as that! That, I believe, is just what causes the examples I've cited to be either recognizably limited in relation to full language forms or of doubtful value. Very extreme Ritual, Ritual that is too nearly *total*, is not only addressed to no one, it's entirely expressive, entirely self-contained. Such language cannot exist in any fully meaningful sense *between* persons, unless by accident some word or words is so important to the recipient, the auditor, that he forces meaning into it. If I say,

> Blue, slim, cool doves,
> Soft smoke, evening doom

and you find that a description of evening high in the Alleghenies, it will be by symbolic accident. An accident for which those two lines can take no credit. The meaning was apparently so strong in you that the merest trigger released it. And if I go to the extreme of saying,

> Raceasy the room fall-spinning
> Dark hot blur scream the whole
> Wall people bank money-proud curse
> The well poor and sickest of the legion
> For earth the coverer dealt and called.

I have uttered gibberish. There are total subjectivists, perhaps, who will say that these lines are meaningful to those who find meaning in them. My answer is that, as audience, I must not only experience the meaning but be able to point out, at least vaguely, the relationship between that experience and the language. That relationship is the element of Rhetoric, of reason, of language used interpersonally, of language that defines and marks out boundaries. There is necessarily a subjective element, for meaning is experientially based; but complete subjectivism makes isolated and meaningless beings of us all.

In the case of the rhetorical extreme, language goes through a fading process in which the Ritual disappears. And, as with the ritualistic extreme, there are efficient and useful forms that exist in this gray area. Chief among them are the artificial languages, particularly mathematics. Mathematics is an efficient sign system for some purposes, and clearly it's a system that contains very little Ritual. Very little, but some. The comments of persons such as British mathematician and physicist Paul Dirac, who said, "It is more important to have beauty in one's equations than to have them fit experiment,"[146] indicate that mathematics is not without an element of Ritual, at least for the truly creative mathematicians. Still we would quickly agree that $8 + 7 = 15$ is almost entirely without an intrapersonal, or poetic, or constitutive element. Similarly, such things as telephone directories are part of language, but they contain an exceedingly small amount of Ritual. They are not beyond language, but neither can they be considered language in the full sense of that word.

This notion of partial or faded language is especially important as applied to the rhetorical extreme, because it is there that we face a peculiar oddity of our times. Because for several centuries science has been worshipped with ever-increasing fervor in the Western world, and because the essential "language" of science is mathematics, the idea has developed that mathematics is the purest, the most efficient, the highest form of language. Mathematics is looked to as the system that is accurate, precise, and that makes truly effective communication possible.

[146] Koestler, p. 329.

Conversely, natural language is regarded as that sloppy, vague, ambiguous, and inefficient form of communication that is vastly inferior to mathematics. In Chapter 1, I pointed out that mathematics is not equipped to deal with matters of love, or loneliness, or honor, and that it seemed odd to call a system so ill-equipped a "language." Here I'll content myself with the observation that it's odd indeed to begin with language as we all know it, the natural language of man, to abstract from that language certain qualities, and then to maintain that that simplified and partial system is somehow best, or purest, or most efficient. How do you laugh mathematically? Or cry?

From a different viewpoint, I want to repeat my contention that my notions of Rhetoric and Ritual include all language acts. The statement is sometimes made that the four basic types of discourse are poetic, rhetorical, philosophical, and scientific. This statement apparently means that these four types of discourse are equally basic, that none of them is the foundation of any of the others. My position is that Ritual (poetic) is the most basic language process, but that Ritual and Rhetoric combine to form what we call natural language. In the extreme stages in which either of these processes is absent, or nearly so, language is fragmenting, deteriorating, beginning to fade into the completely felt but inexpressible reality of "total" Ritual or the entirely objective and impersonal (and therefore inexpressible) reality of "total" Rhetoric.

I would argue that philosophical and scientific discourse certainly exist, but that they are in no sense basic language processes. Most of the examples I've used in this book have no scientific dimension, and only a few of them possess a philosophical dimension. These two types of discourse seem to me to be distinctly secondary and tertiary language functions, i.e., they are added-on features of language in the sense that all language *must* be ritualistic and rhetorical, but *may* be philosophical or scientific as well.

Scientific discourse is a tertiary language form identifiable by its method, *not* its content. We use scientific discourse whenever we define and investigate *objectively*, whenever we consider something to be part of *objective reality*. Thus, scientific discourse is employed in psychology, sociology, etc., as well as physics and chemistry. As I've indicated, it's too often forgotten that the scientists who examine this objective reality operate within their own rhetorical and ritualistic biases. Biases less obvious, perhaps, than those of the humanist, but biases nonetheless. The scientist has, after all, *chosen* to be a scientist, and specifically to be a chemist, biologist, physicist, etc. That choice is a rhetorical-ritualistic act, and it leads to the further, rhetorical-ritualistic acts of finding importance in certain problems, certain aspects of nature, etc. In addition, scientists are ritualists in that they find beauty, elegance in the problems with which they're concerned, as witness the comment by Paul Dirac. So, it is only after the ritualistic and rhetorical fact that the scientist becomes scientist, that he attempts objective and impersonal observations, measurements, and predictions. And it is because of their ritualistic and rhetorical beginnings that scientists will always fail, in one sense. For, as Koestler points out,

Einstein's space is no closer to reality than Van Gogh's sky. The glory of science is not in a truth "more absolute" than the truth of Bach or Tolstoy, but in the act of creation itself. The scientist's discoveries impose his own order on chaos, as the composer or painter imposes his; an order that always refers to limited aspects of reality and is biassed by the observer's frame of reference, which differs from period to period, as a Rembrandt nude differs from a nude by Manet.[147]

The scientist's behaviors are first sermonic (rhetorical) and creative (ritualistic), then scientific.

Philosophical discourse presents something of a different problem. It's been argued, and well argued, that philosophical discourse does not depend on any other form of discourse, but is, rather, a means of examining those forms as objects.[148] It's been argued that philosphy examines art, Rhetoric, and science, but that philosophy doesn't become any of these things; instead, there are philosophies of art, science, and Rhetoric. Further, it's been argued that philosophical discourse exists separate and apart from any persuasive element in such discourse, and that philosophical arguments call for no action of any sort, not even the action of assenting; it's even been argued that philosophical discourse may be addressed to an audience of peers or to no audience at all.[149]

I would argue, as I have, that such views of philosophy conflict with the most basic characteristics of language. True, such views establish philosophy as the primary intellectual discipline, for if all other disciplines can be examined by philosophy, philosophy must be the *a priori* mode of thought. But in so establishing philosophical discourse, the very nature of language has been distorted; the philosopher uses language with no intent to persuade, and he uses language that does not even need an audience. How can his language have meaning unless it is based on his experiences, and if it *is* so based, how can it be used at all without presenting an attitude or point of view—without persuading? If he talks to no audience, why does the philosopher talk at all? For the simple joy of doing so? But that would make him a ritualist! And if he talks to an audience of his peers, he must attempt to persuade them of the rightness, the validity of his ideas.

In my opinion, there's a tendency on the part of some philosophers to equate philosophy with reasoning or logical thought. That definition is entirely too broad, for it makes all ordered discourse into philosophy. There's no room for anything other than philosophy, except perhaps art, and even that is questionable.

The answer, I think, is one that places philosophy a bit more narrowly, but still nobly, among the various disciplines. Philosophical discourse is the sort that deals with presuppositions, that draws parallels and relationships between disciplines, that unites areas of study previously thought to be incompatible and thereby enriches them. I turn once again to Professor Langer:

[147] *Ibid.*, p. 252.
[148] Henry W. Johnstone, Jr., "The Relevance of Rhetoric to Philosophy and of Philosophy to Rhetoric," *Quarterly Journal of Speech* LII, 1: 42.
[149] Maurice Natanson, "Rhetoric and Philosophical Argumentation," in *Philosophy, Rhetoric and Argumentation,* ed. Maurice Natanson and Henry W. Johnstone, Jr. (University Park, Pa.: The Pennsylvania State University Press, 1965), p. 150.

The serious philosophical need of our day is a conceptual structure that may be expanded simply by modification (not metaphorical extension) of definitions in literally meant scientific terms, to cover wider fields than physics and chemistry proper, so that the exploration of those problematic domains—biology, with its special areas of genetics, evolution theory, neurology, etc., psychology, already departmentalized into animal and human, normal and abnormal, educational, social, and so on, the complex disciplines, mainly economic, that deal with values, and whatever other fields claim to be future "ologies"—may proceed as so many developments of our most exact systematic knowledge. To construct such concepts is, I believe, the task of professional philosophers; it is too large to be done by other intellectual workers on a basis of incidental insights reflected on in leisure hours. It requires familiarity with philosophical ideas, both general and technical reading in many fields, and logical training to the point of a liberated logical imagination; competences which may be demanded of philosophers, but hardly of anyone else.[150]

Here is a role for philosophical discourse that is a high one, indeed. And, while I don't wish to imply that Professor Langer would agree with my order of priorities, it seems to me that such a role gives philosophy precedence of a sort over all other disciplines save one—save language, save Rhetoric and Ritual. For it's in and with these two processes that the philosopher himself works. It's the function of philosophy, of philosophical discourse, to deal with generalities, but to *end* rather than *begin* with those generalities. It is the arduous task of the philosopher to assimilate the content of various fields and *then* to arrive at generalizations that relate or unite those fields.[151] Thus philosophical discourse is a *secondary* language form. It follows and is dependent on the primary form Rhetoric-Ritual; but it precedes and is more basic than the tertiary form scientific discourse. Philosophy can explore the presuppositions on which science rests (chief among which is the assumption of a mechanistic universe), but in the depths of language there are no metaphorical, or rhythmical, or dramatic presuppositions for philosophy to investigate.

For all men, philosophers, scientists, poets, war-makers, politicians, bigots, schizophrenics, language is basic. My order of priorities, then, begins with language, and within language, Ritual is basic to Rhetoric. Then comes the secondary form, philosophical discourse. And after that the tertiary form, scientific discourse.

Rhetoric and Ritual are the processes that are fundamental to all others, and they make up the realm of language. That realm includes (beginning with the faded or partial rhetorical extreme) labels and names such as appear on street signs; lists of such items, as telephone directories and dictionaries; mathematics and other nonverbal sign systems; precise and scholarly discourse; the speeches, essays, and books that present knowledge of men and things; the pleas for social action; the passionate cries for betterment of the human condition; (then moving into the realm of Ritual) stories, plays, and novels that are strongly involved in social reality;

[150] Langer, *Mind: An Essay on Human Feeling*, p. xxii.
[151] *Ibid.*, p. xxi.

narrations and descriptions of people in conflict with themselves and each other; explorations of the interior reality—the dreams—of man; lyric statements of joy or sadness; the nonverbal but translatable forms of dance and pantomime; and ending with the faded or partial ritualistic extreme, the symbolic arts of painting, sculpture, dance, and music. All these are part of the domain of Rhetoric and Ritual, or of what Kenneth Burke has called "logology"—the study of symbolic action,[152] though my definition may be broader than his. But that broadness, that inclusiveness is, in my judgment, profoundly needed, for we have fragmented our language and ourselves far, far too much.

## Rhetoric: A Synthesis

In Chapter 2, I pointed out that the neo-Aristotelian approach to Rhetoric resulted in a too manipulative and mechanistic view of the process of persuasion, that the assumption that a speaker or writer *could* persuade an audience led to the assumption that that alienated audience merely reacted passively to the rhetorician's prodding, and that such notions dehumanized both audiences and rhetoricians. In this chapter I've argued that Ritual is both inseparable from and basic to Rhetoric, that intrapersonal communication is the foundation of the interpersonal, and that poetic language is the ground against which practical language figures.

All this seems to me to mean that the larger view of Rhetoric that I wish to present now must center the persuasive process on the *persons* involved; that is, Rhetoric must be an intensely *personal* act for *both* listeners and readers *and* speakers and writers. There must be no alienation that results from Rhetoric, and that means that all those involved in rhetorical events must be equally free and equally powerful. To precisely the extent that one person is not free or is powerless, the Rhetoric that I'm going to propose will be flawed; and to precisely the extent that one person is limited in his ability *to choose* to behave or believe in a certain way will that Rhetoric be without worth.

These are brave words. The problem, of course, is to make them work. And to do that I need to deal with the notion of persuasion in some (new) detail.

### Persuasion Reconsidered

The ideas about persuasion that I presented in Chapter 1 are *unsatisfactory* but *indispensable*. It would be foolishness to maintain that we don't attempt to persuade others, or that we don't use the processes called Invention (including ethical, emotional, and logical proofs), Disposition (including the ordering of statements and supports), and Style (including the individual and rhetorical aspects of that dimension of language). It might well prove desirable to change some of these elements about a bit, and I'm going to do that a little further on, but it would be idle to pretend that any of them can be eliminated. When I argue for or against some point of view, I *do* employ all these processes: I do attempt to establish an ethical relationship between myself, my subject, and my audience; I do attempt to adapt my discourse to the audience, and thereby to create an emotional impact; I

[152] Burke, *Language as Symbolic Action*, p. 47.

do use evidence and argument, principally definition, in what I presume to be logical ways; I do organize my discourse into some sort of introduction, a main part that contains the central ideas supported in various ways, and a conclusion that summarizes and briefly restates the importance of what I've said; and I surely do use language in a way that constitutes my very being and in a way that creates or results in the rhetorical act itself. It seems absolutely apparent to me that all these ingredients exist in my own and others' discourses. Yet by themselves these ingredients result in an alienating and manipulative Rhetoric, because they make persuasion a one-way process in which the rhetorician *acts on* the audience, while the audience merely *reacts to* the rhetorician.

The first change, then, must be to acquire equality for the audience, to make them *actors,* not *reactors* and that means that the audience can never *be persuaded* (a passive and static condition), but must *persuade* (an active and dynamic process). Such a notion is immediately remarked as an oddity: an *audience* that *persuades* is very nearly a contradiction in terms, so accustomed have we become to the active and passive roles of rhetorician and audience. And the next question is obvious: If the audience persuades, *whom* do they persuade? Themselves?

Yes! Exactly! Audiences must persuade themselves! Just that! I've already said as much, of course, in arguing that we must always listen to ourselves. The seemingly simple and neat notion that audiences *listen to* speakers and writers leads directly to the idea that audiences are *persuaded by* speakers and writers, and it's that idea that turns listeners and readers into passive, machine-like creatures whose responses to the stimuli of the rhetoricians' language are automatic and mindless.

But it's not enough to insist that audiences must be as active and as powerful as rhetoricians. Even if you can with some ease accept the idea that persuasion is self-directed and that the very nature of meaning requires that *all* users of language listen to themselves, there still is no clear role for the rhetorician in this "new" Rhetoric. What is the function of the speaker or writer who addresses audiences that listen to and persuade themselves? Clearly his function is not that of the traditional, neo-Aristotelian persuader. Rather it's the apparently contradictory twin role of the one who wishes to bring about change and, at the same time, to protect the audience's (and his own) freedom of choice.[153]

There's an extremely simple experience that is familiar to all of us and that illustrates the rhetorical function that I'm trying to describe: in the midst of heated arguments we've all been faced by the spectacle of someone giving in and agreeing for what seemed to be the *wrong reason.* Our responses then went something like, "I don't want you to do it *for me,*" or "I don't want you to say yes *just to please me—I want you to want to do it.*" Homey as this sort of experience may seem, it's the basis of the rhetorical process that I'm describing in this section, for it's an unmistakable example of a Rhetoric in which agreement *per se* is not enough!

Let me try to put this simple experience into broader terms. I've defined Rhetoric as *the theory and practice of persuasion by reasoned discourse.* The word "persuasion" obviously means a desire or an attempt to change audience attitudes,

[153] Thomas H. Olbricht argues just this point of view in "The Self As A Philosophical Ground of Rhetoric," *Pennsylvania Speech Annual XXI:28-36.*

and as I've said, it would be absurd to pretend that rhetoricians do *not* wish to bring about such changes. What has been forgotten far too often, however, is that it would be even more absurd to pretend that rhetoricians can afford to ignore the means by which attitudes and actions are changed. To go at once to the ultimate horror of such a point of view, if changes at any cost are the goal of Rhetoric, Adolf Hitler must be reckoned among the greatest rhetoricians of history. He "persuaded" many millions of Jews to die.

Such a notion is grotesque. Gassing and torturing human beings is not Rhetoric. Those uses of force rest squarely on the power of one person to control the behavior of another, and that power is the absolute opposite of Rhetoric. Henry W. Johnstone, Jr. puts this idea excellently:

> When we wish to control the action or belief of another person, but either lack an effective means of control or have an effective means that we nevertheless do not wish to use, we argue with the person. Argument is therefore not effective control. To argue with another is to regard him as beyond the scope of effective control, and hence is precisely to *place* him beyond the scope of effective control, providing he is a person capable of listening to argument and knows how it is that we are regarding him. We give him the option of resisting us, and as soon as we withdraw that option we are no longer arguing. *To argue is inherently to risk failure, just as to play a game is inherently to risk defeat. An argument we are guaranteed to win is no more a real argument than a game we are guaranteed to win is a real game.* (italics mine)[154]

Rhetoric requires that audiences be free to *choose* to agree *or* disagree with the writer or speaker, to *choose* to persuade *or* not to persuade themselves. There can be no manipulation of the audience, no control over them, no power that is vested solely in the rhetorician.

And yet Rhetoric *is* an attempt to persuade, an attempt by the speaker or writer to persuade his listeners or readers. The conflict between the freedom that is necessary to avoid mechanistic notions and the intentional act of persuasion can be resolved by borrowing an idea from the province of Ritual. In Chapter 4, I talked about the intentional fallacy, pointing out that the mere assertion by an author that a poem or play meant this or that was totally worthless as a basis for evaluating the merit of that piece of Ritual. I did *not* argue that poets or playwrights don't intend that their works be important, significant, or memorable, but simply that those intentions play no part in valid critical appraisals of those works. It seems quite obvious that the makers of Ritual do intend that their creations have certain meanings, and equally obvious that those intentions must be disregarded.

In an entirely analogous fashion, a rhetorical discourse, say, this book, is what it is and means, not because of the author's *intentions,* but because of the actions of both rhetorician and audience. I intend that this book mean many good and important things, and I intend to persuade you to agree with me. Those intentions are real, entirely so, and yet they indicate precisely nothing about the value of this

[154] Henry W. Johnstone, Jr., "Some Reflections on Argumentation," *Philosophy, Rhetoric and Argumentation,* ed. Maurice Natanson and Henry W. Johnstone, Jr. (University Park, Pa.: The Pennsylvania State University Press, 1965), p. 1.

rhetorical event. This and all other rhetorical discourses will succeed or fail, not because of the rhetorician's intentions, but because a *basis* has or has not been provided *for the conscious exercise of free choice* by the audience.

And that, in my judgment, is both the role of the rhetorician and the core of the rhetorical process—*to provide a basis on which hearers and readers can consciously exercise freedom of choice*. Bound up in this concept are three further notions that I must deal with now: First, if the audience must be free to accept or reject the rhetorician's views, must not a similar freedom be possessed by that rhetorician? a freedom to accept or reject his *own* ideas? Second, how shall a writer or speaker go about the business of getting an audience to consciously exercise freedom of choice? And third, how shall we evaluate the worth, the success or failure of rhetorical discourses in relation to specific actions, issues, and beliefs?

*The Rhetorician and His Rhetoric*      If I must listen to myself, it must follow that I can and do persuade myself. And once again, the notion of persuasion as an *active* process is the key. I persuade myself because it's *only* by listening to myself that I can know what I mean. Indeed it may well be that it's only in the act of listening to myself that I find out what I've said. Think for a moment of the situations in which you've *changed* a statement or an idea in the very process of uttering it. For me one of the most frequent language frustrations is the fact of finding myself somewhere in the middle of a sentence and realizing that I've wandered off on a tangent and have completely forgotten how the sentence started, or how I might be able to end it. That realization comes because it's the act of *using* language that brings knowledge or meaning. Of course I may use language silently: I may sit and think a sentence to myself. But whether silent or oral, it's the *action* of symbolizing that *is* meaning. The symbols, verbal and nonverbal, that we employ *are* our meanings, and there is no meaning apart from or prior to those symbols. It's only in the act of saying something that I can know what I want to say or what I'm going to say. That act may be complexly or simply structured, but it's in the doing, the forming, the putting together that knowledge and meaning lie.

Again, extreme statements. Do I mean that before starting this sentence I possessed no knowledge of how I wished this sentence to go? Yes, I mean just that! Remembering, of course, that I may have "started" this sentence in a very private, silent, inner language of my own, and that that "starting" may have occurred immediately before I wrote down the first word(s) or quite a long time before that writing down. The *writing down* was secondary, for I owned, I actively held and experienced that first word(s) somewhere inside myself before I could *write it down*. The only sense in which I must qualify this idea concerns the singular form of the word "word"; I do *not* mean that I create sentences *one* word at a time, like sausages ground out by a machine. Rather the words come in clusters, in clumps, even, at times, in sentences. Some such word grouping I necessarily experienced actively before I could do any writing down, and it was in that action, that experience that I discovered what I was saying and what I meant.

This idea of knowledge in action is complicated enough as it is, but the waters get even muddier when you consider the rhetorician who undergoes changes, who persuades himself *while* facing an audience. It's this sort of self-persuasion that may seem most dramatic, for the thought of a speaker who interrupts his own discourse to admit to errors or simply to say that he has changed his mind can be a startling one. *Most* of the time, however, such changes are pretty unobtrusive, for they take place over a fairly long period of time and between a rhetorician and his unseen audience. This book is the perfect example of long-term self-persuasion. I turned in to my publishers what I fondly thought of as the final draft early in January 1969. With my enthusiastic approval, the editor-in-chief had suggested having the book reviewed by three or four people in the field whose opinions I trusted; I would be free, of course, to react as I wished to the reviewers comments—to ignore them or to observe them in whole or in part. I'd chosen good people to do the reviewing; when the manuscript was sent off I was innocently positive that I could do any rewriting that would be indicated by their minor criticism in a very short time.

The comments came back. It's now over a year and a half later. And I'm just finishing what I now think of as a final draft—a very different one from the first final draft. The point is that I didn't have to do it; I didn't have to do any rewriting at all. But when the comments arrived, there were two sets of them that were too insightful for me to ignore. Those two reviewers pointed out basic flaws in the book that required a complete rewriting. I tried my damndest to forget those reviews, to convince myself that they were wrong. For a week or two, I fought those reviews furiously. Then, little by little, I persuaded myself that they were right, despite the extra work that I knew they'd cost me. The people involved were too intelligent to make such gross errors. Slowly I let myself realize that the dialectic had been a good and necessary one, that the thesis (my first final draft) and the antithesis (the reviewers' blunt and accurate ciriticisms) had paved the way for what could be a valuable synthesis (this version of the book, I hope). But it was all *my* doing, and all my *doing.* That is, I persuaded myself, and I did so by the act of inviting criticism and the further act of responding to that criticism. (From the viewpoint of the critics, it was *their* doing, self-persuasion on *their* part.) The entire process was an active one. Even the week or two of trying to decide not to rewrite was a time of action, and an exhausting action at that. And at every step I changed my mind in one way or another, seeing, as I wrote a paragraph or a chapter, that it worked and fit cleanly into place or that it hung loosely in its niche and fitted poorly into the larger design. Constantly I tried to look ahead, to plan the next step. And constantly I failed. Oh, I'd get some rough outlines right now and then, but it was always a matter of juggling parts, smoothing edges, reworking details, and finding that it was ever the act of writing that told me what I wanted to write.

As I said, these were long-term changes. And it's nearly always this sort of change that's involved as the rhetorician influences himself. But what of that dramatic form of change that *might* occur when a speaker faces an audience, finds that he no longer believes his own words, and is honest enought to proclaim his disbelief. Rare as such an occurrence may be, it seems to me to be absolutely necessary in any viable Rhetoric, for the rhetorician who cannot undergo or admit to such change is locked into a system that is too rigid and too unyielding. The freedom to change one's views in midstream is profoundly needed, even though that freedom be exercised most infrequently. Consider a rhetorical system without that freedom: it would closely resemble that paradigm case of rhetorical dishonesty, the formal debate as practiced on college campuses; the debater argues for or against a proposition *no matter what his opponents say;* and without the freedom to change his views *as he states them,* the rhetorician is doomed to argue for or against a proposition *no matter what he himself says.* In the case of the debater, it surely requires no special insight to understand that there will necessarily be times when the opposing team will have presented the better case. That is, the debater himself will *know* that the opponents have constructed superior arguments. When that debater clings to his own point of view, a point of view that he realizes is not tenable, I think that his behavior is quite clearly dishonest. And in the case of the writer or speaker who cannot change his mind in response to his own statements, the system is equally dishonest. Such a man must stick to whatever position he chooses at the beginning, no matter whether he finds that position defensible or not. He cannot know whether or not his argument for, say, open admission to colleges and universities is sound until he constructs that argument. Yet he must stand by his argument, sound or unsound. No matter how many problems he may discover in building his argument, no matter how flimsy that argument turns out to be, he is doomed to state and restate it endlessly unless he can change his mind.

I spend this much time on a rhetorical extreme because it illustrates the principle so clearly. Think of the impact on an audience that would result if the speaker were to stop in the middle of his discourse and say directly to his audience, "Ladies and gentlemen, I've just thought of something that seems to me very important. And it seems to contradict many of the things I've already told you. So, at this moment, I don't really know where I stand on these issues, but if you'll bear with me, I'll try to explain my own conflicting ideas." Would we not trust such a speaker at once?

And again, I'm not arguing that such changes in mid-discourse occur constantly, or even frequently. Far oftener there will be changes between one discourse and the next, as there were changes in my attitudes between my first book and the second one, and between the second and the present one. (Of course, in the sense in which I described it in Chapter 2, such rhetorical events fuse together into an over-all discourse.) Speakers who face audiences frequently, particularly holders of political office who face the *same* audience repeatedly, are instantly suspect if they do not change in the *process* of holding office. The politician who chooses some ideological vantage point and refuses to budge despite the press of new events, who mouths his same platitudes regardless of a changed situation, who takes pride in his own unwillingness to change, is a rhetorically shabby, unskilled, and dishonest being. To oppose or support the Vietnam war in 1965 was one thing; to do so in 1970 was something else; and the politican who rides his rhetorical ass resolutely down the years, because to change steeds would somehow be unAmerican or unmanly, is a fool—and a dangerous one. On the other hand, the rhetorician who is willing to hear himself, to listen to the strengths and weaknesses in his own arguments, is one to whom we should all listen.

*The Rhetorical Road to Freedom of Choice*     But as a rhetorician, how do you go about the business of getting an audience to consciously exercise freedom of choice? A practical and basic question, especially since I've ruled out any and all sorts of manipulation, of getting the audience to do what you want them to. What's left?

What's left is, I think, the most difficult sort of honesty in the world—the honesty that's indicated by a willingness to confront and reveal yourself. The word "honesty," of course, is an invitation to all sorts of rhetorical disasters, for the bigot, the chauvinist, the killers of the children and women of our "enemies" in Vietnam, the suppressors of freedom can all maintain that they are absolutely honest. But theirs I've noticed is an honesty of a different sort. They are quite willing to tell the rest of us what to do and how to do it, but I don't find that they are willing to admit their own mistakes, their fears, even their hates. And I mustn't overstate the case (or rather, I mustn't make it one-sided): it's not only the political conservatives that avoid self-confrontation. Indeed I think that it's that very fault in the so-called liberals that paves the way for the conservative regimes. In universities throughout the country (most of which can reasonably be called liberal), faculties avoided the painful forms of self-confrontation such as the elimination of incompetent teachers, the removal of unjustifiable courses, the termination of government contracts; finally, legislatures and students began to attack the very problems that faculties themselves should have dealt with.

Honesty, in the sense of self-confrontation and self-revelation, is for me the prime rhetorical good. I talked earlier of the need to confine the realm of philosophy so that it doesn't absorb all orderly thought processes, and that point is relevant here. In an article on the differences between Rhetoric and philosophy, Henry W. Johnstone, Jr., states that Rhetoric is necessarily secretive and deceptive while philosophy is necessarily open and undisguised, and that

> in the rhetorical situation, disagreement exists only to be overcome through the exploitation of an initial agreement, and *the desire of an audience to reach its own conclusions must be circumvented.* In philosophical discussions, on the other hand, whether there is an initial agreement or not, it cannot be exploited to overcome disagreement, since the latter is radical, permitting no compromise. *What must be exploited is just the desire of each participant to reach his own conclusions. A conclusion has no philosophical use if is not reached freely. To be philosophically useful, it must represent the unconstrained attempt on the part of its advocate to fulfill his obligation to defend and clarify his position. Thus philosophical discussion is, in effect, a collaborative effort to maintain the conditions under which disagreement is possible.* [155] (all italics mine)

I disagree with this view on two important grounds: first, it simply defines all open, nonmanipulative discussion that leaves individual freedom of choice unrestricted as philosophical, and all other forms of discourse become tainted by secrecy, disguise, or hypocrisy; second, it strongly implies that the rhetorician *can* manipulate his audience, *can* circumvent "the desire of an audience to reach its own

[155] *Ibid.,* "Persuasion and Validity in Philosophy," p. 146.

conclusions." I believe both objections are valid, although I find the desire to center such open, honest discourse in one's own field entirely understandable. After all, I'm doing the same thing. But the notion of manipulating audiences, the notion of preventing audiences from reaching freely chosen conclusions leads you right back to prescriptive, mechanistic attitudes toward persuasion and language—attitudes that simply are not viable.

So, if you will agree that the sort of honesty I'm describing is not the special province of philosophy, but is instead a characteristic of language used ethically, the answer to the problem is completed. As a rhetorician you function best, you help your audience to achieve the highest level of consciously exercised free choice by the honesty of self-confrontation and self-exposure. You make your argument as clear as you can as you go along; you avoid all hidden pressures and prejudices; you point out consequences of given viewpoints whether they are favorable or unfavorable to your cause (the two-sided persuasion of Chapter 1); you explain your own thought processes, the ways that you arrived at the belief in question; and you always, always make it totally apparent that the audience must consciously and freely make its own choices.

*As a rhetorician you function within an eternal dialectic: on the one hand, you attempt to persuade an audience; on the other, you demand that that audience choose freely for itself.*

Two things must be emphasized here. First, I want to say once more that I'm not implying that the rhetorician holds neutral, impersonal views toward his subject. Not at all! Language is sermonic. To use language is to persuade. Rhetorical discourses, at their best, are exciting just because the speaker or writer believes as strongly as he does and still leaves his audience free to choose their beliefs. The great rhetorician keeps no secrets: he admits his own biases and his desire that the audience share them, and at the same time he insists that the audience make their own choices. Second, there is today in America an attitude among some that makes any examination, disclosure, or confrontation of the self into a weakness. Those who are willing to admit that as Whites they share responsibility for White racism, or that as Americans they share responsibility for the grotesque years in Vietnam are accused of being weaklings, of indulging in pitiable orgies of self-blame. This strikes me as an argument for a form of John Wayneism, or "those bullets don't really hurt." The notion that strength consists of maintaining the rightness of your position no matter what, and that to admit faults, flaws, errors is somehow weakness seems an eerie one to me. I've never found it particularly easy to admit my own White racism, my own overly rigid attitudes toward the young, or my own cowardice in refusing to confront others who behave in those ways. On the contrary, those admissions are very often quite painful. Obviously then, I see the sort of honest self-confrontation I'm describing as strength, and strength of one of the most valuable sorts.

But a question arises once again. If the goal of rhetorical discourse is the conscious exercise of free choice by the audience, and if the rhetorician can best reach that goal by open self-confrontation and self-disclosure, how shall we evaluate rhetorical discourses as to success or failure? It's a good question, and I think there's a good answer.

*The Success or Failure of Rhetoric*    The problems are, you remember, that very often there are no observable immediate effects of rhetorical discourse, so that it's impossible to say that the discourse did or did not achieve its goal; frequently the rhetorician could not have persuaded his audience no matter what he did, as in cases where the audience is committed to a contrary view; quite often we call discourses fine examples of Rhetoric although they have failed to sway an audience (the Pitt speech on the taxation of the American colonies, for instance); much of the time (in a sense, all the time) the rhetorician is interested in presenting a way of thinking, a viewpoint, a new terminology, and though changes of this verbal or symbolic sort may be observable, they are so subtle and they occur over such long time periods that there may be no possible means of measurement immediately following the rhetorical act (the Frost essay is an example); and lastly, the very notion that the rhetorician can bring about such immediate and observable results plunges us instantly into the problems of the powerless, passive, and puppet-like audience versus the powerful, active, and manipulative rhetorician. And yet we will wish to say that certain discourses were successful in one or many senses, and that others were failures. And we can.

We can *if* we postulate, as the rhetorician's basic goal, the conscious exercise of free choice by his audience (and, of course, himself), for we may then proceed easily to the statement that *those rhetorical discourses are successful which provide a basis on which the audience may consciously and freely choose to agree or to disagree with the rhetorician.* Instantly Pitt's speech becomes a success, for *he set forth his reasons* for opposing taxation with great clarity. And though his audience chose to disagree, it must be said that the audience either made its choice on the basis of Pitt's argument or that that argument *was* advanced and did in fact constitute a basis for the exercise of free choice, and that that's all that can be expected of a rhetorician. Milton Mayer's "The Children's Crusade" and Paul Ehrlich's "Eco-Catastrophe" are at once successful, for they provide bases on which attitudes and actions may be based. And Professor Friedenberg's "The Generation Gap" is immensely successful, for it creates a grid, a matrix of insights into the treatment of the young in this country. These discourses are successful because audiences can use them to construct attitudes and outlooks of their own, and they remain successful no matter whether the audience attitudes agree or disagree with those of the speaker or writer.

By contrast, all discourses by Richard Nixon in 1968 (at least all those reported in the mass media) were unsuccessful, although he was elected president. They were unsuccessful because they did not present to audiences bases on which to choose freely. Think back to what he said. There was the constant repetition of "law and order," but what did that mean? Surely we were all familiar with the fact of crimes, crowded courts, graft, etc. "Law and order." Evidently it did *not* mean that holders of high office should be rewarded for lawful and ethical conduct and punished for its opposite, since Mr. Nixon was instrumental in proposing Judges Haynsworth and Carswell for the Supreme Court and removing Henry Morgenthau from his job as U.S. Attorney in New York. These and other examples indicate that Mr. Nixon takes a rather particular view of "law and order." Witness the spectacle of the Nixon Administration going in to court in 1969 and 1970 to ask that the desegregation of Southern schools be delayed or slowed down—*desegregation that was ordered in 1954!* Now of course it is inevitable that Mr. Nixon, and all of us, hold particular and personal views on this and all issues. But he did not make his views known. There was always the specter of racism lurking behind his words because he refused to show to his audience his own reasoning, the steps by which he arrived at his conclusions, and the doubts and fears that any intelligent man must harbor about his own ideas.

You will note my own prejudices in this matter. I'm not an admirer of Mr. Nixon, as you could easily have predicted. And the question therefore arises as to whether or not I'm simply finding some means by which to condemn officially those rhetorical events that I don't like and to praise those with which I agree. My answer is that I think it's not merely a matter of personal prejudice (though the possibility that I've fooled myself troubles me from time to time), because I think I can point to the specific element in discourses that makes possible the conscious exercise of free choice by audiences.

I talked at some length earlier of ethical appeals. Now, as I promised way back in Chapter 2, I want to put some added stress on the ethical dimension of Rhetoric. That there must be an ethical dimension is, I hope, quite clear. Without it we are back at the problem of results, and torture is far more efficient than reasoned discourse if all you're interested in is results. It's the old ends-means controversy that is capable of only one resolution: there are no such things as "ends" and "means." What we call "means" are in fact "ends." If we allow it to be otherwise the ends inevitably become more important or all important. If the end is to sell you a bunch of ideas, the means, no matter how I may fight to prevent it, will decline in importance until it is simply the end, the results that count. To avoid this trap I must view as *ends* both the sale of the ideas and the honest or ethical means used in the selling; if I don't I find myself sliding toward the goal of selling my notions honestly *or* dishonestly, but selling them!

Ethics, honesty—these are big words. Often they are vague and difficult to measure or pin down. But there is one factor that is fundamental to an ethical consideration of any subject, any issue, any problem. That factor is *the willingness to accept responsibility both for what is and what should be.*[156] Any rhetorical event in which the rhetorician refuses to accept or only partially accepts these responsibilities will fail, wholly or in part. And the failure will occur simply because there is no basis for the exercise of free choice until responsibility for change and for what needs to be changed is accepted. So long as a rhetorician argues that it's not really *our* fault, that it wasn't *our* doing, and that *we're* not individually responsible for *Vietnam, racism, poverty, urban disaster,* and *environmental pollution* he can offer us no possibility of making changes, of solving those problems. So long as I believe that *I* am not responsible for the war in Vietnam, I

[156] The idea of responsibility as a vital element of human behavior is strongly stated by Lionel Rubinoff in *The Pornography of Power* (New York: Ballantine Books, 1969), especially pp. 35-40.

can easily escape any responsibility to end that war; only after I have accepted the responsibility *for* it can I accept the responsibility to *end* it. Another extreme-sounding proposition, but I think it works.

When I say "responsibility," I don't mean it in a 100% or all-or-nothing sense. I *am* responsible for the war in Vietnam; so are you. I *am* responsible for White racism in America; so are you, if you're White (Black racism is an odd invention of White racists a few of whom have black skins). And I *am* responsible for the horrors of our cities and the incredible fact of hungry children in this grotesquely affluent society; and so are you.

Responsibility is shared in all but the most wildly extreme cases: infants are not responsible for being dropped, or ignored, or poorly fed; but even prisoners in concentration camps had some slight degree of responsibility for their own starvation, since suicide was a possible alternative. And in all the usual human affairs of war, peace, education, unemployment, the rot of our cities, and the oppression of some of our citizens *the responsibility is shared by all of us.* To deny that fact is to invite inaction, apathy, unconcern, and to offer no basis for the conscious exercise of free choice. Hence the horror of the Ohio grand jury that found only the students responsible for the deaths at Kent State.

Responsibility is shared. Not equally, but it's shared. We are so used to pointing out the ways in which we *differ* from the extreme bigot, the hired killer, the corrupt politician, that we ignore the ways in which we are *alike*. It's true that I am far less racist than George Wallace, but it's also true that I share *some* of his racism, and that makes me responsible for the plight of Black Americans. Less responsible perhaps, but it's the basic shared responsibility that must be admitted before I, or you, can afford the luxury of talking about degrees of responsibility. When we ignore the traits and responsibilities that we share and concentrate on differences between our own (relative) innocence and the others' (relative) guilt, we end by disclaiming responsibility altogether. "I don't oppress Black people; as a matter of fact, I think they ought to have the same rights I do." "I was never in favor of Vietnam; I argued against it from the start." "Sure, cities are in a mess, and there are too many poor people; something ought to be done." How often have you heard such things? And have you noticed that those statements are almost inevitably followed by, "But what can *I* do?" Or "What do they want from me?" Or "You act like it's *my* fault!" And that these latter statements are followed by a lack of action? The reason is simple enough: there's been no acceptance of responsibility, and therefore there's been no ground laid for change or for the exercise of free choice.

Some examples now, for it's been a long time since I've made any of these notions specific by using illustrations. Here are two discourses. With the first of the two I am about to commit the foolishness of asking you to deal with a rhetorical act, the full text of which I do not provide. I choose to commit this foolishness because the discourse in question does an extraordinary job of allowing, even requiring the audience to accept responsibility and to consciously exercise freedom of choice, and it does that job by first admitting the powerlessness of the rhetorician. An unusual procedure, surely! But this is a most unusual discourse; it was created by what may well be the finest rhetorical and philosophical mind in the world. (The complete text does not follow because, despite the most determined efforts, I've been unable to obtain reprint rights.)[157]

On May 2, 1967, Jean-Paul Sartre delivered the Inaugural Address at the Bertrand Russell War Crimes Tribunal in Stockholm. His opening words were: "We are here to discover whether or not the charges of war crimes brought against the United States are justified."*

Sartre then addressed himself to the question of the Tribunal's "legitimacy." And he faced an immediate and major problem. You will remember that the Russell War Crimes Tribunal that met in Stockholm and Copenhagen in 1967 predated the period in which there was widespread opposition to the Vietnam War in the United States. And although many Europeans took the Tribunal and its findings quite seriously, that body, and its judgment, was systematically ignored in the United States. Obviously, then, the fundamental question that the Tribunal had to face at the outset, particularly in relation to the U.S. and its allies, was the matter of its own legitimacy.

To the frustration of international jurists, the United States has refused to ratify nearly every international agreement that would have bound it to the observance of world law. The United States has refused to contractually commit itself to observe the Kellogg-Briand Pact, the Hague Convention, the principles involved in the Nuremberg Trials, and, of course, the Geneva Accords that pertained directly to Vietnam. Clearly, the first step had to be a discussion or statement about the basis on which this small group of individuals presumed to consider themselves a War Crimes Tribunal.

How *might* Sartre have argued that he and his fellows constituted a legitimate international body? On moral grounds, of course! He could easily have argued that, regardless of the legal question, the Tribunal had an unassailable moral right to place the United States on trial. There has certainly been no lack of testimony from many, many countries as to the simple fact that the war in Vietnam was, from the outset, morally indefensible. And the Nuremberg Trials are an impressive moral precedent, no matter what their legal worth may be. But to have argued on this ground would have been disastrous, for it would have plunged the Tribunal into the maze of claims and counter-claims that have surrounded the Vietnam War for years. You can imagine the cries: "The U.S. is honoring its obligations to those brave citizens of South Vietnam who want to be free"; "The U.S. is cold-bloodedly slaughtering Vietnamese men, women, and children in a war that is of its own making." And on and on, back and forth.

Sartre avoided all this. He avoided it by a six-part argument that is both simple and unassailable morally and rhetorically.

First, he pointed out that the establishment of the Nuremberg Tribunal in 1945

[157] Because of copyright restrictions, I am forced to use excerpts of Jean-Paul Sartre's Inaugural Address to the Bertrand Russell War Crimes Tribunal that come from three different sources. Asterisks indicate my own translation of segments of the address that appeared in "Jean-Paul Sartre Déclare: 'Nous sommes des jurés, non des juges,'" *Le Figaro*, May 3, 1967. Two asterisks indicate an excerpt from a translation of the address printed in *The Los Angeles Free Press*, August 11, 1967. Three asterisks indicate an excerpt from a translation published in *Against the Crime of Silence*, ed. John Duffett (New York: O'Hare Books, 1968), pp. 40-45. The full text can be found in the last two sources.

marked a profound change—a change from attempts to set down the "laws of war" to an attempt to formulate "laws against war." And he emphasized the fact that the Allies, horrified at Nazi excesses, were apparently unaware that they were laying the groundwork for their own condemnation.

Second, he stressed the fact that the legitimacy of the Nuremberg trials has been strongly questioned, that they have been called a "diktat" of conquering nations, and that they were not truly international. He asked whether the Nuremberg judges should have been citizens of neutral countries, and answered that that was uncertain, but that it was quite certain that the Germans were not convinced of the legitimacy of the trials. And that means that both the procedures at Nuremberg and the decisions reached there have consistently been called illegitimate. Further, it has been claimed that Nuremberg was possible only because of the fortunes of war and that, given a different outcome of the war, an Axis Tribunal might well have judged and condemned the Allies for their excesses—the bombing of Dresden and Hiroshima, for example.

Third, in a rhetorical master stroke, Sartre argued that it would have been quite simple to establish the legitimacy of the Nuremberg Tribunal. All that would have been required was to make the Tribunal *a permanent body*, or to make it a part of the United Nations—a part *permanently empowered* to judge all charges of war crimes, no matter what nation or nations were charged. In this fashion the universality and legitimacy of Nuremberg could easily have been established. Instead, fast upon the heels of the last German who disappeared into prision, the Tribunal itself disappeared and has not been heard from since.

Fourth, he asked whether there has been a need for an International War Crimes Tribunal since 1945, whether any nation has practiced violence against another, whether any country's sovereignty has been threatened or destroyed, whether we have been innocent for the past two decades. And he answered: "Since the Nuremberg Trials, war crimes have regularly been committed in the course of the historic events involving the struggle of the Third World, and never since Nuremberg has such a Tribunal been so necessary."*

Fifth, Sartre reminded us that history cannot be rolled back, that no one can retreat to pre-Nuremberg, that whenever a small or poor country is the object of aggression by a larger, stronger one, people cannot be prevented from thinking, "but it is exactly this that was condemned at Nuremberg." The disappearance of the Nuremberg Tribunal, he added, created a vacuum in international life—a vacuum that can be filled in only two ways: some state or states could take the initiative in setting up a new Nuremberg, but few would dare propose a body whose first job would surely be an investigation of a war waged by so powerful a country as the United States; or a genuine court of the people could take the revolutionary step of re-establishing the Nuremberg Tribunal, but the people, separated and fragmented by frontiers, have no way of imposing on various governments a true international court. Thus the dilemma: Nuremberg occurred; after it came a void that requires a new Tribunal; yet the only two sources of power, the state and the people, are unable or unwilling to act.

Sixth, Sartre stated that the Russell Tribunal grew out of the contradiction between the necessity for an International Tribunal made explicit at Nuremberg and the powerlessness of states or people to create such an international body. The Russell Tribunal, he acknowledged, had received no mandate of any sort; but that was because no one could give that mandate. The Russell Tribunal was not recruited or established by any government, and no government invested it with power. However, that is not to say that its legitimacy was in question, for the very real power held and exercised by the Nuremberg Tribunal did not result in uncontested legitimacy for that body. The legitimacy of the Russell Tribunal derived, not from its power, but from its powerlessness—its powerlessness and its universality. "We have neither the power to condemn nor the power to acquit."*

Powerlessness was the legitimacy of the Russell Tribunal, for "the tribunal is powerless and universal, and it is that fact that guarantees the independency and the liberty of our conscience. We receive orders from no one."*

Given that powerlessness, the Tribunal would pass no sentence, for "what could a condemnation mean, even the mildest of condemnations, if we do not possess the means to see it carried out? *We will limit ourselves therefore, if that is what turns out to be necessary, to stating that such and such an act falls under the jurisdiction of Nuremberg.*"** (italics mine.) The Russell Tribunal, in other words, would decide that certain acts were or were not war crimes according to the standards set up at Nuremberg and would proclaim that those acts would or would not have been judged war crimes *if* the laws applied at Nuremberg were applied in this case. And, quite clearly, those who wish to question the legitimacy of the Russell Tribunal must first question the legitimacy of the Nuremberg Tribunal and then the legitimacy of a permanent International War Crimes Tribunal. From a position of openly admitted powerlessness, Sartre has moved to a position of enormous moral and ethical strength.

The purpose of the Bertrand Russell War Crimes Tribunal was, Sartre said, to indicate how acts of war taking place at the time it convened *would have been judged* at Nuremberg, and thereby to increase the recognition that a permanent International Tribunal is urgently needed. Sartre closed by pointing out that, unlike Nuremberg, the Russell Tribunal was indeed international, including members from the country accused, but he added that the mere desire for universality and impartiality on the part of the members of the Tribunal was certainly no reason for considering it a legitimate enterprise. Rather, he asked that its legitimization come after the fact, retroactively, as the public absorbed the workings of the Tribunal through the reports of the press; and he expressed his profound hope that the public would

> discover together with us . . . the documents, the testimony, that they will evaluate them and make up their minds about them . . . together with us. We want the conclusion . . . to be drawn by each individual in his own mind at the same time as we draw them ourselves; even beforehand perhaps.***

Sartre's final words were: "We are jurors, not judges. The peoples of the world will judge the conclusions to which we come."*

For me, this discourse is perhaps the most ethical rhetorical event of our time. Not only does Sartre state that the public has the power to choose freely, and not only does he insist that the audience use its power, he argues that the exercise of free choice by the audience is the *only* way the Tribunal can become legitimate. And the reverse is equally true: only through the free choice of the audience can the Tribunal lose forever any claim to legitimacy.

I know of no clearer instance, and I can imagine no clearer instance, of a rhetorician proclaiming the right of, and the necessity for, his audience to consciously exercise its freedom of choice. I urge you to read the full text in one of the sources cited.

It has seemed very strange to me, but now and then people have said that Sartre's discourse really meant very little, because he and the other members of the Tribunal had already made up their minds that the United States was guilty. I have yet to meet anyone familiar with the evidence introduced at the Tribunal (the evidence is recorded in *Against the Crime of Silence*) who would say that, and I can only assume that because the Tribunal *did* find the United States guilty, and because Sartre, Russell, and other members of the Tribunal were known to be unsympathetic to many aspects of the United States' foreign policy, some critics were led to think the discourse insincere or manipulative. My immediate question in such cases has been: "If you think Sartre was dissembling, that he was trying in some way to load the case against the United States, it must follow that he was trying to get you, his reader, to agree that the United States was the villain. What evidence did he use to try to persuade you of this?" The reply is usually a slow, "Well, none." And that is the key to the nature of this discourse. *Sartre does not pretend to neutrality*, but he makes it quite clear that the audience will determine the legitimacy and the worth of his position. The Tribunal is, as he puts it, a "common enterprise," an enterprise for which both rhetorician and audience bear responsibility.

And the question of responsibility here is a troubling one, for in 1967 the charges made at the Russell Tribunal seemed (to the few who bothered to read them) extreme. By now they have all been documented and confirmed by the commercial press. The infamous "Pentagon Papers" are simply the most complete such documentation. What shall we say, then, of a discourse or a Tribunal that provided a clear basis on which to freely choose a position? And what shall we say of ourselves—of those of us who carefully chose to ignore the evidence? In my view, it is not Sartre who is at fault here.

This is, I think, the highest level on which rhetorical discourse can exist. There is no hint of a right or proper answer that is the property of the speaker and that will be communicated to the audience. Instead, the audience is a full partner, an active partner, and a partner that must create its own answer just as the members of the Tribunal do, or "even beforehand perhaps."

Such willingness to honor the power, the responsibility, and the right of the audience to choose freely, without implying for a moment that the Tribunal did not have its own attitudes and beliefs, is found far too rarely in the rhetorical events of our time. Compare this address with the statements of politicians who insist that they seek office, not for any personal motives, and certainly not because they would enjoy such positions and such power, but only because they "have been called on to serve." Or compare it with the regular proclamations about the high moral quality of those who hold political posts—proclamations accompanied by headlines about grand jury investigations into the morally and legally dubious activities of those same persons.

Or compare it with the following essay by an author whose reputation is towering, but who does not, in this discourse, measure up to the ethical standard that Sartre has set.

### Of Revenge

Revenge is a kind of wild justice; which the more man's nature runs to, the more ought law to weed it out, for as for the first wrong, it doth but offend the law, but the revenge of that wrong, putteth the law out of office. Certainly, in taking revenge, a man is but even with his enemy, but in passing it over, he is superior; for it is a prince's part to pardon; and Solomon, I am sure, saith, *It is the glory of a man to pass by an offense.* That which is past is gone and irrevocable, and wise men have enough to do with things present and to come; therefore they do but trifle with themselves that labor in past matters. There is no man doth a wrong for the wrong's sake, but thereby to purchase himself profit, or pleasure, or honor, or the like; therefore, why should I be angry with a man for loving himself better than me? And if any man should do wrong merely out of ill-nature, why, yet it is but like the thorn or briar, which prick and scratch, because they can do no other. The most tolerable sort of revenge is for those wrongs which there is no law to remedy; but then let a man take heed the revenge be such as there is no law to punish, else a man's enemy is still before hand, and it is two for one. Some, when they take revenge, are desirous the party should know whence it cometh. This is the more generous; for the delight seemeth to be not so much in doing the hurt as in making the party repent; but base and crafty cowards are like the arrow that flieth in the dark. Cosmus, Duke of Florence, had a desperate saying against perfidious or neglecting friends, as if those wrongs were unpardonable. *You shall read,* saith he, *that we are commanded to forgive our enemies; but you never read that we are commanded to forgive our friends.* But yet the spirit of Job was in a better tune: *Shall we,* saith he, *take good at God's hands, and not be content to take evil also?* and so of friends in a proportion. This is certain, that a man that studieth revenge keeps his own wounds green, which otherwise would heal and do well. Public revenges are for the most part fortunate; as that for the death of Caesar; for the death of Pertinax; for the death of Henry the Third of France; and many more. But in private revenges it is not so; nay, rather, vindictive persons live the life of witches, who, as they are mischievous, so end they unfortunate.

—Francis Bacon

These two rhetorical acts differ a great deal. Sartre was concerned with an immediate social issue, Bacon with a philosophical or psychological description of human character as he thought it should be. Both, however, present a point of view and plead a cause, i.e., both are rhetorical events. Bacon's essay is rhetorically inferior because he neither discloses himself nor honors his audience as fully as Sartre does. Part of the time he argues in practical terms: the least objectionable sort of revenge is for acts that the law cannot or does not punish—but if you take such revenge be sure that there is no law against your vengeful act or your enemy will have gotten at you twice. But, inconsistently, he also says that it's more "generous" to let your enemy know the source of the vengeance than to do it secretly—hardly a practical matter. And it would seem difficult to believe his statement that there's really no reason to feel vengeful because your enemy must have been trying to help himself by hurting you, and because that's a human and understandable motive. Lastly, the idea that "public revenges are for the most part fortunate" rings a grotesque note in an era that has seen the assassinations of Malcolm X, John F. Kennedy, Martin Luther King, Jr., and Robert Kennedy, plus an unknown number of less famous persons.

No, Bacon's essay won't do. Ethically the flaws are too many and too serious. He doesn't admit the human need for revenge that we have all felt, nor does he contrast that need with the social need for control of extreme behaviors. He doesn't inquire into the bases of what he calls "public revenges." And most importantly, he neither makes clear his own reasoning, his own attitudes about the subject nor gives his audience responsibility for deciding that he has argued well or poorly. It is, I'm afraid, an unimpressive rhetorical effort.

For other comparisons look back to discourses quoted earlier. Lincoln's Second Inaugural, for example, can stand the scrutiny. As I pointed out, Lincoln, as leader of the country, assumed responsibility for the war in the name of the entire country. He thus made it possible for both North and South to join together to heal the nation. That they did not do so can hardly be called a fault in Lincoln's address. And his extraordinary rhetorical effort indicates some of the reasons for which we revere him.

Frost's essay, "The Figure A Poem Makes," can stand the comparison, too, though the ethic there is less resounding. He makes it pretty clear that he accepts the responsibility for his own work and at the same time shares that responsibility with his audience. He exposes himself honestly, telling of the ways in which he finds his own poetry. But I find most impressive in that essay the high style, the near-poetic style with which Frost achieves, not merely the statement of a point of view, but the demonstration of one. And this same quality of writing makes it possible for the audience to judge for itself the merits of Frost's case. I want to repeat that there is far more Ritual in this rhetorical act than in many others, including Sartre's.

Milton Mayer's "The Children's Crusade" was strongly ethical. The open admission that the author was one of the elders of whom he spoke and that he was terrified of the young had a searing honesty.

Professor Ehrlich's "Eco-Catastrophe" left his readers free to choose. He dramatized his case, but there was nothing manipulative in his address.

Professor Friedenberg's "The Generation Gap" shone with its own ethic. He faced his contemporaries, declared his sympathies, and exposed much of the ugliness we heap on our young.

And all the other discourses in Chapter 1 had notable ethical values, though none, I think, can quite equal Sartre's speech.

I have set the case high, obviously. All the illustrative rhetorical efforts in the first chapter are to be admired. For somewhat varying reasons of course, but they are all worthy. And none is ethically shabby. Still, I would say that all of them are inferior to the opening address at Stockholm delivered by Jean-Paul Sartre.

Now, what have I said by saying that? Have I set a standard so high that it's almost never reached? Yes, I have. I have indeed. What else is there to do in a day and place in which a Vice President can attack the intellectual and academic communities to the applause of what is called "the silent majority"? What else is there to do in a country whose President ignores or opposes the claims of minorities to equal human rights? What else is there to do in a society that corrupts itself by worshipping financial profit and then proceeds to worship its own corruption?

We live in a nation whose gross national product is reckoned in dollars. A gross reckoning, surely. And the need for those dollars is a force that distorts us all. It has been pointed out that one of the basic dilemmas in the United States is that its citizens *must use symbols as their society wishes* if they are to enjoy their share of the material goods the society provides. And the society wants from the citizen a very specific kind of symbolization—a *profitable* one, for,

> his society is committed to turnover, to production and consumption in ever-increasing amounts. And words are more important now to turn over than things. Merchandising is of greater value to the economy that manufacture, which can be handed over to robots or semi-robots. Craftsmanship has become vestigial.
>
> The gifted American, then, must learn how to merchandise his talents. His talents must be bought, or else he will "starve"—get enough to eat perhaps but share none of the prestige or excitement of the new society. Today we do not live Platonically off slave labor, or Benedictinely on a feudal farm, or Jeffersonianly next door to wilderness; we live Madisonianly by the sale of our wits. And our wits must be packaged attractively or they go unnoticed. Our wits express themselves in symbols, but the symbols must seem real if anyone is to pay real dollars for them. If this means that symbols must be aimed at customers, at the worst and weakest in customers, so that a steady stream of real dollars may be obtained (and it does mean just this, with mathematical precision), we begin to understand an inherent ethical catch in the new technical order, its obligation to rely on the *misuse of symbols.*
>
> This catch is most obvious in politics and commerce, but it also exists in art and science. In academic life it usually takes discrete forms: excessive specialization, excessive avoidance of value-judgments, and similar devices of shrewd hedging and unnoticed secession from the concerns of other men. These evasions of responsibility become inevitable as soon as morality becomes social, not personal. In a highly technicalized society morality becomes more and more social and less and less personal. It is easier to fool

society than one's inner voice, as long as that anachronism remains audible.[158]

That is one of the most frightening descriptions of our culture that I have ever read. And I find it true. What else can explain the madness behind advertisements about cyclones in soap and doves in detergents *that pretend to be real.* What else explains the horror of using Ritual to sell cars—"We wish you a merry Chrysler"—or the insanity behind one hundred years of White riots against Blacks that suddenly finds Blacks to be racists when they attempt to protect themselves. And what else is there that will make sense of the fearful intensity with which we proclaim the rightness of a way of life that includes war waged against a people because they might take over a country, and that might influence another country, and that other country might act on yet another, so that, somewhere down the line, we might find ourselves menaced—a menace that we must remove now by fighting a war.

It is not a credibility gap but a gulf of madness that threatens to swallow us all. And the ugly words we hear from the callous speakers and writers who always, always assure us that the blame lies elsewhere must be branded for what they are—the most shameful lies. There is no better way to fight for social health than to restore Rhetoric to the position described at the beginning of the first chapter: "When one man speaks honestly and openly to other men, it can be a thing of wonder and magic"; and "for a man to speak his thoughts, his feelings, his desires and needs to others requires bravery, for in so speaking that man becomes vulnerable."

I have set the case high. It must be high if I am to avoid the obscenity of calling advertisements Rhetoric, or if I am to escape the need to find rhetorical worth in Richard Nixon's first inaugural address. And I *must* exclude the former from my concerns and disdain the latter if I am to deal with language and with myself in ways that give pride and pleasure. The rhetorical process is and must be intensely personal. I see the symbolic corruption around me, but it is my secret terror that I may not perceive my own merchandising, my own dishonesty. For I am part of this system that has done so much damage to us all. I see its faults and I want them changed. And the changes may be drastic. But at the same time, I must admit that there is a sense in which I am committed to this system. I want, for example, to be a fine professor in a fine university. And if that sort of commitment is deep enough, it may well be my undoing.

As I face the world around me, I want the case set high for Rhetoric, for the rhetorical act at its best, or even near its best, is a noble one. And surely we find nobility too rarely and in too weak and diminished forms. Rhetoric must reason well, must use evidence appropriately, must argue with grace. But most of all it must ring with the clear, sounding ethic that admits responsibility and demands that audiences retain their humanity by choosing freely. In that quality lies much of our salvation. The rest is found in Ritual.

[158] Gerald Sykes, "The New Salvation," *The Center Magazine* II, 5:27.

## Ritual: A Synthesis

It feels strange and yet fitting that this is the penultimate section of my discourse and that, though I have said much about Ritual, have argued that it is the basis of and is inseparable from Rhetoric, and that it is primarily intrapersonal and poetic, I have not yet defined Ritual. I've described it in several ways, but so far no definition. Nothing comparable to "Rhetoric is the theory and practice of persuasion by reasoned discourse."

The word itself says much. Ritual, that which is prescribed in some formal sense, a ceremony, a performance, a rite. The central notion here is the business of repeatability. That is, repeatability for pleasure, not mere mechanical and unfeeling repetition. In the simplest sense Ritual includes all those processes in the repetition of which we find joy, or beauty, or satisfaction, or pleasure. One of the barest and simplest Rituals in my life occurs every morning when I walk our dog. My wife is usually finishing her makeup in her bathroom, and as I leave I call out, "We'll be back, Honey." I may have started to do this so that my wife would know I'd left and would answer the phone if it rang instead of waiting for me to do it. Or I may have had some other rhetorical reason. Whatever the beginnings, the act has become ritualistic now. I call a slurred-together "Wilbybackhoney," and I wait for the sound of her voice. It's a small thing, but I find a certain pleasure in it; I enjoy this small matin of mine. But there's more to it: I'd feel odd if I were to leave silently, for there is some sense in which this Ritual, slight as it is, has become necessary.

Ritual is the sum of those processes that are formed or prescribed in such a way as to give us pleasure, a "necessary" pleasure, when we repeat them. (I don't want to advance that as a formal definition though.) Working still on the simplest level, the reason that some people think of literature as being necessarily written is clear enough; in the confusion and complexity in which we exist, few of us would have the time or energy to acquire, to possess, to retain large amounts of oral literature. And yet we frequently find that snatches of poetry, song, or novels that we have never read, but have heard only, remain with us for many years. The written verse, or play, *seems* so much more clearly formed; it is set down on paper and can magically be taken up from that paper and repeated by he who holds the keys to language. Hence, the near-awe of the written word.

But a little thought convinces us that it is not the fact of writing or printing that is of primary formal value. There *are* such visual values, as I mentioned in talking about free verse in Chapter 3, but they are not basic to Ritual. A poem that is never written down but that is repeated aloud many times is, of course, a poem; and the folk tales of heroes and forlorn maidens are narratives despite the fact that they are told orally; and surely, an author who creates, say, some lines of verse without writing them down *has*, in fact, created that verse. We certainly will not wish to say that these things become poetry, narrative, and verse *only after* they are written down. When they are formed, when they become language forms, they exist, and their existence doesn't depend on writing. (Except of course in such highly unusual cases as the following:

<pre>
                        A
                      tree
                  is not per-
               haps the most beau-
              tiful thing in the world,
             yet it grows with grace, and
            offers shelter to the traveller, and
           it is neither cruel nor wanton nor too
          convinced of its own right. In all these
         ways man *may* be like a tree, though most
        are not; but one further thing the two *must*
         share—both die from the top down.
</pre>

There's a good bit of doubt about the ritualistic value of this example, but if there is such value it would seem that visual form plays a necessary part.)

Ritual is formed symbolic action—action so prescribed that we can repeat it pleasurably. And in saying that a large step is taken toward the solution of the problem described in Chapter 4. There, you'll recall, I talked about the separation of people and Ritual, about the fact that only drama included people (in the form of characters), and about the fact that prose and poetry (the other two major literary forms) were far too easily thought of as objects. Now I've said that Ritual, *all* Ritual, is symbolic action so formed and prescribed that we find pleasure in repeating it. That *must* mean that the very *form* of Ritual not only includes human beings but is appropriate to human action; if the pleasure we find in repeating Ritual is the key, then Ritual must allow for and fit itself to the human act of repetition. And although there's been no evidence advanced for it yet, the idea that drama (the only literary form that does include people) may well provide clues to the approach I'm seeking certainly seems plausible. The next step then—find the sense in which Ritual must be seen as a *human act* that can be repeated for pleasure, keeping an eye on the possibility that drama, as we conventionally know it, may provide some or all of the answers.

### Ritual as Drama

In Chapter 3, I said that the elements that distinguished drama from other symbolic processes were characterization and conflict, and that the two fused to become characters-in-conflict. I said too that these dramatic ingredients made it *possible* for drama to be performed, to be acted, because *the performer was given something to act, some behavior, some actions to perform.* For my present purpose those words are mightily important.

Formally, conventional drama is suited to its purpose, for it consists of the names of characters followed by the words that those characters utter, that they behave. We know at once, as we read drama, that *we are performers.* Probably we'll want to differentiate between the kind of performance we go through as we sit and read a play silently and the kind the actor goes through on the stage, but there is no doubt that, in some imaginative, quiet, but formal sense, we are performing, are feeling the characters' tensions and joys, are *being* those characters. To say that we are not is to say that we are not reading drama, for we do, in fact, utter the characters' words.

Two arguments are significant at this point: first, there is a broad, developmental sense in which language itself is dramatic; second, there is a narrower, more specific sense in which all Ritual is formally similar to conventional drama.

*Language as Drama*    To be human is to use and be used by language. The idea of a human being without language is simply a contradiction in terms. On our deepest language levels, our deepest symbolic levels, we perceive beauty and ugliness, danger and comfort in the sounds, sights, textures, and motions of the world around us. Without these primal, nonverbal, symbolic processes we could not possibly be considered human.

Language is always an *active* process, and all users of language—readers, writers, listeners, speakers, and thinkers—are symbolically active. There's no possibility of *using* language *passively*, as the underlined words indicate.

These two notions fit together: to be human is to engage and be engaged in the active process of language.

Next it must be emphasized again that in our active language processes we act on the world, on our environment. We do *not* merely *react* passively to it. I first said that as long ago as the Introduction and illustrated it with quotations from Arthur Koestler. Let me turn to Mr. Koestler again for what is a near-perfect description of our acting on the world around us:

> The lowliest creature and the highest, the moment it is hatched or born, lashes out at the environment, be it liquid or solid, with cilia, flagellae, or contractile muscle fibre; it crawls, swims, glides, pulsates; it kicks, yells, breathes, feeds, and sucks negative entropy from its surroundings for all it's worth.[159]

And the words used in the Introduction, like so many of Koestler's statements, bear repeating (i.e., attain a certain ritualistic quality?):

> In fact, the animal does not merely adapt to the environment, but constantly adapts the environment to itself. It eats environment, drinks environment, fights and mates environment, burrows and builds in the environment; and even in observing environment, it modifies, dismantles, analyses, and resembles it after its own fashions, converting "noise" into "information."[160]

What striking statements of an aspect of ourselves that we rarely consider! I'm led instantly to think of my pencil acting on the page as I write these words, of my fingers acting on the pencil, etc. And the various larger forms of acting on the environment loom endlessly once we begin to look: the food eaten, the furniture arranged, the walls painted, and on and on.

And this concept links with the previous two, so that to be human is to

[159] Koestler, p. 447.
[160] *Ibid.*, p. 448.

engage and be engaged in the symbolic process of acting on the environment.

The beginning of drama emerges from this action on the environment, for in so acting we behave in a protagonist-antagonist sense. Our language behaviors are always personal, always individual; the outer world is impersonal, unfeeling, massive. Language then is a matter of pitting man against matter, the personal against the impersonal; language is a matter of trying to bring some sort of order out of chaos. The environment is not a submissive pudding that yields when we prod it. The world resists our symbolic maneuvers and manipulations so that we must, in Koestler's terms, "lash out" at it if we are to restructure it and make of it a habitable place.

The conceptual string now reads, to be human is to be involved in the symbolic process of acting on an antagonistic universe.

But this acting on the environment is a two-edged process. By acting on the world about us we act on ourselves in the sense that we constitute ourselves. From early infancy onward this process continues. The baby who begins to feel a rattle or ball as some sort of vague *thing* is starting to separate himself from his environment and to constitute himself as a creature able to feel, and hear, and see. The young child who asks endless questions and who can be satisfied with almost any answer (the moon is yellow because it's up so high) is equipping himself with the marvelous discovery that questions have answers. The boy or girl who probes curiously into the surrounding environment is fitting him or herself with the traits of the investigator or explorer. And the adult who seizes and is seized by a poem, or play, or story is refining and elaborating on those qualities that make him unique; he's sharpening his sensitivity to a particular sort of tragic or comic situation, or discovering tastes that lead him in one direction rather than another, or increasing his understanding of his own emotional processes. It's in these symbolic behaviors that we create ourselves, for in using language we become conscious that we are language users. Language processes are reflexive; they carry with them self-consciousness. Thus our self-awareness exists in, and is created by language. The views of ourselves that we hold dear or frightening are symbolic structures. And our beliefs in our own frailty or fierceness we build of our language.

The chain now reads, to be human is to constitute oneself by symbolically acting on the antagonistic environment.

Finally, it's in the active, double-edged, symbolic processes of language that drama is fully born, for as humans we are doomed to the inevitable and futile struggle to break the bonds of language. It's here that the primal dramatic act is found, not in religion or the need for emotional catharsis. First man forms himself by acting on his world; he becomes conscious of himself as separate from the out-there, and in the process he becomes conscious of his own consciousness. Then man sees himself as separated from the world, as set apart and isolated; and he cannot bear his uniqueness, for to be literally isolated is literally to die. The eternal conflict between the need to exist, to be separate from the world, and the need to unite with, to draw strength and comfort from the world *is* drama.

This conflict can be seen in Suzanne Langer's description of the manner in which language (and man) may have begun.

(Language) could only have arisen in a race in which the lower forms of symbolistic thinking—dream, ritual, superstitious fancy—were already highly developed, i.e., where the process of symbolization, though primitive, was very active. Communal life in such a group would be characterized by vigorous indulgence in purely expressive acts, in ritual gestures, dances, etc., and probably by a strong tendency to fantastic terrors and joys.[161]

Professor Langer speaks of the probability that language began as a sort of vocal and gestural play, a symbolic game, and then says:

In a sociable species this game would presumably become a joint affair almost at once. The word uttered by one pre-Adamite would evoke a fuzzy, individual conception in another; but if the word, besides stimulating that conception, were tied up to the same *object* for the hearer as it was for the speaker, the word would have a common meaning for both of them. The hearer, thinking his own thought of the object, would be moved thereby to say the word, too. The two creatures would look at one another with a light of understanding dawning under their great brow-ridges, and would say some more words, and grin at some more objects. Perhaps they would join hands and chant words together.[162]

These conjectures about the first fringes of symbolic behavior are impressive because they offer not only a plausible explanation of the earliest and crudest attempts at language, but also a description that includes those qualities most apparent in fully developed language. Both at the beginning and now, it's these qualities that are fundamental: suggestibility or impressionability ("a strong tendency to fantastic terrors and joys"), the individuality and separation ("the hearer, thinking his *own* thought"), the need to unite, to overcome the felt isolation ("they would join hands and chant words together"). Always, it seems, the confines of language have been felt and fought against. Today these are our most commented-on characteristics: our readiness to react to "fantastic terrors and joys" is seen in Shakespeare's lines quoted before, "The lunatic, the lover, and the poet/ Are of imagination all compact"; our prisoned individuality has been described by Thoreau, "The mass of men lead lives of quiet desperation"; and our need to join together, to reach beyond ourselves is perhaps reflected most clearly in such invitations to dramatic partnerships as these lines from the Prologue to *Henry V*:

> Think when we talk of horses that you see them
> Printing their proud hooves i' the receiving earth.
> For 'tis your thoughts that now must deck our kings,
> Carry them here and there, jumping o'er times,
> Turning the accomplishment of many years
> Into an hourglass.

As humans we look out at the world and each other with and through language, and we know that our language is, that *we are*, a prism that bends what is

[161] Langer, *Philosophy in a New Key*, p. 114.
[162] *Ibid.*, pp. 119-20.

seen. But there is no possibility of breaking through language and seeing our world *as it is*, for without language we do not exist. Thus we must depend totally on the very process that binds us. The most we can do is to turn that process back on itself, *on ourselves*, to create the symbolic miracle of metaphor. We may come to Richards' point of realizing that all specific metaphors "are super-imposed upon a perceived world that is itself a product of earlier or unwitting metaphor," i.e., that the primal metaphor is the fusion of the symbolic act of seeing and the thing seen. But there is no going beyond this point; all attempts to deal directly with naked reality are futile; worse, they are self-defeating. Language, like tragedy, leads to ultimate defeat. No matter whether we labor to see clearly and understand scientifically the objective reality that surrounds us or whether we work dramatically and passionately to bridge the gaps that distance us, we are, at the last, returned to ourselves.

It's at this depth that the hugely embedded foundation of drama must first be seen. Here the very act of perception is a conflict between viewer and viewed, for neither the universe nor the acts of man are passive or impersonal. The perceiver acts on and against a resistant world, and in doing so he creates and sustains himself. Soon he realizes that simple direct contact with anything beyond himself is impossible, for such contact would violate his own symbolic nature. Yet he cannot sit submissively in his language chains, he must stretch out his hand to his brothers and to the scenes in which they move. He struggles, and from these struggles there develops first the glint of awareness that his brothers' symbolic state is like his own, then, the earliest attempts to break his symbol-bonds by joining together in rude Ritual performed on the shared ground where understanding is possible. Many, many years later he is led by this symbolic need to stand on the stage, separated by actuality and artifice from those who watch, and to reach across the footlights in the dramatic act that has come closer than any other to uniting human beings.

*Ritualists as Actors*     Turning now to the narrower sense in which language is drama, the sense in which all Ritual is formally similar to conventional drama, the first statement to be made is that all Ritual involves *personae*. That is, just as traditional drama involves characters, all forms of Ritual are based on the existence of imaginary persons, speakers, *personae*. The term *persona* has been used for some years by literary critics, and I'm going to adopt it because it is so close to "person" *and* to the *dramatis personae* of conventional drama.[163]

Every ritualistic act, poem, play, or story, is a statement that can appropriately be uttered by some *persona*. The acts fits or is suited to the character and personality of a fictitious being, just as rhetorical acts are, we say, appropriate to actual persons. The *personae* of Ritual exist in, are embodied in the ritualistic act, and they must be discovered by exploring that act. What is misleading, or what we have allowed to become misleading, is that the literary or recorded *form* of

---

[163] In an earlier book, *The Speaking and the* Speakers *of Literature* (Belmont, Calif.: Dickenson Publishing Company, Inc., 1967), I used the term "speaker" in dealing with the notion of the dramatic bases of literature. I've decided that the label *persona* is more profitable simply because it pulls so urgently toward both the "person" of the reader-speaker-thinker and the *dramatis personae* of formal drama. And that double pull is, I believe, a revealing one.

some ritualistic acts clearly discloses the *persona,* while the literary *form* of others does so less clearly.

For instance, it's quite obvious that this act, these words, indicates the existence of a *persona:*

> RICHARD: Now is the winter of our discontent
> Made glorious summer by this sun of York:
> And all the clouds that lowered upon our house
> In the deep bosom of the ocean buried.
> Now are our brows bound with victorious wreaths;
> Our bruiséd arms hung up for monuments;
> Our stern alarums chang'd to merry meetings,
> Our dreadful marches to delightful measures.
> Grim-visag'd war hath smoothed his wrinkled front:
> And now—instead of mounting barbéd steeds
> To fright the souls of fearful adversaries,—
> He capers nimbly in a lady's chamber
> To the lascivious pleasing of a lute.
> But I—that am not shap'd for sportive tricks,
> Nor made to court an amorous looking-glass;
> I, that am rudely stamped, and want love's majesty
> To strut before a wanton ambling nymph;
> I, that am curtail'd of this fair proportion,
> Cheated of feature by dissembling nature,
> Deform'd, unfinish'd, sent before my time
> Into this breathing world scarce half made up,
> And that so lamely and unfashionable
> That dogs bark at me as I halt by them;—
> Why, I, in this weak piping time of peace,
> Have no delight to pass away the time,
> Unless to spy my shadow in the sun,
> And descant on mine own deformity:
> And therefore,—since I cannot prove a lover,
> To entertain these fair well-spoken days,—
> I am determinéd to prove a villain,
> And hate the idle pleasures of these days.

Reading these lines of the opening speech of *Richard III* we know at once that there is a *persona,* a character here. And we have no difficulty in assuming that these words tell us something, perhaps a great deal, about the *persona;* in other words, we assume that the *persona* is to be discovered in what he says, in the act of speaking. We find that the anger and bitterness that Richard expresses when he speaks of his deformity, his hunched-back, is a significant part of his character. And in some sense we understand that he must lash out at those around him, that he must play the only part he feels he can play—the villain; in some sense, that is, we understand Richard.

Because we've seen this sort of thing performed on stage and in film, we react to it as a character, or characters, behaving in a certain way. We talk about Richard as a character, a *persona*, not merely about lines in a play. As pointed out in Chapter 4, the difference is most important, for Richard the *persona* is alive, dynamic, while lines in a play are objects.

But we are *not* used to finding a persona, a character, in lines like these:

### Sonnet CXXXVIII

When my love swears that she is made of truth,
I do believe her, though I know she lies,
That she might think me some untutored youth,
Unlearnéd in the world's false subtleties.
Thus vainly thinking that she thinks me young,
Although she knows my days are past the best,
Simply I credit her false speaking tongue.
On both sides thus is simple truth suppressed.
But wherefore says she not she is unjust?
And wherefore say I not that I am old?
Oh, love's best habit is in seeming trust,
And age in love loves not to have years told.
   Therefore I lie with her and she with me,
   And in our faults by lies we flattered be.

—William Shakespeare

Yet a *persona* exists in and behind these words just as surely as Richard existed in his. The difference is simply that one is explicitly labeled, the other implied. An attitude is expressed here, and attitudes can be held and expressed only by people. Or, to repeat one of my basic and recurring notions, because to use language is to be human, *this* use of language betokens some sort of person. A fictitious one, and therefore a *persona*.

In this case the *persona* is easy enough to see, for there are personal pronouns that are clear indicators: "*my* love," "*I* do believe her, though *I* know she lies," etc. The "I" is the *persona*. And his ritualistic act, his act of speaking, shows him to us. A man who is too distant from his woman in years, who needs her too much or too urgently, who knows the fear of not being loved; a man who is bitter at his own inability to face the lies both he and his love have told; and that bleak pun on "lie-lies" in the final couplet surely discloses a man who is at the mercy of a love that is more punishment than pleasure.

One more example—this one of a kind in which we are even less likely to look for a *persona:*

### USA [164]

X marks the spot where the body lies in time,
Bloody blotch that fell through the howling air:

By love betrayed, the letter read and burned?
Darling, I'm sorry, can't we just be friends?

[164] Reprinted by permission of Paul Engle.

By grim phone call at night, the stranger's voice
Muffled through cloth, but harder than a fist?
By dark disease, hidden from family,
But x-rays absolute proof: look, that gray blur—
With antiseptic shrug and surgical smile—
Six months, maybe a year?
                              Is there a note,
Scrawled like a scream on paper?
                              I tried, I tried!
I thought it would work. Only myself to blame.
Best years of my life. I still can't figure out
Where it went wrong. Good-bye.
                              Or a woman's name
Dropped on the pale page like dripping sound,
That one word loud as if it were live blood.

Or an address hinting it would tell all,
That proved to be his lodge, happy to send a wreath,
A bench of brothers to mourn.
                              Or a paragraph
Neat as an order book, thought out for days,
A model to be used by the next man
Tagged for the territory, giving the car,
His guns and tackle, to his oldest boy,
And all insurance to his wife (he'd been
Well-covered, naturally).
                              Or not one word,
Just silence leering from an empty room,
To hint that after liquor, drugs, and girls
He'd given up and let the lesion take him—
Guilt like an old wound groaning with the weather.
Nothing to show the weasel, conscience, snarled
Once before he grabbed it, cage and all,
And jumped into the glittering cage of air?
Nothing: no next room salesman to report
He'd heard a yell, as if one heard the blind
Cyclops bellow into his astonished cave.

But look—the cops are calling. Give im air.
Let the poor bastard breathe. He's coming to.

He's tougher than we thought—some broken bones,
Not much for a fall like that, he'll soon be back
Good as ever, one of the boys, to bounce
History on his knee like a bold blonde.

                                        —Paul Engle


There are no "I's" or "me's" here that point to the *persona*. The word "I" is
used several times, but it refers to someone the *persona* is describing. Just as I may
say a sentence such as, "He looked up and said through the longest pain on earth, '*I*

can't love her because that might make her love me!'" in which "I" refers to a person being described rather than to myself, a *persona* may use "I" in speaking of someone else.

There is an attitude expressed in these lines, an attitude toward a man who attempts suicide. It's the *persona* who holds that attitude, who describes the would-be dead one. And as with the previous examples the *persona* can be found by exploring the attitude and the act that is this ritualistic event. This *persona* is an observer, not a participant. He looks on, sees human pain, but keeps himself aloof from that pain and the man who suffers it. There's even a sort of humor, especially in the last lines—a kind of satirical smile at the live one who wanted to be dead, but who'll soon be back "to bounce/History on his knee like a bold blonde." It's not a cruel humor; rather, it seems that this *persona* sees all the human frailties that surround him, accepts them, but cannot refrain from pointing them out wryly. A feeling man, this *persona*, but one who is armored against too much sympathy.

And so it is with all Ritual. There are *personae* in every Ritualistic act—some obvious, others only dimly limned.

A *persona* of course is *not* the author. There is no necessary relationship between the two. Richard III is not Shakespeare; the watcher who smiled faintly at the attempted suicide is not Paul Engle. To equate the *persona* with the author is to return to the depths of the intentional fallacy, for an understanding of the *persona* then demands an understanding of the author. If the two are one I must always turn to history and biography to determine who the author-*persona* is; and such concerns, no matter how important to the biographer or historian, are not the stuff of Ritual. Proof of this pudding is found in the simple fact that we can and do enjoy and involve ourselves in all kinds of Ritual without knowing a thing about given authors.

A *persona* is an imaginary being created on the one hand by an author and on the other by a reader. Arthur Koestler puts this point well:

> Thus the figments of Bovary, Little Lord Fauntleroy, and Alyoshe Kara-
> mazov which float around us in the air are projections which body forth from
> our intimate selves, like the medium's ectoplasm. The author has created the
> prototype-phantoms, and the reader creates out of himself a copy, which he
> assumes to be like the original, though this is not necessarily the case. Whe-
> ther the Elizabethans saw Shylock in tragic or grotesque light, my own Shy-
> lock is a tragic figure—he has a great hook nose like mine, not a snub nose like
> to thine.[165]

Here is both the core of the difference between Rhetoric and Ritual *and* the heart of Ritual as drama. Rhetoric is discourse addressed to an audience; in some fashion, to some degree, Rhetoric brings a speaker or writer and an audience together. Ritual is not discourse and is not addressed to an audience; the *personae* are a middle ground in the ritualistic event, a stage wrought by an author and worked by readers who move beyond themselves to become, to empathically inhabit, those imaginary beings. It's the consummatory, the constitutive act of

[165] Koestler, p. 346.

becoming *personae* that opens Ritual to all who can or wish to enter. And it's exactly that act that removes or solves the problem of treating Ritual as objects. So long as I consider a ritualistic event as an object I'm limited to thinking or talking *about* that object—poem, story, or play. But as soon as I view it as a *persona* I have something to do, someone to become; I can then *behave* Ritual, just as actors *behave* or perform their roles. Indeed the way is open for me to *act* Ritual, to look at poems and stories, as well as plays, as actions that I can perform. The stories, poems, and plays remain distinguishable forms, but they share the dramatic dimension that makes them Ritual.

Now to some of the ways of discussing and becoming *personae*.

Since Ritual always involves *personae*, the primary question is always "Who?" But that question is often answered by the secondary ones—"What?" "Where?" "When?" and "How?" These questions have been suggested by various writers as techniques for exploring the dramatic nature of Ritual,[166] and they all refer to some aspect of the Ritualistic act.

The What? is simple enough. The *persona* is discovered through his act, through his words. But it must be understood that this is not all the same as the notion that Ritual is an "it" and that the first problem is to find *what* "it" means. Instead the problem is always to discover the *persona*, and the What? is merely one way of doing so. In some cases it's the simplest way. The *persona* of this short excerpt, for instance, is revealed pretty clearly through what he says:

from "Exploration by Air, Part II"[167]

For we are talking about a kind of existence, the newly tenanted sky, the bird's aspect of the world to which you have by now grown used. To the groundling the sky is a venture above him always prohibited, and the wind is a force and a motion; he sees it over the airport as the straightening wind-sock, as a shower of leaves, as spiralling dust. But for you the wind is your step, is your stairway; and you gun the engine and streak forward into it, and with a single giant stride you are in it, climbing; the wind is a place you inhabit.

—Fleming MacLeish

He's talking about flying, and he obviously knows what it is to fly. His feelings about the sense of power, the sense of freedom, that comes with inhabiting the wind are *his*, and they disclose him. Although he makes no direct comparison between himself and the groundlings, the implication that he isn't one of them is unmistakable.

As a brief aside, notice that this is not *discourse* despite the fact that the *persona* is speaking *to* someone. The difference is that discursive language (Rhetoric) is always addressed to a *real* audience, an audience of persons. These words are addressed to an *imaginary* audience, an audience of *personae*, in the same sense that a speech of Othello's is addressed to Desdemona. Direct address, address

[166] See Geiger, Chapter 6.
[167] Reprinted by permission of Hawthorn Books.

between author and real audiences, violates the nature of Ritual. Northrop Frye comments on the results of such interference by authors in their own works:

> As soon as it is felt that a writer is showing off, that he is taking his eye away from his form and is beginning to introduce things that he cannot resist, a barrier goes up at once. The reason is that a self-conscious cleverness interrupting the unity of the form is an intervention from the ordinary personality, with its claims to attention, a kind of attempt at direct address, from the author as "man." The barrier is a sign that direct address, which has no place in literature as such, is being resisted.[168]

The *persona* of Ritual must not be displaced by the person, the writer or speaker, of Rhetoric. When that happens audiences are deprived of the dramatic process of responding to and becoming the *persona* and are jolted into the self-persuasive role of rhetoricians. Even in such balanced forms as propagandistic plays (say, 50% Rhetoric, 50% Ritual), there's room for only a limited amount of direct address between author and audience; there is an odd form of direct address in such cases, but it's between *personae* and audiences. And in the heavily ritualistic acts even that is forbidden, and direct address can occur only between one *persona* and another. (But because there is no "pure" Rhetoric or Ritual, because I'm discussing a continuum, not a dichotomy, I must stress again the constant overlapping that occurs.[169] In rhetorical discourse the ritualistic element enters when the speaker or writer is withdrawn, aloof, distant, or reserved; in ritualistic acts Rhetoric is involved because those acts, though not addressed *to* a real audience, are performed *by* real people *for* a real audience [even when performer and audience are one].)

Back to the subsidiary questions that disclose the *persona*, the Who? After the What? the next question is likely to be Where? I am who I am depending in good part on where I am; I'm one person talking to my wife at breakfast, another talking to a class, another trying to tell a policeman that the light didn't really turn red before I drove into the intersection. Hopefully there's some continuity in these behaviors, and it's that continuity that distinguishes them from the roles I play in Ritual. In the latter there need be no continuity, no relationship between one role and another. A *persona*, too, is who he is depending a great deal on where he is. For example:

### from "The Garden of Proserpine"

> Here, where the world is quiet,
>     Here, where all trouble seems
> Dead winds' and spent waves' riot
>     In doubtful dreams of dreams;
> I watch the green field growing
> For reaping folk and sowing,
> For harvest-time and mowing,
>     A sleepy world of streams.

[168] Frye, p. 121.
[169] There is an article that deals with the idea of the *personae* implied by rhetorical acts, developing the notion of rhetorical-ritualistic overlap in an unusual and interesting way: Edwin Black, "The Second Persona," *Quarterly Journal of Speech* LVI, 2: 109-119.

> I am tired of tears and laughter,
>     And men that laugh and weep;
> Of what may come hereafter
>     For men that sow to reap:
> I am weary of days and hours,
> Blown buds of barren flowers,
> Desires and dreams of powers,
>     And everything but sleep.

—Algernon Charles Swinburne

I find this *persona* through what he says, and what he says depends directly on where he says it. In this case, the first stanza describes the locale in which the *persona* exists, and he could not utter the second stanza if that locale were different. Imagine the first lines describing "a city where winding hollows, and narrow deep-set streets, explode with sound that follows and ruins all retreats." Not impressive lines of course, but you could surely be tired of all such things. *Not* "tired of tears and laughter," though, or even of "desires and dreams and powers." The utter weariness in the second stanza depends on the Where? of the first. And the *persona*, a man or woman who wants no more of the world, also depends on that first stanza. Another *persona* might resent or resist his environment, but his resentment or resistance would vary with that environment. The Where? as well as the What? is an important key to the Who?

Perhaps less frequently, or at least less frequently of major significance, is the question When? It's similar to the What? in the sense that *personae* differ because of the time in which they live. It's one thing to be an American in 1971, and it was quite a different thing to be an American in 1941, or 1841, etc. The When? of Ritual is often less clear than the What? or Where?, but it's always there and always of some value in disinterring the Who? Here's a fairly obvious When?:

### Astrophel and Stella

> Loving in truth, and fain in verse my love to show
> That she, dear she, might take some pleasure of my pain—
> Pleasure might cause her read, reading might make her know,
> Knowledge might pity win, and pity grace obtain—
> I sought fit words to paint the blackest face of woe,
> Studying inventions fine, her wits to entertain,
> Oft turning others' leaves, to see if thence would flow
> Some fresh and fruitful showers upon my sunburnt brain.
> But words came halting forth, wanting Invention's stay;
> Invention, nature's child, fled step-dame Study's blows;
> And others' feet still seemed but strangers' in my way.
> Thus, great with child to speak, and helpless in my throes,
> Biting my truant pen, beating myself for spite,
>     "Fool," said my Muse to me, "look in thy heart, and write!"

—Sir Philip Sidney

Perhaps the simplest thing to say is that this *persona* is not speaking now, for he doesn't talk the way persons or *personae* do today. His language marks him in time, puts him in no single year, decade, or even century, but surely places him several centuries into the past. He doesn't speak from the twentieth or nineteenth centuries. The syntax is old—"knowledge might pity win," "studying inventions fine," etc.; today we'd reverse these and say, "knowledge might win pity" and "studying fine inventions." The metaphors are old, too—"But words came halting forth, wanting Invention's stay" (notice the capital "I" Invention—a reference to the classical canon of Rhetoric); it still works as metaphor, but the almost personalized use of "Invention" sounds through a thick layer of years. And even the vocabulary—"thence," "oft," "thy," "step-dame"—indicates that this *persona* is far before the age of anxiety, of nuclear tension, of the flip, fragmented phrase. Put together with the What?, this When? reveals a *persona* who struggles to be loved in a time more formal, more ornate, and more gilded than our own.

The last question, How?, is a complicated one. By How? I *don't* mean the way in which a *persona* says what he says, and that's what the question could be misunderstood to mean. "How does he say it? Why, angrily, or sadly, or brusquely, or whiningly." I don't mean that sort of How? because all qualities of that sort are part of the What? As I've said several times, you can't separate matter and manner; you can't utter a word without uttering it in some fashion. So the notion that a word or words can be artificially isolated from its or their manner of utterance is unjustifiable. If I yell an angry and loud "Shut up!" the anger and volume is not one thing and the perceived acoustical events something else.

By the question How? I mean the symbolic form the *persona* uses, the ritualistic form that he employs. I said in Chapter 3 that the basic forms of Ritual were prose, poetry, and drama; in this chapter I've emphasized the importance of drama as the basis of *all* Ritual. Now, without discarding any of this, I want to talk about the How? by describing the secondary forms that are superimposed on the dramatic base of Ritual and the *personae* that exist in those secondary forms.

*The Personae of Poetry, Prose, Verse, and Nonpoetry*    The three terms, "poetry," "prose," and "verse," can be most confusing. Conventionally, "poetry" and "prose" are used as near-opposites—"poetry" meaning imaginative language dependent on metaphor and rhythm, and "prose" (of the ritualistic sort, not the rhetorical kind that is based on reasoned efforts to persuade) meaning imaginative language that is descriptive or narrative in nature. "Verse" is traditionally used to mean either one sort of poetry or simply as a synonym for poetry. In Chapter 3 these terms were so used.

That these meanings aren't entirely satisfactory seems evident if you examine the following examples. This is a verse:

> Thirty days hath September,
> April, June and November, etc.

So is this:

> There was a young lady named Bright
> Who travelled much faster than light.
> She went out one day
> In her relative way,
> And returned on the previous night.

This is poetry:

## I Knew A Woman Lovely in Her Bones[170]

I knew a woman, lovely in her bones,
When small birds sighed, she would sigh back at them;
Ah, when she moved, she moved more ways than one:
The shapes a bright container can contain!
Of her choice virtues only gods should speak,
Or English poets who grew up on Greek
(I'd have them sing in chorus, cheek to cheek.)

How well her wishes went! She stroked my chin,
She taught me Turn, and Counter-Turn, and Stand;
She taught me Touch, that undulant white skin:
I nibbled meekly from her proffered hand;
She was the sickle; I, poor I, the rake,
Coming behind her for her pretty sake
(But what prodigious mowing we did make.)

Love likes a gander, and adores a goose:
Her full lips pursed, the errant note to seize;
She played it quick, she played it light and loose;
My eyes, they dazzled at her flowing knees;
Her several parts could keep a pure repose,
Or one hip quiver with a mobile nose
(She moved in circles, and those circles moved.)

Let seed be grass, and grass turn into hay:
I'm martyr to a motion not my own;
What's freedom for? To know eternity.
I swear she cast a shadow white as stone.
But who would count eternity in days?
These old bones live to learn her wanton ways:
(I measure time by how a body sways.)

—Theodore Roethke

To say that these three selections are all the same thing—verse, or poetry, or verse and poetry—seems strange. "I Knew a Woman Lovely in Her Bones" possesses qualities of word-magic, of the mystery of metaphor, of the newness of poetry. To call this the same as the limerick and "Thirty Days Hath September" contradicts all my (our?) basic language responses. I feel a huge symbolic injustice in lumping these works together.

This is prose:

## from "On the Origin of Inequality"

A famous author, reckoning up the good and evil of human life, and comparing the aggregates, finds that our pains greatly exceed our pleasures:

[170] "I Knew a Woman," copyright 1954 by Theodore Roethke, from *The Collected Poems of Theodore Roethke.* Reprinted by permission of Doubleday & Company, Inc.

so that, all things considered, human life is not at all a valuable gift. This conclusion does not surprise me; for the writer drew all his arguments from man in civilization. Had he gone back to the state of nature, his inquiries would clearly have had a different result, and man would have been seen to be subject to very few evils not of his own creation. It has indeed cost us not a little trouble to make ourselves as wretched as we are. When we consider, on the one hand, the immense labours of mankind, the many sciences brought to perfection, the arts invented, the powers employed, the deeps filled up, the mountains levelled, the rocks shattered, the rivers made navigable, the tracts of land cleared, the lakes emptied, the marshes drained, the enormous structures erected on land, and the teeming vessels that cover the sea; and, on the other hand, estimate with ever so little thought, the real advantages that have accrued from all these works to mankind, we cannot help being amazed at the vast disproportion there is between these things, and deploring the infatuation of man, which, to gratify his silly pride and vain self-admiration, induces him eagerly to pursue all the miseries he is capable of feeling, though beneficent nature had kindly placed them out of his way.

—Jean-Jacques Rousseau
(translated by G. D. H. Cole)

And this:

### from "The Comic Spirit"

If you believe that our civilization is founded in common sense (and it is the first condition of sanity to believe it), you will, when contemplating men, discern a Spirit overhead; not more heavenly than the light flashed upward from glassy surfaces, but luminous and watchful; never shooting beyond them, nor lagging in the rear; so closely attached to them that it may be taken for a slavish reflex, until its features are studied. It has the sage's brows, and the sunny malice of a faun lurks at the corners of the half-closed lips drawn in an idle wariness of half-tension. That slim feasting smile, shaped like the long-bow, was once a big round satyr's laugh, that flung up the brows like a fortress lifted by gunpowder. The laugh will come again, but it will be of the order of the smile, finely-tempered, showing sunlight of the mind, mental richness rather than noisy enormity. Its common aspect is one of unsolicitous observation, as if surveying a full field and having leisure to dart on its chosen morsels, without any fluttering eagerness. Men's future upon earth does not attract it; their honesty and shapeliness in the present does; and whenever they wax out of proportion, overblown, affected, pretentious, bombastical, hypocritical, pedantic, fantastically delicate; whenever it sees them self-deceived or hoodwinked, given to run riot in idolatries, drifting into vanities, congregating in absurdities, planning short-sightedly, plotting dementedly; whenever they are at variance with their professions, and violate the unwritten but perceptible laws binding them in consideration one to another; whenever they offend sound reason, fair justice; are false in humility or mined with conceit, individually, or in the bulk; the Spirit overhead will look humanely malign, and cast an oblique light on them, followed by volleys of silvery laughter. That is the Comic Spirit.

—George Meredith

But again, the two are different in important ways. The Rousseau excerpt is a reasoned view of the human condition; it's a statement deploring man's ability to make himself miserable; it's Rhetoric. The Meredith piece is a view of the human condition too, but an imaginative view, a dramatic view, the view of a *persona;* it's Ritual.

There's a four-way distinction that needs to be made here and in all Ritual. "Thirty Days Hath September" and the limerick are verse, but they are *not* poetry. "I Knew a Woman Lovely in Her Bones" is verse, and it *is* poetry. The Rousseau excerpt is prose, but *not* poetry. And the Meredith selection is prose, and it *is* poetry. Simply because language is in verse form doesn't mean that it's poetry; and the fact of being poetry doesn't mean that the thing is verse. Similarly, prose can be poetry or nonpoetry, and what is nonpoetic can be either verse or prose.

There are four labels, and *two* of them are needed to label any work, for the choice is always between verse-poetry, verse-nonpoetry, prose-poetry, and prose-nonpoetry. Or, put differently, there is no verse, only verse-poetry or verse-nonpoetry—no prose, only prose-poetry or prose-nonpoetry, etc. Here's an illustrative schematic device.

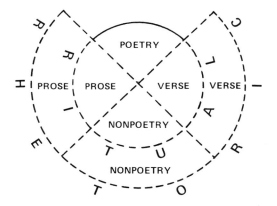

By this rather cumbersome figure, I mean to indicate the two realms, the rhetorical and the ritualistic, with the processes of prose, verse, and nonpoetry extending from one into the other, and only the area of poetry sealed off from Rhetoric and confined to Ritual. (Notice that Ritual is at the center, the core, of Rhetoric.)

But there's a further problem. The categories of prose, verse, and nonpoetry exist both within and beyond the limits of Ritual. I talked earlier of the difference between rhetorical and ritualistic prose. And analogously there is rhetorical and ritualistic verse, and rhetorical and ritualistic nonpoetry (non-poetry has only negative connotations when used alone). Thus "Thirty Days Hath September" and the limerick are not only examples of verse that are not poetry, they're examples of verse that are not even Ritual. And the excerpt from Rousseau is nonpoetry that is also nonritualistic (always remembering that there's a hint of Ritual in the most extreme Rhetoric, and *vice versa.*) The problem, then, is to see whether these forms all exist *within* the boundaries of Ritual, for a comparison between symbolic processes that are ritualistic and others that are rhetorical is not what I'm up to at this stage.

Examples are immediately wanted, but I'm going to assume that the matter of prose is self-evident. Prose such as the Meredith excerpt seems so obviously ritualistic that I don't think further evidence is needed. But I said that that selection was prose *and* poetry, was prose-poetry. The first question then, "Is there Ritual in the form of nonpoetry, say prose-nonpoetry?"

Yes.

## The Learned Giant

Teng Pi, whose cognomen was Po I, was a man of Chin. He was seven feet high. Both his eyes had crimson corners, and they blinked like lightning flashes. In feats of strength he was cock of the walk; and once when his neighbour's bulls were locked in fight, with a blow of his fist he broke the back of one of them and sent it rolling on the ground. The stone drums of the town, which ten men could not lift, he could carry about in his two hands. He was, however, very fond of liquor, and given to quarreling in his cups; so that when people saw him in this mood they would keep out of his way, saying that it was safer to be at a distance from such a wild fellow.

One day he was drinking by himself in a tea house when two literati happened to pass by. Teng Pi tried to make them join him; but they, having a rather low opinion of the giant, would not accept his invitation.

"Gentlemen," cried he in a rage, "if you do not see fit to do as I ask, I will make an end of the pair of you, and then seek safety in flight. I could not brook this treatment at your hands."

So the two had no alternative but to walk in. Teng Pi took the place of honour himself, and put his guests on each side of him. He called for more liquor, and began to sing and make a noise. And at last, when he was well tipsy, he threw off his clothes and began to attitudinize. He drew a knife, and flung it down with a bang on the table; at which the two literati, who were aware of his weakness, rose to take leave.

"Stop!" shouted Teng Pi, detaining them. "I too know something about your books. What do you mean by treating me as the spittle of your mouth? If you don't hurry up and drink, I fear my temper will get the better of me. Meanwhile, you shall ask me anything you like in the whole range of classical literature, and if I can't answer, I will imbrue this blade in my blood."

To this the two literati agreed, and forthwith gave him a number of the most difficult allusions they could think of, taken from the Classics; but Teng Pi was equal to the occasion, and repeated the full quotation in each case without missing a word. Then they tried him on history, covering a period of three thousand years; but here again his answers were distinguished by accuracy and precision.

"Ha! ha!" laughed Teng Pi, "do you give in now?" At which his guests looked blankly at each other, and hadn't a word to say. So Teng Pi shouted for wine, and loosed his hair, and jumped about, crying, "I have floored you, gentlemen, today! Of old, learning made a man of you; but today, all you have to do is to don a scholar's dress and look consumptive. You care only to excel with pen and ink, and despise the real heroes of the age. Shall this be so indeed?"

Now these two literati were men of some reputation, and on hearing Teng Pi's words they were greatly shamed, and left the tea house, hardly knowing how to put one foot before the other. On arriving home they made further inquiries, but no one had ever seen Teng Pi at any time with a book in his hand.

—Sung Lien
(translated by H. A. Giles)

It seems most unlikely that this story would be labeled as primarily rhetorical. The matters of spinning the tale, the descriptions of the characters, and the odd switch at the end are so clearly ritualistic. There's no contact between a real author and a real audience here; instead we read of, react to, and become the *persona*. The *persona* is neither Teng Pi nor the two literati. He is the storyteller, the narrator, the one who observes Teng Pi and the learned ones; he is the one who accepts the wildness of Teng Pi and who sees the need for affection or admiration in the giant; he is the one who repeats the story.

Second question, "Is there Ritual in the form of verse-nonpoetry?"
Yes again.

The Unknown Citizen[171]
(To JS/07/M/378—This Marble Mounment is Erected by the State)

He was found by the Bureau of Statistics to be
One against whom there was no official complaint,
And all the reports on his conduct agree
That, in the modern sense of an old-fashioned word, he was a saint,
For in everything he did he served the Greater Community.
Except for the War till the day he retired
He worked in a factory and never got fired,
But satisfied his employers, Fudge Motors Inc.
Yet he wasn't a scab or odd in his views,
For his Union reports that he paid his dues,
(Our report on his Union shows it was sound)
And our Social Psychology workers found
That he was popular with his mates and liked a drink.
The press are convinced that he bought a paper every day
And that his reactions to the advertisements were normal in every way.
Policies taken out in his name prove that he was fully insured,
And his Health-card shows that he was once in hospital but left it cured.
Both Producers Research and High-Grade Living declare
He was fully sensible to the advantages of the Installment Plan
And had everything necessary to the Modern Man,
A phonograph, a radio, a car and a frigidaire.
Our researchers into Public Opinion are content

That he held the proper opinions for the time of year;
When there was peace, he was for peace; when there was war, he went.
He was married and added five children to the population,
Which our Eugenist says was the right number for a parent of his generation.
And our teachers report that he never interfered with their education.
Was he *free*? The question is absurd:
Had anything been wrong, we should certainly have heard.

—W. H. Auden

This is verse; there's an obvious rhythmic pattern based on phrases that are of unequal lengths but that are clearly marked by the rhyme scheme. It's not poetry, for there's no metaphor, none of the newness of poetic creation. Compared with Meredith's "The Comic Spirit," for instance, there's nothing here that corresponds in any poetic sense to the density of metaphor in sentences such as, "That slim feasting smile, shaped like the long-bow, was once a big round satyr's laugh, that flung up the brows like a fortress lifted by gunpowder." It's verse-nonpoetry, but it's still Ritual. There's a *persona* here who speaks bitingly of the horrors of our society. He speaks about a man who has died but whose death really occurred years before his heart stopped. The calm, searing satire shows this *persona* as a man who feels violent anger at the ugly, dehumanizing culture in which he lives, but whose anger is controlled and scathing.

So, prose, verse, and nonpoetry all exist in Rhetoric; and they all exist in Ritual. Specifically, they can be described as follows: verse and prose are opposites—verse is language characterized by a sustained and perceptible rhythmic pattern, prose, language characterized by the absence of such a pattern; poetry and nonpoetry are opposites—poetry is language whose meaning depends primarily on metaphor, nonpoetry, language whose meaning is not expressed primarily in metaphor. (I'm using the term metaphor broadly still, as in Chapter 3.) And as forms of Ritual they all share the qualities of being dramatic in that they present *personae,* of being self-constituting and self-pleasing in that they are their own reasons for being and in that they bring pleasure in the simple act of repetition, and of being language processes that resonate at the earliest and deepest levels of our development as individuals and as a race.

But there remains a further step to take: as prose-poetry, prose-nonpoetry, verse-poetry, and verse-nonpoetry are forms of Ritual, it must follow that they embody discernibly different *personae.* And it turns out that those differences are fairly simple.

Beginning with prose-nonpoetry, the *personae* here see and act more directly than those of the other forms. They are *personae* whose attitudes, conflicts, actions are not presented in terms of any added form. When compared with verse or poetic forms, the term "prose-nonpoetry" acquires positive comparative values. But when considered alone that term merely means Ritual in its simplest state. All other forms (verse-nonpoetry, prose-poetry, and verse-poetry) bring additional symbolic values to this basic ritualistic form. Thus, viewed as *personae*, the differences seem to me to be as follows: the *persona* of prose-nonpoetry acts directly and freely because he is bound by the demands of neither metaphor nor rhythm; the *persona* of verse-nonpoetry acts within the formal limitations of a rhythmical structure, and his behavior is therefore more tightly disciplined and is likely to have a somewhat great impact: the *persona* of prose-poetry is committed to the new, is tied by and strengthened by metaphor, and his words may well pierce more deeply than the first two *personae*; and a *persona* of verse-poetry submits himself to the most demanding of symbolic processes—the double restriction of metaphor and rhythm—and his act may well be the most tautly worked and deeply imaginative. All these *personae* are the beings I (or you) become as I engage in the ritualistic act. So the above comments should be understood to mean that as the *personae* of prose-poetry, verse-poetry, etc., I (or you) will involve myself more or less deeply.

Thus the traditional forms of Ritual, prose, poetry, and drama, become verse-poetry, prose-poetry, verse-nonpoetry, and prose-nonpoetry, united by the dramatic foundation from which they all rise and separated by the varying *personae* that constitute each form. As Ritual these forms must be seen as *personae* in action, in conflict; as different forms of Ritual, they are the *personae* that the nature and requirements of their actions make them.

And the next issue, naturally, has to do with the relationships between these *personae* and persons, audiences, listeners and readers.

### The Hierarchies of Ritual

The four forms function in ordered or patterned sequences. That is, prose-nonpoetry, verse-nonpoetry, prose-poetry, and verse-poetry cannot be meaningfully arranged in just any order, but must in fact be arranged either as I've just listed them or in exactly the reverse fashion.

To start this argument I'll point out that prose-nonpoetry of the rhetorical sort is the kind of language we use in our ordinary rational attempts to deal with the world and each other and that the prose-nonpoetry of Ritual is the closest to this everyday language, is the most familiar-seeming of the forms of Ritual, and is likely to be thought of as the easiest sort of Ritual to deal with or understand. Put differently, if I think of my most frequent language acts as the usual, or normative, or even "real" ones, I'm likely to think of ritualistic prose-nonpoetry as the closest or most similar to those usual or "real" acts. The following lines are ritualistic prose-nonpoetry, but they are as close to poetry as language can be without crossing that thin, movable, arbitrary dividing line. Indeed it may be that these lines are as equally divided between poetry and nonpoetry as the examples given earlier that were 50% Rhetoric and 50% Ritual. This is another excerpt from *Cyrano de Bergerac*, and these lines are from a scene in which Cyrano, hidden by shadows, speaks of his aching love for Roxane, who thinks that it is her lover, Christian, uttering these words[172]:

[172] From *Cyrano de Bergerac* by Edmond Rostand, Brian Hooker Translation. Copyright 1923 by Holt, Rinehart and Winston, Inc. Copyright 1951 by Doris C. Hooker. Reprinted by permission of Holt, Rinehart and Winston, Inc.

CYRANO: Night, making all things dimly beautiful,
       One veil over us both—You only see
       The darkness of a long cloak in the gloom,
       And I the whiteness of a summer gown—
       You are all light—I am all shadow! . . . How
       Can you know what this moment means to me?
       If I was ever eloquent—
ROXANE: You were
       Eloquent—
CYRANO: —You have never heard till now
       My own heart speaking!
ROXANE: Why not?
CYRANO: Until now,
       I spoke through . . .
ROXANE: Yes?—
CYRANO: —through that sweet drunkenness
       You pour into the world out of your eyes!
       But to-night . . . but to-night, I indeed speak
       For the first time!
ROXANE: For the first time—Your voice,
       Even, is not the same.
CYRANO (passionately—moves nearer):
       How should it be?
       I have another voice—my own,
       Myself, daring—
       (he stops, confused; then tries to recover himself)
       Where was I? . . . I forget! . . .
       Strange—like a dream . . .
ROXANE: How, strange?
CYRANO: Is it not so
       To be myself to you, and have no fear
       Of moving you to laughter?
ROXANE: Laughter—why?
CYRANO (struggling for an explanation):
       Because . . . What am I . . . What is any man,
       That he dare ask for you? Therefore my heart
       Hides behind phrases. There's a modesty
       In these things too—I come here to pluck down
       Out of the sky the evening star—then smile,
       And stoop to gather little flowers.
ROXANE: Are they
       Not sweet, those little flowers?
CYRANO: Not enough sweet
       For you and me, to-night?
ROXANE (breathless): You never spoke
       To me like this. . . .
CYRANO: Little things, pretty things—
       Arrows and hearts and torches—roses red,
       And violets blue—are these all? Come away,

And breath fresh air! Must we keep on and on
Sipping stale honey out of tiny cups
Decorated with golden tracery,
Drop by drop, all day long? We are alive;
We thirst—Come away, plunge, and drink, and drown
In the great river flowing to the sea!
ROXANE: But . . . poetry?
CYRANO: I have made rimes for you—
Not now—Shall we insult Nature, this night,
These flowers, this moment—shall we set all these
To phrases from a letter by Voiture?
Look once at the high stars that shine in heaven,
And put off artificiality!
Have you not seen great gaudy hothouse flowers,
Barren, without fragrance? Souls are like that;
Forced to show all, they soon become all show—
The means to Nature's end ends meaningless!
ROXANE: But . . . poetry?
CYRANO: Love hates that game of words!
It is a crime to fence with life—I tell you,
There comes one moment, once—and God help those
Who pass that moment by!—when Beauty stands
Looking into the soul with grave, sweet eyes
That sicken at pretty words!
ROXANE: If that be true—
And when that moment comes to you and me—
What words will you? . . .
CYRANO: All those, all those, all those
That blossom in my heart, I'll fling to you—
Armfuls of loose bloom! Love, I love beyond
Breath, beyond reason, beyond love's own power
Of loving! Your name is like a golden bell
Hung in my heart; and when I think of you,
I tremble, and the bell swings and rings—
"Roxane!"—
"Roxane!" . . . along my veins, "Roxane!" . . .


There are several fascinating things that take place in these lines. First of all
this is Cyrano speaking—Cyrano the poet, the lover of words. And this is the first
time he has been able to declare his love for Roxane; before this he had spoken
only through the love letters that he had written for Christian. And even though in
this scene Roxane thinks that it is Christian speaking, the very act of uttering these
words, of hearing himself utter them, is almost miraculous to Cyrano. He says that
"to-night, I indeed speak/ For the first time!" Obviously this is not a moment in
which Cyrano will think lightly of words; they are, in fact, the ultimate reality, for
it is with words that he has created his love. And yet look at his own utterance a
few moments later:

> Love hates that game of words!
> It is a crime to fence with life—I tell you,
> There comes one moment, once—and God help those
> Who pass that moment by!—when Beauty stands
> Looking into the soul with grave, sweet eyes
> That sicken at pretty words!

What a magnificently clear cry! Cyrano's words have brought him a moment of triumph, and yet he finds those very words insufficient. The Ritual fails him, and he needs desperately to go beyond words. And in spite of that desperate need, when Roxane asks him how they shall face their moment of truth, what words he will then offer, Cyrano replies, incredibly:

> All those, all those, all those
> That blossom in my heart, I'll fling to you—
> Armfuls of loose bloom!

What a wildly contradictory and beautiful scene! Cyrano, the master ritualist, builds his love of words; he understands utterly that that utter dependence is an incompleteness, a weakness; and at the same time he cannot go beyond his own words except into even more riotous "armfuls of loose bloom."

Here is a very clear statement by a character who puts enormous value on the verbal and on the need to go beyond the verbal. He finds in the ultimate twinings of language that the verbal is empty without the nonverbal, that the verbal leads to the nonverbal, but that the nonverbal leads on even further to other areas of the verbal.

It was out of a belief in the interdependency of words and nonwords that I chose the subhead of this chapter:

> singing forever
> a song made
> of silent as stone silence of
> song

I understand that heading to mean that Ritual is in the final stage made of silences, not words, or of words that are based on silences.

But I've gotten myself off the track, except for the sense in which my argument can be taken to mean that Ritual such as these lines by Cyrano is the most directly related to the "real" or basic human condition. I cited these words as an example of prose-nonpoetry, a ritualistic form that seems closest to the language processes of my everyday. Typography must not be allowed to mislead here; Cyrano's lines can be written out exactly like this paragraph:

CYRANO: Night, making all things dimly beautiful, one veil over us both— you only see the darkness of a long cloak in the gloom, and I the whiteness of a summer gown—You are all light—I am all shadow! . . . How can you know what this moment means to me? If I was ever eloquent—

And the *persona* is not altered importantly. He is a creature of Ritual, but he seems almost my neighbor because there is neither metaphor nor rhythm fierce enough to separate us. (There are many metaphors in these lines, obviously, but the meaning, the *persona* is not directly dependent on or expressed through them.)

By contrast, this sort of Ritual is further away from my daily being.

### Reuben Bright[173]

Because he was a butcher and thereby
Did earn an honest living (and did right)
I would not have you think that Reuben Bright
Was any more a brute than you or I;
For when they told him that his wife must die,
He stared at them and shook with grief and fright,
And cried like a great baby half that night,
And made the women cry to see him cry.
And after she was dead, and he had paid
The singers and the sexton and the rest,
He packed a lot of things that she had made
Most mournfully away in an old chest
Of hers, and put some chopped-up cedar boughs
In with them, and tore down the slaughter-house.

—Edwin Arlington Robinson

This is verse-nonpoetry. Ritual surely, for it's a powerful and imaginative work, and the *persona* who observes and feels Reuben Bright's pain moves us, absorbs us in his tenderness. Verse, yes, for the lines march evenly along punctuated by the rhyme. But not poetry, for there's little metaphor here and none that is central to the meaning.

Perhaps I should stress the fact that Ritual of this sort does not become unworthy because it's nonpoetry. It's quite possible to use the ritualistic forms in an evaluative sense, but such evaluations can be made only after granting the splendor of such prose-nonpoetry as *Madame Bovary*, the glitter and magic of such verse-nonpoetry as Robert Frost often wrote, the power of such prose-poetry as *The Lady's Not For Burning*, and the incandescence of such verse-poetry as Cummings' or Millay's or Wordsworth's lyrics. By definition, all forms within this realm are most, most worthy.

Back to "Reuben Bright," this is not the symbolic stuff of my ordinary hours. The rhythm gives it a framework that closes it partially away from me.

And even further from my usual language is this act:

### Quest[174]

Always when I see Italian marble
and great burnished mahogany sitting quiet
and ruthless in the indulgence of five centuries,

[173] "Reuben Bright" is reprinted with the permission of Charles Scribner's Sons from *The Children of the Night* by Edwin Arlington Robinson (1897).
[174] © *The Moral Circus: Poems, 1955,* and © *The Gazabos: Forty-One Poems, 1959.* Reprinted by permission of Edwin Honig.

always I ask whose is the skull
set in jewels grinning there in shadow
who thrust all this from him feverishly
as the white dove flew nimbly from the mouth
and the feathers made great onslaughts
against the mind, loosening, flattening himself
to dive into the eye of the needle.

—Edwin Honig

Prose-poetry this time. The *persona* here exists in his metaphors; take them away and there is no meaning, no *persona*, no poem. There's no rhythmical pattern (although the typography suggests it), but the interlaced metaphors ("great burnished mahogany sitting quiet/and ruthless in the indulgence of five centuries") are at a far remove from my ordinary symbolic behaviors.

And at the greatest distance from the usual "real" me lies this form:

Snowy Heron[175]
What lifts the heron leaning on the air
I praise without a name. A crouch, a flare,
A long stroke through the cumulus of trees,
A shaped thought at the sky—then gone. *O rare!*
Saint Francis, being happiest on his knees,
Would have cried *Father!* Cry anything you please.

But praise. By any name or none. But praise
The white original burst that lights
The heron on his two soft kissing kites.
When saints praise heaven lit by doves and rays,
I sit by pond scums till the air recites
Its heron back. And doubt all else. But praise.

—John Ciardi

The *persona* here functions within the demanding forces of verse and poetry. He combines the discipline of rhythm with the need to mint awareness newly. He does not speak as I do "normally." His vision is sharper, deeper, more disturbing, and more profitable than mine. His drive to reach beyond himself, to find beauty and meaning in the heron's flight is stronger and more fiercely shaped than mine. Simply, he is far from me.

The four forms become steps, a ladder that leads away from the familiar, the normal, the everyday, in a sense the "real" language acts that constitute me.

And concurrently, the four forms create a sequence, a stairway that leads in precisely the *opposite* direction. They make up a *second* hierarchy that moves in direct and startling contrast to the first, for the basic form, the most fundamental

[175] From *I Marry You* by John Ciardi. Copyright 1958 by Rutgers, The State University. Reprinted by permission of the author.

*Rhetoric*

form in that second hierarchy is verse poetry. To repeat two quotations from Arthur Koestler:

> Thus, rhythm and assonance, pun and rhyme are not artificially created ornaments of speech; the whole evidence indicates that their origins go back to primitive—and infantile—forms of thought and utterance, in which sound and meaning are magically interwoven, and association by sound-affinities is as legitimate as association by other similarities.[176]

> And just as rhythm is not an artificial embellishment of language but a form of expression which predates language, so visual images and symbols are not fanciful embroideries of concepts, but precursors of conceptual thought. The artist does not climb a ladder to stick ornaments on a facade of ideas—he is more like a pot-holer in search of underground rivers.[177]

Verse-poetry reaches back "to primitive—and infantile—forms of thought and utterance." As a *persona* of verse-poetry I'm not hanging pretties on "a facade of ideas." Rather, I'm "like a pot-holer in search of underground rivers," and in those rivers run currents of rhythm and metaphor. When I become the *persona* of a verse-poem I tap into those currents, I touch the oldest (or youngest) and deepest parts of my being. In the rhythm of verse-poetry I caress myself as I did when I was an infant engaging in joyous and meaningless sound-play; and in its metaphor I return to that creature who prefigured man millenia ago by seeing the world in the colors of his own feelings. I caress and return in such acts as this from *Macbeth*:

> Tomorrow, and tomorrow, and tomorrow,
> Creeps in this petty pace from day to day,
> To the last syllable of recorded time;
> And all our yesterdays have lighted fools
> The way to dusty death. Out, out brief candle!
> Life's but a walking shadow; a poor player,
> That struts and frets his hour upon the stage,
> And then is heard no more: it is a tale
> Told by an idiot, full of sound and fury,
> Signifying nothing.

In this *persona* are enclosed something of the small one who was me nearly half a century ago and of the old one who pointed the way to me thousands of centuries ago. The small and old ones have not disappeared; they exist in me. And when I act with words like these they are awakened. These words reach deep; they penetrate the years and centuries and discover the sleeping ones at my core.

Not quite as deeply rooted is prose-poetry. This, for example:

from *The Egoist*
Chapter V: Clara Middleton

(Sir Willoughby) looked the fittest; he justified the dictum of Science. The survival of the Patternes was assured. "I would," he said to his admirer, Mrs.

[176] Koestler, p. 315.
[177] *Ibid.*, p. 325.

Mountstuart Jenkinson, "have bargained for health above everything but she has everything besides—lineage, beauty, breeding: is what they call an heiress, and is the most accomplished of her sex." With a delicate art he conveyed to the lady's understanding that Miss Middleton had been snatched from a crowd, without a breath of the crowd having offended his niceness. He did it through sarcasm at your modern young women, who run about the world nibbling and nibbled at, until they know one sex as well as the other, and are not a whit less cognizant of the market than men; pure, possibly; it is not so easy to say innocent; decidedly not our feminine ideal. Miss Middleton was different: she was the true ideal, fresh-gathered morning fruit in a basket, warranted by her bloom.

Women do not defend their younger sisters for doing what they perhaps have done—lifting a veil to be seen, and peeping at a world where innocence is as poor a guarantee as a babe's caul against shipwreck. Women of the world never think of attacking the sensual stipulation for perfect bloom, silver purity, which is redolent of the Oriental origin of the love-passion of their lords. Mrs. Mountstuart congratulated Sir Willoughby on the prize he had won in the fair-western-eastern.

"Let me see her," she said; and Miss Middleton was introduced and critically observed.

She had the mouth that smiles in repose. The lips met full on the centre of the bow and thinned along to a lifting dimple; the eyelids also lifted slightly at the outer corners and seemed, like the lip into the limpid cheek, quickening up the temples, as with a run of light, or the ascension indicated off a shoot of colour. Her features were playfellows of one another, none of them pretending to rigid correctness, nor the nose to the ordinary dignity of governess among merry girls, despite which the nose was of a fair design, not acutely interrogative or inviting to gambols. Aspens imaged in water, waiting for the breeze, would offer a susceptible lover some suggestion of her face: a pure smooth-white face, tenderly flushed in the cheeks, where the gentle dints were faintly intermelting even during quietness. Her eyes were brown, set well between mild lids, often shadowed, not unwakeful. Her hair of lighter brown, swelling above her temples on the sweep to the knot, imposed the triangle of the fabulous wild woodland visage from brow to mouth and chin, evidently in agreement with her taste; and the triangle suited her; but her face was not significant of a tameless wildness or of weakness; her equable shut mouth threw its long curve to guard the small round chin from that effect; her eyes wavered only in humour, they were steady when thoughtfulness was awakened; and at such seasons the build of her winter-beechwood hair lost the touch of nymph-like and whimsical, and strangely, by mere outline, added to her appearance of studious concentration. Observe the hawk on stretched wings over the prey he spies, for an idea of this change in the look of a young lady whom Vernon Whitford could liken to the Mountain Echo, and Mrs. Mountstuart Jenkinson pronounced to be a "dainty rogue in porcelain."

—George Meredith


That long, intricate, totally metaphorical description of Miss Middleton pulls me to a *persona* very near my own beginnings, for this *persona* perceives as I did in infancy, physiognomically. There's no hint here of impersonal or objective description, but rather a description made in terms of the describer's feelings. The case can seem overstated I suppose, but this sort of language shares much with the infant's act of seeing a chair in the dark *as a frightening shape,* not as a chair. Both are metaphorical on the most basic level, both cloak "reality" in the emotions of the observer, and both see reality as emotional. Miss Middleton is "a dainty rogue in porcelain," and that is strangely close to the child's teddy bear that *is* comfort and warmth. Not driven quite as deeply as the combination of rhythm *and* metaphor pushed the lines from *Macbeth,* this act still reaches far into my symbolic structure.

Less probing is verse-nonpoetry.

from "An Essay on Criticism"

'Tis hard to say, if greater want of skill
Appear in writing or in judging ill;
But, of the two, less dang'rous is th' offence
To tire our patience, than mislead our sense.
Some few in that, but numbers err in this,
Ten censure wrong for one who writes amiss.

—Alexander Pope

As this sort of *persona* there is a certain move away from everyday language "reality." This is a "me" who lies below the surface. But not far below. This *persona* is related to the old, small one of metaphor and rhythm, but distantly so. The rhythm is in a sense "separable" from this language. [178] The word "skill" can be changed to "ability," "sense" to "intelligence," and "amiss" to "poorly" and much of the rhythm is destroyed. Not all of it, but much. And that seems to mean that the quality of rhythm in this sort of material (verse-nonpoetry) is not as tightly woven into the language as it is in verse-poetry or as metaphor is intertwined throughout all poetry.

Closest to the surface, to the "unreal," ordinary me is prose-nonpoetry. This example:

She went into the room quietly, closed the door, and waited.

"Yes?" The blow fell gently but deliberately. There was no help, no warmth in the word.

She told herself hurriedly that she'd known it would be hard, that no help was to be expected. But her mind rocked gracefully back to an old view, a painful one, but known and familiar. The first whisper in her head was careful, nudging only. "Maybe you'd better wait till another time." "I can't." "Sure, you can, and it might even be easier then." "But—" "No point in doing it one way just because it's the hardest."

She listened, and knew that by listening she had lost, that once more the inner prophet had led her to a land of endless and richly deserved pain.

"Sorry—I was looking for—" She went out.

Here I'm led away from the surface only by a *persona.* That fact is important of

[178] Geiger treats the business of the separability of rhythm most perceptively, I think. See his fourth chapter.

course, but it's important, too, that this *persona* speaks pretty much as I do. He (she) is not separated from me by rhythm or metaphor.

' These distinctions between verse, prose, and poetry (and, by implication, nonpoetry) are far from new. In *The Poetics*, Aristotle wrote:

> . . . it is the way with people to tack on "poet" to the name of a metre, and talk of elegiac-poets and epic-poets, thinking that they call them poets not by reason of the imitative nature of their work, but indiscriminately by reason of the metre they write in. [179]

and (once again) later:

> The distinction between historian and poet is not in the one writing prose and the other verse—you might put the work of Herodotus into verse, and it would still be a species of history; it consists really in this, that the one describes the thing that has been, and the other a kind of thing that might be. Hence poetry is something more philosophic and of graver import than history, since its statements are of the Nature rather of universals, whereas those of history are singulars. [180]

Northrop Frye writes:

> . . . there is the rhythm of a regularly repeated pattern of accent or meter, often accompanied by other recurring features, like rhyme or alliteration. This regularly recurring type of rhythm is what I mean by verse. "Poetry," however indispensable a word in literary criticism, can hardly be used in the technical sense of a verbal structure possessing a regular, recurrent, and in general, predictable rhythm. [181]

And Babette Deutsch has drawn together the ideas of several theorists in saying:

> The distinction between poetry and verse is as least as old as Sidney, who spoke of the latter as "but an ornament and no cause to Poetry, sith there have beene many most excellent Poets that never versified, and now swarme many versifiers that neede never aunswere to the name of Poets . . . it is not riming and versing that maketh a Poet, no more than a long gowne maketh an Advocate, who though he pleaded in armor should be an Advocate and no Souldier." For Sidney poetry lay in "delightful images" and "delightful teaching," though he admitted that "the Senate of Poets hath chosen verse as their fittest rayment . . ." Eliot, without defining the difference, implies that verse is merely a matter of structure, while poetry is marked by intensity of feeling and gravity of import, which find expression in a musicianly concern for resonance in both the sounds and the associations of the words chosen. The distinguishing feature of verse is its formal aspect, that of poetry is its imaginative power. [182]

[179] Aristotle *De Poetica*, trans. Ingram Bywater, *The Works of Aristotle*, Vol. XI (London: Oxford University Press, 1946), i. 1. 1447b. 12-16.

[180] *Ibid.*, i. 9. 1451b. 1-8.

[181] Frye, p. 143.

[182] Babette Deutsch, *Poetry Handbook* (New York: Grosset & Dunlap, 1957), pp. 112-13.

It's interesting that the verse-prose-poetry-nonpoetry distinction has been held for so long by so many people and is still a minority view. I want to argue for the validity of that view, but far more important, I want to stress the existence of the two hierarchies and the tension that quivers between them.

We are born (and descend from) verse-poets, and we grow to the adult and necessary but artificial state of prose-nonpoets. Thus, in Ritual, what is closest to symbolic reality (prose-nonpoetry) on one level is, on another, the most distant from it. And what is most directly tuned to our inner symbol systems (verse-poetry) on one level, creates, on another, the most discord.

All selves cannot be honored. As one is allowed precedence, another is suppressed. The verse-poet opposes the prose-nonpoet. If we accept the surface of our symbolic natures as "real" or preferable, we cut ourselves off from our well-springs of metaphor and rhythm. And if we choose the reality of the depths, we deny the prose-poetry surface that brings us close to the world of Rhetoric.

We must, I'm afraid, ricochet back and forth between the interfaces of the two hierarchies like crazed shuttlecocks seeking a rest position that is nowhere to be found. We're pulled both ways, and as we near one face, the force of the other is stronger. Always, there's some sense in which we must move on; this is drama—the basis of all Ritual—and the qualities forever absent in this realm are simple facticity and a fixed and static permanence. It's no accident that this continual pulling, this *motion*, occurs in the symbolic process directly concerned with *emotion*. This is the ritualistic dialectic, *the act by which we create and please ourselves in repetitions that leave us always newer and richer than we were and always, somehow, not quite satisfied.* (That is, at last, the definition of Ritual that I have to offer.)

It is this dialectic that leads to the final statements of this discourse, to a final view of the larger dialectic that pits Rhetoric and Ritual against each other.

## Ritual versus Rhetoric

Rhetoric and Ritual are inseparable; Ritual is the basis of Rhetoric; Rhetoric and Ritual include all language; Rhetoric must directly involve the self in an ethical and responsible fashion; language develops dramatically; Ritual is a dramatic form that must be understood in terms of *personae;* and the *personae* of Ritual pull against each other, conflict with each other. All these matters have been treated dialectically in one sense or another. The attempt has been to start analytically and to move to dialectical notions—notions that do not split off one part of the symbolic process of man-in-language and treat it as a real, and separate, and independent entity. What remains is to emphasize the dynamic relationship between Rhetoric and Ritual, the sense in which each act *both* involves and implies the other *and* pulls strongly away from the other.

Because it is the symbolic act that allows us to deal most directly with the world outside our own skins, we are constantly pulled toward Rhetoric, for we need to treat that world, to organize it so that we can find it intelligible. Thus we must reason. We *cannot* go to the extreme of observing and describing that world and considering our own observations and descriptions as simple, objective reality, for they are, after all, *our* observations and descriptions. It's not that they are necessarily ours in the sense that we have originated or created them; we may well adopt them from what we take to be the observations and descriptions that have been made by others. Still, once we accept them or use them, they become ours. And we cannot ignore the fact that we have committed the act of observing or describing, and that in so doing we have put something of ourselves into the "real" world. To think of our own reasoned statements about the world as objective in any thorough sense is to think of those statements as separate from ourselves, to think of our language as separate from us. In that direction lies eventual disavowal of our own meaning.

Our need to recognize the outer world and to cope with it draws us constantly toward rational processes. Since the rationality is our own and not some detached, impersonal, logical act, it is necessarily persuasive, necessarily rhetorical. Rhetoric, then, is a permanent and necessary fact of our symbolic life; it is that process in which we orient ourselves in regard to the world. In Rhetoric, we face the problems of coexistence with other beings—problems that require cooperation because we cannot solve them alone. In Rhetoric, we face the problems of adjusting the environment so that we can exist more comfortably—again, problems that we cannot solve alone. And in Rhetoric, we face the problems of changing ourselves so that we fit more easily into our environment, and even with these problems we need the help of others. Thus, Rhetoric always pulls us toward the world and the people around us. Or, better, it's in Rhetoric that we *need* to move toward the world and the people around us.

But even as we concern ourselves with the world—with friends, colleagues, jobs, racism, home, money, war, clothes, schedules, and all the details of the outer world that demand our attentions and our actions—we create an inner tension. The simple fact of turning our attention outward means that we are ignoring (for some time, or to some degree) the inner world. And our needs to deal with that world are even greater and more insistent than our needs to consider outer reality.

Inwardly, in Ritual, we face the problem of power, for we want very much to be recognized as able chemists, insightful writers, or fine professors, as those who think cleanly and with grace—and to be so recognized is to possess power. And we face the problem of beauty, for we want our notions to be more than accurate, we want them to be aesthetic. And we face the problems of fear, for always we run the risk of being wrong, or foolish, or unloved. And we face the problem of time, for there are not enough years for what we need to do. We can solve none of these problems rhetorically, for they are not susceptible to rational approaches. The only hope is ritualistic self-definition—definition in acts that bring pride and pleasure: to love without guarantees, to be worthy of good and beautiful things, to look tenderly and with knowledge at all art—that source of so much comfort, to accept our weaknesses and fears without self-condemnation. It is only in such acts as these that enrichment and renewal are possible, and in these very acts we find the need for further enrichment and renewal, for the repetition of pleasing and self-constituting processes—the repetition of Ritual. Yet we cannot simply turn inward, for by doing that we would negate our rhetorical needs. *Negate* them, and that is something we must not do—at least not fully.

"Negation" is a key term in language, and it's particularly important in the dynamic between Rhetoric and Ritual. [183] In Rhetoric negation operates on several levels: words, for instance, refer to what they are not, for the word "tree" is not my, or your, experiences with the thing "tree"; we must define in terms of negation, for it's by pointing out limits or boundaries beyond which a thing does *not* go that definitions are made. In Ritual negation operates variously, too: there is the negation of metaphor in which one term negates another; dramatically there is the negation of *personae* already described, and there is the negation of the person by the *persona*, wherein become characters in Ritual and are no longer the ordinary, everyday Paul Campbell, John Warren, etc. As Kenneth Burke points out tellingly, man is the inventor of the negative, and the negative is a particularly symbolic act, for there are no negatives in the objective world. [184] All these are important instances of negation, but the most significant function of the negative occurs in the rhetorical-ritualistic tension. As we honor our rhythms and inward pleasures, we are *not* facing those aspects of outer reality that seem urgent; we are negating them, yet we feel their urgency. And as we honor our needs to reason persuasively, we are negating all the metaphors we want to be, to create; we are negating them, yet that want *remains*.

So turn as we may, we negate some part of ourselves, and that act stirs up currents that draw us to an opposite shore. It's as if we were elastically bound to both realms so that the further we moved in either direction, the stronger would be the opposing pull. Why not the middle then? Why not an even mixture of Rhetoric and Ritual for all seasons? Simply because that's only one symbolic process, and probably far from the richest or most exciting. An even blend of Rhetoric and Ritual will do little to help us explore the stars, end war, find the courage to love, or heal our loneliness; all these require strongly rhetorical or deeply ritualistic acts. It seems that we must move to the areas that are primarily rhetorical or ritualistic and that by doing so we create our own needs to move away from the very symbolic land we inhabit.

Once more, the rhetorical pull is always a little weaker, the ritualistic always a little stronger. Another way of saying that it's Ritual that's basic. Think of the limitless examples: cars that sell because of their styling, fashions in clothing that have nothing to do with utilitarian values, architecture that is art rather than simple construction, psychologically and socially deviant behavior that is obviously impractical but clearly rewarding to the behavers, honors and titles preferred above material rewards, the act of dying for one's country or for a cause. These processes seem so obviously ritualistic at bottom, though there are clear-cut rhetorical dimensions in nearly all of them.

There even seems to be neurological evidence that points to the tensions that make us seesaw back and forth between Rhetoric and Ritual.[185] It's with our "old" brain inherited from reptilian and lower mammalian ancestors, that we *feel*, and that brain has apparently changed little during the entire course of evolution.

[183] Burke, *Language as Symbolic Action*, pp. 419-479.
[184] *Ibid.*, pp. 9-13.
[185] Arthur Koestler, *The Ghost in the Machine* (New York: The Macmillan Company, 1967), Chapter 16.

But it's with our "new" brain, the neocortex, that we think, and that brain has developed with an explosive (and unstable) speed over the last half million years or so. And the fact of the matter seems to be that the two brains are not very well coordinated; the term "schizophysiology" has been used to describe the conflicts between the structure and function of the two brains. [186] In my own terms, it's the battle and the back-and-forthness between Rhetoric and Ritual—the two symbolic states that make it possible for a *reasoning* man to have *faith*, and for a *faith*-full man to *reason*.

Last, and certainly not least (perhaps even most), I want to talk about *god-terms* as a final version of the rhetorical-ritualistic conflict. The notion of *god-terms* is another borrowing from Kenneth Burke, [187] though I shall use his concept in several of my own ways. Burke talks about the human act of titling and points out that there is a symbolic drive in us to find ever more inclusive titles. We may, for instance, make up names or titles for, say, one hundred different items; as soon as we do we feel the need for a title of titles, for a title of all one hundred of those items. We may then make up titles for a second group of, say, one hundred items; again, as soon as we do we need a title of titles, a title for the whole group. Each of these titles of titles is a minor *god-term*. But with two such terms we need at once a higher title of titles, a title for *both* titles of one hundred items. In this fashion we may create titles for *all things;* at that point we need a supreme *god-term*, a title for all titles. But if we create it we will immediately need a title for the opposite, for all not-things or for all nonexistent things. If we create that we need another and higher *god-term*, or title for both the title of all titles of things and the title of all titles of not-things. And of course, if we create that *god-term* we need another for its opposite. And on and on.

Burke says that this sort of symbolic drive for ever more comprehensive *god-terms* is seen most clearly in theological terminology. There, he points out, the supreme *god-term* is "god," and he talks of the fact that we can work toward or away from *god-terms*. If we start with *god-terms* (as the Bible does by simply inserting the word "God," into the first sentence, most of what we do thereafter is simply a spinning out of the implications of those terms, just as I have spun out the implications of the title of this book. If we work toward *god-terms* we go through the process described above.

*God-terms* function in personal and dramatic ways too. As individuals we create *god-terms* for ourselves, and there are never more than a few of these titles of titles. Mine are *urgency, power, love,* in the verbal realm. But *god-terms* can be nonverbal; they can be visual, or auditory, or kinaesthetic images. I sometimes carry inside me a *god-term* that is the sight and feeling of a fencer lunging; and in the past I have been possessed by the *god-term* that was the picture of a small boy cowering in a corner. Similarly, we create and assign *god-terms* to *personae.* Hamlet's most usual title of titles is "the man who couldn't make up his mind" or

[186] *Ibid.,* 284-88.
[187] Kenneth Burke, *The Rhetoric of Religion: Studies in Logology* (Boston: Beacon Press, 1961), pp. 1-40.

"the melancholy Dane." They've always seemed to me to be perfectly worthless as god-terms, for given the circumstances, how could he have made up his mind or been anything but melancholy? Rather, Hamlet is "a closed curve" for me; which is to say, I become a closed curve when I am Hamlet. That's the nonverbal *god-term* I see as Hamlet. For the one who stops by those famous woods on a snowy evening, my *god-term* is "a dark mirror." For Holden Caulfield, "a silent scream." And on through my world of *personae*.

The next step is perhaps predictable. Our ritualistic *god-terms* conflict with our rhetorical *god-terms*. Our titles of titles for *personae* and for ourselves clash with our titles of titles for the outer world. One of my own *god-terms*, you remember, is *urgency*; for the world of others one of my *god-terms* is the quality of frightened coldness and detachment; the two do not mesh well or easily. And the result is that both will change in the fusion that is needed if I am to be a single, intact person. I will always play my roles, but I have the larger role of the one who plays the particular roles that I play—my dramatic *god-term*.

It is in the move from rhetorical and ritualistic *god-terms* to titles for *both* those titles, to names for *both* those *god-terms*, that we face hope or despair as individuals and as a race. It is with Ritual that we first harm ourselves, for it is in our secret and subjective symbolic processes that we feel the fear of the man with a different colored skin or of the nation with a different culture. But it is in Rhetoric that we harm ourselves further, for we reason (we say) our way to conclusions that we already hold, and we find what we persuade ourselves to accept as evidence for our beliefs that the man or the country is dangerous or inferior. And if, metaphor-like, we are to join the rhetorical and ritualistic dimensions of ourselves in such a way that whole beings emerge, we must run the rhetorical risk first, then the ritualistic. We must be willing to confront ourselves and to expose ourselves to others, asking always that they choose freely for themselves. And we must be willing to accept the reality of our own pleasures and fears, and yet to become the *personae* that seem contradicted by those pleasures and fears. It is only through the *personae* of our Ritual that we can come to comprehend the reality of our Rhetoric. And only then can our halves heal.

The strange history of man may simply continue on its downward path. There is, after all, no reason to expect any change. We have bred hundreds upon hundreds of generations of increasingly schizoid creatures. Now we can face the prospect of destroying ourselves, even face it bravely, in the name of democracy, and honor, and America, and unconsidered god.

# *Epilogue*

> measureless cool flames of making
> —E. E. Cummings

There is little basis for hope. And I am not hopeful.

Yet metaphors are never predictable. They happen, and a new word is born. If even a few men could shape their utterances so that they themselves as utterers were included therein, the hope might come. For those men and those utterances would produce the mightiest of new words, the mightiest of metaphors.

The change will not come from our philosophies or psychologies, our logic or science. It will not even come from art. We've tried these, and we've failed.

We've only one thing left.

The change will come, if it comes, from the deepest symbolic processes of our language.

# Bibliography

You remember that a simple list of items is what I've called partial or faded language. Most of this bibliography will be just that, but I want the first few entries to be something more, because they're works that seem to be extremely important.

I've referred to Kenneth Burke's writings several times. He's written more insightfully about the symbolic process than anyone else, in my judgment. Some of his books are hard reading, mostly because we're so analytically conditioned; but they're all very, very profitable and provocative reading. I think that a good starting place would be:

*Language as Symbolic Action: Essays on Life, Literature, and Method,* Berkeley, Calif., 1968.

This is a collection of his essays that make for a good introduction to many of his basic ideas. Then I'd suggest:

*The Rhetoric of Religion: Studies in Logology,* Berkeley, Calif., 1970.

This book provides a brilliant symbolic comparison of the linguistic and theological processes. Next, I'd turn to:

*Counter-Statement.* Chicago, 1931.

Burke deals with critical theory in this book, but critical theory is an integral part of language theory as he uses those terms. And his criticism of specific works always gives valuable clues to the language process itself. Then read:

*The Philosophy of Literary Form,* Baton Rouge, 1941.

Here's more literary and critical theory, but always with an eye to the symbolic function. One essay in this book, "The Rhetoric of Hitler's 'Battle,' " is especially worthy because it explicates so well facist Rhetoric. Following this, read:

*Attitudes toward History,* Boston, 1937.

This is a work that suggests the delightful proposition that history should be viewed as comedy. Finally, read the two books that are Burke's basic works. They provide the theoretical structure for nearly everything else he's written. The problem is that they're extraordinarily difficult, and if you start with them you're likely to throw up your hands in dismay. They're available singly, but also bound together:

*A Grammar of Motives* and *A Rhetoric of Motives,* Cleveland, 1962.

All Burke's writing, but especially the above two books, is symbology: he is always concerned with the nature of the symbol-user, the symbol, and what is symbolized. And he offers more to the student of language that any other theorist I know. Many people complain that Burke is difficult to deal with because he insists on stressing relationships, cross-references, blendings together. He does indeed, and that is precisely his strength.

In previous pages, I've also mentioned Susanne Langer a good many times. For me, her works are second in importance only to Burke's. (And I think it's amazing that the two never refer to each other.) Langer's three major books must be read in the following order, for they constitute a logical sequence. Start with:

*Philosophy in a New Key*, New York, 1942.

In this book she sets up a frame of reference for the study of the symbolic modes of language, ritual, myth, and art. And though it's a small book, it contains enormous amounts of theoretical gold. Then move to:

*Feeling and Form*, New York, 1953.

Here Langer describes the various symbolic processes of art. All of them are excitingly done, but the treatment of *poesis* (language art) is the part that I find most important. Last, study:

*Mind: An Essay on Human Feeling*, Baltimore, 1967.

This is perhaps the most difficult book of all those listed in this bibliography. Here Langer argues that all living (human and nonhuman) beings or organisms, and particularly all human reality, have form, that that form is analogous to what is commonly called "feeling," and that both must be viewed as "acts," acts which do *not* require actors or agents. It's an amazing book, and it's worth the hard reading it requires.

Next, I urge you to read two books by Arthur Koestler, both of which I've mentioned earlier. Actually, they might be read before Burke and Langer, for they provide a kind of overview of man's symbolic arrangement of himself and his world. They are:

*The Act of Creation*, New York, 1964, and
*The Ghost in the Machine*, New York, 1967.

I think both these books have been under-rated, despite Koestler's fame. The first one is a brilliant study of three fundamental human processes: art, science, and humor. And Koestler argues that the creative act is the same in all three. The second one describes man an as aberrant species, as an organism gone wrong. And it's sobering, to say the least.

Then two books by Northrop Frye, both of which combine literary criticism and language theory in exciting ways.

*The Well-Tempered Critic*, Bloomington, Indiana, 1963, and
*Anatomy of Criticism*, New York, 1967.

The first one combines the notion of rhythm and the notion of style in sucy a way as to unify language study; the second describes the major modes of critical thought, and argues that art is the basis of society or culture.

Moving backward in time, there is a three-volume work by Ernst Cassirer that's of great importance for the student of language. The books were written in the 1910's and 20's, but translated into English much later.

*The Philosophy of Symbolic Forms, Volume 1: Language*, New Haven, 1953;

*Volume 2: Mythical Thought,* 1955; *Volume 3: The Phenomenology of Knowledge,* 1957. The three volumes constitute a bridge from Kant to philosophers and symbologists such as Langer and Burke. Here are most of the concepts which Langer has refined and which Burke has developed into symbology itself.

Then you must read three books by Owen Barfield. They're all simply written, but they deal with basic issues: the nature of poetry, the way new words change our thinking, and the way we affect ourselves by our views of god and nature. The books are:

*Poetic Diction,* London, 1928.

*History in English Words,* Grand Rapids, Michigan, 1967.

*Saving the Appearances: A Study in Idolatry,* New York, no date.

Next a book by William Barrett. It's about the ways in which we do *not* behave rationally, and it's appropriately titled:

*Irrational Man: A Study in Existential Philosophy,* New York, 1958.

Then a book by a scientist who recognizes the limits of science, and who argues that man's knowledge is far from "scientific": here is a book that carries special weight because of the ethical appeal of the author, Michael Polanyi:

*The Study of Man,* Chicago, 1958.

Many books of readings or collections of essays by various authors are spotty—a few good items, many that are dull. But there's an anthology by Max Black that's unusually good. All the essays are about language, and nearly all of them are excellent:

*The Importance of Language,* Englewood Cliffs, N.J., 1962.

Now a book that is an utter *must.* It's by Thomas Szasz, and it's about the symbolic function of insanity in this society. Szasz argues that we *use* insanity in almost the same way that the puritans used witches and witchcraft:

*The Manufacture of Madness,* New York, 1969.

In a different vein, a book that reveals the symbolic reality of society, especially in relation to language and literature, is one by Hugh Duncan:

*Language and Literature in Society,* New York, 1969.

In a still different vein, the symbolic values involved in the conflict between the youth movement and the establishment are exposed with startling clarity by Theodore Roszak. By all means read:

*The Making of a Counter Culture,* New York, 1969.

Finally, one of the many novels that clarifies the symbolic nature of reality, of human behavior, and of mental suffering is a work by Hannah Green. It's a beautifully and brilliantly written book, and it offers extraordinary insights into the seductive world of madness. Read and re-read:

*I Never Promised You a Rose Garden,* New York, 1964.

And finally, finally, read, read again and again a book by Kate Millett that illustrates searingly the symbolic nature and symbolic distortion built into such basic and unexamined notions as "man," "woman," "sex," "biology," "personality," and "society."

*Sexual Politics,* New York, 1970.

And now for a fairly lengthy list of writings that are pertinent to symbology. All of them are of value.

Ackoff, R.L., "Toward a Behavioral Theory of Communication," *Management Science*, Vol. IV (1958), pp. 218-324.

Aldridge, J. W., ed., *Critiques and Essays on Modern Fiction: 1920-1951. Representing the Achievement of Modern American and British Critics.* New York, 1952.

Alexander, S., *Beauty and Other Forms of Value*, London, 1933.

Allen, W., *The English Novel: A Short Critical History*, London, 1954.

——— *Reading a Novel*, New York, 1949.

Allers, R., *The Psychology of Character*, New York, 1943.

Allport, G. W., *Personality: A Psychological Interpretation*, New York, 1937.

Alston, W. P., *Philosophy of Language*, Englewood Cliffs, New Jersey, 1964.

Altmann, S. A., ed., *Social Communication Among Primates*, Chicago, 1966.

Ames, V. M., *Aesthetics of the Novel*, Chicago, 1928.

Anshen, R. N., ed., *Language: An Enquiry into Its Meaning and Function*, New York, 1957.

Aristotle, *Aristotle's Theory of Poetry and Fine Arts*, trans. S. H. Butcher, New York, 1951.

Arnheim, R., "The Gestalt Theory of Expression," *Psychological Review*, Vol. LVI (1949), pp. 156-171.

Auerbach, E., *Mimesis: The Representation of Reality in Western Literature*, trans. Willard Trask, New York, 1957.

Austin, J. L., *Philosophical Papers*, ed. J. O. Urmson and G. J. Warnock, Oxford, 1961.

———, *Sense and Sensibilia*, Oxford, 1962.

Ayer, A. J., *Language, Truth and Logic*, 2nd ed., London, 1946.

Babcock, H., *Time and the Mind*, Cambridge, Massachusetts, 1941.

Bach, E., *An Introduction to Transformational Grammars*, New York, 1964.

Back, K. W., "Influence through Social Communication," *Journal of Abnormal and Social Psychology*, Vol. XLVI (1951), pp. 9-23.

———, "Social Research As a Communication System," *Social Forces*, Vol. XLI (1962), pp. 61-68.

Baker, E., *The History of the English Novel*, Vols. 1-IX, London, 1924-1938.

Bar-Hillel, Y., *Language and Information*, Reading, Massachusetts, 1964.

Barnlund, D., *Interpersonal Communication: Survey and Studies*, New York, 1968.

Bartlett, F., *Thinking*, London, 1958.

Basler, R. P., *Sex, Symbolism, and Psychology in Literature*, New Brunswick, New Jersey, 1948.

Bate, W. J., ed., *Criticism: The Major Texts*, New York, 1948.

Bateson, F. W., *English Poetry and the English Language: An Experiment in Literary History*, Oxford, 1934.

Baum, P. F., *The Principles of English Versification*, Cambridge, Massachusetts, 1922.

Beach, J. W., *American Fiction: 1920-1940*, New York, 1948.

———, *The Twentieth Century Novel: Studies in Technique*, New York, 1932.

Beardsley, M. C., *Problems in the Philosophy of Criticism*, New York, 1958.

Becker, E., *The Birth and Death of Meaning*, New York, 1962.

Becker, G. J., "Realism: An Essay in Definition," *Modern Language Quarterly*, Vol. X (1949), pp. 184-197.

Beloff, J., *Existence of Mind*, London, 1962.

Bentley, M. and E. J. Varnon, "An Accessory Study of Phonetic Symbolism," *American Journal of Psychology*, Vol. XLV (1933), pp. 76-86.

Berg, J., "Cooperation Without Communication and Observation," *Journal of Social Psychology*, Vol. IV (1955), pp. 287-296.

Bergson, H., *The Creative Mind*, trans. Mabelle L. Adison, New York, 1946.

Berko, J., "The Child's Learning of English Morphology," *Word*, Vol. XIV (1958), pp. 150-177.

Berlo, D. K., *The Process of Communication*, New York, 1960.

Berlyne, D. E., "Knowledge and Stimulus-Response Psychology," *Psychological Review*, Vol. LXI (1954), pp. 245-254.

Berne, E., "Concerning the Nature of Communication," *Psychiatric Quarterly*, Vol. XXVII (1953), pp. 185-198.

Bernstein, B., "Language and Social Class," *Journal of Sociology*, Vol. XI (1960), pp. 271-276.

———, "Linguistic Codes, Hesitation Phenomena and Intelligence," *Language and Speech*, Vol. V (1962), pp. 31-46.

Bever, T. G., J. A. Fodor, and W. Weksel, "Is Linguistics Empirical?" *Psychological Review*, Vol. LXXII (1965), pp. 493-500.

———, ———, and ———, "On the Acquisition of Syntax: A Critique of 'Contextual Generalization," *Psychological Review*, Vol. LXXII (1965), pp. 467-482.

Birkhoff, G. D., *Aesthetic Measure*, Cambridge, Massachusetts, 1933.

Black, M., *Language and Philosophy: Studies in Method*, Ithaca, New York, 1949.

———, *Models and Metaphors: Studies in Language and Philosophy*, New York, 1962.

Blair, H., *Lectures on Rhetoric and Belles Lettres*, London, 1783.

Blackmur, R. P., *Language as Gesture, Essays in Poetry*, New York, 1952.

———, *The Lion and the Honeycomb: Essays in Solicitude and Critique*, New York, 1955.

Bloomfield, L., *Language*, New York, 1933.

Boas, F., "Language," in *General Anthropology*, Franz Boas, ed., Boston, 1938.

Bonner, J. T., *Morphogenesis: An Essay on Development*, Princeton, New Jersey, 1952.

Booth, W., *The Rhetoric of Fiction*, Chicago, 1961.

Boring, E. G., *The Physical Dimensions of Consciousness*, New York, 1933.

———, *Sensation and Perception in the History of Experimental Psychology*, New York, 1942.

Bosanquet, B., *Three Lectures on Aesthetics*, New York, 1915.

Bowers, F., *Textual and Literary Criticism*, New York, 1959.

Brain, W. R. "The Cerebral Basis of Consciousness," *Brain*, Vol. LXXIII (1950), pp. 465-479.

Braine, M. D. S., "The Ontogeny of English Phrase Structure: The First Phrase," *Language*, Vol. XXXIX (1963), pp. 1-13.

Brickell, H., *Writers on Writing*, New York, 1949.

Broadbent, D., *Perception and Communication*, New York, 1958.

Brodbeck, A., and O. Irwin, "The Speech Behavior of Infants Without Families," *Child Development*, Vol. XVII (1946), pp. 145-156.

Brooks, C., and R. Warren, *Understanding Fiction*, New York, 1943.

Brosnahan, L., *The Sounds of Language*, Cambridge, 1961.

Brown, R., *Words and Things*, New York, 1958.

———, "Linguistic Determinism and the Parts of Speech," *Journal of Abnormal and Social Psychology*, Vol. LV (1957), pp. 1-5.

———, and U. Bellugi, "Three Processes in the Child's Acquisition of Syntax," *Harvard Educational Review*, Vol. XXXIV (1964), pp. 133-151.

——— and J. Berko, "Word Association and the Acquisition of Grammar," *Child Development*, Vol. XXXI (1960), pp. 1-14.

Buchler, J., *Toward a General Theory of Human Judgment*, New York, 1951.

Buermeyer, L., *The Aesthetic Experience*, Merion, Pennsylvania, 1924.

Buhler, C., *The First Year of Life*, New York, 1930.

———, *The Mental Development of the Child*, New York, 1930.

Campbell, K., "The Rhetorical Implications of the Philosophy of Jean-Paul Sartre," Unpublished Ph.D. dissertation, University of Minnesota, 1968.

Campion, G., and G. Elliott-Smith, *the Neutral Basis of Thought*, New York, 1934.

Carmichael, L., H. P. Hogan, and A. A. Walter, "An Experimental Study of the Effect of Language on the Reproduction of Visually Perceived Form," *Journal of Experimental Psychology*, Vol. XV (1932), pp. 73-86.

Carnap, R., *The Logical Syntax of Language*, London, 1937.

———, *Meaning and Necessity*, Chicago, 1947.

———, "Meaning and Synonymy in Natural Languages," *Philosophical Studies*, Vol. VII (1955), pp. 33-47.

Carr, H., *Psychology: A Study of Mental Activity*, New York, 1925.

Carroll, J., "Communication Theory, Linguistics and Psycholinguistics," *Review of Educational Research*, Vol. XXVIII (1958), pp. 79-88.

———, *Language and Thought*, Englewood Cliffs, New Jersey, 1964.

———, "An Operational Analysis of Language Behavior," *Anthropological Linguistics*, Vol. 1 (1959), pp. 37-54.

———, *The Study of Language*, Cambridge, Massachusetts, 1953.

Cartier, F., and K. Harwood, "On the Definition of Communication," *Journal of Communication*, Vol. III (1953), pp. 1-10.

Caton, C., *Philosophy and Ordinary Language*, Englewood Cliffs, New Jersey, 1964.

Caudwell, C., *Illusion and Reality*, London, 1937.

Chandler, A., *Beauty and Human Nature: Elements of Psychological Aesthetics*, New York, 1934.

Chappell, V., ed., *Ordinary Language*, Englewood Cliffs, New Jersey, 1964.

Chauchard, P., *Language and Thought*, trans. N. Kent, New York, 1964.

Cherry, C., *On Human Communication*, New York, 1957.

Child, C., *Physiological Foundations of Behavior*, New York, 1924.

Chisholm, R., "Intentionality and the Theory of Signs," *Philosophical Studies*, Vol. III (1952), pp. 56-63.

Chomsky, N., *Aspects of the Theory of Syntax*, Cambridge, Massachusetts, 1965.

―――, "A Review of B. F. Skinner, 'Verbal Behavior'," *Language*, Vol. XXXV (1959), pp. 26-58.

―――, *Syntactic Structures*, The Hague, 1957.

Cofer, C., "An Experimental Analysis of the Role of Context in Verbal Behavior," *Transactions of the New York Academy of Sciences*, Vol. XXII, Series 2 (1960), pp. 341-347.

―――, and B. Musgrave, ed., *Verbal Learning and Verbal Behavior*, New York, 1961.

Cohen, A. M., W. G. Bennis, and G. Wolkon, "The Effects of Changes in Communication Networks on the Behavior of Problem Solving Groups," *Sociometry*, Vol. XXV (1962), pp. 177-196.

Cohen, A. R., "Upward Communication in Experimentally Created Hierarchies," *Human Relations*, Vol. XI (1958), pp. 41-53.

Cohen, B., H. I. Kalish, J. R. Thurston, and E. Cohen, "Experimental Manipulation of Verbal Behavior," *Journal of Experimental Psychology*, Vol. XLVII (1954), pp. 106-110.

Cohen, L., *The Diversity of Meaning*, London, 1962.

Cohen, M., "Social and Linguistic Structure," *Diogenes*, Vol. XV (1956), pp. 38-47.

Comfort, A., *The Novel and Our Time*, London, 1948.

Conklin, H., "Linguistic Play in Its Cultural Context," *Language*, Vol. XXXV (1959), pp. 631-636.

Cook, A., *The Meaning of Fiction*, Detroit, 1960.

Cooke, D., *The Language of Music*, London, 1959.

Craik, K. J., *The Nature of Explanation*, Cambridge, 1943.

Crane, R. S., ed., *Critics and Criticism Ancient and Modern*, Chicago, 1952.

―――, ed., *The Language of Criticism and the Structure of Poetry*, Toronto, 1953.

Croce, B., *Aesthetic as Science of Expression and General Linguistic*, trans. Douglas Ainstie, London, 1922.

Crowley, T., *Modern Communication*, New York, 1962.

Daiches, D., "Problems for Modern Novelists," in *Accent Anthology*, New York, 1946.

―――, *The Novel and the Modern World*, Chicago, 1960.

Dance, F., ed., *Human Communication Theory*, New York, 1967.

Darlington, C., "The Genetic Component of Language," *Heredity* (1947), pp. 269-286.

Dart, R., "On the Evolution of Language and Articulate Speech," *Homo*, Vol. X (1959), pp. 154-165.

Davies, R., "Art and Anxiety," *Partisan Revue*, Vol. XIV (1945), pp. 310-321.

Davison, W., "On the Effects of Communication," *Public Opinion Quarterly*, Vol. XXIII (1959-1960), pp. 343-360.

Davitz, J., *The Communication of Emotional Meaning*, New York, 1964.
———, and L. J., Davitz, "The Communication of Feeling by Content-Free Speech," *Journal of Communication*, Vol. IX (1959), pp. 6-13.
———, and ———, "Nonverbal Vocal Communication of Feeling," *Journal of Communication*, Vol. XI (1961), pp. 81-86.
DeLaguna, G., *Speech: Its Function and Development*, New Haven, Conn., 1927.
DeVoto, B., "The Invisible Novelist," *Pacific Spectator*, Vol. IV (Winter, 1950), pp. 30-45.
Deutsch, K., "Communication Theory and Social Science," *American Journal of Orthopsychiatry*, Vol. XXII (1952), pp. 469-483.
Dewey, J., *Art As Experience*, New York, 1934.
Dexter, L., and D. M. White, eds., *People, Society and Mass Communications*, New York, 1964.
Di Vesta, F. J., and D. O. Stover, "The Semantic Mediation of Evaluative Meaning," *Journal of Experimental Society*, Vol. LXIV (1962), pp. 467-475.
Dobzhansky, T., *Mankind Evolving*, New Haven, Conn., 1962.
Dollard, J., and N. Miller, *Personality and Psychotherapy*, New York, 1950.
Dorchester, D., Jr., "The Nature of Poetic Expression," *Poet Lore*, Vol. V (1893), pp. 81-90.
Downey, J., *Creative Imagination*, London, 1929.
Drew, E., *The Modern Novel: Some Aspects of Contemporary Fiction*, New York, 1926.
DuBrul, E. L., *Evolution of the Speech Apparatus*, Springfield, Illinois, 1958.
Duncan, H., *Communication and the Social Order*, New York, 1962.
Eccles, J., ed., *Brain and Conscious Experience*, New York, 1966.
Edel, L., *The Psychological Novel*, Philadelphia, 1955.
Edelman, M., *The Symbolic Uses of Politics*, Urbana, Illinois, 1964.
Edgar, P., *The Art of the Novel: From 1700 to the Present Time*, New York, 1933.
Eisenstadt, S. N., "Communications Systems and Social Structure," *Public Opinion Quarterly*, Vol. XIX (1955), pp. 153-167.
Eliot, T. S., *On Poets and Poetry*, New York, 1957.
———, *The Sacred Wood: Essays on Criticism and Poetry*, London, 1920.
———, *Selected Essays, 1917-1932*, New York, 1932.
Empson, W., *Seven Types of Ambiguity*, London, 1930.
Ervin, S. M., "Changes with Age in the Verbal Determinants of Word-Association," *American Journal of Psychology*, Vol. LXXIV (1961), pp. 361-372.
Faber, S. M., and R. H. Wilson, eds., *Control of the Mind*, New York, 1961.
Fairbanks, G., "A Theory of the Speech Organism as a Servosystem," *Journal of Speech and Hearing Disorders*, Vol. XIX (1954), pp. 133-139.
Farber, I., "The Things People Say to Themselves," *American Psychologist*, Vol. XVIII (1963), pp. 185-197.
Farber, M., "Subjectivity in Modern Fiction," *Kenyon Review*, Vol. VII (1949), pp. 645-652.
Fearing, F., "Toward a Psychological Theory of Human Communication," *Journal of Personality*, Vol. XXII (1953), pp. 71-88.

Feidelson, C., *Symbolism and American Literature*, Chicago, 1953.

Festinger, L., "Informal Social Communication," *Psychological Review*, Vol. LVII (1950), pp. 271-282.

———, *A Theory of Cognitive Dissonance*, New York, 1957.

Fillenbaum, S., L. V. Jones, and J. M. Wepman, "Some Linguitic Features of Speech from Aphasic Patients," *Language and Speech*, Vol. IV (1961), pp. 91-108.

Finley, J. R., and A. Staats, "Evaluative Meaning Words as Reinforcement Stimuli," *Journal of Verbal Learning and Verbal Behavior*, Vol. VI (1967), pp. 193-197.

Firth, J. R., *Papers in Linguistics 1934-1951*, New York, 1957.

Fischer, J. L., "Social Influences in the Choice of a Linguistic Variant," *Word*, Vol. XIV (1958), pp. 47-56.

Flavell, J. H., *The Development Psychology of Jean Piaget*, Princeton, 1963.

———, "Meaning and Meaning Similarity: A Theoretical Reassessment," *Journal of General Psychology*, Vol. LXIV (1961), pp. 307-319.

Flew, A., ed., *Logic and Language*, First Series, Oxford, 1951.

———, ed., *Logic and Language*, Second Series, Oxford, 1953.

Fodor, J. A., and J. J. Katz, eds., *The Structure of Language: Readings in the Philosophy of Language*, Englewood Cliffs, New Jersey, 1964.

Forester, E. M., *Aspects of the Novel*, London, 1927.

Foss, M., *Symbol and Metaphor in Human Experience*, Princeton, New Jersey, 1949.

Foster, R., *The New Romantics: A Reappraisal of the New Criticism*, Bloomington, Indiana, 1962.

Frank, L. K., *Feelings and Emotions*, New York, 1954.

Freud, S., *On Aphasia*, New York, 1953.

Friedman, M., *Stream of Consciousness: A Study in Literary Method*, New Haven, Conn., 1955.

Friedman, N., "Imagery from Sensation to Symbol," *Journal of Aesthetics*, Vol. XII (1953), pp. 24-37.

Frye, N., ed., *Sound and Poetry*, New York, 1957.

Garnett, A. C., *Reality and Value*, New Haven, Connecticut, 1937.

Garvin, P., ed., *Natural Language and the Computer*, New York, 1963.

Geiger, D., *The Sound, Sense, and Performance of Literature*, Palo Alto, California, 1963.

Gellner, E., *Words and Things*, London, 1959.

Ghiselin, B., ed., *The Creative Process: A Symposium*, New York, 1955.

Gibson, E., "A Systematic Application of the Concepts of Generalization and Differentiation to Verbal Learning," *Psychoanalytic Review*, Vol. XLVII (1940), pp. 196-229.

Gleason, H. A., Jr., *An Introduction to Descriptive Linguistics*, Rev. ed., New York, 1961.

Goffman, E., *The Presentation of Self in Everyday Life*, New York, 1959.

———, *Encounters: Two Studies in the Sociology of Interaction*, Indianapolis, 1961.

Goldstein, K., *Language and Language Disturbances*, New York, 1948.

Goodenough, F., "Semantic Choice and Personality Structure," *Science*, Vol. CIV (1946), pp. 451-456.

Goodenough, W., "Componential Analysis and the Study of Meaning," *Language*, Vol. XXXII (1956), pp. 155-216.

Goodglass, H., and J. Mayer, "Agrammatism and Aphasia," *Journal of Speech and Hearing Disorders*, Vol. XXIII (1958), pp. 99-111.

Goodman, P., *The Structure of Literature*, Chicago, 1954.

Gottschalk, L. A., G. Gleser, and G. Hambridge, "Verbal Behavior Analysis," *A.M.A. Archives of Neurology and Psychiatry*, Vol. LXXVII (1957), pp. 300-311.

Greenberg, J. H., *Essays in Linguistics*, Chicago, 1957.

———, ed., *Universals of Language*, Cambridge, Massachusetts, 1963.

Greenough, J. B., and G. L. Kittredge, *Words and Their Ways in English Speech*, New York, 1906.

Grice, H. P., "Meaning," *Philosophical Review*, Vol. LXVI (1957), pp. 377-388.

Grootaers, W. A., "Language Behavior of an Individual During One Day," *Orbis*, Vol. I (1952), pp. 126-129.

Guthrie, E. R., "Association by Contiguity," in *Psychology A Study of a Science*, Vol. III, S. Koch, ed., New York, 1959.

Hall, A., *A Glossary of Important Symbols*, Boston, 1912.

Hall, E. T., *The Hidden Dimension*, New York, 1966.

———, *The Silent Language*, New York, 1959.

Hall, R., "Assuming One Set of Positing Words," *Philosophical Review*, Vol. LXVII (1958), pp. 52-75.

Hamilton, C., *Materials and Methods of Fiction*, Norwood, Massachusetts, 1909.

Hampshire, S., *Thought and Action*, London, 1959.

Harlow, H., and C. Woolsey, eds., *Biological and Biochemical Bases of Behavior*, Madison, Wisconsin, 1958.

———, and R. Stagner, "Psychology of Feelings and Emotions. II. Theory of Emotions," *Psychological Review*, Vol. XL (1933), pp. 184-195.

Harrah, D., *Communication: A Logical Model*, Cambridge, Massachusetts, 1963.

Harris, Z., "Co-Occurrence and Transformation in Linguistic Structure," *Language*, Vol. XXXIII (1957), pp. 283-340.

———, "Discourse Analysis," *Language*, Vol. XXVIII (1952), pp. 1-30.

———, "From Morpheme to Utterance." *Language*, Vol. XXII (1946), pp. 161-183.

Hartshorne, C., "The Intelligibility of Sensations," *The Monist*, Vol. XLIV (1934), pp. 161-185.

———, *The Philosophy and Psychology of Sensation*, Chicago, 1934.

Head, H., *Aphasia and Kindred Disorders of Speech*, New York, 1926.

Henle, P., ed., *Language, Thought and Culture*, Ann Arbor, Michigan, 1958.

———, ed., *Structure, Method and Meaning*, New York, 1951.

Herdan, G., *Quantitative Linguistics*, London, 1964.

Herrick, C., *The Evolution of Human Nature*, New York, 1961.

———, *Introduction to Neurology*, Philadelphia, 1931.

Hicks, G., ed., *The Living Novel*, New York, 1957.

Hilgard, E. R., "Human Motives and the Concept of the Self," *American Psychologist*, Vol. IV (1949), pp. 374-382.

———, *Theories of Learning*, London, 1957.

Hingston, R. W. G., *Problems of Instinct and Intelligence*, New York, 1928.

Hjelmslev, L., *Prolegomena to a Theory of Language*, Madison, Wisconsin, 1961.

Hockett, C., *A Course in Modern Linguistics*, New York, 1958.

Hocking, W., *The Self, Its Body and Freedom*, London, 1928.

Hoggart, R., *The Uses of Literacy*, Boston, 1962.

Hoijer,H., ed., *Language in Culture*, Chicago, 1954.

Holloway, J., *Language and Intelligence*, London, 1951.

Hovland, C. I., "A 'Communication Analysis' of Concept Learning," *Psychological Review*, Vol. LIX (1952), pp. 461-472.

———, I. L. Janis, and H. Kelley, *Communication and Persuasion*, New Haven, Connecticut, 1953.

Howes, D.H., "On the Relation between the Probability of a Word as an Association and in General Linguistic Usage," *Journal of Abnormal and Social Psychology*, Vol. LIV (1957), pp. 75-85.

Humphrey, G., *Thinking*, London, 1951.

Hunt, E. B., *Concept Learning*, New York, 1962.

Hunter, W. S., *Human Behavior*, Chicago, 1928.

Huxley, A., *The Doors of Perception*, New York, 1954.

Huxley, J., *Evolution, the Modern Synthesis*, New York, 1943.

Hymes, D., ed., *Language in Culture and Society*, New York, 1964.

Irwin, O. C., "Infant Speech: Development of Vowel Sounds," *Journal of Speech and Hearing Disorders*, Vol. XIII (1948), pp. 31-34.

Jacobson, E. R., L. Kahn, F. Mann, and N. Morse, eds., "Human Relations Research in Large Organizations," *Journal of Social Issues*, Vol. VII (1951), pp. 1-74.

Jakobovits, J., and W. E. Lambert, "Mediated Satiation in Verbal Transfer," *Journal of Experimental Psychology*, Vol. LXIV (1962), pp. 346-351.

Jakobson, R., C. G. M. Fant, and M. Halle, *Preliminaries to Speech Analysis: The Distinctive Features and Their Correlates*, Cambridge, Massachusetts, 1963.

James, D. G., *Skepticism and Poetry: An Essay on the Poetic Imagination*, London, 1937.

James, H., *The Art of Fiction and Other Essays*, ed. Morris Roberts, New York, 1948.

James, W., *The Principles of Psychology, Vol. 1*, New York, 1890.

Jaspers, K., *Reason and Existenz*, New York, 1955.

Jenkins, J. J., "A Mediational Account of Grammatical Phenomena," *Journal of Communication*, Vol. XIV (1964), pp. 86-97.

Jesperson, O., *Growth and Structure of the English Language*, New York, 1955.

———, *The Philosophy of Grammar*, London, 1951.

Johnson, A., *Treatise on Language*, ed. David Rynin, Berkeley, California, 1947.

Jones, L. V., M. F. Goodman, and J. M. Wepman, "The Classification of Parts of Speech for the Characterization of Aphasia," *Language and Speech*, Vol. VI

(1963), pp. 94-107.

———, and J. M. Wepman, "Dimensions of Language Performance in Aphasia," *Journal of Speech and Hearing Disorders*, Vol. IV (1961), pp. 220-232.

Jones, R., *The Dramatic Imagination*, New York, 1941.

Joos, M., ed., *Readings in Linguistics*, Washington, D. C., 1957.

———, "Semiology: A Linguistic Theory of Meaning," *Studies in Linguistics*, Vol. XIII (1958), pp. 53-70.

Jung, C. G., *Contributions to Analytical Psychology*, trans. H. G. and C. F. Baynes, New York, 1928.

———, *Modern Man in Search of His Soul*, London, 1933.

———, *Man and His Symbols*, Garden City, New York, 1946.

Kaplan, A., "Definition and Specification of Meaning," *Journal of Philosophy*, Vol. XLIII (1946), pp. 281-288.

Kasanin, J. S., ed., *Language and Thought in Schizophrenia*, New York, 1946.

Katz, J. J., and J. A. Fodor, "The Structure of a Semantic Theory," *Language*, Vol. XXXIX (1963), pp. 170-210.

———, and P. Postal, *An Integrated Theory of Linguistic Description*, Cambridge, Massachusetts, 1964.

Kausler, D. H., ed., *Readings in Verbal Learning*, New York, 1966.

Kellmer, P., and M. Tanner, "The Effects of Early Deprivation on Speech Development," *Language and Speech*, Vol. 1 (1958), pp. 269-287.

Kepes, G., *Language of Vision*, Chicago, 1944.

Kjeldergaard, P., "The Psychology of Language," *Review of Educational Research*, Vol XXXI (1961), pp. 119-129.

Korzybski, A., *Science and Sanity; An Introduction to Non-Aristotelian Systems and General Semantics*, Lakeville, Connecticut, 1933.

Laftal, J., *Pathological and Normal Language*, New York, 1965.

Laird, C., *The Miracle Language*, Greenwich, Connecticut, 1957.

Laird, J., *Problems of the Self*, The Shaw Lectures of 1914, London, 1917.

Lambert, W. E., and L. A. Jackobovits, *The Case for Semantic Satiation*, Montreal, 1963

———, R. Hoogson, R. Gardner, and S. Fillenbaum, "Evaluational Reactions to Spoken Languages," *Journal of Abnormal and Social Psychology*, Vol. LX (1960), pp. 44-51.

Langfield, H. S., *The Aesthetic Attitude*, New York, 1920.

Lantz, D., and V. Stefflre, "Language and Cognition Revisited," *Journal of Abnormal and Social Psychology*, Vol. LXIX (1964), pp. 472-481.

Lasswell, H. D., and D. Lerner, *The Comparative Study of Symbols*, Stanford, California, 1952.

Leach, M., and J. Fried, eds., *Dictionary of Folklore, Mythology and Legend*, 2 Vols., New York, 1947.

Leggett, H. W., *The Idea in Fiction*, London, 1934.

Lenneberg, E. H., and J. M. Roberts, "The Language of Experience," *International Journal of American Linguistics*, 1956. Memoir 13.

———, and ———, "A Probabilistic Approach to Language Learning," *Behavioral*

*Science*, Vol. II (1957), pp. 1-13.

———, and ———, "Understanding Language without Ability to Speak: A Case Report," *Journal of Abnormal and Social Psychology*, Vol. LXV (1962), pp. 419-425.

Lesser, S. O., *Fiction and the Unconscious*, Boston, 1957.

Lewis, C. D., *The Poetic Image*, New York, 1947.

Lewis, C. S., "Psychoanalysis and Literary Criticism," *Essays and Studies of the English Association*, Vol. XXVII (1941), pp.7-21.

Lewis, M. M., *Infant Speech*, New York, 1951.

Lewis, R. W. B., *The Picaresque Saint: Representative Figures in Contemporary Fiction*, New York, 1959.

Liddell, R., *A Treatise on the Novel*, London, 1947.

Lindsley, D. B., "Brain Potentials in Children and Adults," *Science*, Vol. LXXXIV (1936), p. 354.

Linsky, L., *Semantics and the Philosophy of Language*, Urbana, Illinois, 1952.

Loeb, L., *The Biological Basis of Individuality*, Springfield, Illinois, 1945.

Lorenz, K. L., *On Aggression*, London, 1966.

Lowenthal, L., *Literature and the Images of Man: Sociological Studies of the European Drama and Novel, 1600-1900*, Boston, 1957.

Lucas, F. L., *Literature and Psychology*, London, 1951.

Luria, A. R., *The Role of Speech in the Regulation of Normal and Abnormal Behavior*, Oxford, 1961.

McCarthy, D., *The Language Development of the Preschool Child*, Minneapolis, 1930.

———, "Language Development in Children," ed. L. Carmichael, *Manual of Child Psychology*, New York, 1964.

McCarthy, M., "The Fact in Fiction," *Partisan Review*, XXVII (Summer, 1960), pp. 438-458.

McGeoch, J., *The Psychology of Human Learning*, New York, 1942.

MacKaye, J., *The Logic of Language*, New York, 1965.

McKellar, P., *Imagination and Thinking*, London, 1957.

McKeon, R., "The Philosophic Bases of Art and Criticism," *Modern Philology*, Vols. XLI-XLII (1943-1944).

Maclay, H., and C. Osgood, "Hesitation Phenomena in Spontaneous English Speech," *Word*, Vol. XV (1959), pp. 19-44.

Markey, J. F., *The Symbolic Process*, London, 1928

Mason, S., ed., *Signs, Signals and Symbols*, London, 1963.

Mayo, B., " 'Rules of Language," *Philosophical Studies*. Vol. II (1951), pp. 1-7.

Mead, G. H., *Mind, Self and Society*, Chicago, 1934.

Medawar, P. B., *The Uniqueness of the Individual*, New York, 1957.

Mendilow, A. A., *Time and the Novel*, New York, 1952.

Meyerhoff, H., *Time in Literature*, Los Angeles, 1955.

Miller, G. A., *Language and Communication*, New York, 1956.

———, "Some Psychological Studies of Grammar." *American Psychologist*, Vol. XVII (1962), pp. 748-762.

Miller, N. E., and J. Dollard, *Social Learning and Imitation*, New Haven, Connecticut, 1941.

Monrad-Krohn, G. H., "Dysprosody or Altered Melody of Language," *Brain*, Vol. LXX (1947), pp. 405-415.

Moore, A. R., *The Individual in Simpler Forms*, Eugene, Oregon, 1945.

Morris, C., *Signs, Language and Behavior*, New York, 1946.

Morris, D., *The Biology of Art*, New York, 1962.

Moulton, R. G., *The Modern Study of Literature*, Chicago, 1915.

Mowrer, O. H., "The Autism Theory of Speech Development and Some Clinical Applications," *Journal of Speech and Hearing Disorders*, Vol. XVII (1952), pp. 263-268.

———, "The Psychologist Looks at Language," *American Psychologist*, Vol. IX (1954), pp. 660-694.

———, *Learning Theory and the Symbolic Processes*, New York, 1960.

———, *Learning Theory and Behavior*, New York, 1960.

———, *Learning Theory and Personality Dynamics*, New York, 1950.

Muller, H., *The Science of Language*, London, 1891.

Myers, E., *The Foundations of English*, New York, 1940.

Myklebust, H. R., *The Psychology of Deafness: Sensory Deprivation, Learning, and Adjustments*, New York, 1960.

Nafe, J., "The Psychology of Felt Experience," *American Journal of Psychology*, Vol. XXXIX (1927), pp. 367-389.

Nida, E. A., "The Analysis of Immediate Constituents," *Language*, Vol. XXIV (1948), pp. 168-177.

Nielsen, J. M., *Agnosia, Apraxia, Aphasia: Their Value in Cerebral Localization*, 2nd ed., New York, 1946.

Noble, C. E., "An Analysis of Meaning," *Psychological Review*, Vol. LIX (1952), pp. 421-430.

Ogden, C. K., and I. A. Richards, *The Meaning of Meaning*, 5th ed., New York, 1938.

Ortega Y Gasset, J., *The Dehuminization of Art*, trans. Willard Trask, Garden City, New York, 1956.

Osborne, H., *Aesthetics and Criticism*, London, 1955.

Osgood, C. E., and M. S. Miron, *Approaches to the Study of Aphasia*, Urbana, Illinois, 1963.

———, *Contemporary Approaches to Cognition*, Cambridge, Massachusetts, 1957.

———, and G. J. Suci, "Factor Analysis of Meaning," *Journal of Experimental Psychology*, Vol. L (1955), pp. 325-338.

———, ———, and P. H. Tannenbaum, *The Measurement of Meaning*, Urbana, Illinois, 1957.

———, *Method and Theory in Experimental Psychology*, New York, 1953.

———, "The Nature and Measurement of Meaning," *Psychological Bulletin*, Vol. XLIX (1952), pp. 197-237.

———, "On Understanding and Creating Sentences," *American Psychologist*, Vol. XVIII (1963), pp. 735-751.

——, and T. A. Sebeok, eds., *Psycholinguistics*, Bloomington, Indiana, 1965.

Paget, R., *Human Speech*, London, 1930.

Parker, D., *The Analysis of Art*, New Haven, Connecticut, 1926.

Pei, M., *The Story of English*, Philadelphia, 1952.

——, *The Story of Language*, Rev. ed., Philadelphia, 1965.

Pell, O. A., *Value Theory and Criticism*, New York, 1930.

Penfield, W., and L. Roberts, *Speech and Brain Mechanisms*, Princeton, 1959.

Perky, C. W. "An Experimental Study of Imagination," *American Journal of Psychology*, Vol. XXI (1910), pp. 422-452.

Peyre, H., *Writers and Their Critics: A Study of Misunderstandings*, Ithaca, New York, 1944.

Pfuetze, P. E., *The Social Self*, New York, 1954.

Piaget, J., *The Language and Thought of the Child*, trans. M. Gabain, 2nd ed., London, 1932.

——, *The Psychology of Intelligence*, trans. M. Piercy, New York, 1950.

Pierce, J. R., *Symbols, Signals, and Noise*, New York, 1961.

Pike, K., "Language as Particle, Wave, and Field," *The Texas Quarterly*, Vol. II (1959), pp. 37-54.

Pillsbury, W. B., and C. L. Meader, *The Psychology of Language*, New York, 1928.

Pollio, H. R., "Word Association As a Function of Conditioned Meaning," *Journal of Experimental Psychology*, Vol. LXVI (1963), pp. 454-460.

Pommer, H. F., and W. M. Sale, Jr., *The Use of Language*, New York, 1947.

Prall, D., *Aesthetic Analysis*, New York, 1936.

Prescott, F. C., *Poetry and Myth*, New York, 1927.

Pronko, N. H., "Language and Psycholinguistics: A Review," *Psychological Bulletin*, Vol. XLIII (1946), pp. 189-239.

Quine, W., *Word and Object*, Cambridge, Massachusetts, 1960.

Rader, M., *A Modern Book of Aesthetics*, 2nd ed., New York, 1952.

Rahv, P., "Fiction and Criticism of Fiction," *Kenyon Review*, Vol. XII (1950), pp. 189-218.

Reid, J. R., *A Theory of Value*, New York, 1938.

Richards, I. A., *Practical Criticism: A Study of Literary Judgment*, London, 1929.

——, *Principles of Literary Criticism*, New York, 1924.

Roback, A. A., *Destiny and Motivation in Language*, Cambridge, Massachusetts, 1954.

Robinson, R., *Definition*, New York, 1950.

Rosenberg, S., ed., *Directions in Psycholinguistics*, New York, 1965.

Rosenblith, W. A., ed., *Sensory Communication*, Cambridge, Massachusetts, 1961.

Russell, B., *The Analysis of Mind*, London, 1921.

——, *An Inquiry into Meaning and Truth*, New York, 1940.

Salzinger, K., "Experimental Manipulation of Verbal Behavior: A Review," *Journal of General Psychology*, Vol. LXI (1959), pp. 65-94.

Sanford, F. H., "Speech and Personality," *Psychological Bulletin*, Vol. XXXIX (1942), pp. 811-845.

Santayana, G., *The Life of Reason: Or, The Phases of Human Progress*, N.Y., 1905.

Sapir, E., *Language*, New York, 1921.

Saporta, S., ed., *Psycholinguistics*, New York, 1961.

Sartre, J., *Against the Crime of Silence: Proceedings of the Russell International War Crimes Tribunal*, ed. J. Duffett, New York, 1968.

———, *The Age of Reason*, trans. E. Sulton, New York, 1948.

———, *Anti-Semite and Jew*, trans. G. J. Becker, New York, 1948.

———, *Baudelaire*, trans. M. Turnell, Norfolk, Connecticut, 1950.

———, *Being and Nothingness*, trans. H. E. Branes, New York, 1956.

———, *Black Orpheus*, trans. S. W. Allen, Paris, 1963.

———, *The Communists and Peace*, New York, 1968.

———, *The Condemned of Altona*, trans. S. and G. Leeson, New York, 1961.

———, *The Devil and the Good Lord and Two Other Plays*, New York, 1960.

———, *The Emotions, Outline of a Theory*, trans. B. Frechtman, New York, 1948.

———, *Essays in Aesthetics*, trans. W. Basking, New York, 1963.

———, *Existential Psychoanalysis*, trans. H. Barnes, Chicago, 1966.

———, *Existentialism*, trans. B. Frechtman, New York, 1947.

———, *Existentialism and Human Emotions*, trans. H. Barnes, New York, 1957.

———, *Existentialism and Humanism*, trans. P. Mairet, London, 1957.

———, "Forgers of Myths: The Young Playwrights of France," *Theatre Arts*, Vol. XXX (June, 1946), pp. 324-335.

———, *The Ghost of Stalin*, trans. M. Fletcher, New York, 1968.

———, *Imagination: a Psychological Critique*, trans. F. Williams, Ann Arbor, Michigan, 1962.

———, *Iron in the Soul*, trans. G. Hopkins, London, 1960.

———, *Literary and Philosophical Essays*, trans. A. Michelson, New York, 1967.

———, *Nekrassov, A Farce*, trans. S. Leeson and G. Leeson, London, 1956.

———, *No Exit and Three Other Plays*, trans. S. Gilbert, New York, 1956.

———, *The Psychology of Imagination*, trans. B. Frechtman, New York, 1961.

———, *The Reprieve*, trans. E. Sutton, New York, 1947.

———, *Saint Genet, Actor and Martyr*, trans. B. Frechtman, New York, 1963.

———, *Sartre on Cuba*, New York, 1961.

———, *Search for a Method*, trans. H. Barnes, New York, 1963.

———, *Situations IV*, trans. B. Eisler, New York, 1965.

———, *The Transcendence of the Ego: An Existentialist Theory of Consciousness*, trans. F. Williams and R. Kirkpatrick, New York, 1948.

———, *The Wall and Other Stories*, trans. L. Alexander, New York. 1948.

———, *What Is Literature?* trans. B. Frechtman, New York, 1965.

———, *The Words*, trans. B. Frechtman, New York, 1946.

Savory, T. H., *The Language of Science*, London, 1953.

Sayce, A. H., *Introduction to the Science of Language*, London, 1880.

Schaefer, K. E., ed., *Environmental Effects on Consciousness*, New York, 1960.

Schoenberg, A., *Style and Idea*, New York, 1950.

Schuell, H., and J. Jenkins, "The Nature of Language Deficit in Aphasia," *Psychological Review*, Vol. LXVI (1959), pp. 45-67.

Searle, J., "Meaning and Speech Acts," *Philosophical Review,* Vol. LXXI (1962), pp. 423-432.

Shannon, C. E., and W. Weaver, *The Mathematical Theory of Communication,* Urbana, Illinois, 1949.

Sholl, D. A., *The Organization of the Cerebral Cortex,* London, 1956.

Shwayder, D. S., "Uses of Language and Uses of Words," *Theoria,* Vol. XXVI (1960), pp. 31-43.

Simpson, G., *The Meaning of Evolution: A Study of the History of Life and of Its Significance for Man,* New Haven, Connecticut, 1949.

Skinner, B. F., *The Behavior of Organisms,* New York, 1938.

———, *Science and Human Behavior,* New York, 1953.

———, *Verbal Behavior,* New York, 1957.

Smith, A. E., *Communication and Culture,* New York, 1966.

Smith, F., and G. Miller, *The Genesis of Language,* New York, 1966.

Smith, J. H., and E. W. Parks, eds., *The Great Critics: An Anthology of Literary Criticism,* New York, 1951.

Spitz, R. A., *No and Yes: On the Genesis of Human Communication,* New York, 1957.

Spitzer, L., *Linguistics and Literary History,* Princeton, 1948.

Staats, A. W., *Learning, Language and Cognition,* New York, 1968.

———, "Learning Theory and Opposite Speech," *Journal of Abnormal and Social Psychology,* Vol. LV (1957), pp. 268-269.

Staats, C. K., and A. W. Staats, "Meaning Established by Classical Conditioning," *Journal of Experimental Psychology,* Vol. LIV (1957), pp. 74-80.

———, and ———, *Complex Human Behavior,* New York, 1963.

Stang, R., *The Theory of the Novel in England, 1850-1870,* New York, 1959.

Stevenson, C. L., *Ethics and Language,* New Haven, Connecticut, 1944.

Taffel, C., "Anxiety and the Conditioning of Verbal Behavior," *Journal of Abnormal and Social Psychology,* Vol. LI (1955), pp. 496-501.

Tatz, S. J., "Symbolic Activity in Learning Without Awareness," *American Journal of Psychology,* Vol. LXXIII (1960) pp. 239-247.

Thorburn, J., *Art and the Unconscious,* London, 1934.

Thorndike, E. L., "The Origin of Language," *Science,* Vol. LXXVII (1933), pp. 173-175.

Tillotson, K., *The Tale and the Teller,* London, 1959.

Tillyard, E. M. W., *The Epic Strain in the English Novel,* London, 1958.

Trager, G. L., "Paralanguage: A First Approximation," *Studies in Linguistics,* Vol. XIII (1958), pp. 1-12.

Tuve, R., *The Elizabethan and Metaphysical Imagery: Renaissance Poetic and Twentieth-Century Critics,* Chicago, 1947.

Ulmann, S., *Semantics: An Introduction to the Science of Meaning,* New York, 1962.

Underwood, B. J., and R. W. Schulz, *Meaningfulness and Verbal Learning,* Chicago, 1960.

Urban, W. M., *Language and Reality: The Philosophy of Language and the*

*Principles of Symbolism*, New York, 1951.

Van Ghent, D., *The English Novel Form and Function*, New York, 1953.

Vendryes, J., *Language*, New York, 1925.

Vivas, E., "The Esthetic Judgment," *Journal of Philosophy*, Vol. XXXIII (1936), pp. 57-69.

———, "A Note on Value," *Journal of Philosophy*, Vol. XXXIII (1936), pp. 568-575.

Vygotsky, L. S., *Thought and Language*, trans. E. Haufmann and G. Vaker, Cambridge, Massachusetts, 1962.

Waissman, F., *The Principles of Linguistic Philosophy*, ed. R. Harre, New York, 1965.

Walsh, D., "The Cognitive Content of Art," *Philosophical Review*, Vol. LII (1943), pp. 433-451.

Ward, A. C., *Foundations of English Prose*, London, 1931.

Warnock, G. J., "Verification and the Use of Language," *Revue Internationale de Philosophie*, Vol. V (1951), pp. 317-322.

Warren, A., and R. Wellek, *Theory of Literature*, New York, 1949.

Watson, J. B., "Is Thinking the Action of Language Mechanism?" Part V. *British Journal of Psychology*, Vol. XI (1920), pp. 87-104.

Weir, R., *Language in the Crib*, The Hague, 1962.

Weisenberg, T., and K. McBride, *Aphasia*, New York, 1935.

Weiss, A. P., *A Theoretical Basis of Human Behavior*, Columbus, Ohio, 1925.

Weller, R., and W. Austin, *Theory of Literature*, New York, 1949.

Wells, R., "Immediate Constituents," *Language*, Vol. XXIII (1947), pp. 81-117.

Werner, H., and B. Kaplan, *Symbolic Formation*, New York, 1964.

Wever, E. G., *Theory of Hearing*, New York, 1949.

Wheelwright, P., *Metaphor and Reality*, Bloomington, Indiana, 1962.

White, L. A., "Symboling: A Kind of Behavior," *Journal of Psychology*, Vol. LIII (1962), pp. 311-317.

Whitehead, A. N., *Symbolism: Its Meaning and Effect*, New York, 1927.

Whitney, W. D., *Language and the Study of Language*, New York, 1867.

Whorf, B. L., *Language, Thought and Reality*, ed. J. B. Carroll, Cambridge, Massachusetts, 1956.

Wiener, N., *Cybernetics: Or Control and Communication in the Animal and the Machine*, New York, 1948.

———, "Speech, Language and Learning," *Journal of the Acoustical Society of America*, Vol. XXII (1950), pp. 696-697.

Wilson, G. A., *The Self and Its World*, New York, 1926.

Wilson, R., *The Miraculous Birth of Language*, New York, 1948.

Wodehouse, H., "Language and Moral Philosophy," *Mind*, Vol. XLVII, 1938.

Woodward, F. R., "Recovery from Aphasia; Report of Two Cases," *Bulletin of the Los Angeles Neurological Society*, Vol. X (1945), pp. 73-75.

Woodworth, R. S., *Dynamics of Behavior*, New York, 1958.

Yngve, V., "A Model and an Hypothesis for Language Structure," *Proceedings of the American Philosophical Society*, Vol. CIV (1960), pp. 444-466.

Young, P. T., *Emotion in Man and Animal*, New York, 1943.

———, *Motivation and Emotion: A Survey of the Determinants of Human and Animal Activity*, New York, 1936.

Ziff, P., *Semantic Analysis* Ithaca, New York, 1960.

Zipf, G. K., *The Psycho-Biology of Language*, Boston, 1935.

Zuckerkandl, V., *Sound and Symbol*, New York, 1956.

# Index

## A

Analogy    58
Analysis    1-2
Anthony, Susan B.
  "On Woman's Right to
    Suffrage"    90-91
Argument    66-81
  deductive    67-68
  definitional    70-73
  enthymematic    67-69
  inductive    69-70
Aristotle    1, 179, 266
Auden, W. H.
  "The Unknown
    Citizen"    255-256
Audience adaptation    39-55
  and free choice    224-225
Authoritative testimony    56-57

## B

Bacon, Francis
  "Of Revenge"    233
*Book of the Dead*    137
Burke, Kenneth    206, 207
Butler, Samuel
  "The Way of All Flesh"    177-178
Byron, George Gordon, Lord
  "So, We'll Go No More
    A-Roving"    199-200

## C

Catullus
  "My Sweetest Lesbia"    137-138
Ciardi, John
  "Snowy Heron"    262
Creeley, Robert
  "The Language"    144-145
*Cyrano de Bergerac*    166-169, 258-259

## D

Definition    70-81
Description    150-154
Deutsch, Babette    266
Dialectic    2-5
Dickens, Charles
  *A Tale of Two Cities*    193-194
Disposition    81-95
  as emphasis    85
  in the Body    86
  in the Conclusion    86
  in the Introduction    86
  transcending parts    82-90
  statements    83-86
  supports    8
Donne, John
  "Song"    147

## D

Drama    165-171
  characterization and conflict
    in    165-171
Drew, Elizabeth    179-180
Duncan, Hugh Dalziel    205-206

## E

*Ecclesiastes*    14
Ehrlich, Paul
  "Eco-Catastrophe"    43-52
Emotional proofs    36-55
  versus facts    38, 40-55
"Enemy, The"    163-165
Engle, Paul
  "USA"    244-245
Ethical proofs    22-36
Evidence    56-66
Examples    57
Exposition    149-150

## F

Facts    58-59
  versus emotional appeals    38, 40-55
Friedenberg, Edgar Z.
  "The Generation Gap"    107-114
Frost, Robert
  "The Figure A Poem Makes"    92-94
Fry, Christopher
  *The Lady's Not For
    Burning*    169-171
Frye, Northrop    101-103, 247-248, 266

## G

Geiger, Don    180
God-terms    270-271
Gogol, Nikolai
  "Apostrophe"    151

## H

Henry, Patrick    12-13
Herrick, Robert
  "Upon Julia's Clothes"    174
Honig, Edwin
  "Quest"    261-262
Hugo, Victor
  Speech on the anniversary
    of Voltaire's death    191-193

## I

Ibn Khaldún
  "Observations on History"    150
Ibn Kolthúm
  "Pour Us Wine"    134
Imagery    150-154
"Indra, the Supreme God"    133-134

Invention    22-81

### J

James, Henry
  "The Pilgrim in Oxford"    152-153
Johnstone, Henry W., Jr.    220, 224

### K

Kakinomoto no Hitomaro    133
Kennedy, John F.    12
Killens, John O.
  "Black Man's Burden"    76-79
Koestler, Arthur    208-209, 215-216,
  239, 246, 263

### L

Langer, Susanne    198, 206-207, 208,
  211, 216-217, 240-241
Language
  and man    6
  and reality    9
  as drama    239-242
  as intrapersonal process    201-206
  as poetic process    206-211
  as Rhetoric and Ritual    211-218
  as rhythmic and metaphorical
    209-211
  constitutive    99-101
  discursive forms of    215-218
  partial or faded    212-215
  verbal and nonverbal    6-9
Lenneberg, Eric    20-21
Lien, Sung
  "The Learned Giant"    254-255
Lincoln, Abraham
  Second Inaugural    104-105
Listening    201-206
Logical proofs    55-81

### M

MacLeish, Fleming
  "Exploration by Air"    247
Mayer, Milton
  "The Children's Crusade"    26-33
Meaning    171-181
Meredith, George
  "The Comic Spirit"    252
  *The Egoist*    263-264
Metaphor    145-149
Miller, Vassar
  "The Resolution"    138

### N

Narration    154-162
  point of view in    158-162
Negation    269-270
Nonpoetry    256

### O

"Of An Old Passion"    154-158
Omar Khayyám
  "The Rubiyat"    134

### P

*Personae*
  and authors    246-247
  of literature    242-250
  of poetry, prose, verse, and
    nonpoetry    250-257
Persuasion
  as self-persuasion    219, 221-223
  nature of    16-22
  one-sides versus two-sided    24-36
  versus informing    16-22
Pitt, William
  Speech on taxing the
    Ameeican colonies    74-75
Plato    1
Poe, Edgar Allen
  "Annabel Lee"    212
Poetry
  and nonpoetry, prose, and
    verse    250-257
  defined    256
  form of    140-149
  metaphor in    145-149
  rhythm in    140-145
"Poor Cat, Rich Cat"    133
Pope, Alexander
  "An Essay on Criticism"    265
Prose
  a combined form    163-165
  and nonpoetry    256-257, 266
  defined    256
  description in    150-154
  exposition in    149-150
  form    149-165
  imagery in    150-154
  narration in    154-165
  poetry    261-262, 263-265

### R

Ransom, John Crowe
  "Blue Girls"    173
Rhetoric
  and freedom of choice    220-237
  and Ritual as the limits of
    language    211-218
  and the rhetorician    221-224
  as discourse    180
  as inseparable from Ritual    190-200
  as persuasion    16-22
  as rational    15-16
  definition of    15
  ethics of    124-128
  history of    14-15
  major problems in neo-
    Aristotelian Rhetoric    120-128
  minor problems in neo-
    Aristotelian Rhetoric    118-119
  nature of    15-22
  negation in    269

neo-Aristotelian    15
one-directionality    121-122
philosophical problems in    122-123
separateness of    120-121
successful and unsuccessful    124-128,
    226-237
versus Ritual    267-271
Richards, I. A.    210
Ritual
    and Rhetoric as the limits
        of language    211-218
    and the intentional fallacy    186-187
    as drama    238-242
    as inseparable from Rhetoric    190-200
    as nondiscursive language    180-181
    as the ground of Rhetoric    201-211
    content of    171-181
    defined    267
    dehumanized    188
    description of    237-238
    drama    165-171
    forms of    139-171
    god-terms in    270-271
    hierarchies of    257-267
    negation in    269-270
    poetry    140-149
    prose    149-165
    rhythmic distortion    185-186
    the *personae* of    250-257
    universality of    179-181
    versus Rhetoric    267-271
Ritualists as actors    242-250
Robinson, Edwin Arlington
    "Reuben Bright"    261
Roethke, Theodore
    "I Knew A Woman Lovely in
        Her Bones"    251
Roosevelt, Franklin D.
    Declaration of War speech    19-20
Rousseau, Jean-Jacques
    "On the Origin of
        Inequality"    251-252

S

Sappho
    "Mother, I Cannot Mind My
        Wheel"    137
Sartre, Jean-Paul
    Speech at the War Crimes
        Tribunal    228-233
Shakespeare
    *Henry IV, Part I*    134-136
    *Julius Caesar*    13
    *Macbeth*    263
    *Richard III*    243
    *Sonnet CXXXVIII*    244
    *Henry V*, Prologue    241
*Shi King*    132
Sidney, Sir Philip
    "Astrophel and Stella"    249
Socrates    13
"Song of Solomon"    136-137
Statistical statements    57-58
Stendahl
    "My Mother's Death"    160
Style    96-115
    as direct address    103-104
    as inseparable from substance    96-99
    as ornamentation    96
    individual    99-101
    rhetorical    101-115
Swinburne, Algernon Charles
    "The Garden of Proserpine"    248-249
Symons, Julian
    "Pub"    143

V

Verse
    and prose, poetry, and
        nonpoetry    250-257
    free    142-145
    metrical    140-142
    nonpoetry    261-265
    poetry    262, 263
Voltaire
    "The Way the World Goes"    161-162
"Vulnerable One, The"    158-159